'*The Gift of Song* is highly original, brilliantly conceived, and engagingly written. Its description of how music and dance are used to create and reactivate relationships across time, space, and ethnicity is a major contribution to studies of Aboriginal song and repatriation, as well as to the fields of ethnomusicology and the performing arts.'

Anthony Seeger,
Distinguished Professor of Ethnomusicology,
Emeritus, UCLA

'A superb piece of work, consummately showing the rich musical life of Western Arnhem Land, its interconnectedness to emotion, sociality, and the ritual and sacral, as well as the ability of music both to sustain deep elements of traditional culture and to connect across to Balanda and global cultural interests.'

Nicholas Evans,
Distinguished Professor of Linguistics,
Australian National University

'A major contribution to the field of ethnomusicology, and an important source for linguists, anthropologists, art critics, dance scholars and historians working with indigenous languages and cultures in Australia.'

Allan Marett,
Emeritus Professor,
The University of Sydney

The Gift of Song

The Gift of Song: Performing Exchange in Western Arnhem Land tells the story of the return of physical and digital cultural materials through song and dance. Drawing on extensive, first-person ethnographic fieldwork in western Arnhem Land, Australia, Brown examines how Bininj/Arrarrkpi (Aboriginal people of this region) enact change and innovate their performance practices through ceremonial exchange. As Indigenous communities worldwide confront new social and environmental challenges, this book addresses the following questions: How do Indigenous communities come to terms with legacies of taking and collecting? How are cultural materials in digital formats received and ritualised? How do traditional forms of exchange continue to mediate relationships? Combining ethnomusicological analysis and linguistically and historically informed ethnography, this book reveals how multilingualism and musical diversity are maintained through *kun-borrk/manyardi*, a major genre of Indigenous Australian song and dance. It retheorises the core anthropological concept of 'exchange' and enriches understanding of repatriation as a process of re-embedding tangible objects through intangible practices of ceremony and language.

Reuben Brown is a non-Indigenous (Settler/Balanda) applied ethnomusicologist specialising in Indigenous song and dance practices from western Arnhem Land (*kun-borrk/manyardi*). Brown has co-authored publications with Indigenous Australian ceremony leaders as well as musicologists, linguists, anthropologists, and historians on the relationship between language and song and the reuse of archival recordings to support transmission of Indigenous knowledge. Brown is an ARC DECRA research fellow at the Research Unit for Indigenous Languages, Faculty of Arts, University of Melbourne. His DECRA project investigates how ceremonial performance at Indigenous festivals in northern Australia enacts diplomacy between Indigenous and non-Indigenous participants, and between different clan and language groups.

SOAS Studies in Music
Series Editors:
Rachel Harris, *SOAS, University of London, UK*
Rowan Pease, *SOAS, University of London, UK*

Board Members:
Angela Impey *(SOAS, University of London)*
Henry Spiller *(University California)*
Kwasi Ampene *(University of Michigan)*
Linda Barwick *(University of Sydney)*
Martin Stokes *(Kings College London)*
Moshe Morad *(Tel Aviv University)*
Noriko Manabe *(Temple University)*
Richard Widdess *(SOAS, University of London)*
Suzel Reily *(Universidade Estadual de Campinas)*
Travis A. Jackson *(University of Chicago)*

SOAS Studies in Music is today one of the world's leading series in the discipline of ethnomusicology. Our core mission is to produce high-quality, ethnographically rich studies of music-making in the world's diverse musical cultures. We publish monographs and edited volumes that explore musical repertories and performance practice, critical issues in ethnomusicology, sound studies, historical and analytical approaches to music across the globe. We recognize the value of applied, interdisciplinary and collaborative research, and our authors draw on current approaches in musicology and anthropology, psychology, media and gender studies. We welcome monographs that investigate global contemporary, classical and popular musics, the effects of digital mediation and transnational flows.

Dhrupad
Tradition and Performance in Indian Music
Ritwik Sanyal and Richard Widdess

The Art Song in East Asia and Australia, 1900 to 1950
Edited By Joys Hoi Yan Cheung and Alison Tokita

Reform, Notation and Ottoman music in Early 19th Century Istanbul
Euterpe
Mehmet Ali Sanlıkol

The Gift of Song
Performing Exchange in Western Arnhem Land
Reuben Brown

For more information about this series, please visit: https://www.routledge.com/music/series/SOASMS

The Gift of Song
Performing Exchange in Western Arnhem Land

Reuben Brown

NEW YORK AND LONDON

Designed cover image: Stanley Gameraidj, Jason Brown, Harrison Cooper and Charlie Mangulda (singing and playing clapsticks), Isaac Galaminda, Roy Mangirryang (dancing with mamurrng), Solomon Nangamu, Maurice Gawayaku and Rupert Manmurulu perform a mamurrng ceremony for the author Reuben Brown. Photograph by Martin Thomas.

First published 2024
by Routledge
605 Third Avenue, New York, NY 10158

and by Routledge
4 Park Square, Milton Park, Abingdon, Oxon, OX14 4RN

Routledge is an imprint of the Taylor & Francis Group, an informa business

© 2024 Taylor & Francis

The right of Reuben Brown to be identified as author of this work has been asserted in accordance with sections 77 and 78 of the Copyright, Designs and Patents Act 1988.

The Indigenous/Bininj/Arrarrkpi knowledge in this book is the Indigenous cultural intellectual property (ICIP) of *kun-borrk/manyardi* ceremony leaders and custodians. This knowledge and associated recordings should be used with consent of the intellectual property owners and with proper attribution.

All rights reserved. No part of this book may be reprinted or reproduced or utilised in any form or by any electronic, mechanical, or other means, now known or hereafter invented, including photocopying and recording, or in any information storage or retrieval system, without permission in writing from the publishers.

Trademark notice: Product or corporate names may be trademarks or registered trademarks, and are used only for identification and explanation without intent to infringe.

Library of Congress Cataloging-in-Publication Data

Names: Brown, Reuben (Ethnomusicologist), author.
Title: The gift of song: performing exchange in Western Arnhem land /Reuben Brown.
Description: New York, NY: Routledge, 2024. | Series: SOAS studies in music | Includes bibliographical references and index.
Identifiers: LCCN 2023047814 (print) | LCCN 2023047815 (ebook) | ISBN 9781032106366 (hardback) | ISBN 9781032106502 (paperback) | ISBN 9781003216339 (ebook)
Subjects: LCSH: Aboriginal Australians—Australia—Arnhem Land (N.T.)—Music—History and criticism. | Folk music—Australia—Arnhem Land (N.T.)—History and criticism. | Folk dance music—Australia—Arnhem Land (N.T.)—History and criticism. | Aboriginal Australians—Australia—Arnhem Land (N.T.)—Social life and customs. | Aboriginal Australians—Australia—Arnhem Land (N.T.)—Rites and ceremonies. | Ceremonial exchange—Australia—Arnhem Land (N.T.)
Classification: LCC ML3770.7.A75 B7 2024 (print) | LCC ML3770.7.A75 (ebook) | DDC 781.62/9915—dc23/eng/20231020
LC record available at https://lccn.loc.gov/2023047814
LC ebook record available at https://lccn.loc.gov/2023047815

ISBN: 978-1-032-10636-6 (hbk)
ISBN: 978-1-032-10650-2 (pbk)
ISBN: 978-1-003-21633-9 (ebk)

DOI: 10.4324/9781003216339

Typeset in Times New Roman
by codeMantra

Access the Support Material: www.routledge.com/9781032106366

For kun-borrk and manyardi songmen, dancers and leaders, past, present and future, and for Eli and Mira

Contents

List of figures	*xiii*
List of tables	*xv*
Audio and video examples	*xvi*
A note on cultural sensitivity	*xx*
Acknowledgements	*xxi*
A note on use, spelling, and pronunciation of Aboriginal words	*xxiii*
Glossary of terms, abbreviations, and symbols	*xxiv*
A note on recordings, transcriptions, and support material	*xxviii*

Prologue: Receiving the gift   1

1 **Following footsteps**   6
  Regenerating ancestral connections through kun-borrk/manyardi *9*
  Singing, dancing, and exchanging gifts 11
  Repatriation and archival returns of Indigenous song and dance 13
  The 1948 recordings and media 16
  Multilingual kun-borrk/manyardi *18*
  Locating the track 22
  The archival record of kun-borrk/manyardi *25*
  Performing ethnography (and writing an ethnography of performance) 27

2 **'They Still Help Us': Legacies of exchange**   39
  The journey to Amartjitpalk 39
  Histories of encounter and exchange 43
    European contact and the mission era 45

x Contents

    Musical setting of kun-borrk/manyardi *48*
        Performance context 48
        Song inheritance 49
        Song conception 50
        Songs and song structure 51
        Song order 53
        Melodic contour 54
        Rhythmic mode 54
    Doing 'performance-conscious' ethnography 55
    Following their footsteps at Amartjitpalk 58
        Calling out 58
        Dispersing and marking the beat 58
        Coming together, lifting, stamping, and pausing 60
        Following the lead songman 60
    Flexibility and complementarity in the ordering of songs 61
    Conclusion: singing and dancing the past into the present 64

3 'You Belong to Gunbalanya': A reburial ceremony   71
    Receiving the bones 71
    The 1948 American-Australian Scientific Expedition to
        Arnhem Land and its legacy 75
    Where did the spirits go? 77
    You came a long way 79
    Orienting them home 82
        The procession 86
        Dancing them into the grave 87
        Saying 'bobo' 89
        Covering the grave 92
        Smoking and cutting ties 94
    Conclusion: kun-borrk/manyardi *as repatriation 95*

4 'It's a Secret, For You': A Mamurrng ceremony   102
    A sensory overload 102
    Mamurrng diplomacy with Balanda 107
    The Warruwi Mamurrng 108
    Exchanging inalienable gifts 112
    Stages of the Warruwi Mamurrng 113
        Warming up 114

Handing over 117
Saying 'thanks' 122
Conclusion: kun-borrk/manyardi *as belonging 124*

5 **'That Spirit Changed My Voice': A funeral ceremony for Nakodjok**   129
Nakodjok returns 129
Song and the life cycle 132
Coming together for Nakodjok 135
  Paying respects through song 140
  Intervening spirits 142
  Circulating songs 146
Conclusion: kun-borrk/manyardi *as a conduit 148*

6 **'I'll Tell You This Corroboree Song': An intercultural exchange in 1948**   153
Playing it back 153
Reconstructing the exchange 160
Curating the record of kun-borrk/manyardi *in 1948 166*
Diversity of song in 1948 169
  Song texts recorded in 1948 171
  Continuity and change 177
Conclusion: kun-borrk/manyardi, *then and now 180*

7 **'Join in and Dance': Festivals and new forms of exchange**   186
Exchanges on the dance ground 186
Indigenous cultural festivals in the contemporary era 193
Fast one for bininj; slow one for daluk 195
Taking kun-borrk/manyardi to the stage 201
Conclusion: new expressions for old songs 209

8 **'We're All Family Now': Understanding the exchange**   214
Tracing the footsteps of kun-borrk/manyardi *215*
  Treatment of rhythmic mode and song order 216
  Staying on the right track: cross-repertory/cross-event musical analysis 218
  Relative weighting of different repertories within a performance 218

*Aural identity of repertories signalled through rhythmic
    mode 219
Preferred tempo bands 220
Cross-repertory tendency to sequence songs by rhythmic
    mode 221*
*Diversity and flexibility 221
Modes of exchange 223
Adaptability and innovation 224
The path ahead 225*

Epilogue: Returning the gift   230

References   *235*
Index   *249*

Figures

0.1	Photo of a recording of *manyardi* at Injalak Hill, Gunbalanya, 2011	3
1.1	Map of western Arnhem Land, showing languages and communities referred to in the book	19
1.2	Photo of Russell Agalara, Alfred Gawaraidji, Tommy Madjalkaidj, and Solomon Nangamu making a recording of Marrawiwi/Inyjalarrku at Adjumalarl waterfall near Gunbalanya, 2012	25
2.1	Photo of manyardi performance at Amartjitpalk, Goulburn Island, 2012	41
2.2	Solomon Nangamu and Russell Agalara's inheritance of the Mirrijpu song-set	49
2.3	Components of a performance event in western Arnhem Land, showing the structure of song IL01 (AVEx 4.2) and its place within the performance	52
2.4	Rhythmic modes featured in *kun-borrk/manyardi* songs analysed in the book	56
2.5	Relationship between dance and musical structure in a *manyardi* Mirrijpu song in fast doubled rhythmic mode (AVEx_2.2)	59
2.6	Music transcription of Marrwakara songs MK01 and MK02 'joined together', performed by Harold Warrabin at Amartjitpalk, 2012 (AVEx_2.3)	63
3.1	Photo of AASEAL members at base camp in Gunbalanya (Oenpelli), 1948	76
3.2	Music Transcription of Inyjalarrku *Nigi* no. 1, song IL50 (AVEx_3.4)	94
4.1	Photo of Roderick Lee helping to cover Reuben Brown in red ochre in preparation for the Mamurrng	105
4.2	Photo of George Winunguj performing a Rom ceremony for Axel Poignant in 1952	107
4.3	Photo of Recipients of the Warruwi Mamurrng in 2012	112

xiv *Figures*

4.4	Photo of Roy Mangirryang presenting the *mamurrng*	120
5.1	Photo of the construction of a bough shelter or 'shade' for the body of Nakodjok at Mikkinj Valley outstation	139
5.2	Excerpt from vocal part of 'old' Mirrijpu song MP18 (AVEx_5.1)	147
5.3	Music transcription of vocal part excerpt of 'new' Mirrijpu dream-composed song MP21 (AVEx_5.2)	148
6.1	Photo of Larry Marawana and group listening to recordings of *kun-borrk/manyardi* made at Red Lily billabong, Gunbalanya, 1948	162
7.1	Photo of Matter of Soul Band from Goulburn Island performing at the 2012 Stone Country Festival in Gunbalanya	190
7.2	Map showing the order of ceremonial performance at the Stone Country Festival, 2012	197
7.3	Photo of Toby Cooper from Croker Island dancing to rhythmic mode 5c in Milyarryarr song MR04 (AVEx_7.3)	200
9.1	Photo of the author with Solomon Nangamu, Lynize, Jamie Milpurr, Jenny Manmurulu, David Manmurulu, Rupert Manmurulu, and Renfred Manmurulu at Twin Hill Station after a Mamurrng ceremony, 2016	231

Tables

1.1	Summary of song-sets performed during fieldwork (2011–13) in western Arnhem Land	28
3.1	Summary of *kun-borrk/manyardi* song items performed for a reburial ceremony, Gunbalanya, 2011	83
4.1	Musical structure of Inyjalarrku song IL02 (AVEx_4.3)	116
5.1	Summary of the main stages of the funeral ceremony for Nakodjok involving ritual song and dance	137
5.2	Summary of Mirrijpu song items performed by Solomon Nangamu and Russell Agalara at Mikkinj Valley for Nakodjok funeral ceremony	143
6.1	Summary of recordings at Gunbalanya in 1948, showing the song origin, song-set, language, conception, and details of recording	170
6.2	Music transcription of Itpiyitpy song, MA24 Cut 2 (AVEx_6.8)	175
6.3	Music transcription of Kunbarlang song, MA24 Cut 6 (AVEx_6.9)	176
6.4	Changes in rhythmic mode in Kurri song by Frank Djendjorr/Philip Nayuku, MA24 Cut 10 (AVEx_6.10)	179
7.1	The ordering of song groups at the Stone Country Festival in 2011 and 2012 and Mahbilil Festival in 2011 and 2013	196
7.2	MR05 song structure and changes in rhythmic mode (AVEx_7.2)	199
7.3	MR04 song structure and changes in rhythmic mode (AVEx_7.2)	199
7.4	Summary of bands that performed at the Stone Country and Mahbilil Festivals in Gunbalanya and Jabiru in 2011 and 2012	202
8.1	Summary of considerations in the performance of *kun-borrk/manyardi* affecting song order, rhythmic mode, and tempo	216
8.2	Number of song items and weighting of song-sets performed across events	219

Audio and video examples

Reference	AVEx DOI/URL	Description	Dur.
AVEx_0.1	https://dx.doi.org/10.26278/EY6F-6452	Audio of Johnny Namayiwa clarifying didjeridu rhythms and practising Milyarryarr song MR01	01:05
AVEx_2.1	https://dx.doi.org/10.26278/9Q67-4C60	Video of Reuben Brown, Brendan Marrgam, Maurice Gawayaku dancing to Mirrijpu song MP06 at Amartjitpalk	01:54
AVEx_2.2	https://dx.doi.org/10.26278/6Z6Z-C904	Video of Reuben Brown, Brendan Marrgam, Maurice Gawayaku dancing to Mirrijpu item MP26 at Amartjitpalk, Goulburn Island	01:18
AVEx_2.3	https://dx.doi.org/10.26278/YPEN-8833	Audio of Harold Warrabin singing Marrwakara songs MK01 and MK02 together at Amartjitpalk, Goulburn Island	01:34
AVEx_2.4	https://dx.doi.org/10.26278/VFE7-1N35	Video of Solomon Nangamu singing Mirrijpu song MP25 and Harold Warrabin dancing comically	01:46
AVEx_3.1	https://dx.doi.org/10.26278/MQ8R-7P72	Video of Karrbarda dancers dancing the bones in to the gravesite to song KB01 for a reburial ceremony at Gunbalanya, 2011	00:32
AVEx_3.2	https://dx.doi.org/10.26278/KSAV-N217	Audio of Eric Marrday and SD performing Karrbarda *ngalbadjan* 'mother' song KB14	01:32
AVEx_3.3	https://dx.doi.org/10.26278/MGFC-VK27	Audio excerpt of Solomon Nangamu singing '*bobo*' to complete a performance.	00:08
AVEx_3.4	https://dx.doi.org/10.26278/VRJ9-TS69	Video of James Gulamuwu dancing 'farewell' by the graveside.	01:16
AVEx_3.5	https://dx.doi.org/10.26278/V6D2-ED20	Video of Solomon Nangamu, Alfred Gawaraidji, and Russell Agalara performing Mirrijpu songs MP06 and MP04 ('mother song') for a smoking ceremony	02:06

(*Continued*)

Audio and video examples xvii

Reference	AVEx DOI/URL	Description	Dur.
AVEx_4.1	https://dx.doi.org/10.26278/M0DA-KV14	Audio of Inyjalarrku singing song IL05 for Mamurrng ceremony, Goulburn Island	01:16
AVEx_4.2	https://dx.doi.org/10.26278/WB4Z-YS67	Video of Inyjalarrku group performing song IL01 as part of opening warm-up evening for Mamurrng ceremony, Goulburn Island.	01:37
AVEx_4.3	https://dx.doi.org/10.26278/E4FT-EH66	Audio of Inyjalarrku singing song IL02	01:05
AVEx_4.4	https://dx.doi.org/10.26278/5D2S-0D84	Video of dancers revealing the *mamurrng* for the first time dancing to Yanajanak song YJ03	02:13
AVEx_4.5	https://dx.doi.org/10.26278/JT96-6A04	Edited video of Inyjalarrku handing over *mamurrng* with David Manmurulu dancing as *yumparrparr* (giant)	03:13
AVEx_4.6	https://dx.doi.org/10.26278/GMRE-7Z37	Video of Allan Marett and Linda Barwick performing *wangga* as 'thanks' for the Mamurrng.	00:58
AVEx_5.1	https://dx.doi.org/10.26278/92ND-QM77	Solomon Nangamu, Russell Agalara, and Alfred Gawaraidji performing Mirrijpu song MP18 at a funeral ceremony for Nakodjok Nayinggul	02:06
AVEx_5.2	https://dx.doi.org/10.26278/18ZM-0431	Solomon Nangamu, Russell Agalara, and Alfred Gawaraidji performing Mirrijpu song MP21 at a funeral ceremony for Nakodjok Nayinggul	02:43
AVEx_6.1	https://dx.doi.org/10.26278/691D-C745	Archival video of Bininj/Arrarrkpi skinning buffalo in 1948. Original file details: filmed by Howell Walker in 1948, National Geographic collection R01R02-O-04	02:44
AVEx_6.2	https://dx.doi.org/10.26278/8PXR-C641	Archival video of women collecting red apple with Margaret McArthur. Original file details: filmed by Howell Walker in 1948, National Geographic collection R09R10-O-25.	01:58
AVEx_6.3	https://dx.doi.org/10.26278/QQAC-8J21	Archival video (spliced with matching archival audio from Simpson) of Larry Marawana explaining Kolobarr song to Colin Simpson and listening to playback of songs. Original file details: filmed by Howell Walker in 1948, National Geographic collection R01R02-O-05, audio-recorded by Colin Simpson and Ray Giles ABC Radio Archives disc MA24 Cut 7	01:39

(*Continued*)

xviii *Audio and video examples*

Reference	AVEx DOI/URL	Description	Dur.
AVEx_6.4	https://dx.doi.org/10.26278/RMWW-VD47	Archival recording of saltwater (Nganaru) song from North Goulburn Island sung by Billy Namunurr recorded in 1948. Original file details: recorded by Colin Simpson and Ray Giles ABC Radio Archives disc MA24 Cut 1	01:57
AVEx_6.5	https://dx.doi.org/10.26278/CSRB-HF79	Archival recording of saltwater Marrwakara (goanna) song from Goulburn Island. Original file details: recorded by Colin Simpson and Ray Giles ABC Radio Archives disc MA24 Cut 12	01:13
AVEx_6.6	https://dx.doi.org/10.26278/J01N-6S87	Archival recording of Kolobarr song sung by Larry Marawana. Original file details: recorded by Colin Simpson and Ray Giles ABC Radio Archives disc MA24 Cut 7	01:25
AVEx_6.7	https://dx.doi.org/10.26278/A47F-Z684	Archival recording of wangga song sung by Mung.gi or Billy Mandji. Original file details: recorded by Colin Simpson and Ray Giles ABC Radio Archives disc MA24 Cut 3	00:45
AVEx_6.8	https://dx.doi.org/10.26278/FESP-P266	Archival recording of Stone country Itpyitpy song sung by Paddy Bull and Ilarri. Original file details: recorded by Colin Simpson and Ray Giles ABC Radio Archives disc MA24 Cut 2	01:52
AVEx_6.9	https://dx.doi.org/10.26278/1MQ3-B996	Archival recording of Kunbarlang song sung by Balir Balir and Bilinyarra. Original file details: recorded by Colin Simpson and Ray Giles ABC Radio Archives disc MA24 Cut 6	02:50
AVEx_6.10	https://dx.doi.org/10.26278/RWNX-MR02	Archival recording of Kurri song sung by Frank Djendjorr Namornkodj and Philip Nayuku. Original file details: recorded by Colin Simpson and Ray Giles ABC Radio Archives disc MA24 Cut 10	04:30
AVEx_7.1	https://wildflowerband.bandcamp.com/track/kabbari	'Kabbari' by Wildflower Band	00:46
AVEx_7.2	https://dx.doi.org/10.26278/M1GM-5X70	Audio of Johnny Namayiwa singing Milyarryarr songs MR05_MR04_MR05 at Stone Country Festival in 2011	04:32

(*Continued*)

Audio and video examples xix

Reference	*AVEx DOI/URL*	*Description*	*Dur.*
AVEx_7.3	https://dx.doi.org/10.26278/8183-4Q09	Video of Toby Cooper dancing to Milyarryarr song MR05_MR04_MR05 at Stone Country Festival in 2011	00:47
AVEx_7.4	https://dx.doi.org/10.26278/Z57Q-EN95	Harold Warrabin sings 'Long Grass Man' from the album 'Best of Warruwi 2003'	03:00

A note on cultural sensitivity

This book contains names and images of people who have passed away. Their names have been included so as to recognise their contribution to the research. Readers are advised it may be appropriate when discussing the deceased to use skin and clan names rather than personal names, and to be guided by family members around use.

Acknowledgements

This book was researched, conceived, and written on Boonwurrung, Woiwurrung, Dja Dja Wurrung, Gadigal, Larrakia, Gundjeihmi, Mengerrdji, Erre, Urningangk, Mawng, and Kunwinjku country. I pay my respects to all Elders, past and present, and acknowledge that Indigenous sovereignty has never been ceded.

My first thanks go to the people of Gunbalanya, Warruwi, and Jabiru and surrounding outstations who hosted me on their country and to the Bininj and Arrarrkpi ceremony leaders, custodians, and knowledge holders who generously contributed to this book through their performances, insights, guidance, and expertise. This includes Jimmy Kalarriya†, Jacob Nayinggul†, Connie Nayinggul, Alfred Nayinggul, Solomon Nangamu, Russell Agalara, Alfred Gawaraidji, David Manmurulu†, Jenny Manmurulu, Rupert Manmurulu, Renfred Manmurulu and their family, Johnny Namayiwa, Tommy Madjalkaidj, Eric Mardday†, James Gulamuwu†, Harold Warrabin, Micky Yalbarr, Maurice Gawayaku, Brendan Marrgam, Don Namundja, Isaiah Nagurrgurrba†, and Joey Nganjmirra. A special thanks to Donna Nadjamerrek and her family Lois Nadjamerrek, Rhonda Nadjamerrek, Hagar Nadjamerrek, and June Nadjamerrek. Donna warmly adopted me and my partner into their family and helped me to integrate into Bininj society, assisting with my learning of their language of Bininj Kunwok, and always keeping in touch during periods spent away from Gunbalanya. At Injalak Arts and Crafts where I based myself for much of this research, Andrew Manakgu patiently helped me to transcribe and translate interviews and conversations in Kunwinjku.

Thank you to Linda Barwick, Martin Thomas, and Paul Dwyer who supervised me for the PhD thesis, upon which much of the research in this book is based. I am extremely grateful to Linda Barwick, who taught me valuable skills in conducting fieldwork in intercultural settings, managing recordings, and undertaking transcription and musical analysis. Special thanks to Martin Thomas for support at all stages, from the original research to developing the ideas for the book and guidance through the publication process. This research was supported by the team on the ARC Discovery Project 'Intercultural Inquiry in a Trans-National Context: Exploring the Legacy of the 1948 American-Australian

Scientific Expedition to Arnhem Land' (DP1096897) including Linda Barwick, Martin Thomas, Allan Marett, and Amanda Harris and enriched by their research. Financial support from the University of Melbourne and the University of Sydney and in-kind support from Gundjeihmi Aboriginal Corporation, Injalak Arts and Crafts, and Bininj Kunwok Language Centre also helped me in the researching and writing of this book.

I am grateful for the generous feedback on draft manuscripts of this book, valuable advice, and insights into the publishing process I received along the way from Allan Marett, Tony Seeger, Nick Evans, Ric Knowles, Sally Treloyn, Nick Tochka, Murray Garde, Ruth Singer, Isabel O'Keeffe, Amanda Harris, Bruce Birch, Michael Walsh, Glen McGillivray, and Cathy Falk. Thanks also to Bill Ivory, Justin O'Brien, Alex Ressel, Lorna Martin, Andrish Saint-Clare, and Joel Saint-Clare for their advice, support, and encouragement in the field.

Thanks to Henry Reese, Fregmonto Stokes, Celeste Macleod, Nick Ward, Julia Miller, and Jodie Kell for assisting me in preparing the manuscript and accompanying recordings and metadata for archiving in PARADISEC. Thank you to Samantha Owens for support with the index, and to Constance Ditzel, Hanna Rowe, Assunta Petrone and the team at Routledge for their guidance and patience throughout the publication process. The path to writing this book was filled with unexpected bumps, twists, and turns. Thanks to my family for their constant encouragement, patience, and support, and my parents Christine and Mark Brown for helping me to buy a 4WD *mutika* that proved an extremely valuable asset for fieldwork in Arnhem Land! Finally, I thank my partner, Rachel Orzech, for her calm commitment throughout the process of bringing this book to life and unwavering support through the ups and downs of fieldwork and starting a family as early career researchers. To our two *wurdjow/warranyngiw* (children) Nakodjok Eli and Ngalkodjok Mira, thank you for motivating me to share the gift of *kun-borrk/manyardi* with you and future generations—I hope your experiences with the songs and languages of this Country will enrich you as it has me.

A note on use, spelling, and pronunciation of Aboriginal words

Throughout this book, Aboriginal words in different languages are indicated in italics and English translations are glossed in brackets the first time the word appears in the text. A glossary of words in Indigenous languages commonly used in this book follows. My intention in adopting select local terms rather than using their English equivalents is to convey the way in which conversations with Bininj/Arrarrkpi were conducted with Balanda like me. I encourage readers to have a go at sounding out the word upon first encounter and use https://bininjkunwok.org.au and https://www.mawngngaralk.org.au as a guide. The orthography used for Kunwinjku (K) is based on the Standard Kunwinjku Orthography developed by Steve Etherington and used in the bilingual programme in Gunbalanya in the 1980s. The orthography used for Mawng (M) is the same as that adopted by linguist Heather Hewett working with Mawng elders and used today at Warruwi school. The main difference between Bininj Kunwok and Mawng spelling is that Mawng uses a *p, j*, and *y* to indicate a bilabial stop, palatal stop, and palatal approximants, respectively, whereas Kunwinjku uses a *b, dj*, and *j*; Mawng also uses the palatal approximant *w*. The main vowels in Mawng are *a, i,* and *u* (*e* and *o* are less common). For a guide to pronouncing Kunwinjku and Mawng words, see Support Material Figure i.i.

Following Bininj Kunwok spelling conventions, for ease of legibility, long words in Bininj Kunwok are broken up using hyphens to separate particular morphemes. These include noun class prefixes, e.g. *kun-borrk* (K: public dance-accompanied song tradition), *man-berlnginj* (K: clapsticks); pronominal prefixes, e.g. *karri-bedjekmerren* (we [1pl incl]-splatter with white ochre), *ngarri-borrkke* (we [1pl excl] dance); and the hither marker -m-, e.g. with the pronoun *ngam-re* (I-hither-go). Exceptions include if the word is a proper noun, e.g. Kundjeyhmi (dialect of Bininj Kunwok), as well as 'lexically frozen' prefixes, e.g. *Namarrkon* (lightening spirit). A series of colons is sometimes used to represent the length of a vowel in speech or in song, as in the following example:

You came a lo::::::ng way.

Glossary of terms, abbreviations, and symbols

Indigenous language terms commonly used in this book

bakki	K: tobacco/cigarettes
bim	K: rock art painting
Bininj/Arrarrkpi	K/M: Indigenous person/human
bininj/arrarrkpi	male person
bobo	Kriol: goodbye
bunggurl/manikay	central and northeast Arnhem Land public ceremony
daluk/warramumpik	K/M: woman
delek	K: white ochre
djang	K: sacred site
junba	public ceremony from the Kimberley region
kobah-kobanj	K: old people
korroko	K: a long time ago
kun-borrk/manyardi	K/M: western Arnhem Land public ceremony; dance/song
kurrula	K/M: saltwater
mako/arrawirr	K/M: didjeridu
mamurrng	K/M: ceremonial pole/diplomacy ceremony
mimih	K: stone country spirits
man-berlnginj/nganangka	K/M: clapsticks
manme/walij	K/M: food; tucker
namorrorddo/yumparrparr	K/M: giant
ngalbadjan/nigi:	K/M: mother song
nulatparlangkat	M: fast tempo songs
nulatparlilil	M: slow tempo songs
wardde-ken	K: stone country
wangga	public ceremony from Daly region
yawkyawk	K: young woman; female water spirit/mermaid
yawurrinj	K: young men/boys

Glossary of terms, abbreviations, and symbols xxv

Musical abbreviations

Bpm	Beats per minute
CS	Clapstick
Dj	Didjeridu
FT	Free translation
GG	Gurrumba Gurrumba [*bunggurl*]
IL	Inyjalarrku [song-set]
IT	Itpiyitpi [song-set]
IS	Instrumental Section
KB	Karrbarda [song-set]
KL	Kunbarlang [song-set]
KU	Kurri [song-set]
KR	Kurrula [song-set]
LW	Lambudju wangga
MAN	Manikay [unclassified clan songs]
MD	Morrdjdjanjno
MK	Marrwakara/Mularrik Mularrik [song-set]
MP	Mirrijpu [song-set]
MR	Milyarryarr [song-set]
MS	Melodic sequence
MW	Marrwakani [song-set]
MX	Marrawiwi [song-set]
MY	Mimih/Yawkyawk [song-set]
NK	Nabarlek [song-set]
SF	Saltwater Fish [song-set]
ST	Song text
Vc	Vocals
YJ	Yanajanak [song-set]

Language abbreviations

Eng.	English (ISO 639-3 code: eng)
K	Kunwinjku (ISO 639-3 code: gup)
M	Mawng (ISO 639-3 code: mph)
Mdj	Mengerrdji (ISO 639-3 code: zme)
Kr	Kriol (ISO 639-3 code: rop)

Interlineal glossing

Interlineal glossing is provided for some songs in 'ordinary language' discussed in Chapter 6.

xxvi *Glossary of terms, abbreviations, and symbols*

Glossing of pronominal prefixes

1s	first person singular ('I')
2s	second person singular ('you')
3s	third person singular ('he/she')
1du incl	first person dual inclusive ('you and me')
1du excl	first person dual exclusive ('me and another person [not addressee]')
1du+1	first person dual + another ('you and me and another person')
2du	second person dual ('you two')
3du	third person dual (them two)
1pl incl	first person plural inclusive ('we' [including addressee])
1pl excl	first person plural exclusive ('us mob' [not addressee])
2pl	second person plural ('you all')
3pl	third person plural ('they all')
3>12	they to us [subject/object]

Other glossing abbreviations

BEN	benefactive case
DIREC	Directional
exclm.	Exclamation
FUT	Future
IMP	imperative mood
IRR	Irrealis
min	minimum subject
NP	Nonpast tense suffix
P	past tense
Q	NQuestion
R	Realis

Other abbreviations and symbols

†	Indicates the person is now deceased (the first time the name appears in the text)
AASEAL	American-Australian Scientific Expedition to Arnhem Land
ABC	Australian Broadcasting Commission
AIATSIS	Australian Institute of Aboriginal and Torres Strait Islander Studies
ARC	Australian Research Council
CI	Chief Investigator
CMS	Church Missionary Society
DP	Discovery Project
GAC	Gundjeihmi Aboriginal Corporation

Glossary of terms, abbreviations, and symbols xxvii

GBM	General Business Manager
IAC	Injalak Arts and Crafts Association
PARADISEC	Pacific and Regional Archive for Digital Sources in Endangered Cultures
SCF	Stone Country Festival
WALSP	Western Arnhem Land Song Project

Key to symbols used in song inheritance kinship diagram

△	Male
○	Female
△ (crossed)	Male (deceased)
⌀	Female (deceased)
⌐⌐	Sibling relationship
⌐⌐	Spouse relationship

A note on recordings, transcriptions, and support material

Select audio/video examples (AVEx) discussed and analysed in this book are accessible via a QR code DOI link in this book. To view/listen, readers need to sign in or create a free account with paradisec.org.au. Audiovisual examples are cited with a chapter number followed by a sequential number. For example, **(AVEx_3.1)** indicates Chapter 3, audio/video example 1. A PDF of Support Material including additional figures, music analysis, and details relating to the performance events and recordings analysed in each chapter can also be found in the Support Material tab for this book at routledge.com.

Music transcriptions are based on the author's close listening to the recording and, in some instances, on the interviews with singers who offered line-by-line sung or spoken versions of the song text and may need to be checked for further accuracy with singers and corrected in the future. Transcriptions of didjeridu rhythms are to be taken as indicative; the aim is to show how the clapstick, didjeridu, and vocal parts interact and how the music is organised, rather than provide a detailed musical transcription for performance. A gloss and free translation of the song text is provided where the song text is in spoken language; for song texts in spirit language, no translation was offered although some words have meaning for singers, as discussed in Chapter 2.

A summary of song items relating to events analysed in each chapter is provided in this book and the Support Material. This may include the song item/recording; song ID; rhythmic modes; tempi (in beats per minute); corresponding rhythmic mode; a brief description of the 'action'—dance, ritual, social activity, etc.—that took place; and tempo changes in the performance.

A summary of the author's field recordings and recordings by others referenced in this book can be found in Support Material Appendix i and Appendix ii. Other fieldwork recordings referenced in this text—including sung performances and spoken interviews—can be accessed via DOI links provided in footnotes and by signing into paradisec.org.au. Citations from fieldwork interviews include the speaker, name of recording, and time code. Full or partial transcripts (.eaf and .txt files) of recorded interviews can also be accessed alongside the recording.

Prologue
Receiving the gift

It was during one of my first trips to western Arnhem Land in the dry season of 2011 that I received the gift. Of course, I didn't realise it had been given until sometime after the event. I sat with four Mawng ceremony leaders at the foot of Injalak Hill, across the billabong from the town of Gunbalanya. As with many other occasions, I was accompanied by men, who are responsible for singing songs in ceremony in this region. This small excursion out of town had been instigated by Solomon Nangamu, who fetched fellow songmen James Gulamuwu and Johnny Namayiwa, and didjeridu player Alfred Gawaraidji for the occasion (see Figure 0.1). Together, they helped me navigate my utility vehicle/pickup—or 'ute' as it is commonly referred to in Australia—to the other side of the billabong and around the hill to a quiet place where we sat to record and discuss their songs. They explained that they would sing first, then talk afterwards. Later, I would learn that this was an important convention—alongside calling out using the ancestral language of the country one enters—which helps to establish one's presence, and lets the spirits of Country know who is there.[1] They held a quiet discussion to decide on the number and order of songs that they would perform, and began by helping the eldest singer, James Gulamuwu, to 'practise' his songs for the recording. When they had finished playing and singing Gulamuwu's songs, they passed around *bakki* (K: tobacco/cigarettes) and talked about how they had learned the songs by following their fathers and male relatives, who would travel to different ceremonies around western Arnhem Land where they had been invited to sing:

> JG: *Yoh* [K/M: yes], our fathers used to sing—like, his [Solomon Nangamu's] father used to sing, my father used to sing that song I sing now, and his [Alfred Gawaraidji's] father used to play didjeridu.

They took it in turns performing four songs each from the repertories that they had inherited; while one singer sang his songs, the other two would beat the clapstick rhythms that went with that song, sometimes singing along quietly in support of the main singer. Throughout, Gawaraidji accompanied on the didjeridu with a steady flow of air, aided by circular breathing from deep within the diaphragm. The lead singer would listen to the sound of the *mako/arawirr* (K/M: didjeridu; a log hollowed out by termites), at the beginning of the song before 'tuning in' his voice, as they put it—humming or singing along to the fundamental tone with an open vowel: 'oh-e-i'. Then, he would commence beating the *man-berlnginj/nganangka* (K/M: clapsticks; two pieces of carved hardwood). The rhythm of the *mako*, which at this point felt unstable, would adjust to sync with the rhythm of the *man-berlnginj*. This musical dialogue continued throughout the song: occasionally, Gawaraidji's flow of air paused, coinciding with the end of the singer's vocal phrase, and then it would start up again, before finally coming to an end, leaving the lead singer to strike two or three solitary beats of the *man-berlnginj* to finish the song (listen to **AVEx_0.1**).

AVEx_0.1 https://dx.doi.org/10.26278/EY6F-6452

After one singer finished performing his repertory, the next singer would quietly rehearse aspects of his song with the others—mouthing the sound of the didjeridu while lap slapping to keep the beat of the clapstick—previewing both the didjeridu and clapstick rhythms accompanying the vocal phrase. Gulamuwu remembered the advice that the *kobah-kobanj* (K: old people) used to give them about 'holding on' to the songs they had been given:

> Long time, old people used to tell us, "You gotta sing. Whenever you want to sing, sing all the time so that you have that thing strong and your voice will be good. On and on—can't leave it"… Even didjeridu too: play, play, play—your lungs get better and your own tune of the didjeridu for the song [will get better].[2]

He recalled his father's words:

> "When I die, son, you keep that song", or "you keep that didjeridu [i.e. memorise and perform the accompaniment]"… So we are carrying it on… "You follow, like footsteps. Don't lose it—keep it".[3]

Prologue: Receiving the gift 3

Figure 0.1 Photo of a recording of *manyardi* at Injalak Hill, Gunbalanya, 2011. Clockwise from left: James Gulamuwu, Alfred Gawaraidji, Johnny Namayiwa, and Solomon Nangamu at Injalak Hill, 2011. Photograph by Reuben Brown.

The twelve songs that Gulamuwu, Gawaraidji, Namayiwa, and Nangamu recorded at Injalak Hill through my recording device were a gift to future generations. The event led me to some of the questions that motivate this book: how does one nurture and sustain the gift of a song? How is it passed on? How is it given back? Yorta Yorta/Dja Dja Wurrung songwoman Dr Lou Bennett reflects on the responsibility of the receiver to nurture songs that are gifted:

> To gift a song to another is to establish a relationship that is bound in locality. There is the responsibility of custodianship and with this comes an unspoken agreement. It does not matter if this is an exclusive agreement. The song maker may gift the same song to many; however, in return it is expected that the song be taken care of as a family member—nurtured, protected, loved, and honoured[4]

Bennett's idea of songs establishing relationships that are bound in locality highlights for me my responsibility as a Balanda researcher, not only to document and analyse songs but also to nurture recordings so that the next generation of singers can continue singing. Even at this early stage of my fieldwork, I had come to find myself entangled in a web of relationships bound up in song and place. I had brought with me digitised media of songs and archival footage and photos made by members of the 1948 American-Australian Scientific Expedition to Arnhem Land. Then within weeks of commencing fieldwork, I was invited to help with a ceremony at Gunbalanya to return and rebury human bones belonging to the community's ancestors, which had been stolen from Injalak Hill in 1948 by Frank Setzler, the archaeologist on the Expedition. I volunteered with the logistics, catering, and other tasks as part of a large-scale community event involving a number of different groups and organisations. This allowed me to get to know Bininj and Balanda from the community, and to build relationships with Bininj people and *kun-borrk/manyardi* songmen. Injalak Arts and Crafts (IAC) at Gunbalanya became a base for my fieldwork, where Bininj could watch and listen to the archival media and hold discussions with elders and artists working at the centre. Like many non-profit remote Aboriginal art organisations, IAC was the cultural hub of the community, coordinating everything from rock art tours to the local festival, and operating with scant resources. It had one computer which I used for playback and access to the recordings from 1948 as well as contemporary recordings we made. I installed an iTunes database and organised a library of *kun-borrk* using the metadata fields to allow community members to search for songs by singer, song-set, language, or event where this information was available. In addition, my supervisor Linda Barwick—leader of the project supporting my research alongside Allan Marett, Martin Thomas, and Amanda Harris—had previously met and recorded Nangamu and his late brother Solomon Ganawa singing Mirrijpu at Warruwi in 2006.[5]

This early exchange at Injalak Hill—the same place where researchers in 1948 had camped, recorded songs, and taken bones without permission—would lead to further events involving sharing, recording, and exchanging song and dance and the return of physical and digital cultural materials that I describe in this book. In tracing these ceremonial exchanges, and my own role in receiving and reciprocating, this book aims to trace broader networks of gifting and exchanging that honour and renew the songs and sustain Bininj/Arrarrkpi[6] relations with Balanda and others.

Notes

1 Following Indigenous scholars and Bininj/Arrarrkpi interlocutors, throughout this book I capitalise 'Country' when referring to the Indigenous understanding of Country as sentient, multidimensional, alive, and both nourishing of and reliant on Aboriginal people and cultural practices. See Deborah Bird Rose, *Nourishing Terrains: Australian Aboriginal Views of Landscape and Wilderness* (Canberra: Australian Heritage Commission, 1996).
2 [James Gulamuwu, 20110903-RB_07.wav, https://dx.doi.org/10.26278/NWFE-VJ78, 00:03:50–00:04:45].
3 [James Gulamuwu, 20110903-RB_07.wav, https://dx.doi.org/10.26278/NWFE-VJ78, 00:05:38.633–00:06:05.666].
4 Lou Bennett, "Black fulla, White fulla: Can there be a truly balanced collaboration?" in *Musical Collaboration between Indigenous and non-Indigenous People in Australia: Exchanges in the Third Space*, ed. Katelyn Barney (New York: Routledge, 2022), 12.
5 See Reuben Brown and Solomon Nangamu, "'I'll show you that manyardi': Memory and lived experience in the performance of public ceremony in Western Arnhem Land," in *Music, Dance and the Archive*, ed. Amanda Harris, Linda Barwick and Jakelin Troy (Sydney: Sydney University Press, 2022), 29.
6 'Bininj' means Aboriginal person in the language of Bininj Kunwok. It has a second meaning (indicated in this book in italics and no capitals) of 'man', as opposed to *daluk* (woman). In Mawng language, 'Arrarrkpi/*arrarrkpi*' has the same meaning as 'Bininj/*bininj*' (the word in Mawng for woman is *warramumpik*).

1 Following footsteps

'Following footsteps' is a common idiomatic expression used by Bininj/Arrarrkpi songmen in English and in western Arnhem Land languages to describe their *kun-borrk/manyardi* song repertories. In Bininj Kunwok, the verb *-kadjung* means literally to 'follow/chase', but is also used in the sense of 'to sing a [secret] ceremonial song' or 'to follow a text and melody in other public song [*kun-borrk*]'.[1] In Mawng language, the verb *-yarru* has a similar meaning, 'to follow', but is often used in the metaphorical sense (as in English) of 'doing something as someone else has done before'.[2] Mawng people tell the ancestral story of the quoll and the moon, who were both Arrarrkpi (M: human) during the Dreamtime, and who fought to the death. The moon rose again and became immortal, but the quoll died. As Lazarus Lamilami tells it, the quoll said:

> *"Ngapi nganamin kapin Arrarrkpi*
> *Ngarrunpayarrun amparrkamparr ta kanipa ta kunak ta*
> *nakapa kutpamajupa naka ngapi ngarrunpanayarrun"*
>
> "I'm going to be like humans.
> You will all follow me, everyone on earth, you'll all die.
> You'll follow in my footsteps and die like me"[3]

Each singer's repertory consists of a number of different songs, collectively called a 'song-set'.[4] These song-sets are named after particular animals and plants, or after song-giving spirits that live in the ancestral country of the singer—in the rocky Arnhem Land plateau, or in the mangroves along the coast of Arnhem Land. These animals, plants, and spirits are evoked and enacted in designs painted on the body with *delek* (K: white ochre), and in the rhythms and melodies of the songs. Dancers associated with the plateau country paint themselves with a white clay splatter design called *bedjekbedjek* in Bininj Kunwok, which is said to imitate the mischievous *mimih* rock spirits that inhabit the caves of the plateau, while dancers associated with the saltwater country (the coast and surrounding islands) may paint themselves with designs that represent the wings of a bird.[5]

DOI: 10.4324/9781003216339-2

The movement that accompanies *kun-borrk/manyardi* also 'follows' the animals, plants, and spirits that the song-set is named after. For example, when *daluk* (K: women) dance Karrbarda (K: long yam), they imitate digging the yam and carrying it above their heads with their dillybags. As the late singer for the Karrbarda song-set Eric Mardday explained, '*kabirri-melme and kabirri-karung karrbarda*' (K: 'they [the dancers] stamp their feet [in the style that imitates the *mimih* spirits] and dig the long yam').[6] Other statements by western Arnhem Land songmen recorded over the course of my fieldwork about the sounds of the didjeridu and voice reveal the extent to which this idea of 'following' phenomena from the natural and ancestral world permeates the song and dance tradition:

- "Me, I follow that Marrawiwi [M: name of song-set], this one [demonstrates the dancing], *yarrmanaya* [M: large hardyheads], that's me—I dance." (Tommy Madjalkaidj)[7]
- "They dance, follow that seagull and fish." (Alfred Gawaraidji)[8]
- "I follow that trevally [body design]."(Alfred Gawaraidji)[9]
- [The vocables in the Mularrik Mularrik (M: frog) song] follow that, like how that frog she talk, they play the didj [didjeridu] the same like frog [demonstrates frog sounds][10]—"That tidal wave like... that tidal that come, that *kurrula* [M: sea], they [the women dancers] follow that beating [of the clapstick].[11] (Solomon Nangamu)

Franca Tamisari observes that for Yolngu (Aboriginal people of eastern Arnhem Land), stories, kinship, songs, painting, and dances are 'footprints' of ancestral activity that can be conjured up in the present:

> *Djalkiri* or *luku* (literally 'foot' and by extension 'footprint' and 'step') is the term often used to refer to different aspects of Yolngu Law (*rom*) which originated from ancestral journeys and actions that shaped the land[...] These visible marks or 'footprints' are continuously manifested and retraced in paintings (*dhulang*), songs (*manikay*) and dances (*bunggurl*)... In phenomenological terms the 'footprint', I assert, is a 'living body' and a 'knowing body', an embodied consciousness and perception of and in the world, simultaneously a fragment and an agent of place, a product and actor of social relations, a subject and object of action and experience.[12]

The metaphor of footsteps also relates to the way the western Arnhem Land performance tradition is handed down over generations; it acknowledges both the agency of *kobah-kobanj* in guiding ceremonial performance and of *yawurrunj* carrying on and innovating the song and dance practice they have inherited. When you follow someone's footsteps, you follow their particular path, while at the same time creating fresh footsteps for the next person to follow. In a similar way, as I will explore in this book, songmen not only perform the same songs and teach the same dances that their relatives gave them but also refresh the repertories they have inherited over time by lending their own singing style to the songs. Occasionally, they receive new songs in dreams which they add to the repertory of inherited songs. These songs come from ancestral spirits residing in Country, or spirits of relatives including those that taught them to sing and dance when they were growing up.[13] As Solomon Nangamu explained to me while staying in his family home in Gunbalanya after a recent trip to his ancestral home of Goulburn Island:

> Myself, I can listen to that clapstick. Somebody watch me, but they sing it for me. They give me that song and I sing that song. I got a couple of new songs now, when I was living there [Goulburn Island]. And I got it in my dream. My ancestors, they talked to me, and I listen, that they're going to give me something—a present, like a gift.[14]

Yet even these 'new' gifted songs contain the same song words, melodies, and rhythms as the 'old' songs, and are performed in a manner and order established by previous generations. As the late singer for the Karrbarda (K: long yam) song-set, Eric Mardday explained, songs that have been recently conceived in dreams are still considered the same as those songs that came before. The recipient then starts 'practising' and 'working up' this 'new' song to be performed in ceremony:

> We can't change [...] Karrbarda (K: long yam song-set) [it's] from grandfather footsteps. We go back to grandfather footstep all the way. If my kids, they learn [to sing Karrbarda songs], they still go back [i.e. to sing the old songs], they can't change. Like if they keep going [singing and dancing], they might get from dream, *yi-beng[kan]* (K: you understand), like when old people [spirits] coming up and singing another song, and they get up, start practising, and then we have like big ceremony [...] and we say 'all right, this another song coming up'. But it's still Karrbarda.[15]

As Allan Marett notes—tracing back to earlier scholarship on Aboriginal Australian music by Catherine Ellis[16]—there is a widespread convention that associates particular melodic forms with Dreamings, and the ancestors, peoples, and countries associated with those Dreamings.[17] Solomon Nangamu similarly discusses how the melody of song-set is retained, even as the song-set is passed down through the generations:

> [We] can't change it, can't get another tune. It stays there forever, until we pass it to a new generation—like our own children, our son, our grandson.[18]

Regenerating ancestral connections through *kun-borrk/manyardi*

The living history of Bininj/Arrarrkpi occupation of western Arnhem Land goes back thousands of generations, and is extensively recorded in beautiful detail all over the Arnhem Land plateau in rocky outcrop caves and 'galleries'.[19] Here, Bininj/Arrarrkpi sheltered for millennia from the sun and the monsoonal rains, and painted *bim* (K: rock art paintings) about their lives and the lives of their ancestors.[20] Some of these *bim* are instructional in nature, displaying a 'menu' of the various edible fish species in the area such as barramundi and catfish, detailing their organs—a style of painting known as 'X-ray art'.[21] Many *bim* record the movement of ancestral creators across the region such as *namarrkon* (K: lightening Dreaming ancestor), depicted with hammers protruding from his knees and elbows which he uses to strike and throw thunder, or *yingarna* (K: creation mother), depicted with numerous dillybags, each representing spirit-children who gave Bininj/Arrarrkpi the different languages of western Arnhem Land.[22]

Other *bim* are about Aboriginal lore, depicting stories about ancestral figures who married the 'wrong skin' (non-eligible marriage partners), and about ceremony and the origins of song and dance. These paintings show *mimih* (stone country) spirits dancing and playing clapsticks and didjeridu, and were painted during the freshwater period (1,500 years ago–present day) when the sea levels receded and the freshwater rivers flooded the plains. As Alice Moyle argues, this suggests that the didjeridu was a relatively 'late intrusion' into the cultural life and song tradition of Aboriginal people of Arnhem Land.[23] Whilst Bininj/Arrarrkpi culture therefore has ancient foundations, it is also dynamic. Just as songmen continue to perform new compositions based on songs passed down to them, artists continue to paint and sculpt innovative works of art inspired by the *bim* of their ancestors.

Reflecting on how his *manyardi* came about, songman Solomon Nangamu remarked:

> Any living thing they was eating, like *kobah-kobanj* [K: old people], like *korroko* [K: a long time ago]—oyster, cockle, anything that lived in that sea—seafood, people who lived on this island, long time. They said "ah, we can't just go eat food? How 'bout we make song about this tucker—bush tucker?". So, they made all this song now, that we're singing now. They talk about land, they talk about the seaside, any living creature that God made, and *kobah-kobanj* they got that thing, and they passed it to me and I try and pass it to my new generation…[24]

Nangamu's explanation resonates with the observations of scholars such as Berndt, Myers, and Stanner on the performative nature of the Dreaming. Anthropologist W.E.H. Stanner gave the first extended explanation of the connection between the ancestral period ('The Dreaming') and the present (the

'Here-and-Now'). Stanner argued that stories from the Dreaming do not provide a literal meaning, nor a definition or truth, but rather a 'poetic key to Reality' or a 'key of Truth':

> The active philosophy of Aboriginal life transforms this 'key', which is expressed in the idiom of poetry, drama and symbolism, into a principle that The Dreaming determines not only what life *is* but also *what it can be*. Life, so to speak, is a one-possibility thing, and what this is, is the 'meaning' of the Dreaming.[25]

The Dreaming, which shaped the country that people inhabit and to which people are linked through their ancestors who had lived in that country since time immemorial, manifests itself in the here-and-now in various forms. Living and natural phenomena such as birds, yam, and the sea are interpreted as manifestations of the ongoing presence and power of The Dreaming. Songs, dances, and ceremony are passed on from ancestral spirits that still dwell in the country such as *mimih* (K: stone country spirits) or *warra ngurrijakurr* (M: little mangrove-dwelling spirit people). In this way, they 'follow up the Dreaming' and re-enact its presence.[26] Like Stanner, Fred Myers argues that it is precisely through the activities that Aboriginal people perform in the *present* that they are able to give meaning to the Dreaming and able to 'hold' their particular ancestral country:

> The meaning of these places, their value, must be understood as constructed—not by the application of some pure cultural model to blank nature... but in activities that constitute relationships within a system of social life that structures difference and similarity among persons.[27]

Ronald Berndt observes that the artist plays a vital role in this interpretation of the Dreaming, as a 're-activator' of the spirits, 'reviving the spiritual' through the paintings, songs, dance, carvings, etc. that he or she creates.[28] Berndt suggests that through metaphoric and symbolic meaning, western Arnhem Land songs 'guide us toward an intellectual appreciation of the world about us'.[29]

Nangamu's insights about song creation allude to the richness of the *kun-borrk/ manyardi* tradition and the many named song-sets that have been performed by various songmen over the generations, all of which pay homage to various 'living creatures' of western Arnhem Land (see Support Material Figure 1.iv for a list of song-sets). *Kobah-kobanj* were keeping alive the very things that they treasured and that sustained them by putting them into a song; 'they got that *thing*'—that inspiration or life force that has its origins in the Dreaming—and they fashioned it in musical form, and then passed it on so that it could continue to be nurtured. His reference to God as creator hints at Arrarrkpi integration of Methodist teachings of Christianity into their spiritual beliefs and understandings about the Dreaming (discussed in Chapter 2).

Today, as in the past, Bininj/Arrarrkpi come together to perform *kun-borrk/ manyardi* in ceremonies that mark a variety of social occasions—funerals, community celebrations, exchanges between language groups (called Mamurrng ceremonies), cultural festivals, and recreational occasions. Ceremony helps people socially, to navigate a way forward and forge new footsteps in changing circumstances. This might involve grieving for a deceased family member; celebrating an achievement in the community; and establishing good relationships between groups that find themselves living or working together for the first time. When their voices are strong, the didjeridu is clear, and the dancing is tight, Bininj/Arrarrkpi also feel spiritually supported by their ancestors. On another occasion (see Chapter 2), Nangamu spoke directly into the camera I had set up to document the performance, delivering his message to a wider audience including future generations of Arrarrkpi and Balanda (Euro-diasporic) who would be reading this book:

> I don't know about today, all this new generation, they don't listen to us, they just ignore us. But our song, you can't leave our song; it's in our hearts, in our minds. And for me, I can't leave my culture, I can't. If I leave it [and] I don't sing, I get sick. Thats mean I lost my culture, everything—I got nothing. But I have to keep my culture strong, always, all the time. Wherever I go, my song is with me all the time.[30]

The gift of a song then represents more than the sum of its parts (the words, melody or 'tune', didjeridu and clapstick rhythm, and dance accompaniment). In Nangamu's words, it is his link to 'culture' and to the *kobah-kobanj* that came before him. To cease practising singing, playing *mako*, and dancing is to go 'off track' from *kobah-kobanj* who first received and then passed on the gift.

Singing, dancing, and exchanging gifts

The idea Nangamu expressed of giving and receiving gifts as a means of activating and maintaining relations is a topic of substantial anthropological and ethnomusicological literature. Malinowski theorised systems of exchange through his analysis of the Kula ring practised by Trobriand islanders, which he described as a 'big, inter-tribal relationship, uniting with definite social bonds a vast area and great numbers of people, binding them with definite ties of reciprocal obligations'.[31] Following on from Malinowski, Mauss analysed Melanesian, Northwest North American, and ancient Eurasian societies, showing how practices of giving, receiving, and returning gifts sustain long-term relations: the gift received remains active as a symbol of the relationship it fosters, thereby creating mutual obligations. Drawing on Maori understanding that *taonga* (goods) possess *hau* (spirit), Mauss theorised gift-giving as about passing on something essential of oneself: 'because the thing itself possesses a soul, is of the soul'.[32]

Weiner argued that rituals of exchange in Melanesian society are essential to processes of regeneration:

> exchange interaction is reflective of the kinds of symbolic and material values a society accords its reproductive and regenerative flow [...] the flow must be "fed" or the system (or part of it) begins to collapse. The modus operandi of this "feeding" is exchange.[33]

More recently, Sykes analyses sounds/musics in the Sri Lankan (Sinhala Buddhist) tradition as part of an exchange with deities whereby sounds originating from gods are given to people, given to other people, and given back to gods, contributing to the idea of sounds/musics not as an expression of one's identity but as 'gifts that must be given as gestures of respect'.[34]

In western Arnhem Land, exchange ceremonies such as the Mamurrng (explored in Chapter 4 of this book) enact not only ties to ancestors and ancestral country but also diplomacy within a regional landscape of variegated language and clan identities. The exchange of gifts is a dynamic, reciprocal, and essentially performative process, rather than a purely commercial transaction. As Ronald Berndt observes, 'the value of the goods themselves is felt to be enhanced and emphasised, in varying degrees, by the elaboration of the ritual of which they are, essentially, the focal point'.[35] The *mamurrng* pole that is exchanged as part of the Mamurrng ceremony represents more than the sum of its parts. It is what Antoinette Weiner refers to as an 'inalienable gift', 'imbued with the intrinsic and ineffable identities of [its owner] which are not easy to give away'.[36] One of these 'ineffable' aspects of the receiver's identity is the lock of hair that is sent to the givers of the mamurrng as an invitation to initiate the ceremony. Both the receiver and the giver also exchange ancestral knowledge through the performance of songs and dances handed down to them. Unlike commodities, which become private property once they are exchanged, inalienable gifts remain attached to the donor, creating a bond between the donor and recipient: 'control over the meaning and inheritance of inalienable possessions accords authority to their owners, and is the seed of differences between groups—they represent enduring social identities'.[37] *Kun-borrk/manyardi* is perhaps the ultimate of inalienable gifts, in that it can be sung/danced for other people, but the performers still own the songs, dances, and body paint designs.

This giving of inalienable gifts in order to create new relationships or renew existing relationships takes place as part of a 'gift economy'.[38] Prior to European colonisation, gift economies were common throughout Aboriginal Australian society and among many Indigenous societies around the world, and—as we will explore in Chapter 6—still persist today in parallel with market-based capitalist economies. Giving places the receiver under an obligation to receive, and to make some kind of (unspecified) return in the future.[39] Each clan may have a number of relationships of reciprocity to other neighbouring clans in different directions, creating an interdependent network of exchange within any given region of Aboriginal society. As Donald Thomson reports in 1949 of his Yolngu informant named Raiwalla, this urge to give as part of a ceremonial network of exchange is stronger and distinct from the gift given in response to a request:

> He conceives his giving within the ceremonial cycle—which is of the type called *wetj*—as due to *marr*, to the force, the ritual urge, (stronger, even, than the desire to retain and possess *gerri* [trade items]) to pass them on and either to increase thereby his own prestige in the *kumur marnda* [trading partner] relationship, or to acquit himself of an existing obligation in the quarter to which he sends it.[40]

Ceremonial exchange creates a form of regional diplomacy by perpetuating obligation between groups and is also important to the way that Aboriginal people identify with Country and make claims to place. As Fred Myers suggests:

> place enters into Aboriginal social life in a fashion similar to other material forms, mediated by social action, as a potential formulation of similarity and difference, a token of identity and exchange.[41]

Informed by a Pintupi worldview, Myers argues that Aboriginal land ownership consists primarily of 'control over the stories, objects, and rituals associated with the mythological ancestors of The Dreaming at a particular place'.[42] One accesses restricted knowledge of these 'esoterica' through instruction by those who have previously acquired it, and possesses the right to 'hold' Country only through other people's acceptance of shared identity with a claimant.[43] Ceremonial exchange plays an essential role in this recognition and acceptance of shared identity, in turning cooperative ties among 'frequent co-residents' of a place into enduring ties between 'countrymen'.[44]

Repatriation and archival returns of Indigenous song and dance

The repatriation of archival collections of song, dance, language, and ceremony to source communities and individuals is now a common research methodology within applied ethnomusicology.[45] Repatriation can serve as a model for dissembling and potentially undoing relations of power inherent in the way that colonised peoples have been represented,[46] and as a tool for revitalising and sustaining endangered song practices and languages.[47] Anthony Seeger defines repatriation in such contexts as 'the return of music to circulation in communities where it has been unavailable as a result of external power differences—often the result of colonialism, but also including differential access to wealth and technology, educational training, and other factors'.[48] Returns may involve providing a copy of a recording, enabling access to a database, conveying legal ownership of an item, or returning original recordings to communities without retaining a copy at the source institution.[49] Barwick et al. argue that culturally appropriate mobilisation of archival materials can have a powerful effect for those that inherit the knowledge they embody, and that 'since archivists, intermediaries, and end users are all involved, doing archival returns cannot help but change archival systems and research practices too'.[50] Indigenous researchers have drawn on local knowledge frameworks and practices in order to reintegrate archival recordings into contemporary practices and relationships. Clint Bracknell (Noongar) emphasises the agency of Country in nurturing song revival from old recordings:

> in the right context, listening to and commenting on performances recorded in the past can enhance social, emotional and personal wellbeing in Aboriginal communities. Repatriated recordings may also reaffirm intimate personal relationships between people and ancestors, Country and kin; contribute to understandings of local history; become useful when integrated into community and public education projects; and demonstrate continuity of tradition, which can be especially useful in the articulation of Indigenous rights[51]

Payi Linda Ford has applied an Indigenous methodology based on the Mak Mak Marranunggu philosophy of the Mirrwana (cycad palm) and Wurrkama (work done including leaching of toxins from the cycad fruit kernel in preparation for consumption at ceremony events) to the process of returning sound recordings of *wali* and *wangga* Indigenous ceremony from the Daly region of Australia:

> The project's Indigenous research methodology started by treating the body of recordings of the ceremonies and the metadata as the equivalent of the unprocessed *pelanggu* [cycad fruit]. *Pelanggu* is not edible without this transformative processing. The individual pieces of information, recordings dispersed both in time and filing location, needed to be assembled in one place and treated in various ways so as to be re-archived and available for re-use in an easily accessible form. The process was analogous to the ways in which the *pelanggu* is processed before being eaten, and ingested, as *lawa* [a sweet flatbread].[52]

This book deals with the return of both physical remains and digital cultural materials to Bininj and Arrarrkpi at Gunbalanya and Warruwi. Bininj and Arrarrkpi similarly brought their own localised rituals to repatriated objects and to historical recordings by reintroducing them to their country and kin through the performance of *kun-borrk/manyardi*. In Chapter 3, the stolen remains of Aboriginal ancestors held in the United States of America for over 60 years are carried through town and reburied on a wave of song and dance. Elder Jimmy Kalarriya reflects on this moment; he can feel that the spirits are happy to be home.

Chapter 6 explores the reaction of Kalarriya and other songmen to the return of recordings originally made on wire as part of the American-Australian Scientific Expedition to Arnhem Land (AASEAL). Kalarriya—who was a teenager living 'in the bush' in 1948 when the Expedition came—calls out in delight as he recognises his uncle singing. He gives his kinship name, language, traditional country, and relationship to family today. In doing so, he re-embeds the digital recordings in the present physical and social environment. The narrative that emerges through this book is therefore about the role of song and dance practice in activating such returns. Repatriation is understood as a process of bringing *subjects*—including voices past and present, and spirits—into dialogue with the living. By understanding *kun-borrk/manyardi* performance, we may better understand the systems of gifting and exchange that originally motivated Bininj/Arrarrkpi to create archival records, and that are essential to the ways in which cultural materials are received, ritualised, and emotionally metabolised within existing relationships today.

This understanding of archival recordings and digital returns as belonging to cycles of gifting and returning is articulated by senior Junba singer and teacher Matthew Martin. As ethnomusicologist Sally Treloyn writes, Wurnan is a law and practice in the Kimberley of sharing, which can also provide a framework to make sense of the relationships between singers, communities, and researchers:

> Far more than a rigid system of exchange, Wurnan is a kinetic place-based, flexible, cultural and economic system shaped by relationships and collaboration between individuals and between individuals and institutions.[53]

Martin explains that his relationship with Treloyn is also Wurnan:

> Wurnan only coming to [us] for sharing. Share a lot of things, like food, Junba. Share, sharing with spears, woomeras, it's sharing. Wurnan is for a gift, you know. Free gift…Like you [Treloyn] are working with me and I got a Wurnan for you. I Wurnan with you see. You do the recording for me and I do the talking and I'm, it's just like Wurnan giving us. I giving you the stories and you work with me. It's a gift. Recording—that's a gift. You record things.[54]

Understood through the lens of Wurnan, the archival record of Bininj material and intangible culture—dispersed across multiple collections around the globe—might be characterised as a series of exchanges in which goods were shared (or in the case of ancestral bones, stolen) awaiting return or reciprocation. Numerous *kun-borrk/manyardi* songs have been gifted to the archive over the decades; each associated with different song-sets and languages of this polyglot community, stemming from diverse ceremonial events, and connected to networks of people and place. When I began this research, much of this context was missing or lay dormant, ready to be reactivated. Whilst the scientists and recordists of the 1948 AASEAL Expedition did not conceptualise their collections as gifts in a system of exchange, the reception of Bininj/Arrarrkpi to physical and digital returns many years later would lead to the formation of new social relations, and ultimately the composition of new songs.

The 1948 recordings and media

The media I returned to western Arnhem Land included photographs by expedition leader and ethnologist Charles Mountford, photographer Howell Walker, and deputy leader and archaeologist Frank Setzler; 'several miles' of colour (silent) film produced by Walker and cine-photographer Peter Bassett-Smith,[55] as well as audio by the Australian Broadcasting Commission's Colin Simpson and Raymond Giles at Gunbalanya, including recordings of *kun-borrk/manyardi*.[56] Much of it was originally cut up and edited for feature films and radio documentaries for Western audiences, before being placed in archival storage. In 1948, the documentary film was still an emerging genre; recording audio in the field was expensive and impractical due to the heavy, cumbersome nature of the devices. Instead, film-makers typically applied voice-overs and soundtrack 'post-production'.[57] Bassett-Smith's footage was later edited together in this manner to produce three films, titled *Arnhem Land*, *Aborigines of the Sea Coast*, and *Birds and Billabongs*.[58] Walker's footage was shot for the National Geographic Society and was intended to accompany public lectures given by Setzler and others.[59] This footage—consisting of short films typically 3–5 minutes long, staging various 'activities' of the Expedition—was saved onto spools of film and remained in the archive at the Smithsonian Institution until it was recently rediscovered and digitised.[60] Similarly, the audio recordings by Simpson and Giles obtained by members of our research team and consisting in part of a sample of public songs recorded at Gunbalanya were initially made for the ABC radio feature *Expedition to Arnhem Land*.

This media represented a curated subset of 'public' material from Gunbalanya, separate from the recordings of a secret men's ceremony that Mountford had commissioned, and which historian Martin Thomas and linguist Murray Garde had earlier auditioned with senior initiated men. As Garde points out, the men that remembered the ceremony regarded this footage with great fondness, but as was made clear to Expedition members at the time, it was never supposed to have been viewed, heard, or discussed publicly.[61] In spite of the Expedition's focus at the time to document secret ceremonies—highly valued by senior initiated knowledge holders who were able to review the footage privately decades later—it would be recordings of public song and footage of everyday events overlooked by the Expedition that would hold value to a broad audience of Bininj/Arrarrkpi today, generate endless discussion, and provide rich material for analysis in this book.

Western Arnhem Land songmen like Nangamu engaged in the playback of archival media and contributed their own knowledge of *kun-borrk/manyardi* in order to address an urgent need—which they identified explicitly—to record and document songs and song knowledge for current and future generations of Bininj/Arrarrkpi, as well as the broader society. There was precedent for this: five years prior to my fieldwork, Mirrijpu singer Solomon Nangamu had recorded and discussed his songs with ethnomusicologists Linda Barwick and Isabel O'Keeffe on two previous occasions at Goulburn Island, while the fathers and grandfathers of singers for the Inyjalarrku and Marrwakara song-sets had made recordings of their songs with anthropologist Ronald Berndt in the 1960s. Berndt wrote of this previous generation of songmen:

> the majority of the older men were well aware that unless we recorded all aspects of their life, in the form in which we saw it at that particular time, it would be irretrievably lost. They recognised that we were, in effect, recording this material for future generations.[62]

Although the narrative of 'salvaging cultures lost' has been a common theme in anthropological research,[63] current songmen seemed interested in creating recordings mostly as an aid to teaching and as part of an ongoing dialogue with past and future recordings, rather than as a means of capturing a 'dying culture'. At the same time, Bininj/Arrarrkpi elders want to preserve their knowledge for posterity. The introduction of archival recordings of *kun-borrk/manyardi* into the fieldwork process enabled Kunwinjku elders such as Jimmy Kalarriya—an expert in the songs and languages of western Arnhem Land and all aspects of traditional life—to share knowledge from an era that very few had lived through. Kalarriya felt that by putting his 'stories' and knowledge on paper (or a digital version of it) he could trade his specialised knowledge and be compensated to support himself and his family:

> I know story from old people, like I trade-im up story from old people. Only I'm the man [with the knowledge], not other people. I like you[64] write-im down paper and you put here Injalak [Arts Centre], so that I get good money.[65]

When Kalarriya passed away in 2012, his loss was felt profoundly by both Bininj/Arrarrkpi families and Balanda who had worked with him. His willingness to 'trade-im up story' while he was still alive meant that he gifted an expansive corpus of Bininj knowledge to the archive for future generations.

By engaging 'outsiders' and researchers like me, Bininj/Arrarrkpi in western Arnhem Land were not only addressing challenges around transmission of important cultural knowledge identified by Nangamu and Kalarriya; they were also engaging something akin to Wurnan described by Matthew Martin. In my first weeks at Gunbalanya volunteering for the reburial ceremony, I formed an important collaboration and friendship with Donna Nadjamerrek. In her role as the Indigenous Engagement Officer at Gunbalanya, Donna taught me, as well as other visiting scholars, teachers, and Government employees about the various traditional owner families that made up the community of Gunbalanya, about aspects of Kunwinjku language, and about the western Arnhem Land kinship system (see Support Material Figure 1.i). Under this system, each individual has a subsection or 'skin name', which is inherited matrilineally, and which determines their relationship to all others in Bininj/Arrarrkpi society. Based on their individual skin names (which belong to either the *ngarradjku* or *mardku* matrimoieties) and their clan name, Bininj/Arrarrkpi know whether to refer to one another as *ngadjadj* (K: uncle), *ngadburrung* (K: sibling), *karrang* (K: mother), etc. They also understand, based on these skin names, whether or not they are suitable marriage partners, or *binjkurrng* (K: in a mother-in-law avoidance relationship), for example. In order for me to have a place in Bininj/Arrarrkpi society, and in order for me to be easily identified by other Bininj/Arrarrkpi that I met in Gunbalanya in the appropriate way, Donna adopted me into her family (of the *Mok* clan estate) as her *darda* (K: little brother), giving me her skin name, *Ngarridj*.[66] This allowed me to perceive the Bininj social world through Donna's eyes so that I would call others by the same name that she gave them, and stand in a similar relationship to them as she did.

Experienced interlocutors such as Kalarriya's nephew Isaiah Nagurrgurrba helped to explain and translate my research project to others, while singers including Nangamu and Eric Mardday encouraged my active learning of Bininj/Arrarrkpi culture by including me in the singing ensemble, introducing me to relations or to the host families at funeral ceremonies, and showing me their country. In exchange, I compensated research collaborators with money for their time, as well as transport to and from events (often travelling long distances for funerals in outstations) and ensured that elders and senior knowledge holders in particular were looked after and catered for with *manme/walij* (K/M: food) whenever we worked or travelled together.

Multilingual *kun-borrk/manyardi*

The region of western Arnhem Land in the Northern Territory of Australia includes the Aboriginal community of Gunbalanya (Oenpelli) and the island communities of Warruwi (South Goulburn Island)[67] and Minjilang (Croker Island) to the north, as well as many small outstations around the central Arnhem Land plateau.[68] The environment and biodiversity of the area is spectacular, ranging from the rocky escarpment country, which feeds freshwater rivers and streams after wet season rains, to tropical savannah woodlands and monsoon rainforest, floodplains and lowland wetlands, and coastal areas. My fieldwork was conducted mainly in the communities of Gunbalanya, Warruwi, and the mining town of

Jabiru, which is located within Kakadu National Park, some 250 km east of Darwin on the Arnhem Highway. Gunbalanya is a further 70 km northeast of Jabiru on the eastern side of the East Alligator River, and the two communities share language, clan, and kinship ties. Warruwi is 290 km east of Darwin and 100 km northeast of Jabiru. Other locations mentioned in the book include Sandy Creek (a camping area) and Mikkinj Valley outstation (see Figure 1.1).

Arnhem Land is an area of great linguistic diversity. Of the 250 or so Indigenous languages spoken in Australian pre-European contact, more than 20 Aboriginal languages are found in Arnhem Land.[69] In this area and elsewhere in Australia, some languages are 'holding on' with very few remaining speakers, as English and other regional lingua francas take over. Today, fewer than 20 Aboriginal Australian languages are considered 'strong'; the rest are either 'extinct'/'dormant' or highly endangered.[70] The fact that these languages are still

Figure 1.1 Map of western Arnhem Land, showing languages and communities referred to in the book. Cartography © Brenda Thornley 2023.[71]

spoken and others are in processes of revival/reawakening, despite the devastating effects of colonisation, says something of the resilience of Aboriginal language and culture. Although the number of speakers of Aboriginal languages has diminished compared with pre-European contact around 1,800, it is important to understand the traditional languages of the country and their boundaries, since Aboriginal people continue to observe such distinctions, and identify with their traditional language groups, even if these languages are no longer spoken. Songmen also associate songs with their ancestors who spoke these language varieties, and with their traditional country.

Mawng is the main language of Goulburn Island and Warruwi community and is spoken by around 400 people of all generations, while the main language spoken today at Gunbalanya community is Kunwinjku with around 1,500 mother-tongue speakers.[72] Mawng is part of the Iwaidjan language family which also includes Amurdak, Iwaidja, the near-extinct/dormant Garig/Ilgar and Marrku, and extinct/dormant Manangkardi and Wurrugu. Kunwinjku is one of a number of dialects referred to collectively as Bininj Kunwok, which means 'people's language'.[73] This dialect chain also includes Kundjeyhmi, Kundedjnjenghmi, Kuninjku, Kune, and Manyallaluk Mayali, and has become a lingua franca for most of western Arnhem Land.[74] Bininj Kunwok belongs to the Gunwinyguan language family (remotely related to Iwaidjan).[75] Both Bininj Kunwok and Mawng are Non-Pama-Nyungan languages, which have different characteristics from the majority of Australian languages (Pama-Nyungan). Bininj Kunwok is an example of a 'polysynthetic' language, meaning that 'it is possible, in a single word, to use processes of morphological composition to encode information about both the predicate and all its arguments [...], allowing this word to serve alone as a free-standing utterance without reliance on context'.[76]

Across western Arnhem Land, multilingualism is the norm; it is not uncommon for some adults to converse in up to half a dozen Australian languages.[77] The conversations I conducted with songmen and other Bininj/Arrarrkpi—characterised by 'code switching' between languages—reflected this multilingual normality. Usually, I asked questions in English and Kunwinjku, and the majority of Mawng songmen would typically converse with one another in Mawng, after which one of them would relate the answer to me in a mixture of Kunwinjku, Northern Aboriginal Kriol, and English. One of the reasons that multilingualism persists is because of the ongoing cultural practice of clan exogamy (marriage outside one's own clan). Aboriginal people continue to move between communities—such as Warruwi and Gunbalanya—not only for marriage or relationships, but also for work opportunities, and for ceremony. The community of Warruwi on Goulburn Island has around 400 residents who speak ten different languages; an example of a multilingual community that has fostered language difference in spite of its remoteness and its small population.[78] The traditional country of Mawng speakers includes Goulburn Island as well as a section along the coast opposite the islands, sharing a boundary with Kunbarlang-speaking groups to the east, Iwaidja-speaking groups to the west, and Kunwinjku-speaking groups to the south (refer to Figure 1.1). Because of this history of shared boundaries and ceremony, all of these neighbouring languages are today spoken at Warruwi, along with languages from Maningrida (Ndjébbana) and eastern Arnhem Land (varieties of Yolŋu Matha). In pre-contact times, it is likely that there were at least three dialects of Mawng, including Manangkardi, considered to have been spoken by people on North and South Goulburn Island, Ngurtikin, spoken by people living in the western side of the mainland, and Mayinjinaj, spoken by people living in the eastern side of the mainland.[79] Each of these dialects is associated with the Mirrijpu, Inyjalarrku, and Marrawiwi song-sets, respectively.

Whereas at Goulburn Island the traditional language of Mawng is still spoken, at Gunbalanya the main language of Bininj Kunwok and Kunwinjku dialects originates further east. The traditional languages associated with the area in which Gunbalanya is situated include Mengerrdji, Erre, and Urningangk, classified within the Giimbiyu language family, all of which are no longer commonly spoken.[80] A number of historical factors contributed to the decline of speakers of these languages—namely, the impacts of disease and the establishment of buffalo-shooting camps around the East Alligator River and then the mission at Oenpelli, which brought speakers from lands further to the east into the area.[81] It is not entirely clear why Kunwinjku became the lingua franca at Oenpelli (as opposed to other Bininj Kunwok dialects and neighbouring languages belonging to speakers who moved into the area). Nevertheless, by the time the Anglican Church Missionary Society (CMS, Church of England) arrived in 1925 to establish a mission at Oenpelli, Kunwinjku was the dominant language, and the CMS used Kunwinjku both in the church and as the language in which to translate the Bible, further cementing its status as a lingua franca.[82]

Kundjeyhmi, a dialect of Bininj Kunwok, is the language associated with the Mirarr, who are traditional owners of the Jabiru township. There are fewer adult speakers of Kundjeyhmi compared with Kunwinjku, and many Bininj children at Jabiru speak either Northern Aboriginal Kriol, Kunwinjku, or English.[83] Other languages of the Kakadu National Park area traditionally include Gaagadju and Umbugarla or Ngumbur of the Murumburr and Wirlirrgu clans.[84] However, as with the Giimbiyu languages around Gunbalanya, the establishment of buffalo stations around the Kakadu area and mining communities in Eva Valley to the southeast had the effect of dispersing the population and reducing the speakers of these languages, to the point where these groups no longer converse in the language of their country but in common languages, which for the Murumburr and Wirlirrgu clans are Mayali and English.[85] As Evans suggests, although Kundjeyhmi and Kunwinjku people have common relatives and share the same language (Bininj Kunwok), they identify as distinct groups, most likely due to their post-contact experiences, with the former having grown up on the mission at Oenpelli, and the latter having associated with buffalo camps and interacted with mining communities.[86]

Locating the track

On the occasion of our first recording session at Injalak Hill in 2011, the western Arnhem Land songmen performed four songs each from their song-sets. After undertaking embedded fieldwork over a period of four years in western Arnhem Land learning Kunwinjku (the lingua franca of this region), understanding the kinship system of adopted family, and taking part in public ceremonial life—including learning to dance and sing—I had recorded dozens of other songs from the repertoires of collaborating songmen, and learned of hundreds more belonging to others. A number of questions emerged: how did the living practice of *kun-borrk* match with the archival record? Which song-sets continued to be performed, and which song-sets were remembered but not actively performed today? How many new ('dream-composed' or even 'spontaneous') songs had been conceived by subsequent generations of songmen? How many songs and song-sets might be lost if a singer or didjeridu player passes away, and what would the broader implications be? From the beginning of our collaboration, the singers made their thoughts clear about the challenges they faced, and expressed their anxieties about what they felt would be lost if *kun-borrk/manyardi* songs were no longer performed and passed down. Nangamu asked:

> How about our new generation, how they gonna do, when we die? They gunna see the person dead, no *manyardi*. They just get him and they chuck him in the ground. But *culture*, the main one is our culture. *Na-kobanj* (K: old man/Elder) he talk to us, *yoh*, we listen to him, you can't ignore him, you have to listen while he explains what's the meaning [of] what he says.[87]

Nangamu's insights highlight what is at stake if *kun-borrk/manyardi* is lost: Bininj/Arrarrkpi would not just lose their songs; they would potentially lose diverse modes of exchange with one another and with the spirit world, which help perpetuate the life cycle and regeneration of Country. His comment about 'ignoring' elders also points to the challenges of intergenerational transmission of multimodal practices such as *kun-borrk/manyardi* with complex and layered meanings that are embodied and understood by song experts.

In order to understand what it means to give and receive the gift of *kun-borrk/manyardi,* one might ask: 'what does it mean for Bininj/Arrarrkpi of western Arnhem Land to "follow in the footsteps" of their ancestors and perform *kun-borrk/manyardi*?' I approach this question in two ways: first, by examining how the song tradition operates across a variety of social circumstances. Each chapter centres on a particular historical or contemporary intercultural event in which *kun-borrk/manyardi* plays a central role. The events include

- an elicited recording at Injalak Hill to document *kun-borrk/manyardi* and introduce the author to key songmen and their repertories (Prologue)
- a spontaneous trip to sacred sites on Goulburn Island to perform for ancestral spirits (Chapter 2)
- a reburial ceremony performed more than 60 years after bones were stolen from Gunbalanya in 1948 (Chapter 3)
- a diplomacy ceremony performed for the author and his team of researchers (Chapter 4)
- a funeral ceremony for the traditional owner of Gunbalanya who led the reburial ceremony (Chapter 5)
- a corroboree performed in 1948 for members of the Expedition in Gunbalanya (Chapter 6)
- festivals and public performances in which the author performed with ceremony leaders (Chapter 7)

For each event, I consider:

- which individuals came together in order to make the particular performance event happen, and how was language/clan/kinship expressed through the performance?
- in what ways does the performance event interact with the broader society in which it takes place, and how do past performance events shape the present performance?
- how do Bininj/Arrarrkpi navigate the social, political, and economic dimensions of their contemporary lives through this performance event?

Secondly, the book aims to understand the way that *kun-borrk/manyardi* operates both as a distinct genre of western Arnhem Land and alongside other genres of the Top End, which come together as part of the social event. During our first recording session and discussion at Injalak, I made the observation that whilst songs from eastern Arnhem Land (*manikay*) might begin with unaccompanied vocals, the songs that they sang always started with didjeridu and then clapstick accompaniment, before the singer began to sing. James Gulamuwu answered me: 'yeah, like we all different together. Yolŋu people [of northeastern Arnhem Land] they play different, we play us mob different'.[88] Gulamuwu's characterisation of 'different together' is significant because it suggests a conscious differentiation—within western Arnhem Land song-sets and within the Top End region—that occurs 'together' in a shared ceremonial social space and within a unified musical framework. This dialogism is characterised by Nicholas Evans as the 'constructive fostering of variegation',[89] and can be seen in language, myth, social practices, kin classification, song, and ceremonial practice of Yolŋu and Bininj/Arrarrkpi culture.[90] Through musical analysis, I seek to show how this principle of complementary difference plays out, both aesthetically and socially, in each of the social events examined in the chapters of the book. In particular, I consider the considerations for performance—the footsteps, if you like—that *kun-borrk/manyardi* songmen and dancers follow, and have always followed. These include:

- rhythmic mode—how tempo and clapstick beating change within a song, and how this relates to the dance; how tempo changes from one song to the next and throughout a performance, and how this relates to the environment of the performance event[91]
- dance—how the movement and action that accompanies the songs fits with different elements of the music, including the song-set and its origins, the vocal phrase, tempo, clapstick beating, and didjeridu accompaniment of the song
- song order—how singers of different song-sets belonging to different language groups from western Arnhem Land and from the broader Top End region negotiate their performance and order songs in different social circumstances

Each chapter of the book opens with an ethnographic account in the first person, constructed from field notes that I took during and after the event. These accounts are included to help set the scene for an analysis of the *kun-borrk/manyardi* event, by describing my own participation in it, and allowing the reader to trace my own path to learning about Bininj/Arrarrkpi culture and receiving this gift as a Balanda researcher.

In addition to the events in focus, the book draws on a corpus of my own fieldwork recordings representing some of the main song-sets of western Arnhem Land and recordings made as part of the Western Arnhem Land Song Project and archival recordings from various collections (see Figure 1.2). The primary data therefore relates to both historical and contemporary performance events, as well as interviews that I carried out with key ceremony leaders and elders reflecting on these performance events. Because of the unfolding connections I made in particular with Donna Nadjamerrek and Solomon Nangamu at Gunbalanya and his country of Goulburn Island, the ethnography centres on *kun-borrk/manyardi* at these two communities and surrounding towns such as Jabiru and outstations such as Mikkinj Valley. Other areas where *kun-borrk/manyardi* is performed include Minjilang (Croker Island), Maningrida, Barunga, Beswick,

Figure 1.2 Russell Agalara, Alfred Gawaraidji, Tommy Madjalkaidj, and Solomon Nangamu making a recording of Marrawiwi/Inyjalarrku at Adjumalarl waterfall near Gunbalanya, 2012. Photograph by Reuben Brown.

and Bulman. A summary of performance events is listed in chronological order in Support Material Figure 1.iii.

A number of Bininj/Arrarrkpi consultants interviewed for the book contributed their perspectives on both western Arnhem Land performance and various other topics (see Support Material Figure 1.ii). Whilst my fieldwork focusses primarily on *kun-borrk/manyardi* performed at Gunbalanya and Goulburn Island, it does not necessarily account for all *kun-borrk/manyardi* song-sets and performers in western Arnhem Land, particularly those groups based at Minjilang (Croker Island) and other outstations of Arnhem Land and Kakadu National Park.

The archival record of *kun-borrk/manyardi*

Prior to the period of my fieldwork in 2011, a number of songmen from western Arnhem Land and other areas of the Top End were recorded at Gunbalanya and Warruwi by anthropologists, linguists, and musicologists, singing a diverse range of song-sets. Altogether 19 different song-sets were recorded by

10 different recordists in these locations, including 15 from western Arnhem Land, 3 from eastern Arnhem Land, and 1 song repertory from the Daly. There is a broad subdivision in western Arnhem Land between *wardde-ken* (K: 'of the stone country')—the area including and surrounding the Arnhem Land plateau (indicated in Figure 1.1)—and *kurrula* (M: saltwater country), which stretches along the northwestern coast of Arnhem Land, including the Cobourg Peninsula and Goulburn and Croker Islands.[92] This distinction applies to languages, song repertories, and other aspects of cultural life: most Bininj/Arrarrkpi recognise a song as either *kurrula*, *wardde-ken*, or from another region, even if they are not familiar with the name of the song-set or the singer. Because songmen travel around Arnhem Land to participate in ceremony and live and work in different communities, one is likely to hear both *kurrula* and *wardde-ken* songs sung in places outside of their traditional country of origin.[93] The multilingualism that characterises everyday conversation is also reflected in song; some song texts—such as Karrbarda (K: long yam)—switch between different languages within the same song.[94] Support Material Figure 1.iv shows the different song-sets, their country affiliation, and language (note that *kurrula* [M: sea] is both a subcategory and the name of a specific song-set). Many of these recordings were well known by current songmen and others in the community—some of whom had acquired their own copy of the recordings at some stage.

Whilst many of the song-sets recorded prior to 2011 were no longer being performed at these locations or elsewhere in western Arnhem Land, a significant number were still being performed, along with some song-sets that had not been recorded before at Gunbalanya or Warruwi. The main song repertories analysed in this book were recorded mostly at Gunbalanya and Goulburn Island, including Karrbarda (K: long yam) led by Eric Mardday, Yalarrkuku/Mirrijpu (M: seagull) led by Solomon Nangamu, Milyarryarr (M: black heron) led by Johnny Namayiwa, Marrwakara/Mularrik (M: goanna/green frog) led by Harold Warrabin, and Inyjalarrku (M: mermaid) led by David Manmurulu and now led by his sons Rupert Manmurulu, Renfred Manmurulu and Reuben Manmurulu, James Gulamuwu, and Tommy Madjalkaidj (who also led a song-set connected to Inyjalarrku named Marrawiwi [M: salmon]). Other song-sets listed in Table 1.1, which originate from outside of western Arnhem Land, include clan songs from northeastern Arnhem Land—referred to as *manikay* (song)—and central Arnhem Land, referred to as *bunggurl* (dance). These songs were recorded at festivals and funerals both in Gunbalanya and in other outstations of Arnhem Land. These repertories are mentioned in the descriptions of the events but have largely been left out of the performance analysis, which focusses on western Arnhem Land song.[95] As part of the performance analysis for this book, I itemised songs from a corpus including my own fieldwork recordings, as well as legacy recordings featuring current repertories of western Arnhem Land songs, documented as part of the Western Arnhem Land Song Project, and housed in the PARADISEC archive (see PARADISEC deposit RB2 for a complete list of recordings). In determining the identity of the song, I analysed the song text and the melody in the song, and compared this to other recordings of songs from the same song-set. Where existing song IDs from the Western Arnhem Land Song Project (WALSP) were available (for example, MP06: Mirrijpu song number 6), I have used the same WALSP song IDs, and created new song IDs for newly recorded songs or previously unidentified songs, in order to enable cross-corpora analysis in Chapter 8.

Performing ethnography (and writing an ethnography of performance)

This book traces the 'footsteps' of *kun-borrk/manyardi* in Bininj/Arrarrkpi social life through key performance events analysed in each chapter. I chose to organise the book around performance events (as opposed to *kun-borrk/manyardi* song repertories or other principles of the song tradition such as rhythm, melody, song order, dance) and to present these events in nonchronological order for two reasons: firstly, so as to present *kun-borrk/manyardi* as performance in the sense of what Richard Bauman defines as situated social action;[96] constituted in the patterned behaviour between the performer, participants, and the audience; and embedded in the time, place, and context of the performance. Bauman argues that performance is 'framed' in culturally specific ways by what he calls 'poetically patterned contextualisation cues'.[97] In a western Arnhem Land context, a song performed at the end of a sequence expresses 'goodbye', and is signalled through changes in the music and in the dance that mark the performance in ways that both audience and performer understand. Precisely who is saying goodbye to whom is also dependent on where and when the performance takes place, and whether the song is performed as part of a funeral ceremony, Mamurrng, or some other kind of occasion. Secondly, by understanding contemporary performance events in Chapters 2–5 and 7, the reader is better positioned to appreciate historical events and analysis of performances recorded more than 60 years prior in Chapter 6.

The songs and dances discussed mainly belong to a category of untranslatable 'spirit language' song-sets, although I also analyse some songs in 'ordinary' languages in Chapters 6 and 7. In the absence of a translatable song text, the 'contextualisation cues' of the performance are perhaps even more vital in understanding what the song is communicating. As Marett observes, the metalanguage used to describe Aboriginal performance may also be elliptical, in which case transcription and analysis become 'invaluable in isolating elements

28 *Following footsteps*

Table 1.1 Summary of song-sets performed during fieldwork (2011–13) in western Arnhem Land

Song-sets	Affiliation/genre	Language	Lead singer/s
Mirrijpu/Yalarrkuku (seagull)	*kurrula manyardi*	Spirit language associated with Manangkardi	Solomon Nangamu Russell Agalara
Inyjalarrku (mermaid)	*kurrula manyardi*	Spirit language associated with Mawng	David Manmurulu James Gulamuwu
Marrawiwi (salmon), connected to Inyjalarrku	*kurrula manyardi*	Spirit language associated with Mawng	Tommy Madjalkaidj Alfred Gawaraidji
Marrwakara (goanna)	*kurrula manyardi*	Spirit language associated with Mawng	Harold Warrabin
Milyarryarr (black heron)	*kurrula manyardi*	Spirit language associated with Manangkardi, Ilgar Marrku	Johnny Namayiwa
Nabarlek (rock wallaby)	*wardde-ken kun-borrk*	Kundedjnjenghmi Kune	Terrah Guymala
Karrbarda (long yam)	*wardde-ken kun-borrk*	Spirit language associated with Kunwinjku Kunwinjku Kun-barlang	Eric Mardday
Yanajanak (stone country spirits)	*wardde-ken/ manyardi* (mixed)	Spirit language associated with Amurdak	Charlie Mangulda
Wurrkigandjarr clan songs (Marrangu Djinang)	Central Arnhem Land *bunggurl*	Djinang	Stanley Djalarra Rankin
Gurrumba Gurrumba clan songs	Central Arnhem Land *bunggurl*	Ganalbingu	Roy Burnyila Bobby Bunungurr (Ramingining)
Mimih/Yawkyawk (mermaid spirits from stone country)	*wardde-ken kun-borrk*	Kuninjku	Crusoe Kurddal
Galpu clan songs	Eastern Arnhem Land *manikay*	Yolŋu Matha (language group)	Johnny Burrwanga Gurruwiwi family
Yirritja moiety clan songs	Eastern Arnhem Land *manikay*	Yolŋu Matha (language group)	Jason Gunambarr Keith Bascoe

(*Continued*)

Table 1.1 (Continued)

Song-sets	Affiliation/genre	Language	Lead singer/s
Buffalo Dance	Iwaidja-origin dance accompanied by Tiwi ceremony songs	Tiwi	Wesley Kerinaiua
Various Christian hymns	Anglican church music	Kunwinjku English	Rev. Lois Nadjamerrek and congregation

Summary also includes song-sets from outside of western Arnhem Land. The shaded section indicates song-sets that are not analysed in detail in the book.

of musical form and observing how they are used'.[98] Interviewing the singers about their interpretations of the songs also becomes crucial:

> To view performances as repositories of embedded meaning in need of decoding is to foreground the role of the analyst, whereas to view them as enactments of wider cultural forms is to foreground the perspectives of the performers, which the analyst hopes ultimately to integrate into his or her understanding.[99]

As well as integrating Indigenous (specifically Bininj/Arrarrkpi) perspectives and 'ways of knowing', this ethnography emerges from the relationships formed between the author and participants in the research, which I treat as a significant part of the 'data' to be analysed. As Cree scholar Shawn Wilson argues, Indigenous knowledge is 'held in the relationships and connections formed with the environment that surrounds us'.[100] Ceremony enacts knowledge by bringing people together in the same space and strengthening the relationships they share between one another and the environment.[101] Relationships of accountability and reciprocity therefore help sustain knowledge, and are also important in order to conduct respectful and mutually beneficial research.[102] As I explore in Chapter 2, the adoption of outsiders by Indigenous people of western Arnhem Land dates back to the 17th century, when Macassans would travel annually to harvest *trepang* (sea cucumber). By tracing my own connections and role in these events, I aim to understand the web of exchange that takes place around a performance.

Educator and scholar of Yolŋu language and culture Michael Christie argues that archival data of Indigenous song, story, etc. does not contain 'knowledge' but represents 'artefacts of prior knowledge production episodes'.[103] Similarly, this book can also be thought of as a series of 'knowledge production episodes' in which *kun-borrk/manyardi* songmen enact and share their knowledge through the performance event. In Chapters 3 and 6, for example, Bininj/Arrarrkpi enact through performance the reintegration of things that are culturally significant (ancestral remains and recordings of ancestors) into the contemporary social sphere; in Chapters 4 and 5, relationships are strengthened through a diplomacy and funeral ceremony; and in Chapter 7, Bininj/Arrarrkpi 'culture' is enacted through festival performances with tourists.

As Deborah Kapchan suggests, ethnographic research is itself performative because, like telling a story or staging a play, it attempts to provide meaning for experience:

> Performance, like ethnography, is palpable, arising in worlds of sense and symbol. Ethnography, like performance, is intersubjective, depending on an audience, community or a group to which it is responsible, however heterogeneous the participants may be. In its concern with a self-critical methodology that takes account of its effects in the world, ethnography is first and foremost performative—aware of itself as a living script in which meaning is emergent.[104]

Kapchan's description of 'self-critical' ethnography contrasts with the kind of ethnography that the scientists of the Arnhem Land Expedition produced. Their work was indeed performative; it addressed an audience that included their contemporaries in America and Australia and other prominent members of the public who were curious about 'Stone Age' societies. As Amanda Harris argues in analysing the development of an Australian cultural identity reliant on Aboriginal culture during this period, 'non-Indigenous engagement with Aboriginal music in the 1950s was fundamentally self-referential. Non-Indigenous composers looked to writings of non-Indigenous ethnographers, and to non-Indigenous choreography for ideas and inspiration'.[105] Frank Setzler 'meticulously edited' the hours of film from the Arnhem Land Expedition for lectures he gave to the National Geographic Society of America,[106] while diaries from the Expedition members reveal that Expedition leader C.P. Mountford effectively stage-managed aspects of a secret-sacred ceremony at Gunbalanya which he commissioned and filmed: Mountford requested that the performers take off their trousers and wear cotton loincloths or nagas, to create an aesthetic of the 'primitive' more suited to a Hollywood film production.[107] This was not, however, a self-reflective ethnography; it failed to take account of the Expedition's effects on the Aboriginal society it encountered, or to acknowledge the important role that Aboriginal cultural brokers played in helping the team to carry out their research.[108]

The ethnographic records of the Expedition therefore serve as 'performance events' worthy of interrogation. Expedition members were not aware of or able to acknowledge their research in Arnhem Land as a form of exchange, omitting from their official reports the payments exchanged to secure ceremonial performance for example.[109] In contrast, I aim to document the way that my research evolved alongside relationships with the singers, which depended on the exchange of material goods, money, and transport, and to privilege the meanings given to the performance by the performers themselves. It was also important to balance both 'experience-near' concepts derived from within the informant's world (emic analysis) with 'experience-distant' concepts derived from 'outside' the informant's experience (etic analysis).[110] I wanted through this book to not only analyse the structure and musical functions of *kun-borrk/manyardi* but also to describe what it feels like to listen to, dance to, and emotionally experience *kun-borrk/manyardi*, in a particular time and place.

Anthropologist Victor Turner claims that 'one learns through performing, then performs the understanding so gained'.[111] Turner's pedagogical approach was to encourage his anthropology students to act out or 'play' performance rituals, guided by people with experience of the rituals, with the result that students were able to get 'more fully inside the cultures they were reading about in anthropological monographs'.[112] I took a 'performative' approach to fieldwork, adopting the roles of the ethnographer, participant, and, where appropriate, Bininj/Arrarrkpi modes of behaviour, roles, and communication. This meant learning to speak Kunwinjku (the main language at Gunbalanya and 'lingua franca' in western Arnhem Land) with speakers wherever possible, after first studying the language prior to fieldwork with the aid of publications on Bininj Kunwok,[113] and then practising with speakers in the field; adopting cultural norms and Bininj/Arrarrkpi ways of referring—such as using appropriate kinship names for people—and eventually, when invited, preparing for *kun-borrk/manyardi* ceremony and learning to dance. This approach felt like the right way to conduct myself while being hosted on someone else's country, and I believe it ultimately provided rich material for what follows.

Reflecting on the fieldwork experience, I locate the point at which I received the gift not only on that early occasion at Injalak Hill, but also on subsequent occasions at various ceremonies in Gunbalanya, Warruwi, and surrounding outstations, whenever I sat alongside other Bininj/Arrarrkpi and listened, recorded, discussed, danced, and sang with Nangamu, Mardday, Gawaraidji, Gulamuwu, Namayiwa, and other songmen. Although I didn't immediately realise it, they were teaching me about their song tradition by inviting me to follow in *their* footsteps: to engage and learn *kun-borrk/manyardi* through participation in the performance event, in the same way that they had learned from the old people.

Notes

1 Murray Garde, personal communication, 19 March 2015.
2 Ruth Singer, personal communication, 13 March 2015.
3 Lazarus Lamilami, 'Moon and quoll' recorded by Heather Hewett, 1967. For a full transcription of the story, see Ruth Singer, "Agreement in Mawng: Productive and Lexicalised Uses of Agreement in an Australian Language" (PhD thesis, University of Melbourne, 2006), 328. Lazarus Lamilami also gives an account of the story in

Lazarus Lamilami, *Lamilami Speaks, the Cry Went up: A Story of the People of Goulburn Islands, North Australia* (Sydney: Ure Smith, 1974), 46.
4 Following scholars including Barwick, O'Keeffe, and Garde, I adopt the term 'song-sets' to describe western Arnhem Land song repertoires (rather than 'song cycles' or 'song series'), since this does not imply a complete corpus of ordered songs. See Linda Barwick, Isabel O'Keeffe, and Ruth Singer, "Dilemmas in Interpretation: Contemporary Perspectives on Berndt's Goulburn Island Song Documentation," in *Little Paintings, Big Stories: Gossip Songs of Western Arnhem Land*, ed. J. E. Stanton (Nedlands: University of Western Australia Berndt Museum of Anthropology, 2013), 47; Isabel O'Keeffe, "Sung and Spoken: An Analysis of Two Different Versions of a Kun-barlang Love Song," *Australian Aboriginal Studies* 2 (2007): 48; Murray Garde, "The Language of *Kun-borrk* in Western Arnhem Land," *Musicology Australia* 28 (2006): 61.
5 See Garde, "The Language of *Kun-borrk*," 67.
6 [Eric Mardday, 20130913-RB_01.wav, https://dx.doi.org/10.26278/RA1S-DG08, 00:06:36.892–00:06:45.392].
7 [Tommy Madjalkaidj, 20120624-RB_03.wav, https://dx.doi.org/10.26278/P3Q7-VE75, 00:05:06–00:05:13].
8 [Alfred Gawaraidji, 20120624-RB_03.wav, https://dx.doi.org/10.26278/P3Q7-VE75, 00:03:59–00:04:04].
9 [Alfred Gawaraidji, 20120624-RB_03.wav, https://dx.doi.org/10.26278/P3Q7-VE75, 00:05:03–00:05:07].
10 [Solomon Nangamu, 20120729-RB_09_edit.wav, https://dx.doi.org/10.26278/QDQH-P258, 00:11:01–00:11:20].
11 [Solomon Nangamu, 20120624-RB_03.wav, https://dx.doi.org/10.26278/P3Q7-VE75, 00:03:40–00:03:46].
12 Franca Tamisari, "Names and Naming: Speaking Forms into Place," in *The Land Is a Map: Placenames of Indigenous Origin in Australia*, ed. Luise Hercus, Jane Simpson and Flavia Hodges (Canberra: Pandanus Books, 2002), 98. See also Samuel Curkpatrick's discussion about footprints in relation to *manikay* performance and Yolngu education. Samuel Curkpatrick, *Singing Bones: Ancestral Creativity and Collaboration*, Indigenous Music of Australia (Sydney: Sydney University Press, 2020), 56–58.
13 Ronald M. Berndt, "Other Creatures in Human Guise and Vice Versa: A Dilemma in Understanding," in *Songs of Aboriginal Australia*, ed. Margaret Clunies Ross, Tamsin Donaldson and Stephen A. Wild (Sydney: Sydney University Press, 1987), 171; see also Allan Marett, "Ghostly Voices: Some Observations on Song-Creation, Ceremony and Being in North Western Australia," *Oceania* 71, no. 1 (2000): 20–22.
14 [Solomon Nangamu, 20120609-RB_v02.mp4, https://dx.doi.org/10.26278/FP7X-X254, 00:00:01–00:00:34]
15 [Eric Mardday, 20121109-RB_01_02_03.wav, https://dx.doi.org/10.26278/NGTC-GV10, 00:17:01–00:18:01].
16 Ellis identified 'totemic melodies' in Pitjantjatjara ceremony, which cannot fully be understood without reference to the totemic ancestor believed by performers to be present in essence within that melody. Catherine J. Ellis, *Aboriginal Music, Education for Living: Cross-Cultural Experiences from South Australia* (St. Lucia: University of Queensland Press, 1985), 92–93.
17 Allan Marett, *Songs, Dreamings, and Ghosts: The Wangga of North Australia* (Middletown, CT: Wesleyan University Press, 2005), 200.
18 [Solomon Nangamu, 20110903-RB_07.wav, https://dx.doi.org/10.26278/NWFE-VJ78, 00:25:17–00:25:31].

19 An archaeological dig at Malakananja site, located near the road from Jabiru to Gunbalanya in the Mirarr clan estate, found evidence of human occupation dated 50,000–55,000 years old. Richard G. Roberts, Rhys Jones, and M.A. Smith, "Thermoluminescence Dating of a 50,000-Year-Old Human Occupation Site in Northern Australia," *Nature* 345 (1990): 153–56.
20 Carbon dating shows that the tradition of rock art goes back to the pre-estuarine period, over 50,000 years ago. George Chaloupka, *Journey in Time: The 50,000 Year Story of the Australian Aboriginal Rock Art of Arnhem Land* (Chatswood: Reed Books, 1993), 26.
21 Ibid., 104. I am grateful to Kakadu National Park rangers for explaining the 'menu' metaphor, based on knowledge of the Ubirr site provided over time by various traditional owners including 'Big Bill' Neidji.
22 Accounts of the story of *yingarna* vary, depending on the language group. For a detailed account given to Baldwin Spencer by Gaagadju speakers, see Baldwin Spencer, *Kakadu People*, ed. David M. Welch, Australian Aboriginal Culture Series 3 (Virginia: David M. Welch, 2008), 58–63.
23 See Alice M. Moyle, "The Australian Didjeridu: A Late Musical Intrusion," *World Archaeology* 12, no. 3 (1981): 325.
24 [Solomon Nangamu, 20121103-RB_02_edit.wav, https://dx.doi.org/10.26278/TSRV-YY61, 42:52–44:24].
25 W. E. H. Stanner, *The Dreaming and Other Essays* (Collingwood: Black Inc. Agenda, 2009), 61–62.
26 Ibid.
27 Fred Myers, "Ways of Place-Making," *La Ricerca Folklorica* 45 (2002): 106.
28 Ronald M. Berndt, ed., *Australian Aboriginal Art* (Sydney: Ure Smith, 1964), 24.
29 Berndt, "Other Creatures in Human Guise," 189.
30 Solomon Nangamu, [20120609-RB_v02.mp4, https://dx.doi.org/10.26278/FP7X-X254, 00:00:54–00:01:52].
31 Bronislaw Malinowski, *Argonauts of the Western Pacific: An Account of Native Enterprise and Adventure in the Archipelagos of Melanesian New Guinea, Routledge Classics* (1922; repr., London: Routledge, 2014), 819.
32 Marcel Mauss, *The Gift: The Form and Reason for Exchange* (1954; repr., London and New York: Routledge, 2002), 16.
33 Annette Weiner, "Reproduction: A Replacement for Reciprocity," *American Ethnologist* 7, no. 1 (1980): 72.
34 Jim Sykes, *The Musical Gift: Sonic Generosity in Post-War Sri Lanka* (Oxford: Oxford University Press, 2018), 6.
35 Ronald M. Berndt, "Ceremonial Exchange in Western Arnhem Land," *Southwestern Journal of Anthropology* 7, no. 2 (1951): 174.
36 Annette Weiner, *Inalienable Possessions: The Paradox of Keeping-While-Giving* (Berkeley: University of California Press, 1992), 6.
37 Weiner, cited in Ian Keen, *Aboriginal Economy and Society: Australia at the Threshold of Colonisation* (South Melbourne: Oxford University Press, 2004), 352.
38 Ibid., 353.
39 Nicholas Peterson, "Nomads in Clover: Contemporary Murngin Hunters," (1967) [film], cited in Ibid., 337.
40 Donald Thomson, *Economic Structure and the Ceremonial Exchange Cycle in Arnhem Land* (Melbourne: Macmillan, 1949), 78–79.
41 Myers, "Ways of Place-Making," 105.
42 Ibid., 107.

43 Ibid.
44 Ibid.
45 Dan Bendrups, Katelyn Barney and Catherine Grant, "An Introduction to Sustainability and Ethnomusicology in the Australasian Context," *Musicology Australia* 34, no. 2 (2013): 153–58.
46 Sylvia Nannyonga-Tamusuza and Andrew Weintraub, "The Audible Future: Reimagining the Role of Sound Archives and Sound Repatriation in Uganda," *Ethnomusicology* 56, no. 2 (2012): 206–33.
47 Sally Treloyn and Andrea Emberly, "Sustaining Traditions: Ethnomusicological Collections, Access and Sustainability in Australia," *Musicology Australia* 35, no. 2 (2013): 159–77.
48 Frank Gunderson, Robert C. Lancefield and Bret Woods, "Pathways toward open dialogues about Sonic Heritage: An Introduction to *The Oxford Handbook of Musical Repatriation*", in *The Oxford Handbook of Musical Repatriation*, ed. Frank Gunderson, Robert C. Lancefield and Bret Woods (Oxford: Oxford University Press, 2019), xliv.
49 Linda Barwick, Jennifer Green, Petronella Vaarzon-Morel and Katya Zissermann, "Conundrums and Consequences: Doing Archival Returns in Australia," in *Archival Returns: Central Australia and beyond*, ed. Linda Barwick, Jennifer Green and Petronella Vaarzon-Morel, Indigenous Music of Australia (Sydney: Sydney University Press; Honolulu: University of Hawai'i Press, 2020), 3.
50 Ibid., 21.
51 Clint Bracknell, "Connecting Indigenous Song Archives to Kin, Country and Language," *Journal of Colonialism and Colonial History* 20, no. 2 (2019): 12.
52 Linda Payi Ford, "The Indigenous Australian Knowledge Traditions: New Ways for Old Ceremonies—a Case Study of Aboriginal Final Mortuary Ceremonial Practices in the Northern Territory," *International Journal of Asia-Pacific Studies* 16, no. 2 (2020): 15.
53 Sally Treloyn, Matthew Dembal Martin and Rona Googninda Charles, "Cultural Precedents for the Repatriation of Legacy Song Records to Communities of Origin," *Australian Aboriginal Studies* 2016, no. 2 (2016): 99.
54 Matthew Martin in conversation with Sally Treloyn, 7 November 2014. Cited in Ibid.
55 Charles P. Mountford, ed., *Records of the American-Australian Scientific Expedition to Arnhem Land*, 4 vols. (Melbourne: Melbourne University Press, 1956–64).
56 In this book, I refer to Simpson's recordings from Gunbalanya as they are identified in ABC Radio Archives disc MA24. The recordings were originally published as a set of twelve 12-inch discs, PRX2809–10, PRX2645–52, by Colin Simpson in 1949 under the title *Aboriginal Music from the Northern Territory of Australia, 1948, with Annotations by Professor A.P. Elkin* (Sydney: Australian Broadcasting Commission, processed by Columbia Gramophone, 1949). A number of recordings from Oenpelli were then given to Mountford and published under his own name. See Charles P. Mountford, *American–Australian Scientific Expedition to Arnhem Land 1948* (nine 78 rpm discs) (Sydney: Australian Broadcasting Commission, 1949). For further details on the provenance of Simpson's 1948 recordings, see Linda Barwick and Allan Marett, "Snapshots of Musical Life: The 1948 Recordings," in *Exploring the Legacy of the 1948 Arnhem Land Expedition*, ed. Martin Thomas and Margo Neale (Canberra: ANU E Press, 2011), 364.
57 See Anthony Linden Jones, "The Circle of Songs: Traditional Song and the Musical Score to C.P. Mountford's Documentary Films," in *Circulating Cultures: Exchanges of Australian Indigenous Music, Dance and Media*, ed. Amanda Harris (Canberra: ANU Press, 2014), 48.

58 Charles P. Mountford, "Aborigines of the Sea Coast" (Lindfield: Film Australia, 1951), YouTube video, uploaded by NFSA Films, 26 May 2013, <https://www.youtube.com/watch?v=seh0-_JMBuQ>; Mountford, "Arnhem Land" (Sydney: Australian Commonwealth Film Unit; Film Australia, 1950), videorecording; Mountford, "Birds and Billabongs" (Canberra: National Film and Sound Archive Australia, 1951), YouTube video, uploaded by NFSA Films, 28 June 2010, <https://www.youtube.com/watch?v=R09Cy0CMi-c>.

59 See Martin Thomas, "Expedition as Time Capsule: Introducing the American-Australian Scientific Expedition to Arnhem Land," in *Exploring the Legacy of the 1948 Arnhem Land Expedition*, ed. Martin Thomas and Margo Neale (Canberra: ANU E Press, 2011), 10; Joshua Harris, "Hidden for Sixty Years: The Motion Pictures of the American–Australian Scientific Expedition to Arnhem Land," in *Exploring the Legacy of the 1948 Arnhem Land Expedition*, ed. Martin Thomas and Margo Neale (Canberra: ANU E Press, 2011), 241.

60 For details of provenance, see Harris, "Hidden for Sixty Years."

61 Murray Garde, "The Forbidden Gaze: The 1948 Wubarr Ceremony Performed for the American–Australian Scientific Expedition to Arnhem Land," in *Exploring the Legacy of the 1948 Arnhem Land Expedition*, ed. Martin Thomas and Margo Neale (Canberra: ANU E Press, 2011), 413.

62 Ronald M. Berndt, *Love Songs of Arnhem Land* (Melbourne: T. Nelson, 1976), xix.

63 See discussion in Martin E. Thomas, *The Many Worlds of R. H. Mathews: In Search of an Australian Anthropologist* (Crows Nest: Allen & Unwin, 2011), 1–15.

64 In this instance, Kalarriya may have translated from Kunwinjku phrase 'nga-djare', which can mean 'I desire/want'.

65 [JimmyKalarriya,20120610-RB_v05.mp4,https://dx.doi.org/10.26278/645C-Y746, 00:02:44.900–00:03:06.800].

66 In Kunwinjku, na- is the male prefix and ngal- is the female prefix (hence Donna's skin name is *ngal-ngarridj* and clan name *ngal-mok*). The kinship system of western Arnhem Land in Kunwinjku can be found at https://bininjkunwok.org.au/information/kinship

67 Gunbalanya is a former buffalo station and mission, which was called Oenpelli. This name is an approximation of *Uwunbarlany*, the place name in the local language, Erre. Unless referring to the former mission or buffalo station, I adopt throughout the book the name Gunbalanya—the cognate place name in Kunwinjku—now the official name of the town. See Bruce Birch, "The American Clever Man (Marrkijbu Burdan Merika)," in *Exploring the Legacy of the 1948 Arnhem Land Expedition*, ed. Martin Thomas and Margot Neale (Canberra: ANU E Press, 2011), 313. Throughout the book, 'Goulburn Island' refers to South Goulburn Island where the community of Warruwi is situated (reflecting common usage).

68 Outstations refer to a collection of small dwellings on clan country, which can range from 10 to 100 people, and may include a school.

69 Patrick McConvell and Nicholas Thieberger, *State of Indigenous Languages in Australia—2001*, State of the Environment Second Technical Paper Series (Natural and Cultural Heritage) (Canberra: Department of the Environment and Heritage, 2002), 16; M. M. Brandl and M. Walsh, "Speakers of Many Tongues: Toward Understanding Multilingualism among Aboriginal Australians," *International Journal of the Sociology of Language* 36 (1982): 72.

70 McConvell and Thieberger, *State of Indigenous languages in Australia*, 3. Whilst languages that are no longer spoken are often referred to in the literature as 'extinct', from an Indigenous perspective such languages tend to be described as 'dormant', reflecting an understanding of their ongoing presence in the country, and their capacity to be revived and 'woken up'.

71 Map uses location information from Maningrida Language Map (Margaret Carew, 2018), Kakadu and Western Arnhem Land map (Bininj Kunwok Regional Language Centre, 2022), and draws on research by Reuben Brown in collaboration with western Arnhem Land ceremony leaders.
72 Ruth Singer, Nita Garidjalalug, Rosemary Urabadi, Heather Hewett, and Peggy Mirwuma, *Mawng Dictionary* (Canberra: Aboriginal Studies Press, 2021); Murray Garde, ed., *Bininj Gunwok Talk about Health: Medical Terms and Vocabulary for Health Professionals* (Jabiru: Gundjeihmi Aboriginal Corporation, 2010).
73 Previously, the language was spelled with a G (i.e. 'Bininj Gunwok') recognising differences in orthography between dialects; however, in 2015 following community consultation, one single spelling system was adopted for all dialects in the chain. See Nicholas Evans, *Bininj Gun-wok: A Pan-Dialectal Grammar of Mayali, Kunwinjku and Kune*, 2 vols (Canberra: Pacific Linguistics, 2003), xxiii Evans, *Bininj Gun-wok*, xxiii and Murray Garde, "Orthography—How to Write Words," Bininj Kunwok webpage, <https://bininjkunwok.org.au/information/orthography/>, accessed 19 July 2021.
74 Evans, *Bininj Gun-wok*, 6.
75 The Gunwinyguan language family has three subgroups: western, comprising Warray and Jawoyn, central, comprising Bininj Kunwok and Dalabon, and eastern, comprising Rembarrnga, Ngalakan, and Ngandi. Ibid., 33.
76 Nicholas Evans and Hans-Jürgen Sasse, eds., *Problems of Polysynthesis* (Berlin: Akademie Verlag, 2002), 3.
77 Evans, *Bininj Gun-wok*, 41; Nicholas Evans, *Dying Words: Endangered Languages and What They Have to Tell Us* (Chichester: Wiley-Blackwell, 2010), 9.
78 See discussion of language ideologies at Warruwi in Ruth Singer and Salome Harris, "What Practices and Ideologies Support Small-Scale Multilingualism? A Case Study of Warruwi Community, Northern Australia," International Journal of the Sociology of Language 241 (2016): 163–208.
79 Singer, "Agreement in Mawng," 7.
80 Lauren Campbell, "A Sketch Grammar of Urningangk, Erre and Mengerrdji: The Giimbiyu Languages of Western Arnhem Land" (Honours thesis, Department of Linguistics and Applied Linguistics, University of Melbourne, 2006), 7–8. See also Bruce Birch, *A First Dictionary of Erre, Mengerrdji and Urningangk: Three Languages from the Alligator Rivers Region of North Western Arnhem Land, Northern Territory, Australia*, (Jabiru: Gundjeihmi Aboriginal Corporation, 2006), 3–6. Conversely, Singer attributes the survival of Mawng at Warruwi to 'the fact that Mawng people are a majority and own the land … [and] that some missionaries used Mawng to communicate with aboriginal people … and that a conscious effort by influential Mawng people to retain Mawng in the sixties and seventies… resulted in… the establishment of the bilingual school program'. Singer, "Agreement in Mawng," 10.
81 With contact between Bininj/Arrarrkpi and the Macassar of South Sulawesi predating the arrival of Europeans in the area, diseases from the Indonesian islands may have contributed to population reduction in areas of Arnhem Land as early as the first half of the 18th century. Birch, *Dictionary of Erre, Mengerrdji and Urningangk*, 7–8; Garde, *Bininj Gunwok Talk about Health*, ix.
82 Berndt reports that by the 1930s, Kunwinjku had become the lingua franca. Ronald M. Berndt and Catherine H. Berndt, *Man, Land and Myth in North Australia: The Gunwinggu People* (East Lansing: Michigan State University Press, 1970), 7; See also Evans, *Bininj Gun-wok*, 7; *God Kanbengdayhke Kadberre* (Canberra: The Bible Society of Australia, 1992).

83 Garde, Bininj Gunwok Talk about Health, ix.
84 The word 'Kakadu', after which the national park is named, is a corruption of 'Gaagadju', and was first recorded by Baldwin Spencer when he met Gaagadju speakers living along the East Alligator River and at Oenpelli in 1912. See Baldwin Spencer, *Kakadu People*, iv; Birch, *Dictionary of Erre, Mengerrdji and Urningangk*, 1.
85 Evans, *Bininj Gun-wok*, 7.
86 The adoption of different orthographies for Kunwinjku and Kundjeyhmi up until 2015 is one of the outcomes of this differentiation. Ibid., 14.
87 [SolomonNangamu,20121103-RB_02_edit.wav,https://dx.doi.org/10.26278/TSRV-YY61, 00:42:52–00:44:24].
88 [James Gulamuwu, 20110903-RB_07.wav, https://dx.doi.org/10.26278/NWFE-VJ78, 00:26:12.555 - 00:26:23.977].
89 Evans, *Dying Words*, 14.
90 See Reuben Brown, David Manmurulu, Jenny Manmurulu, Isabel O'Keeffe, and Ruth Singer, "Maintaining Song Traditions and Languages Together at Warruwi (Western Arnhem Land)," in *Recirculating Songs: Revitalising the Singing Practices of Indigenous Australia*, ed. Jim Wafer and Myfany Turpin (Canberra: Asia Pacific Linguistics, 2017) and Ian Keen, *Knowledge and Secrecy in an Aboriginal Religion: Yolngu of North-East Arnhem Land* (Oxford and New York: Clarendon Press, 1994), 5–7.
91 To analyse tempo, I slowed down the playback of a recording using 'Transcribe!' software and marked the clapstick beat in order to compute the tempo (in beats per minute) between markers in a selection of the recording.
92 For further discussion, see Linda Barwick, Bruce Birch and Nicholas Evans, "Iwaidja Jurtbirrk Songs: Bringing Language and Music Together," *Australian Aboriginal Studies* 2 (2007): 9.
93 See discussion on the origins of songs recorded at Oenpelli in 1948 by Colin Simpson in Chapter 7.
94 See O'Keeffe's discussion of Bob Balir-Balir's Kunbarlang song-set (now a part of the Karrbarda song-set), which is in Mawng, Kun-barlang, and Kunwinjku languages. O'Keeffe, "Sung and spoken," 48.
95 The Mimih/Yawkyawk (K: mimih/mermaid) song-set is also associated with the 'stone country' of western Arnhem Land. I was not able to focus my analysis on this song-set since the main singer Crusoe Kurddal resided in Maningrida.
96 Richard Bauman, "Verbal Art as Performance," *American Anthropologist* 77, no. 2 (1975): 298.
97 Richard Bauman and Charles L. Briggs, "Poetics and Performance as Critical Perspectives on Language and Social Life," *Annual Review of Anthropology* 19 (1990): 69.
98 Marett, *Songs, Dreamings, and Ghosts*, 10.
99 Ibid., 9.
100 Shawn Wilson, *Research Is Ceremony: Indigenous Research Methods* (Halifax, Winnepeg: Fernwood, 2008), 87.
101 Ibid.
102 Wilson, paraphrased in Virginie Magnat, "Can Research become Ceremony?: Performance Ethnography and Indigenous Epistemologies," *Canadian Theatre Review* 151 (2012): 34.
103 Michael Christie, "Aboriginal Knowledge Traditions in Digital Environments," *Australian Journal of Indigenous Education* 34 (2005): 65.
104 D.A. Kapchan, "Performance," *Journal of American Folklore* 108, no. 430 (1995): 483–84.

105 Amanda Harris, *Representing Australian Aboriginal Music and Dance 1930–1970* (New York: Bloomsbury Academic, 2020) 10.
106 Harris, "Hidden for Sixty Years," 239.
107 Frederick McCarthy, Papers of Frederick David McCarthy, Diary 5, Yirrkala Diary No. 2 and Oenpelli, 1948, 1948, MS 3513/14/5, AIATSIS; cited in Garde, "The Forbidden Gaze," 110–11.
108 For example, Gerald Blitner, who facilitated the Expedition's visit to Groote Eylandt, was systematically excluded from filming because of the way his mixed ancestry contravened Mountford's attempts to portray 'untouched' Indigenous culture. See Martin Thomas, "Unpacking the Testimony of Gerald Blitner: Cross-Cultural Brokerage and the Arnhem Land Expedition," in *Exploring the Legacy of the 1948 Arnhem Land expedition*, ed. Martin Thomas and Margo Neale (Canberra: ANU E Press, 2011), 384.
109 These details can be traced in the diaries of the Expedition members. See Garde, "The Forbidden Gaze."
110 Clifford Geertz, *Local Knowledge: Further Essays in Interpretive Anthropology* (New York: Basic Books, 1983), 57.
111 Victor Turner, "Dramatic Ritual/Ritual Drama: Performative and Reflexive Anthropology," *Kenyon Review* 1, no. 3 (1979): 85.
112 Victor Turner and Edith Turner, "Performing Ethnography," in *The Performance Studies Reader*, ed. Henry Bial (New York: Routledge, 2004), 270.
113 References include the following: Evans, *Bininj Gun-wok*; Murray Garde, *Culture, Interaction and Person Reference in an Australian Language: An Ethnography of Bininj Gunwok Communication* (Amsterdam: John Benjamins Publishing Company, 2013); and Garde, Bininj Kunwok webpage, 2012, <http://bininjgunwok.org.au>, updated 2016.

2 'They Still Help Us'

Legacies of exchange

The journey to Amartjitpalk

In November 2012, I travelled with songman Solomon Nangamu from his home at Gunbalanya to his traditional country of Goulburn Island. The purpose of the trip was to fulfil a promise that Nangamu and another Mawng songman—Harold Warrabin—had made, to show me where their *manyardi* came from. 'I'll take you to Goulburn Island and I'll show you that *manyardi*', Nangamu had said on a number of occasions, while recording and discussing his and Warrabin's songsets (Mirrijpu and Marrwakara). A few months earlier, I had visited Goulburn Island with Nangamu and others for a Mamurrng ceremony. A number of people I had met on that occasion took part in this trip in November with Nangamu. These included dancer Brendan Marrgam (the son of senior traditional owner and songman Johnny Namayiwa), dancer Maurice Gawayaku and his two children, *manyardi* didjeridu player Micky Yalbarr, songmen Russell Agalara and Harold Warrabin, and storyteller Sam Wees, a Warruwi local with Torres Strait Island cultural heritage. On this occasion, Nangamu's plan was to show me his father's ancestral country of North Goulburn Island called Weyirra (M: North Goulburn Island) and his mother's country around Sandy Creek on the mainland opposite Goulburn Island called Wajpi (see Support Material Figure 2.i). We would drive from Gunbalanya to Sandy Creek, and then take a boat from Sandy Creek to Goulburn Island.

The movement of a men's ceremony through the region meant that access to the main road up the Coburg Peninsula was temporarily closed. Once we set off, we lacerated a tyre on a sharp rock just before reaching the halfway point of Coopers Creek crossing. After swapping over a spare tyre, we reached Wajpi/Sandy Creek, where we received the news that the 'tinny' (a small boat with an outboard motor) we had been hoping to catch a lift in had been taken out for turtle hunting, along with its owner. Since the *yawurrinj* [K: boys; young men] usually have success hunting turtle at night when the waters are calmer, we would have to wait until the morning for our lift across to Goulburn Island. I regretted forgetting to pack emergency food supplies in the ute, but Nangamu

DOI: 10.4324/9781003216339-3

seemed unfazed; he was happy to be in his mother's country, and called out in Mawng to the *warra ngurrijakurr*—little spirit people who live in the mangroves along the coastline—to let them know we were there so that they would look after us while we camped on the beach for the night. Arrarrkpi say that the *warra ngurrijakurr* are song-giving spirits who walk around together, and can be heard talking to one another when a human approaches.

The following day our lift arrived, and once on the island, we were able to organise an excursion during the short period that we had to stay at Warruwi. We had arrived on a weekend—a time when Arrarrkpi typically enjoy getting out of the town of Warruwi and visiting places along the coast to go fishing and looking for mud crabs. Compared to Gunbalanya, the population of Warruwi is small (around 400); therefore, it proved easier to mobilise everyone in preparation for an excursion out of town. Brendan Marrgam and Maurice Gawayaku arranged with the Shire Services Manager to take the Shire minibus out for a tour of the island and to practise *manyardi*. Gawayaku holds a bus licence and volunteered to drive us all, bringing his two children along for the chance to get out of town and get involved in the *manyardi*. I went and got a pre-paid 'fuel card', some tea and *walij* (M: food), and Nangamu borrowed some clapsticks from (Inyjalarrku singer) Rupert Manmurulu and fetched didjeridu player Micky Yalbarr, who is familiar with his Mirrijpu songs. Soon I found myself bouncing around in the bus on the rough dirt roads with a party of nine locals, who all took delight in pointing out all of the places on the island that were significant to them.

We headed west out of Martpalk Bay where Warruwi township is situated, past the airstrip, to the place where the barge lands at Wiyarla Bay, and supplies are delivered to the island's only shop every week from Darwin. From this point, you can see Sims Island, where *kobah-kobanj* used to brave the saltwater crocodiles and swim out to collect oysters growing on the rocks. We headed back on the northern side of the airstrip and passed the site where a new Bureau of Meteorology weather radar tower was opened in 2012 with a ceremony accompanied by *manyardi*. Going further east along the main road that travels through the middle of the island, we passed by the road leading to ceremony grounds where young men and women come from all around western Arnhem Land every dry season to camp and go through initiation. A little further along, Marrgam pointed out a tin shack off the road in the bush where he used to go to school, before he moved to the main school at Warruwi. We continued through dry savannah woodlands, slowing down several times for feral horses crossing the road to graze. The horses were once used by stockmen in the mission days, but now roam all over the island and come into the town for water and food. Just as I was beginning to become thoroughly disoriented, we emerged from the bush out into the open sand dunes on the northeastern side of the island and stopped at a place called Amartjitpalk, where the group settled on the beach. While I busied myself with the recording gear, Wees, Gawayaku, and Marrgam lit a fire and went to collect cockle (edible saltwater clams), and Maurice's children played in

Figure 2.1 Photo of manyardi performance at Amartjitpalk, Goulburn Island, 2012. Left to right: Brendan Marrgam, Sam Wees, Russell Agalara, Maurice Gawayaku and his son, Micky Yalbarr (didjeridu), Solomon Nangamu, Harold Warrabin. Photograph by Reuben Brown.

the sand dunes, running up and tumbling down. Agalara, Yalbarr, Warrabin, and Nangamu sat themselves down in a circle around the microphone and began the music making (Figure 2.1).

We were positioned directly opposite the island of Weyirra, where Nangamu's Manangkardi-speaking ancestors once lived. Today, it is inhabited mainly by a population of wild goats, who were brought there during the mission days. Whilst no-one lives there permanently anymore, Arrarrkpi visit the island by boat to hunt and collect food. By facing the island as he sang his Mirrijpu songs, Nangamu was singing not only for his immediate audience but also directly towards his Manangkardi ancestors.

Nangamu picked up the didjeridu first, and began playing the rhythm for the Marrwakara (M: goanna) song (MK01). Warrabin announced that they would 'practise' the song first. They performed it once through, and then once again, this time slowing the tempo at the end of the song and changing the didjeridu rhythm to transition into the Mularrik Mularrik (M: green frog) song (MK02). On this occasion (as with others during which a recordist is present), for the benefit of the recording, the musicians made it known to me when they were 'practising' a song. So as not to interfere with the performance event, I would leave the recorder running, to make sure I didn't miss the beginning or end of a song, and later I would listen over the recording and segment the song items. Then, we would all sit down some time after the performance and listen over the segmented songs, and they would select the songs that they preferred for me to compile on a CD, USB, or SD card for local distribution. After editing a few recordings in this way, I reflected on the lack of distinction between 'practice' and 'performance' in *kun-borrk/manyardi* performance. Large sections of the performance could in a sense be considered 'practice': songs are repeated until the feeling of the song, the intention of the singers, and the mood of the audience are focussed. Often, a song that may have been intended as 'practice' turns out to be the best recording of that particular song. After explaining my editing process to Nangamu on the first occasion at Injalak Hill, he relayed the process in Mawng to others who might be recording for the first time.

After they had finished 'practising', Nangamu began blowing a slower tempo rhythm and Agalara led the singing of a Mirrijpu song with Warrabin and Yalbarr backing the singing. They repeated the song three times, finding a meeting point with one another's voices. When this song had finished, Nangamu asked us if we had heard that 'sweet sound', and the other musicians nodded in agreement. It was as though the sound that came out of their mouths, blended with the *arawirr* (M: didjeridu) and the *nganangka* (M: clapsticks), was not entirely of their making, but a part of the environment around them, which was also making the music and responding to their performance. Later on, while listening back over the recording, Nangamu would comment that he felt 'nice and good' to sing, as though a 'whole orchestra' were backing him up.[1] At another stage of the performance after the men had got up to dance, Micky Yalbarr remarked that the waves had swelled, to which Nangamu responded: '*kunak-apa hapi kangmin...*' ('the land/country is happy...') and Marrgam added '*eh hapi kangmin* ('yes it's happy')—on the right track!'[2]

We were staring out at the ocean that separated North from South Goulburn Island, with the waves of the *kurrula* (M: sea) calmly lapping at the water's edge in front of us. The singers fell into a discussion about how the islands were once joined, and the events that had caused them to separate during the Dreaming. It was a story that Nangamu had told me before, when he was explaining how his *manyardi* had come about. The *mirrijpu* (silver gull *Chroicocephalus novaehollandiae*)[3] was once Bininj/Arrarrkpi, as were all of the other birds that can be found at Goulburn Island. *Korroko* (K: long ago), during the period of the ancestors, they were spending their time on Weyirra fishing, when they had unwelcome company in the form of a *waak waak/wurakak* (K/M: black crow):

Yoh [yes], that *mayhmay* [K: bird]... he was like, human too, like, long time. They used to see crow, [he] used to come, just asking around—the black crow, he was a Bininj too. They used to tell him: 'No, you go! Don't come here!' He was scratching around for a scrap of tucker. But they didn't even give it to him. They said, 'nah, we'll give you little rubbish', bone or whatever. He said, 'all right'. And that Island it was only one big Island, South Goulburn. So that crow went and got his axe, that big stone axe. Long time. And [he] split that island in two—north and south—but he's in the middle [now]. They were too greedy for tucker, they never give him [any], and he told them all "I'll teach you a lesson, so you'll be sitting separate, island to island".[4]

Mawng people's *djang* (K: sacred sites) are located not only on the islands, but also underneath the sea, where the trunk of a large paperbark tree that once stood on the united Goulburn Island fell, after the crow chopped it down. The group discussed how when the water is calm, a whirlpool forms in between the islands, indicating that the tree is still growing at the bottom of the ocean floor. Later, we would visit another site near the mangrove swamps on the eastern point of South Goulburn Island, known as *Inyanangatpara* or Whalebone Beach. This site has significance for Galpu clan people from eastern Arnhem Land living at Warruwi who camped with a beached whale until it died (I could still make out the large vertebrae of the enormous creature from the pile of bones). Eventually, our singing excursion would finish on the cliffs of another significant site called *Nganyamirnali*, which looks out to *Ngangkuluk* or 'Bottle Rock', on the western side of the island, before we all loaded back into the minibus and returned to town.

***

This chapter explores the role of *kun-borrk/manyardi* in linking people, place, histories, and ancestors. I suggest that when Arrarrkpi perform on Country such as Amartjitpalk at Goulburn Island, these events 're-activate' memories and 're-generate' spiritual connections to ancestors residing in Country. A brief history of Bininj/Arrarrkpi contact and trade with Macassans from south Sulawesi and the Indonesian Archipelago allows us to better understand Bininj/Arrarrkpi intercultural relations today. I examine the performance at Amartjitpalk as part of an overview of the musical setting of *kun-borrk/manyardi* that will assist with the performance analysis presented in proceeding chapters. I analyse how two musically distinct song-sets—Marrwakara/Mularrik (M: goanna/green frog) and Mirrijpu (M: seagull)—were 'paired' together in performance. I show how this pairing reflects an awareness of what Barwick calls the 'complex whole' of Indigenous Australian performance traditions—made up of interdependent parts including song, dance, and visual art that are linked by ancestral country.[5] Finally, analysis of the way the singers order songs in performance reveals the extent to which *manyardi* draws on an understanding of factors both internal and external to the music and the performance group.

Histories of encounter and exchange

Aboriginal people's history of contact and cultural exchange with non-Aboriginal people predates European exploration and settlement. The precise time that the Macassan seafarers first started visiting western Arnhem Land is not agreed upon, but is believed to be somewhere between the 16th and 18th centuries.[6] The Portuguese and Dutch ('Balanda') who colonised the Indonesian

Archipelago at different times during this period also came in contact with Aboriginal people.[7] In the early 20th century, Malays and Japanese also ventured along the Arnhem Land and northern coasts, searching for pearls and trading goods.[8] Bininj/Arrarrkpi had encounters with these outsiders and documented them in *bim* known as 'contact art'. Not far from the road that we had taken up the Cobourg Peninsula to Sandy Creek is a site called Malarrak at Wellington Range on the Namunidjbuk estate of Mawng-speaking traditional owners, where rock art paintings depict Macassan praus and European luggers and steamers, Macassan knives (*badi*), and smoking pipes, among other subjects.[9] The level of detail in the paintings suggests that the Bininj/Arrarrkpi who painted them did not just see them from afar, but had an intimate knowledge of their subjects.[10] At another site called Ubirr rock on the Bunitj clan estate near the East Alligator River, a painting depicts a Balanda man with a wide-brimmed hat, standing with his hands on hips and smoking a pipe—an image that must have been both ubiquitous and strange for Bininj/Arrarrkpi who first encountered Balanda in their country. Balanda weapons are also depicted in many *bim*, as are paintings of European sailing ships documented by Bininj/Arrarrkpi.

Stories of Macassan annual voyages to western Arnhem Land to harvest *trepang* (sea cucumber, or *bêche-de-mer*) have been passed down to current generations of Bininj/Arrarrkpi. Lazarus Lamilami, a Mawng man who grew up in the bush in his early childhood before the mission was established at Goulburn Island, recalls in his biography how the Macassans would camp along the coast, both at Goulburn Island and on the mainland opposite.[11] They would travel with Aboriginal people in canoes to a place called *widjba* on the Cobourg Peninsula where they would work, boiling the *trepang* with bark from the mangroves and loading it up in bags, before returning home, with the change of sea winds. Some Aboriginal people of Lamilami's parents' generation, including his uncle, travelled back on the praus themselves to Macassar:

> They used to come back with stories about how they were treated there. They said the people were very kind... I think some men had girlfriends in Macassar. Our people liked to go there and see these different things—where they made their dug-out canoes, and the beautiful cloth... and their knives.[12]

Aboriginal-Macassan relations were marked by a curiosity for the different material goods and food they could provide one another (the Macassans introduced Aboriginal people to rice and corn among other foods), a willingness to forge close relationships based around cultural exchange, and a respect for the sovereignty of one another's land.[13] Although there were periods of conflict and violence, Macassans were generally made welcome in western Arnhem Land during their annual visits.[14] The close relationship between Macassans and Aboriginal people of Arnhem Land lasted until around 1907 when Europeans took control of the *trepang* trade.[15] Bininj/Arrarrkpi and Yolngu contact with non-Europeans continued, however, as Japanese pearlers and traders continued to frequent the Arnhem Land coast in the first part of the 20th century, trading with Aboriginal people around the mouths of the Liverpool and King Rivers.[16] The Aboriginal-Macassan relationship therefore provides a template for the way in which Aboriginal kinship networks, diplomacy, and ceremony continue to operate today, incorporating non-Indigenous peoples and practices and rituals.

European contact and the mission era

The history of European contact and colonisation varies considerably in different parts of Australia. The British settlement at Port Essington on the Cobourg Peninsula of western Arnhem Land was abandoned a decade after it was established in 1838. Other settlements at Fort Dundas on Melville Island in the Tiwi Islands (where cattle, buffalo, goats, sheep, and pigs were first introduced from Timor) and Fort Wellington on the northern coast of the Cobourg Peninsula were similarly short-lived.[17] (A timeline of significant European post-contact events in western Arnhem Land is provided in Support Material Figure 2.ii.)

In the late 19th century, pastoralists attempted to take up leases in the Northern Territory, meeting Aboriginal resistance in eastern Arnhem Land and elsewhere after shooting at Aboriginal people, clearing traditional hunting grounds for cattle, and failing to travel along established trade routes.[18] Where they did succeed, they relied on and exploited Aboriginal labour, paying only in food, clothing, and tobacco.[19] During this period, the surveyors Wickham and Stokes encountered organised resistance from Murrinh-Patha at Port Keats after coming ashore, walking through ceremony sites, and shooting their rifles.[20] In western Arnhem Land as elsewhere in Australia, the disease had a dramatic effect on Aboriginal populations in contact situations, spreading beyond the frontier and affecting people living in the bush who were not immune to the various diseases that the British and other outsiders brought with them.[21]

Whereas the early European settlements had failed to bring settlers from the southern states of Australia to build livelihoods that would prove sustainable, in the early 20th century a few individual pioneers would find success in western Arnhem Land by creating small-scale seasonal industries that relied on local resources and Bininj/Arrarrkpi labour. One of these figures was Paddy Cahill, a buffalo shooter who established a buffalo skinning camp at Oenpelli (today Gunbalanya) in 1906 (discussed further in Chapter 6). Around the same time that Cahill was operating his cattle station at Oenpelli, the Methodist Reverend James Watson was searching for a place in western Arnhem Land to establish his mission. Reverend Watson is cast by many Mawng people today as a unifying figure who brought various clans together and resolved tensions or potential violence through his missionary project at Goulburn Island, rather than as a figure who had a destructive impact on Bininj/Arrarrkpi society, culture, and language. During an interview with Mawng songmen Solomon Nangamu, Alfred Gawaraidji, and Tommy Madjalkaidj at Gunbalanya prior to the trip to Amartjitpalk, they had discussed how ceremonial ties observed today between Gumardir and Mawng people can be traced back to Watson's arrival in western Arnhem Land.[22] Watson borrowed horses from Cahill at Oenpelli[23] and was guided on horseback by Gumardir people to Martpalk Bay on South Goulburn Island, where he eventually settled and where the community of Warruwi is situated:

AG: that's why all that Gumardir people there [at Goulburn], when they do the dance they still accompany, they still help us. [They're] like [our] next door neighbour—we share that one creek. They come over—some people got married there—[now] staying at Goulburn—they're from Gumardir

SN: some [Gumardir] people staying here [at Gunbalanya] too

TM: these old people—Gumardir people—when that Balanda came from Adelaide to Darwin to here, this first mission at Gunbalanya, he bin travel right up to Gumardir then he went down to King River, then he cross to Goulburn Island

AG: —crossed to Goulburn Island they bin take him

SN: —that old reverend James Watson… started taking the bible and tame my [Majukudu clan] tribal warriors, because they was wild people, but the bible made them tame, so they all settled down.

AG: older generation [belonging to] me and him [Solomon] bin take that old man now, that Balanda, take him there—Gunbalanya, Gumardir, with the canoe, they take him to Goulburn Island, Warruwi.

TM: …with this Gumardir

SN: …with the canoe, they take him to the other side

TM: …but he bin travel from Adelaide to Darwin, to here [Gunbalanya], to Gumardir then across to Goulburn[24]

The 100-year centenary of Watson's landing by canoe at Goulburn Island was enthusiastically celebrated in 2016, underscoring the significance of the story to the ongoing coexistence of multiple language and clan groups at Warruwi.[25] The Methodists (who also established missions at Milingimbi, Elcho Island, Yirrkala, Darwin, and later Croker Island) chose Warruwi in part because of its isolation from the 'vices' of alcohol and prostitution associated with some of the buffalo camps and Darwin.[26] Perhaps this played a role in converting Arrarrkpi to Christianity (a task that Cahill deemed futile, based on his experience at Oenpelli).[27] While the mission's records do not reveal much about Aboriginal responses to the Methodists, Lazarus Lamilami recalls how many Mawng people fled Goulburn Island initially when Watson arrived and camped at Sandy Creek where they sent 'spies' back to the island to report on what the Balanda were doing with the people who stayed on the island. When favourable reports came back of the story he told about 'Jesus' and the way that he treated people, Mawng returned to the island.[28] One of the incentives for staying on the mission was that Arrarrkpi could learn new skills in farming, lugging, and building:

> A lot of the people worked in the gardens. The missionaries taught them how to grow vegetables, and some of the people they taught how to build. They put up a lot of new buildings, and all the materials were brought in on the boats.[29]

These skills are passed on today through the maintenance of a community garden at Warruwi where singers and dancers such as Maurice Gawayaku and Harold Warrabin work. Arrarrkpi people's history of incorporating the food, culture, skills, crafts, and tools of the Macassans also extended (among many, but not all) to the missionaries when they arrived with their religious message. The fact that the Methodists learned Mawng language and chose not to interfere with ceremony that was taking place in the area also helped them to keep a foothold in Goulburn Island.[30] This contrasts with the experience of some Aboriginal people in other areas of Australia who were not permitted to leave missions or Government reserves, and were discouraged or forbidden to speak their language and practise their ceremonies. Arrarrkpi were allowed to travel to the mainland for holidays, where they would visit other families and maintain cultural practices like hunting and performing *kun-borrk/manyardi*. Lamilami recalls his childhood in the 1920s, visiting camps around Sandy Creek:

> There were a lot of people there, some from the Liverpool River, the Gunavidji [Kunabidji] (people from the Liverpool area). They had a dance that we knew about. It was called *ngulrungbu*.[31] Our people would call out, 'we want *ngulrungbu*!' And these people would come and dance for us... Then they would tell our people that they wanted to see our dance, *mirigbu* [Mirrijpu]—that's the seagull dance. We would dance for them. These dances were for everybody. Anyone could join in, but some people are the main dancers and they are the ones the people want to see. Men and women dance, but the way the people dance on Goulburn Island is different. The [Kunabidji] had a different dance and they do different things. In the [Mirrijpu], the men and the women walk in and are singing, and in the dance they come together in a bunch and then divide up again. The *ngulrungbu* is different. They don't sing as they walk in. They all walk up to the dance-place and sit down. Three men sing and one man plays the didjeridu. Then the men come out and dance, and when they are finished, the women come out and dance in another place. They don't dance together [in the same area of the ceremony ground].[32]

Lamilami's description captures the variegation (or 'different together'-ness) of western Arnhem Land ceremony. It also shows that during the mission era, Bininj/Arrarrkpi continued coming together to exchange song and dance as they had in pre-contact times, and to maintain their individual language identities through various elements of the performance.

Ceremony played an important role in helping formalise new relationships born out of a changing social situation in which various language groups and clans were living together that had previously been more distant. Anthropologist Baldwin Spencer travelled to Oenpelli in 1912 when some language groups were living together for the first time, and described a number of ceremonies that took place during his visit.[33] Spencer observed a corroboree between what he called the 'locals'—the 'Kakadu [Gaagadju] people'—and 'people from the King River to the east', noting that although the visitors 'do not mix in camp' with the Gaagadju and other groups in the 'local' camp, they attended one another's ceremonies.[34]

Lamilami's story highlights how people moved between worlds from the Balanda missions, buffalo camps, and the city of Darwin where they would earn rations and new skills, to outstations and ceremony grounds where they would maintain ceremony. In the decades after the mission era, as Balanda continued to live in places like Gunbalanya and Warruwi—and the Balanda and Bininj/Arrarrkpi worlds merged and became less demarcated—song, dance, and ceremony would remain an important link to the past, and a strategy for dealing with change in the present.

We will now examine the components of western Arnhem Land song, before exploring the performance at Amartjitpalk.

Musical setting of *kun-borrk/manyardi*

Performance context

The *kun-borrk/manyardi* ensemble consists of the lead songman and other men who sing and accompany on didjeridu and clapsticks. Women are responsible for dancing and song knowledge: they influence or direct aspects of the ceremonial performance, and contribute to discussions about the meaning of the songs. In the domain of popular musical styles influenced by *kun-borrk/manyardi* ceremony and associated stories, women have in recent decades led public performance and composition (examples include Wildflower Band and Ripple Effect Band).[35] Formal ceremonial performances are usually held around a dance ground prepared with sand; however, informal or spontaneous performances may take place in intimate settings around the home, around the campfire (Chapter 6),[36] or out of town, as with the performance at Amartjitpalk. *Kun-borrk/manyardi* is also performed at celebrations for important community events within western Arnhem Land (for example, graduation ceremonies or building openings), and circumcision ceremonies outside western Arnhem Land, known as *djabbi* in Yolŋu Matha.[37] The singing ensemble usually sits facing the dancers underneath a 'shade' or bough shelter at the edge of the dance ground made of branches from paperbark trees. The ensemble is flexible; in informal contexts, the main singer may accompany himself with clapsticks, and sit with the didjeridu player. A second or third 'back-up' singer, with or without clapstick accompaniment, usually also joins to complete the ensemble. In contexts involving many participants—funeral ceremonies (Chapters 3 and 5), Mamurrng friendship/gift exchange ceremonies (Chapter 4), and local music festivals (Chapter 7)—three or four singers may sit as part of the ensemble and 'back up' the leading songman if they are familiar with the song-set, and take it in turns to accompany on the didjeridu. The dance ensemble can include any number and age of *bininj/ arrarrkpi* (K/M: men) and *daluk/warramumpik* (K/M: women).

Song inheritance

Kun-borrk/manyardi song-sets are usually passed down from father to son or another male relative, but they can also be inherited matrilineally. Both Eric Mardday (Karrbarda song-set) and Russell Agalara (Mirrijpu song-set) inherited their songs through their mother's father. Figure 2.2 shows inheritance of the Mirrijpu song-set across four generations, from Tom Namagarainmag to his sons Michael Nawudba, Solomon Ganawa, and Solomon Nangamu, and from Nawudba to his daughter Mary to her son Russell Agalara. When I started my fieldwork, Agalara—who is younger than Nangamu—was regarded as the apprentice 'second singer' for the Mirrijpu song-set. He would lead the singing at funeral ceremonies and other formal occasions in Nangamu's absence, and

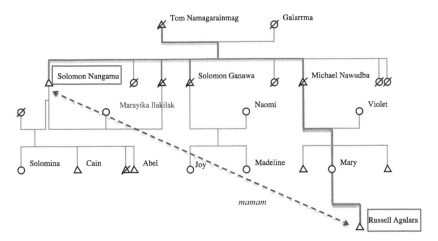

Figure 2.2 Solomon Nangamu and Russell Agalara's inheritance of the Mirrijpu songset. Song inheritance is represented with a bold line, while the dotted line shows *mamam* relationship between Nangamu and Agalara. Kinship diagram by Reuben Brown based on research with Solomon Nangamu. Names used with permission.

will eventually take over as a lead singer and train another apprentice such as Solomon's son Cain Nangamu. Agalara learned the songs from his mother's father Michael Nawudba (Nangamu's older brother, now deceased), and recalls sitting with Nawudba as a toddler and listening to the songs. This meant that Agalara was familiar with the 'old' songs from the song-set that Nawudba used to sing, and his interpretation of those songs is influenced by his memory of Nawudba's singing style and performance. Agalara and Nangamu call each other *mamam*, which is a reciprocal kinship term for one's mother's (classificatory) father or mother's father's sister and, conversely, one's daughter's daughter or daughter's son. (In the kinship system of western Arnhem Land, one's father's brothers are all considered 'father', and one's mother's sisters are considered 'mother'.) Nangamu and Agalara therefore also refer to one another using the English terms 'grandson' and 'granddad'.

Although women do not sing in ceremony, they inherit knowledge of particular song-sets, and may help the songman to perform the songs, and discuss the song's meaning. Mardday's mother Eileen Makanawarra learned to dance Karrbarda from her father Bilinyarra; she describes the Karrbarda song-set as her 'special song'.[38] Marayika Ilakkilak is the former wife of Nangamu's older brother Solomon Ganawa (now deceased) who was the leading songman before he passed on the songs to Nangamu. During my fieldwork, Ilakkilak was present at Nangamu's performances of Mirrijpu, and contributed a great deal to our discussions about the meaning of the song-set and related stories.[39]

Song conception

In western Arnhem Land and elsewhere in Australia, dreams act as a portal through which certain songmen access new songs (or the inspiration for a new song) from song-giving spirits that reside in the traditional country from which the songs originate, or from a deceased spirit who is familiar to them who acts as an intermediary for ancestral spirits in Country and gives the songman the gift of a new song.[40] The songman wakes up, works out the tune, and teaches it to the didjeridu player over a number of days or weeks, as Milyarryarr songman Johnny Namayiwa explains:

> …Because you know when you dream, and then you get up in the morning and you start to think, 'what's the next thing'? It takes a while—say about one or two weeks.[41]

Although singers use the terms 'old' and 'new' to distinguish between inherited *kun-borrk/manyardi* songs and recently conceived/composed songs in their song-set, this may set up a somewhat false dichotomy, since both 'old' and 'new' songs are understood as coming from the same ancestral source.[42] Musical inspiration for 'old' and 'new' songs is often attributed to the same relative who first taught the singer how to sing the songs while they were alive, and then gives the singer a new song in a dream, post-mortem.

In the neighbouring region of the Daly, Marett similarly records detailed descriptions by songmen about songs given to them in dreams by 'song-giving agents'—often the ghosts of deceased songmen who act as intermediaries between dangerous spirit beings and the singer-composer—or, at Wadeye, directly from ancestral spirits (Walakandha and Ma-yawa).[43] The significance of dream-composed songs in Aboriginal Australia has been discussed elsewhere with regard to publicly owned song genres from the Kimberley region[44] and Mornington Island.[45] Barwick, Birch, and Evans have observed that in western Arnhem Land, songs that come from dreams are given the status of 'true' songs, as opposed to songs that come to the singer without spirit intervention.[46] Garde writes that *kun-borrk* songmen establish authority over their song repertories through the way that they interpret songs given by spirits, access 'new' songs through the supernatural, and continue to perform the songs in ceremony.[47] Ronald Berndt similarly observed in 1948 that the 'main singer' of a song-set (or 'cycle' as Berndt calls them) was the one who was recognised as possessing rights to sing the song-set and was 'usually the person most competent to provide both the original rendering and its explanations'.[48]

Songs and song structure

Following Barwick et al., I consider a 'song' to be a defined combination of text, rhythm, and melody that is relatively stable across numerous instances ('song items') in which it is performed.[49] In Mawng, Kun-barlang, and Iwaidja (a language spoken on Croker Island to the north of Gunbalanya), *manyardi* is the general name not only for *song* but also for western Arnhem Land public ceremony.[50] The performance event of *kun-borrk/manyardi* usually consists of a number of song items, interspersed with social interaction between the audience, the dance group, and the singers.[51] The singers perform a selection of songs from their respective song-sets, often repeating a particular song before moving on to the next. In this sense, a song item is only one realisation of the song, just as a performance represents a particular (incomplete) realisation of the singer's song-set. Song items are typically short: between 1 and 2 minutes in duration. When the mood is right and the dancing is going well—as it was at Amartjitpalk when the singers and dancers could feel that Country was happy—the lead singer will perform the next song without a break in the didjeridu accompaniment (see discussion of a performance of Milyarryarr in Chapter 7).

Like *wangga* from the Daly region, most *kun-borrk/manyardi* songs are strophic (verses of the text are sung to the same music, and the melody is coterminous with the song text). Songs typically feature a verse which is repeated two or three times.[52] The verse may consist of one or more phrases of the song text (indicated as 'Text Phrase A, B, C, etc.'), as well as vocables (sung vowels such

52 *'They Still Help Us'*: Legacies of exchange

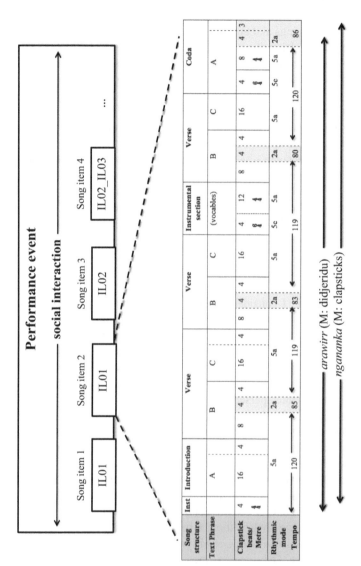

Figure 2.3 Components of a performance event in western Arnhem Land, showing the structure of song IL01 (AVEx 4.2) and its place within the performance. Changes in rhythmic mode and tempo are shown in relation to the musical structure of the song and the division of clapstick beats. The dotted line represents the boundaries of the Text Phrase as well as tempi. 'Inst' indicates Instrumental lead-in to the song. Diagram adapted from Barwick, Birch, and Evans, "Iwaidja Jurtbirrk Songs," 15.

'They Still Help Us': Legacies of exchange   53

as o, a, and i). Some song-sets also feature songs with an Introduction and Coda, which bookend repetitions of the main verse. The clapstick beating in *kun-borrk/manyardi* songs is additive; repetitions of the verse are generally separated by metrical units of clapstick beating—4, 6, or 8 beats—with no singing (represented after the dotted line of Text Phrase C in the 'Clapstick beats/Metre' row of Figure 2.3) or by 'Instrumental Sections' in which the singers sing vocables on the pitch of the didjeridu and the 'tonic', instead of the song text.[53] These sections typically feature more elaborate dancing, as the clapstick beating pattern changes—usually from even to uneven—and the dancers pause their movement as the clapsticks 'skip' the beat. Like some *wangga* and *lirrga* repertoires, *kun-borrk/manyardi* songs usually conclude with the vocal part and didjeridu accompaniment cutting out first, leaving the clapsticks which beat a final 'terminating' pattern to finish the song (represented after the final dotted line in Figure 2.3).[54] Mawng speakers describe this using the phrase *arrin wilpil nganangka,* which can be translated as 'we play the clapstick rhythm that signals the end of the song'.[55] Figure 2.3 illustrates the structural components of a performance of western Arnhem Land *kun-borrk/manyardi*, adapted from Barwick, Birch, and Evans' analysis of Iwaidja *Jurtbirrk* songs of western Arnhem Land. The bottom tier of the diagram shows an expansion of a song item in a performance, in this instance, Inyjalarrku song IL01 (watch AVEx_4.2), which has an Introduction and Coda as well as Instrumental Sections, built around the repetitions of the verse. While this is typical of many Inyjalarrku songs, other song-sets will differ in their structure and in the rhythmic modes that feature in the clapstick part.

AVEx_4.2 https://dx.doi.org/10.26278/WB4Z-YS67

Guide to listening: [0:09] Introduction, [0:19] Text Phrase B, [0:28] Text Phrase C, [0:38] Verse repeat, [0:57] Instrumental Section, [1:05] Verse repeat, [1:23] Coda

Song order

In spite of the popular notion that Aboriginal Australian songs are performed in a strict order or sequence that follows 'songlines'[56] (particular foundational journeys that ancestral beings made during the period of the Dreaming when they created and named the landscape), there is a degree of flexibility in all Aboriginal Australian genres as to the ordering of songs in a performance. Ceremony holders of the Western Desert and Central Australia follow ancestral journeys and 'complex sung maps',[57] singing songs in the order of the sites where ancestors left their mark and embedded the songs in Country. As they recreate these journeys, however, they may choose to omit certain songs associated with less important sites, and performers vary song order according to which aspects of the story they want to emphasise.[58] Similarly, western Arnhem Land song-sets are not performed according to a strict order; indeed, as we will explore in this book, the ordering of songs in each performance event is never the same. Like *wangga* and some *junba* repertoires, they may have an 'ancestral genesis'[59] and connection to *djang* (K: sacred sites). Nevertheless, western Arnhem Land songmen consider multiple factors including Country, kin, occasion, company, mood, performance aesthetics, etc. when ordering songs in a performance.

Melodic contour

The melodic contour of *kun-borrk/manyardi* songs features mainly descending steps along degrees of the scale, but also large intervals. This contrasts with public song from Central Australia and the Kimberley, which is characterised by a series of descents in the melody, with small intervals. The vocal melody of *Kun-borrk/manyardi* songs may begin on the tonic or other degrees of the scale (usually the fifth and seventh), and will always finish on the tonic, resolving with the didjeridu note. A number of melodic modes are represented in various *kun-borrk/manyardi* song-sets. For example, Mirrijpu songs are mainly in major or Dorian melodic mode but also Mixolydian and natural minor mode.[60] Like other Aboriginal Australian genres, *kun-borrk/manyardi* song-sets have one or more characteristic melodic sequences which can be said to constitute their 'aural identity'.[61] The melodic material associated with a song-set, along with particular clapstick patterns, the song text, and the body design, is considered to belong to that song-set.[62] Barwick has suggested that this also enables songs to be identified from a distance when groups approach the ceremony ground and multiple repertoires are being performed, often simultaneously.[63] The practice of retaining melodic features throughout the repertory rests upon 'a convention that is widespread throughout the parts of Aboriginal Australia where song traditions are still strong… that melody encodes relationships between songs, totemic ancestors, Country and kinship'.[64]

Rhythmic mode

Rhythmic modes are an important driving force behind *kun-borrk/manyardi* performance, influencing both the dance, which is in sync with the clapstick beating, and the metre in the vocal part.[65] As Marett observes of their function in *wangga,* rhythmic modes also communicate beyond the dance ground into the spiritual realm:

> It is the association with dance (which can occur in both vocal and instrumental sections) that most strongly underpins the system of rhythmic modes. Through synchronising their movements with the clapstick beating, dancers tread in the footsteps of the ancestral ghosts summoned by the power of song.[66]

Marett et al. define rhythmic modes as a combination of the tempo (the speed of the clapstick beat) and the rhythmic pattern of the clapsticks, which may be either 'even' (steady, unbroken beating of the clapsticks) or 'uneven' (where the clapstick beating skips a beat or a number of beats).[67] Another important component of rhythmic modes is the vocal rhythm and its relationship with the didjeridu rhythm, which complements, but does not replicate, the clapstick rhythm.[68] As Mirrijpu singer Russell Agalara explains, song-sets are recognised in part by the different rhythms in the didjeridu (or 'bamboo') accompaniment:

> [It's] one way, Karrbarda mob, them Yam mob. When they play, they play like, straight line... you can hear that bamboo if you play. But how me and my grandfather [Solomon Nangamu] sings, you can hear that bamboo change— different-different bamboo beats[69]

Songmen also have terms in their own languages to describe tempo ranges or 'bands' relating to the clapstick beat.[70] In Mawng language, for example, songs accompanied with slow beating of the clapstick (approx. 60–100 bpm) are named *nulatparlilil*,[71] while songs accompanied with fast clapstick beating (approx. 120–140 bpm) are named *nulatparlangkat*,[72] and fast doubled clapstick beating (240–300 bpm) is referred to as *kaniwartawkun*. The performance analysis sections of the book will consider ways that songmen choose particular songs and particular rhythmic modes for their function in ceremony. For example, fast songs (rhythmic mode 5; *nulatparlangkat*) may be performed in order to feature dancing involving men/boys, or to enliven the mood of the ceremony, whereas slow-to-moderate songs (rhythmic modes 2, 3, and 4; *nulatparlilil*) may be performed in order to feature dancing involving women/girls, and for a more serious emotional affect (but not necessarily sad).

In order to describe the categories of rhythmic modes of *kun-borrk/manyardi* presented in this book, I have adapted the descriptive system devised by Marett, Barwick, and Ford and originally applied to *wangga* repertories (see Figure 2.4), with some additions necessitated by the data I collected (for example, rhythmic modes 2c, 2d, 3c, 3c[var], 4f, 5f, 5g). In determining which tempo range or band a particular song fits into (and therefore which rhythmic mode), I have also been guided by Marett's analysis of tempo ranges for *wangga* repertories.[73] A summary of tempo bands is presented in Support Material Figure 8.i.v. A comparative analysis of the use of rhythmic modes and tempi for particular song-sets is also presented in Chapter 8.

Doing 'performance-conscious' ethnography

One of the key features of Aboriginal pedagogy is learning through observation and participation. Younger children learn *kun-bork/manyardi* by observing and taking part in repeated performances over time in different contexts, where they are invited (rather than explicitly instructed) to make connections between the

56   'They Still Help Us': Legacies of exchange

Rhythmic mode	Tempo	Clapsticks
Rhythmic mode 1	None (unmeasured)	None
Rhythmic mode 2a	Slow	Even
Rhythmic mode 2b	Slow	Uneven [♩ ♪♩ 𝄽]
Rhythmic mode 2c (Inyjalarrku slow Instrumental mode)	Slow	Doubled uneven ♫♪𝄽♫♪𝄽♩♩♫♫♫♪𝄽
Rhythmic mode 2d (Inyjalarrku 'turnaround' mode)	Slow	Even ♩♩♩♩♩♩♩♩ (underlined beats performed with faster tempo)
Rhythmic mode 2e	Slow	Doubled
Rhythmic mode 3a	Slow moderate	Even
Rhythmic mode 3b	Slow moderate	Doubled
Rhythmic mode 3c (Yanajanak Coda mode)	Slow moderate	Doubled suspended ♫.♫.♫.♩♩𝄽
Rhythmic mode 3c[var] (Milyarryarr Coda mode)	Slow moderate	Even interspersed with doubled suspended 𝄽♩♩♫♩♩
Rhythmic mode 3d	Slow moderate	Uneven (quadruple) [♩ ♪♩ 𝄽]
Rhythmic mode 3e	Slow moderate	Uneven (sextuple) [♩♩ ♪♩ 𝄽]
Rhythmic mode 4a	Moderate	Even
Rhythmic mode 4b	Moderate	Uneven (quadruple) [♩♩♩ 𝄽] or [♩ ♪♩ 𝄽] or [♩♩ ♪♩]
Rhythmic mode 4c	Moderate	Uneven (triple) [♩♩ 𝄽]
Rhythmic mode 4d	Moderate	Uneven (septuple) [♩♩ ♪♩ ♪♩ 𝄽]
Rhythmic mode 4e	Moderate	Uneven (sextuple) [♩♩ ♪♩ ♪♩] or [♩♩♩ ♪♩ 𝄽]
Rhythmic mode 4f (Inyjalarrku moderate Instrumental mode)	Moderate	Moderate uneven interspersed with even (+ didjeridu stop) ♩𝄽♩𝄽♩♩♩♩♩♩♩𝄽♩𝄽 ― ― didjeridu
Rhythmic mode 5a	Fast	Even
Rhythmic mode 5b	Fast	Doubled
Rhythmic mode 5b[var]	Fast	Doubled suspended (♫.♫)
Rhythmic mode 5c	Fast	Uneven (quadruple) [♩♩♩ 𝄽] or [♩ ♪♩ 𝄽]
Rhythmic mode 5c[var] (Milyarryarr fast Instrumental mode)	Fast	Uneven [♩♩♩♩♩ ♪♩ 𝄽.♪]
Rhythmic mode 5d	Fast	Uneven (triple)
Rhythmic mode 5e	Fast	Uneven (sextuple) [♩♩♩♩♩ 𝄽] or [♩♩♩ ♪♩ 𝄽]
Rhythmic mode 5f (Inyjalarrku fast Instrumental mode)	Fast	Uneven interspersed with even (+didj stop) ♩♩♩ ♪♩ 𝄽♩♩♩♩♩♩♩ ♪♩ 𝄽 ― ― didjeridu
Rhythmic mode 5g (Karrbarda fast Coda mode)	Fast	Even interspersed with fast doubled beating (+ didj. stop) ♩♩♩♩♩♩♩♩♫♫♫♫♫♫♫♫♩♩♩𝄽 ――――――――― x didjeridu dance call

Figure 2.4 Rhythmic modes featured in *kun-borrk/manyardi* songs analysed in the book; adapted from Marett, Barwick and Ford, *For the Sake of a Song*, 48.

music, the dance, and the broader cultural and social environment.[74] Musicologist Catherine Ellis suggests that listening to music and participating in song and dance can provide a more straightforward and rewarding foray into another culture:

> [Music] can bridge various thought processes; it is concerned with the education of the whole person; it can stimulate inter-cultural understanding at a deeply personal level, with the result that a person is no longer a member solely of one culture.[75]

For me, learning the song text of *kun-borrk/manyardi* required spending time with the songmen after the performance eliciting the words and their meanings. Conversely, learning the inherent musical language of the *manyardi* sometimes required little conversation, but rather a practice of deep listening, observation, and participation. Other complementary processes of learning were also important: reading published work on the subject, listening back over the recording of the music and other recordings, and transcribing and analysing the music. But these methods alone do not help one to fully understand or describe *kun-borrk/manyardi*. As Barwick observes, 'analysis is a process of understanding rather than a methodology for producing "truth"'.[76]

There was a challenge, however, in embracing my role as a member of the performance group whilst at the same time following the encouragement of songmen: I still needed to ensure I made a good a good quality recording capturing the important elements of the performance, documentation of my observations in the moment, and notes on the recording for future indexing/analysis/discussion. About halfway through the performance at Amartjitpalk, the group had finished eating lunch and were telling amusing stories; the mood seemed relaxed and jovial. Responding to this mood, the singers shifted the music up a gear, stringing together a number of songs in fast doubled rhythmic mode (5b), and Brendan Marrgam and Maurice Gawayaku responded by getting up and dancing. I wanted to follow the cues of the music and join in, but I also had to adjust the microphone so that the singers could be clearly heard in their new configuration, and reposition the camera so that the dancers were in the frame. I observed Gawayaku's son was reluctant to join in the dancing, and felt that the presence of a Balanda filming the performance may have something to do with it.[77] I thought that if I got up and made a fool of myself trying to dance—it was only my second attempt at dancing *kun-borrk/manyardi*—this would surely allow him to feel comfortable enough to join in too. So, in that moment I abandoned the camera and recording gear, and joined Gawayaku and Marrgam who were dancing with their backs to the sea, facing the singers. I tried to synchronise my movements with theirs, jerking and flailing my limbs around, much to the hilarity of the rest of the group (watch **AVEx_2.1**). My plan seemed to work: Gawayaku's son fell to the ground laughing at us all, before getting up again, and joining us.[78] In the process, I gained a deeper appreciation of rhythmic mode and the relationship between dance and song in *kun-borrk/manyardi*.

AVEx_2.1 https://dx.doi.org/10.26278/9Q67-4C60

Following their footsteps at Amartjitpalk

Men and women of all ages take part in *kun-borrk*/manyardi by joining the dancing. In Bininj Kunwok the noun *kun-borrk* literally means 'dance'.[79] Like the term *bunggurl,* which describes a different kind of clan-owned song and dance from central Arnhem Land, *kun-borrk* may also refer to what Franca Tamisari calls the 'dance-event in its totality';[80] a 'corroboree' involving a number of different dance groups. *Kun-borrk/manyardi* movement is highly expressive and individualised, whilst at the same time characterised by moments of unison, when the dancers come together for certain sequences of the song. Since I either sat with the all-male singing ensemble or partook in dancing with other men and boys, my own observations and descriptions of the dance tend to reflect a *bininj/arrarrkpi* rather than *daluk/warramumpik* perspective.

Calling out

To start the dance for a new song item, *bininj/arrarrkpi* come together in a huddle and give an initiating dance call, which triggers the didjeridu player to begin his accompaniment.[81] The vocalisation of this dance call varies, depending on the song-set. The call I became familiar with (associated with Inyjalarrku, Mirrijpu, and Karrbarda song-sets) was vocalised: 'oh:::::: ah:::::::', followed by the dancer striking his legs with a dancing stick or with one hand and yelling 'yi!' in unison with the others, with an index finger pointed to the air. Some dancers such as Marrgam also give a dance call during the song that coincides with and accentuates the end of a vocal phrase or verse. The end of the song item is also signalled with a dance call: on the last beat of the clapstick terminating pattern, the dancers once more strike their legs or hands, and on the next (unaccompanied) beat, call out 'yi!'

Dispersing and marking the beat

After the lead songman commences beating the clapsticks, male dancers spread out and move away from the singing ensemble. Remaining mainly in one spot, they lightly mark the beat of the clapstick with each lift of their feet (every second beat if the rhythmic mode is fast doubled), while keeping an eye on each other and the singing ensemble. As the singing ensemble commence with the

'They Still Help Us': Legacies of exchange   59

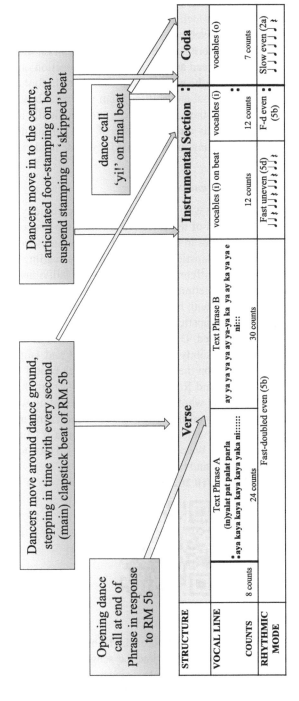

Figure 2.5 Relationship between dance and musical structure in a *manyardi* Mirrijpu song in fast doubled rhythmic mode (AVEx_2.2; 20121103-RB_v10_08_MP26.mp4).

Text Phrase of the verse, the dancers move towards the singers, continuing to mark the clapstick beat with their feet. Then, they vary their dancing to highlight the end of a vocal phrase. For example, Marrgam raised his right foot high to stamp on the first two beats, before holding it out behind him on the third beat and pausing, then swinging his head and torso in another direction on the fourth beat (see Figure 2.5). Sometimes, he would stamp with his right foot and hop on his left foot, holding his thongs out and shifting them with each beat, first from left to right, then above his head, then at waist level, and then finally in a circling motion in front of his chest. This created a sense of forward momentum that complemented the clapstick beating in fast doubled rhythmic mode (5b).

Coming together, lifting, stamping, and pausing

This 'freestyle' dancing contrasts with key moments of synchronicity during the instrumental section and the end of the text phrase where the dancers move in closer together, anchor themselves in one spot, and lift and then scoop the sand with their feet, in time with the clapstick beat, sometimes also calling out 'o:::::::yi!'[82] Again, the movement is different depending on the individual and their relationship to the song-set. Sometimes, Marrgam would come to a stop at the end of his 'hopping' movement with his arms apart and twist his torso, looking away from the singers as the clapstick skipped the beat. Other dancers might pause with their arms outstretched. Dancers would also articulate the stamp in unique ways: Marrgam would subtly stamp his right foot and emphasise the beat by raising a pair of thongs on the pause of the clapstick beat. I would also observe dancers Shannon Lee and Roderick Lee (Chapter 4) emphasising the stamping movement through the whole of their torsos, alternating with the left and right foot while raising the opposite arm. Figure 2.5 shows the moments of synchronicity during the Instrumental Sections and Codas of a Mirrijpu song in fast doubled rhythmic mode. Watch **AVEx_2.2**, where I dance to this song alongside Marrgam, Gawayaku, and his son.

AVEx_2.2 https://dx.doi.org/10.26278/6Z6Z-C904

Following the lead songman

The number of times the verses are repeated, and whether this is followed by an Instrumental Section or Coda, varies each time the song is repeated—such decisions are usually made in the moment by the lead singer. This means that while the dancers have room to improvise during the verse, they must maintain an awareness of the ensemble (the didjeridu player and singers) and the other dancers, in order to anticipate changes in the song and achieve synchronicity at the right moments. When I eventually got up to join the dancing at Amartjitpalk, I found that I was able to intuitively anticipate these moments, because of my familiarity (from earlier recording sessions) with Nangamu's Mirrijpu songs. Often, the lead singer signals his intentions to the group through vocalised instructions. For example, Nangamu would call out *yarakap* (M:'[another] one') before repeating a verse or song, and *nukapa* (M: 'this one') to indicate the final repeat of a verse. Similarly, at Bottle Rock, where the performance finished, Nangamu transitioned to the final mother song by giving the instruction *ja nigi* in Mawng, meaning '[we go to] the mother [song]'.[83]

Flexibility and complementarity in the ordering of songs

The juxtaposition of Mirrijpu and Marrwakara/Mularrik songs in the performance at Amartjitpalk brought up connections not only with people in living memory but also with Country and ancestors.[84] After playing the didjeridu for the first Mirrijpu song at Amartjitpalk (MP14), Micky Yalbarr pointed across the sea to North Goulburn Island, and told us that the song reminded him of a hunting area where he would go fishing and catch 'trevally, skinny fish, any kind'.[85] Nangamu then explained that both the Marrwakara and Mirrijpu song texts refer to this place, which belongs to the country of Manangkardi-speaking people of the Majakurdu clan:

> Any song [with] '*Inyalatpa*'...that's one for us, like all the *manyardi*—'*Linya*' too... Same like Marrwakara [song-set], '*Linya*'. And Mirrijpu [song-set] too, we go same, '*Linya*'... That's *kunred* (K: Country/home)—'*Linya*'.[86]
>
> It's in... Marrwakara, it's in Mirrijpu—in Yalarrkuku—Milyarryarr and Manbam [song-sets]—one. We talk about that one *kunred* (K: home).[87]

According to Nangamu, Linya is the 'short name' for the place name 'Parlalinya'—a dreaming site on Weyirra (North Goulburn Island) associated with the lightning ancestral spirit called *namarrkon* in Kunwinjku, who today assumes the form of a grasshopper. Place names such as these are significant because they are the same both in the spoken language (of Madjukurdu clan Manangkardi speakers who lived in Weyirra) and in the spirit language (originally named by the spirit ancestors). It is not clear whether 'Inyalatpa' is also a specific place name in Manangkardi, or a Manangkardi term for 'home/county', which Nangamu suggests through his translation using the Kunwinjku word *kunred*.[88]

The singers also explained that the Marrwakara/Mularrik songs (MK01 and MK02) 'go together' because the goanna Dreaming and the green frog Dreaming are connected by Mularrik Mularrik Creek on Goulburn Island, which runs through the town of Warruwi (see song item 20121103RB01-03 in Support Material Figure 2.iii).[89] The pair of songs are contrasting in tempo and rhythmic mode (listen to **AVEx_2.3**, where MK02 begins at **01:10**).[90] The songs are also contrasting in the way they mix languages: MK01 is in Manangkardi spirit

62   *'They Still Help Us': Legacies of exchange*

language and has the Manangkardi place name *parlalinya*; MK02 is in Mawng and has the song text: '*mularrik mularrik, mularrik, mularrik k-i[ny-a]ja-ka* [sung as *kinyara*]', translated as 'Frog, she keeps calling out' (see Figure 2.6).[91]

AVEx_2.3 https://dx.doi.org/10.26278/YPEN-8833

'They Still Help Us': Legacies of exchange   63

Figure 2.6 Music transcription of Marrwakara songs MK01 and MK02 'joined together', performed by Harold Warrabin at Amartjitpalk, 2012 (AVEx_2.3; 20121103-RB_01_03_MK01_MK02.wav. Transcription by Reuben Brown based on research with Harold Warrabin and Solomon Nangamu, with contributions from Isabel O'Keeffe.

The flexibility of the *kun-borrk/manyardi* tradition provides scope for learning/instruction and exploration/play within the performance event. At Amartjitpalk, Nangamu frequently took a break from leading the Mirrijpu songs in order to demonstrate the dancing, and to allow Agalara to lead. This gesture took place in the broader context of Nangamu handing over responsibilities as a senior songman to his junior: Nangamu and Agalara spoke about how Agalara had begun leading the songs in funeral ceremonies for the first time in Nangamu's absence. Nangamu also took over the didjeridu accompaniment for a number of songs, allowing Yalbarr and Warrabin to lead, and at the end of the performance, Gawayaku had a turn at playing the didjeridu (see song item 20121103-RB_03_27_MP06.wav, https://dx.doi.org/10.26278/G1FC-5Y24, Support Material Figure 2.iii). During the fast doubled section of dancing, Gawayaku danced in a comical manner that can be expressed in Kunwinjku as *ka-dedjbonghme* (K: he stuck his bum out), perhaps parodying the *warramumpik* (M: female) style of dancing, for the amusement of his children watching on. This involved anchoring his feet in one spot and swinging his bottom from side to side to articulate the beat in an exaggerated way. Harold Warrabin also parodied the men's dancing in the Coda section of MP25, progressively twisting his torso and holding his legs in contorted positions with each articulation of the clapstick beat, before eventually unlocking his twist at the end of the song and making the final dance call, as the other performers collapsed around him in fits of hysterical laughter (watch AVEx_2.4).

AVEx_2.4 https://dx.doi.org/10.26278/VFE7-1N35

Conclusion: singing and dancing the past into the present

Kun-borrk/manyardi has emerged as a unique expression of Bininj/Arrarrkpi culture, which has survived a period of over 50,000 years, fostering innovation and diversity over this time. The performers draw on the knowledge and awareness of their ancestors' occupation and continued presence in Country as they stamp and scoop the sand, sing particular melodies, and beat particular rhythms on the clapstick, which are understood as belonging to Country and to the ancestral spirits that reside in Country. Song and dance are the mediums through which people express the various facets of their identity: in spite of dramatic changes to their lifestyle since European contact, ceremony continues to provide a space in which various language groups from Arnhem Land and elsewhere can come together.

The journey to Amartjitpalk also revealed the centrality of *kun-borrk/manyardi* in the experience of connecting to one's ancestral country. Part of the performance is the act of visiting specific sites, which helps Bininj/Arrarrkpi remember their ancestors, and singing to these ancestors once more in order to activate ancestral powers in Country and enlist them in the performance (by stamping/scooping, calling out, etc.). In the sense that the ancestors who dwell in these places give the current-day songmen inspiration for new songs, the *kun-borrk/manyardi* and the ancestral country associated with it are inseparable, and reliant on one another for regeneration. This idea that *kun-borrk/manyardi* songsets are part of the ecology of places like Goulburn Island, and that this ecology remains fragile, was highlighted in conversations between the songmen, who discussed how the Marrwakara (goanna) is rare on the mainland, along with other species such as the northern quoll and nabarlek that are endangered and under threat of extinction from introduced species such as feral cats and the cane toad. By passing on their songs to the next generation, Bininj/Arrarrkpi are not only sustaining their song tradition but also helping younger people to sustain the ecology to which it belongs.

The principles that underlie *manyardi* are intrinsically flexible, allowing for intergenerational and intercultural participation in the performance. The dance is characterised by individual expression and play, built around key moments of synchronicity; the ensemble is flexible so as to encourage different didjeridu accompanists, backup singers and dancers, and the performance event is built around the particularities of the social occasion. The performance at Amartjitpalk brought together people with connections to Manangkardi, Mawng, and Kunwinjku languages, as well as the Torres Strait Islands. In this context, my presence as an 'outsider'/Balanda in the performance was not at all unusual, and my participation in the dance encouraged, in the same way that Gawayaku's son was encouraged to learn the dances and songs by observing others and trying it out for himself. The story about the crow splitting North and South Goulburn Island apart, and the signs in the landscape of the ongoing presence of the Dreaming, such as the paperbark tree growing under the sea between the islands, serve to remind people of their different ancestral origins and of Manangkardi people who used to live on the island. At the same time, the image of a variety of birds originally together on one island also emphasises people's common origins, and the need for inclusiveness rather than exclusion—a key principle of *kun-borrk/manyardi* performance.

Contemporary songmen such as Nangamu look to old recordings to assist their memory of *manyardi*, and, in the case of Nangamu's Mirrijpu song-set, consciously make new and different recordings, in order to leave another permanent record—a new set of footsteps—for the next generation. Singers nevertheless recognise the musical authorship of the songs that they have learned from their fathers and grandfathers. They pay tribute to those songmen by juxtaposing new dream-conceived songs with the songs they have inherited, following the principles the old people taught them relating to song order and tempi, and continuing to teach the didjeridu accompaniment and song-leading to younger performers. Rather than relying on the recording, *manyardi* rests in the collective memory, to be recreated in performance by a group of expert songmen and countrymen.

In the following chapter, we return to the mainland and to a ceremony that took place early on in my fieldwork to rebury ancestral remains at Gunbalanya.

Notes

1 Solomon Nangamu, conversation with the author; see recording session ID 20121104, https://dx.doi.org/10.26278/E1CZ-4E20
2 [Brendan Marrgam, Solomon Nangamu and Micky Yalbarr, 20121103-RB_03_edit_01.wav, https://dx.doi.org/10.26278/64HC-GZ26, 00:24:49–00:25:44].
3 Although *mirrijpu* means silver gull, Nangamu actually identified the bird after which his song is named as the roseate tern (*Sterna dougallii*).

4 [Solomon Nangamu, 20120609-RB_v01.mp4, https://dx.doi.org/10.26278/98XR-A024, 10:24–10:56]. This is a well-known creation story among Mawng speakers. For a longer version of the story, see Singer, "Agreement in Mawng," 333.
5 Linda Barwick, "Song as an Indigenous Art," in *The Oxford Companion to Aboriginal Art and Culture*, ed. Margo Neale and Sylvia Kleinert (Melbourne: Oxford University Press, 2000), 328.
6 Macknight, for example, first suggested between 1650 and 1750, but revised the date to 1780. See C. C. Macknight, *The Voyage to Marege: Macassan Trepangers in Northern Australia* (Carlton, Vic.: Melbourne University Press, 1976); C. C. Macknight, "The View from Marege: Australian Knowledge of Makassar and the Impact of the Trepang Industry across Two Centuries," *Aboriginal History* 35 (2011): 121–43. A summary of the literature on the topic can be found in Sally K. May et al., "The World from Malarrak: Depictions of South-East Asian and European Subjects in Rock Art from the Wellington Range, Australia," *Australian Aboriginal Studies* 1 (2013): 47.
7 Berndt, "Ceremonial Exchange in Western Arnhem Land," 39.
8 W. E. H. Stanner, 1957, MS3752: Series 1: Item 82, 3. Cited in Bill Ivory, "Kunmanggur, Legend and Leadership: A Study of Indigenous Leadership and Succession Focussing on the Northwest Region of the Northern Territory of Australia" (PhD thesis, Charles Darwin University, 2009), 82.
9 May et al., "The World from Malarrak," 48.
10 Ibid., 51.
11 Lamilami mentions three places where the Macassans would camp: *wighu* on Goulburn Island (northeast of Martpalk where the community of Warruwi is situated), and along the coast on the mainland at a point on the east side of Anuru Bay called Malara, and another place further east along the coast called Guion Point. Lamilami, *Lamilami Speaks*, 71.
12 Ibid., 70.
13 Richard Trudgen, *Why Warriors Lie Down and Die: Towards an Understanding of Why the Aboriginal People of Arnhem Land Face the Greatest Crisis in Health and Education since European Contact* (Darwin: Aboriginal Resource and Development Services Inc., 2000), 16.
14 Lamilami details stories of violence and conflict going back generations, including an account of an Aboriginal man named Wandiwandi who killed a Macassan man and was eventually sentenced and hanged during the early establishment of the Northern Territory government. Lamilami, *Lamilami Speaks*, 73–74.
15 Ronald M. Berndt and Catherine H. Berndt, *Arnhem Land: Its History and Its People* (Melbourne: Cheshire, 1954), 15, cited in Macknight, "The View from Marege," 129.
16 Ronald M. Berndt and Catherine H. Berndt, *The World of the First Australians: Aboriginal Traditional Life, Past and Present* (Canberra: Aboriginal Studies Press, 1999), 496.
17 Glen McLaren and William Cooper, *Distance, Drought and Dispossession: A History of the Northern Territory Pastoral Industry* (Darwin: Northern Territory University Press, 2001), 1.
18 See Trudgen's account of Yolŋu resistance after they were poisoned with horsemeat as revenge for hunting cattle on their traditional lands. Trudgen, *Why Warriors Lie Down and Die*, 18–19.
19 See Ronald M Berndt and Catherine H. Berndt, *End of an Era: Aboriginal Labour in the Northern Territory* (Canberra: Australian Institute of Aboriginal Studies, 1987).
20 See Ivory, "Kunmanggur, Legend and Leadership," 148–53.
21 There were reports of many Aboriginal deaths from influenza in the dry season of 1847 at Port Essington. John Mulvaney, *Paddy Cahill of Oenpelli* (Canberra:

Aboriginal Studies Press, 2004), 54. Birch also speculates that it is 'at least plausible that the transmission of infectious diseases such as yaws, malaria, leprosy, smallpox, and venereal disease, which were all endemic in the Indonesian islands at the time may have resulted in some level of depopulation in Arnhem Land and beyond as early as the first half of the eighteenth century'. Birch, *A First Dictionary of Erre, Mengerrdji and Urningangk*, 7; Judy Campbell, "Smallpox in Aboriginal Australia, the Early 1830s," *Historical Studies* 21, no. 84 (1985): 336–58.

22 Gumardir include Bininj Kunwok– and Mawng-speaking clans who share country along the Gumardir River with Mayinjinaj clans, from the rocky headwaters to the coastal mudflats. Jeremy Russell-Smith, Peter J. Whitehead and Peter Cooke, *Culture, Ecology and Economy of Fire Management in North Australian Savannas: Rekindling the Wurrk Tradition* (Melbourne: CSIRO Publishing, 2009), 72. There are several versions of the Reverend Watson story told today by speakers residing at Warruwi whose ancestors came from Gumardir and further south around Beswick where Watson also stayed.

23 See Mulvaney, *Paddy Cahill of Oenpelli*, 87.

24 [Solomon Nangamu, Tommy Madjalkaidj, Alfred Gawaraidji, 20120624-RB_01. wav, https://dx.doi.org/10.26278/KZ9H-Y326, 00:14:08–00:16:36]

25 See Ruth Singer, "The Wrong T-Shirt: Configurations of Language and Identity at Warruwi Community," *Australian Journal of Anthropology* 29, no. 1 (2018): 70–88.

26 Oenpelli was rejected as a site for a Methodist mission for this reason. Mulvaney, *Paddy Cahill of Oenpelli*, 60.

27 Cahill wrote to the anthropologist Baldwin Spencer that Watson was 'very earnest [...] in his work and has a nice place for his station and all the natives are used to working trepang [...] so from a financial point of view, the place should be success, but, to get the natives to believe in any other religion than their own, well you and I know better than that'. November 18, 1916. Cited in ibid., 115.

28 Richard Trudgen has suggested that because Watson likened the figure of Jesus to creation spirits, he was given a chance to stay and teach, and that the fact that he paid people rations and 'traded fairly' also helped him gain the respect of many Aboriginal people. Trudgen, *Why Warriors Lie Down and Die*, 29.

29 Lamilami, *Lamilami Speaks*, 93.

30 Indeed, Lamilami recalls being taken to his first *ubarr* ceremony by Mr. Keipert (who took over from Watson), and says that the missionaries knew about such ceremonies taking place on Goulburn Island. Ibid., 97.

31 This song-set is not performed today.

32 Lamilami, *Lamilami Speaks*, 118–19.

33 Spencer witnessed and later documented the secret-sacred *ubarr* ('ober') ceremony. He also witnessed a number of public funeral rites.

34 Spencer, *Kakadu People*, 46.

35 See Jodie Kell, Rachel Djíbbama Thomas, Rona Lawrence, and Marita Wilton, "Ngarra-ngúddjeya Ngúrra-mala: Expressions of Identity in the Songs of the Ripple Effect Band." *Musicology Australia* 42, no. 2 (2020): 161–78. https://doi.org/10.1080/08145857.2020.1948730.

36 See also A. P. Elkin, "Arnhem Land Music: Introduction," *Oceania* 24, no. 2 (1953): 85. Such performances are rare today in Gunbalanya, where other forms of entertainment in the home and at the Club have replaced *kun-borrk/manyardi*.

37 Like 'Bininj Kunwok', 'Yolŋu Matha' refers to a group of dialects, in this case spoken in eastern Arnhem Land, and literally means 'people's language'. See Evans, *Bininj Gun-wok*, 12.

38 Eileen Nabageyo, Eric Mardday and Reuben Brown, "*Kun-borrk Kore Kunbarlanja, Korroko dja Bolkkime* (*Kun-borrk* at Gunbalanya, Then and Now)," unpublished

'They Still Help Us': Legacies of exchange

paper presented at Stone Country Festival, Gunbalanya, 2012. Bininj/Arrarrkpi often refer to their song-sets as their 'song'.
39 See 20110903-RB_07.wav, https://dx.doi.org/10.26278/NWFE-VJ78; 20120609-RB_v01.mp4, https://dx.doi.org/10.26278/98XR-A024; 20120609-RB_v02.mp4, https://dx.doi.org/10.26278/FP7X-X254; 20120609-RB_v03.mp4, https://dx.doi.org/10.26278/BB35-BN42, PARARADISEC collection RB2, https://dx.doi.org/10.4225/72/56E97741DD607
40 Ronald Berndt writes that the 'spirit-familiars' which give the singer new songs 'are not the same characters who are or were believed to be responsible for mythic happenings in the ever-present Dreaming, [although] they do have a tenuous connection with such characters; moreover, they are often associated with "traditional" stories… they are intimately concerned with social affairs and have territorial associations'. Berndt, "Other Creatures in Human Guise," 171.
41 [Johnny Namayiwa, 20110825-RB_02.wav, https://dx.doi.org/10.26278/FA3X-VT77, 00:15:29–00:15:44]
42 See Berndt, "Other Creatures in Human Guise," 171.
43 Marett, *Songs, Dreamings, and Ghosts*, 39–45.
44 See Treloyn's discussion of Scotty Martin's *junba* songs, which are dream-conceived: Sally Treloyn, "Scotty Martin's *Jadmi Junba*: A Song Series from the Kimberly Region of Northwest Australia," *Oceania* 73 (2003), 209. See also Raymond Keogh's discussion of the role of 'dream-spirit travels' in the conception *nurlu* genre songs from the Broome area. Raymond Keogh, "Nurlu Songs of the West Kimberleys" (PhD thesis, University of Sydney, 1990), 31. Marett also discusses how *junba* and *balga* genres from the Kimberley involve both ghosts and conception spirits in the form of birds: Marett, "Ghostly Voices," 22.
45 See Paul Memmott and Robyn Horsman, *A Changing Culture: The Lardil Aborigines of Mornington Island*, (Wentworth Falls: Social Science Press, 1991), 184.
46 Barwick, Birch and Evans, "Iwaidja Jurtbirrk Songs," 9.
47 Garde, "The Language of *Kun-borrk*," 86.
48 Berndt, *Love Songs of Arnhem Land*, 44.
49 See Barwick, Birch and Evans, "Iwaidja Jurtbirrk Songs." Western Arnhem Land songmen often use the English term 'song' to refer to the collective group of inherited songs. For clarity, I adopt the term 'song-set' or 'repertory'. In Bininj Kunwok, terms for 'song' are *man-dule* or *duleno*. Garde, "The Language of *Kun-borrk*," 67.
50 See Barwick, Birch and Evans, "Iwaidja Jurtbirrk Songs," 9. This is also the term used for song in Kun-barlang language. See Isabel O'Keeffe, "Kaddikkaddik Kawokdjanganj 'Kaddikkaddik Spoke': Language and Music of the Kun-barlang Kaddikkaddik Songs from Western Arnhem Land," *Australian Journal of Linguistics* 30, no. 1 (2010): 36.
51 Barwick, Birch and Evans, "Iwaidja Jurtbirrk Songs," 13.
52 Ibid.
53 See Allan Marett, Linda Barwick and Lysbeth Ford, *For the Sake of a Song: Wangga Songmen and Their Repertories* (Sydney: Sydney University Press, 2013), 45.
54 See Barwick's observations on *lirrga*. Linda Barwick, "Tempo Bands, Metre and Rhythmic Mode in Marri Ngarr 'Church Lirrga' Songs," *Australasian Music Research* 7 (2002): 73.
55 Ruth Singer and Isabel O'Keeffe, "A Collection of Musical Terms in Mawng and Their Translations Archived with Songs of Western Arnhem Land Australia," *Endangered Languages Archive*, 2012, http://elar.soas.ac.uk/deposit/arnhemland-135103.
56 Popularised by Bruce Chatwin: See Chatwin, *The Songlines* (London: Random House, 1988), 13.

57 Sally Treloyn, "'When Everybody There Together… then I Call that One': Song Order in the Kimberley," *Context* 32 (2007) 117–118. Treloyn's characterisation draws from the work of a number of scholars. See also Catherine J. Ellis and Linda M. Barwick, "Musical Syntax and the Problem of Meaning in a Central Australian Songline," *Musicology Australia* 10, no. 1 (1987) 41–57.
58 Ellis and Barwick, "Musical Syntax and the Problem of Meaning in a Central Australian Songline," 47; Treloyn, "Song Order in the Kimberley," 119.
59 See discussion in Treloyn, "Song Order in the Kimberley," 119.
60 See PARADISEC collection RB2, https://dx.doi.org/10.4225/72/56E97741DD607, and Appendix 4.3 in Brown, "Following Footsteps."
61 Marett, Barwick and Ford, *For the Sake of a Song*, 56. See also analysis of 'core' melodies and their expansion and contraction in order to fit the song text, discussed in the following: Linda Barwick, "Unison and Disagreement in a Mixed Women's and Men's Performance (Ellis Collection, Oodnadatta 1966)," in *The Essence of Singing and the Substance of Song: Recent Responses to the Aboriginal Performing Arts and Other Essays in Honour of Catherine Ellis*, ed. Linda Barwick, Allan Marett and Guy Tunstill, Oceania Monographs 46 (Sydney: University of Sydney, 1995), 101; Raymond Keogh, "Process Models for the Analysis of Nurlu Songs from the Western Kimberleys," *The Essence of Singing and the Substance of Song: Recent Responses to the Aboriginal Performing Arts and Other Essays in Honour of Catherine Ellis*, ed. Linda Barwick, Allan Marett and Guy Tunstill, Oceania Monographs 46 (Sydney: University of Sydney, 1995), 47; Sally A. Treloyn, "Songs that Pull: *jadmi junba* from the Kimberley Region of Northwest Australia" (PhD thesis, University of Sydney, 2006), 204–8.
62 Marett, Barwick and Ford, *For the Sake of a Song*.
63 Linda Barwick, "Musical Form and Style in Murriny Patha Djanba Songs at Wadeye (Northern Territory, Australia)," in *Analytical and Cross-Cultural Studies in World Music*, ed. Michael Tenzer and John Roeder (Oxford: Oxford University Press, 2011), 349; Marett, Barwick and Ford, *For the Sake of a Song*, 63.
64 Marett, Barwick and Ford, *For the Sake of a Song*, 56–57.
65 See Barwick, "Tempo Bands"; Marett, Barwick and Ford, *For the Sake of a Song*, 58–59; Marett, *Songs, Dreamings, Ghosts*, 203–10.
66 Marett, Barwick and Ford, *For the Sake of a Song*, 49.
67 Marett, *Songs, Dreamings, Ghosts*, 204.
68 See Barwick, "Tempo Bands," 72. Precise didjeridu rhythms are difficult to transcribe (and are therefore only approximated in the notation of the didjeridu parts presented here) because of harmonic overtones and rhythmic notes in amplitude and as a result of the player singing into the didjeridu. See Jones, "The Didjeridu."
69 [Russell Agalara, 20110825-RB_03.wav, https://dx.doi.org/10.26278/C9CB-9Y54, 00:07:58.332–00:08:32.943].
70 Barwick, "Tempo Bands," 70.
71 Another meaning for this word is 'weak' or 'tired', as in *nuntakparlilil ta ngaralk* 'having a tired tongue when we talk'. Ruth Singer, "Mawng Dictionary Online," *Mawng Ngaralk* website, http://www.mawngngaralk.org.au/main/dictionary.php, accessed 16 April 2015. Using the program 'Transcribe!', I was able to slow down the playback of a recording and mark the clapstick beat, then highlight a selection of the recording to analyse and record the tempo in beats per minute (bpm) between markers.
72 This word also has the meaning strong, as in *natatparlangkat* 'a strong wind'. Ibid.
73 Marett, Barwick and Ford, *For the Sake of a Song*, 58–59; Marett, *Songs, Dreamings, Ghosts*, 204–05.
74 See Barwick, "Marri Ngarr Lirrga Songs," 13.

75 Ellis, *Aboriginal Music, Education for Living*, 15.
76 Linda Barwick, "Central Australian Women's Ritual Music: Knowing through Analysis versus Knowing through Performance," *Yearbook for Traditional Music* 22 (1990): 60.
77 This dilemma also brings to mind Garde's discussion of the 'participant-observer's paradox' (a recording situation in which natural conversation is skewed or interrupted by the presence of the recordist and recording gear—particularly if the recordist is not participating in the conversation, thereby drawing attention to the recording). Murray Garde, *Culture, Interaction and Person Reference in an Australian Language: An Ethnography of Bininj Gunwok Communication* (Amsterdam and Philadelphia: John Benjamins Publishing, 2013), xiv.
78 [20121103-RB_v10_06_MP06.mp4, https://dx.doi.org/10.26278/T7X5-NM69]
79 See Garde, "The Language of *Kun-borrk*," 65.
80 Franca Tamisari, "Writing Close to Dance: Reflections on an Experiment," in *Aesthetics and Experience in Music Performance*, ed. Elizabeth MacKinlay, Denis Collins and Samantha Owens (Newcastle: Cambridge Scholars, 2005), 170.
81 See discussion with Russell Agalara and Johnny Namayiwa [20110825-RB_01.wav, https://dx.doi.org/10.26278/HQWK-4E25, 00:19:39.300–00:20:19.000]
82 This contributes to an overall impression of tension/pull (during moments of synchronicity in the gapped sections of the dance) followed by release/dispersion (the rest of the time the dancers are dancing).
83 Translations provided by Ruth Singer.
84 For further discussion and a comparison of the melodic sequences of the Marrwakara and Mirrijpu song-sets performed in 2012 with legacy recordings made by Ronald Berndt of the same songs performed by male relatives of the singers in the 1960s, see Brown and Nangamu, 'I'll show you that manyardi', 21–30.
85 [Micky Yalbarr, 20121103_05-RB_20121103_01.wav, https://dx.doi.org/10.26278/G9Y1-SA30, 11:04].
86 [Solomon Nangamu, 20121103-RB_02_edit.wav, https://dx.doi.org/10.26278/TSRV-YY61, 36:40–37:14].
87 [Solomon Nangamu, 20121104-RB_01_XX_edit.wav, https://dx.doi.org/10.26278/QM76-QX91, 00:05:20–00:05:30]. See recording session Item ID 20121104, https://dx.doi.org/10.26278/E1CZ-4E20
88 'Inyalatpa' resembles another Mawng place name 'Inyalatparo' on South Goulburn Island.
89 [Solomon Nangamu and Harold Warrabin, 20121103-RB_02_edit.wav, https://dx.doi.org/10.26278/TSRV-YY61, 26:10].
90 The pairing of fast and slow songs that are thematically linked is a feature of Aboriginal music that has been discussed in relation to *junba* music from the Kimberley and *yawulyu/awelye* (women's ceremony) music of Central Australia. However, it is not as common in *kun-borrk/manyardi*, where a cluster of songs with a similar tempo tend to be performed in sequence. See Treloyn's discussion of song 'mates' in Scotty Martin's *junba* repertory. Treloyn, "Song Order in the Kimberley," 116. See also Linda Barwick's discussion on the paralleling of slow and fast Mungamunga songs, in Linda Barwick, "Performance, Aesthetics, Experience: Thoughts on Yawulyu Mungamunga Songs," in *Aesthetics and Experience in Music Performance*, ed. Elizabeth MacKinlay, Denis Collins and Samantha Owens (Newcastle: Cambridge Scholars, 2005), 8.
91 This song text is discussed in Barwick, O'Keeffe and Singer, "Dilemmas in Interpretation," 55.

3 'You Belong to Gunbalanya'
A reburial ceremony

Receiving the bones

Bill Ivory was up at 6 am, typing away, attempting to reduce the number of emails in his inbox, and replying to endless voicemail messages left on his phone from the day before. Ivory was the Government Business Manager (or 'GBM') for the Department of Families, Community Services and Indigenous Affairs (FaCSIA) in Gunbalanya, but his primary objective, for the time being at least, was managing the business of bones. It had been a busier-than-usual time for the anthropologist, who found himself in the position of go-between for the traditional owners of Gunbalanya and various government, private and community organisations, and their representatives involved in the repatriation. I stayed with Ivory for a period in June–July of 2011 in one of the self-contained air-conditioned transportable buildings or 'dongas' that were part of the GBM's quarters, made up of a couple of offices and visitors' accommodation. In one of these dongas was stored all of the bones that had recently been transported to Gunbalanya from various institutions. They were packaged in grey boxes labelled with numbers that indicated the type of bone, and the site near Gunbalanya from which they had been taken. They appeared innocuous enough, yet Bininj/Arrarrkpi were not keen to go near them.

In the weeks leading to the ceremony, after his morning inbox-clearing routine, Ivory would head out in his Toyota Land Cruiser with notepad and pen to 'cruise around'. This meant attempting to catch up with traditional owners such as Jacob Nayinggul to ask their advice about how they wanted the reburial ceremony to go ahead, then organising with members of the community for the next planning session to be held at the GBM's quarters. Ivory's co-worker Donna Nadjamerrek, the Indigenous Engagement Officer (IEO) at Gunbalanya, would also communicate with various Bininj/Arrarrkpi who were to be involved in the ceremony. Ivory and Nadjamerrek made a good team: both had experienced working and living in both Balanda and Aboriginal societies. Ivory grew up in the Aboriginal community of Maningrida and had a particular understanding of Aboriginal systems of leadership and governance (his PhD thesis topic).[1]

DOI: 10.4324/9781003216339-4

Nadjamerrek has a deep understanding of Bininj culture and experience working and consulting with Balanda (her father, Lofty Nadjamerrek, was a senior ceremony man and a very well-known artist who collaborated with numerous researchers at his clan estate of Kabulwarnamayo). Such skills are critical in the multilingual, multiclan community of Gunbalanya, where various traditional clan-owner groups hold a stake in the decision-making process.

Jacob Nayinggul, the senior traditional owner of the country from which the bones had been taken and one of the last speakers of their traditional language, was to decide how to bury the returned bones once more, in a way that would honour them properly. He too had many years of experience negotiating with Balanda on behalf of his community, around mining, land use, education, and cultural practices. As the date of the ceremony drew closer, Nayinggul's vision for the ceremony became clearer. Many people were now involved, and various logistical challenges continued to present themselves. On the same date as the ceremony, a large group of tourists had pre-booked with IAC to attend a rock art tour of Injalak Hill. In usual circumstances when a funeral takes place in an Aboriginal community such as Gunbalanya, permits to visit are not granted and the town is 'closed' to outsiders until the ceremony has taken place. Rather than requesting that the tour be cancelled, however, Nayinggul invited the tourists to Gunbalanya to attend the ceremony and witness a Bininj cultural event for themselves. This was one of many public gestures he would make in order to bring the process of repatriation out into the open and to demonstrate its significance, both to his own community and to wider society. As a consequence, the event had to now cater for some 200–300 people, including members of the relevant institutions (except the Smithsonian whose representatives had been invited but did not attend), politicians, academics, members of the media and local community, and of course the tourists. Ivory was eager for some assistance on the ground, so when my PhD supervisor Martin Thomas emailed him to let him know that I would be coming to western Arnhem Land to do fieldwork and suggested I help out with preparations for the event, his response was: 'when can Reuben start?'

Not long after I arrived at the GBM's quarters in Gunbalanya, I was greeted with the arrival of boxes of bones—representing the last of the Smithsonian Institution's collection, held in trust at the Museum and Art Gallery of the Northern Territory. Ivory assigned me the task of watching over the bones while he attended a meeting in Darwin. The bones had arrived in Australia unsorted, before physical anthropologist Steven Webb of Bond University had assessed all of the bones and arranged them in bundles according to each individual, identifying males, females, and children, so that they could be buried separately as per tradition. Before missionaries arrived in western Arnhem Land, funeral rites had been generally carried out in two or three stages, with the last of the funeral ceremonies sometimes performed a year or more after the death and the initial interment.[2] Traditional mortuary rites involved rubbing the bones in red ochre and wrapping them in paperbark, before taking them to their final resting place. Some Bininj/Arrarrkpi practised the *lorrkkon* (K: hollow log) ceremony as the final burial ceremony, during which the bones are reinterred in a hollowed-out log painted with intricate clan designs,[3] while others wrapped the bones in paperbark and placed them high up in the rocky shelters of the escarpment—a kind of elevated and protected cemetery—where they could continue to visit them when they passed through the country. The people whose bones had been stolen would have been given these older funeral rites, some of which have since fallen out of practice. Those Bininj/Arrarrkpi in attendance at the reburial in Gunbalanya were aware of this, although they may not have known that the deceased were in some cases just a couple of generations older than them.[4] Many of the Kunwinjku-speaking children, who were born and raised in Gunbalanya but belong to clans whose ancestral country lies to the east, did not necessarily know prior to the ceremony that these people from Gunbalanya had spoken different languages of the country (Erre, Mengerrdji, and Urningangk). Senior law man Jimmy Kalarriya emphasised this point when asked about the significance of the repatriation:

> That bone, they go right back, own country. They buried here, Gunbalanya, because their own country, all the Mengerr and Urningangk. And [those] old people finished[5] [now], and we take im place, Kunwinjku—people staying here, Kunwinjku mob.[6]

Nayinggul decided that they would not be buried with a *lorrkkon* ceremony—that law was also 'finished' at Gunbalanya. A key consideration was whether to place them back in the caves of Injalak and Arrkuluk from which they had been taken. Although this would befit their original burial, Nayinggul decided that this was also unworkable. He was at this time very sick, weak, and wheelchair-bound; he would not have been able to navigate the steep rocky country to get to where the grave sites are situated. It would also have been impossible to bring such a large audience of Bininj/Arrarrkpi and Balanda up to the hills, meaning that few would get to witness the act of (re)interment. Ultimately, Nayinggul decided that they should be buried under the ground at a gravesite south of Arrkuluk camp. Symbolically, this site was where other older people, including some missionaries, had been buried, and was located between the original sites of Injalak and Arrkuluk hills. Buried under the ground and in an area so close to town, the bones were also less likely to be taken again.

Like most funeral ceremonies in western Arnhem Land, the reburial ceremony came together with the assistance of local labour and resources. And like most plans hatched in the extreme and remote environment of Arnhem Land, unexpected challenges arose: the area where the two grave pits for male and female remains were to be dug was filled with unmarked graves and was situated very close to the water table of the nearby billabong. In order to locate an area clear of older graves and the water table, Sally May, an archaeologist specialising in rock art from western Arnhem Land, arranged for a ground penetrating radar machine to be brought in to detect the old grave sites. Workers from the local Gunbalanya Meatworks (meat processing factory) arrived with a backhoe and dug trenches in the spot where Nayinggul wanted the bones to be buried. Earlier, Ivory and I had coordinated a meeting with the traditional owner groups at Gunbalanya and other local organisations to make arrangements for the catering of the ceremony and the speeches. A budget for the catering and transport for guests to the remote community was provided with financial assistance from the Northern Land Council and Museums Victoria.[7] Rangers from Kakadu National Park helped set up marquees to provide a shaded area for the families and guests; the local Meatworks provided meat for the barbecue held after the ceremony for the guests, and the family of Nayinggul caught saratoga and catfish from fishing areas on their country and prepared it for guests in the traditional way, baked in a ground oven. Other volunteers from outside the community also came to lend a hand with catering on the day.[8] The willingness of Balanda to help with the ceremony and the degree of ownership and responsibility taken by both Bininj/Arrarrkpi and Balanda were symbolic of the extent to which the event was an act of reconciliation; of putting right something that had been done that was so clearly wrong. This wrong was not just the theft of bones, but the theft of people's ancestors.[9]

***

For decades, Indigenous communities around the world have voiced their desire to repatriate human remains, ceremonial artefacts, and other significant cultural materials taken from their country by early colonisers and researchers and kept in institutions such as museums or universities, or in private collections.[10] In recent years, these wishes have finally been listened to by some, but not all, governments and private institutions, who have carried out repatriations (often after long periods of consultation with custodians) and changed their policies about keeping skeletal and human remains in their collections.[11] Challenges remain, however, both for Indigenous communities trying to locate and bring home their ancestors—with many institutions still reluctant to part with their collections—and for willing institutions, which require significant resources and time to locate custodians and facilitate repatriation. Reflecting on the ceremony in 2011 to rebury human remains taken from Gunbalanya, this chapter highlights the profound emotional and spiritual significance for Aboriginal communities of repatriating ancestral remains, and gives insight into some of the challenges and decisions that these communities face once the bones of their ancestors are returned. Through a detailed analysis of the performance staged to rebury the bones at Gunbalanya, I show how so-called 'intangible' aspects of culture—language, song, and dance—have a vital role to play in the practical process of repatriating human remains.

Having described the lead-up to the event, the chapter offers Bininj/Arrarrkpi perspectives of the theft and return of their ancestors, and discusses how the ceremony leader Jacob Nayinggul prepared both the community and the spirits of the bones for reburial. An analysis of the main stages of the ceremony at Gunbalanya follows, informed by video rushes provided by Adis Hondo and Suze Houghton, who were working with Thomas on a documentary about the repatriation titled *Etched in Bone*, as well as audio recordings I made, and elicitation interviews I conducted after the event with key songmen who had performed in the ceremony.

The 1948 American-Australian Scientific Expedition to Arnhem Land and its legacy

The Arnhem Land Expedition was a large-scale research venture involving an official party of 17, as well as various Bininj, Arrarrkpi, and Yolŋu guides and helpers who were attached to the Expedition along the way. It also involved much logistical planning; 47 tonnes of gear had to be carried by air, truck, and ship across the width of Arnhem Land to the three main camps—Umbakumba at Groote Eylandt, Yirrkala in northeastern Arnhem Land, and Oenpelli in western Arnhem Land (see Support Material Figure 3.i).[12]

Jointly sponsored by the Australian Government, the National Geographic Society, and the Smithsonian Institution of America, AASEAL was politically and scientifically motivated; an expression of a newfound commitment between two cold-war allies during a period of nation-building in Australia,[13] and an opportunity for Expedition members such as Charles Mountford and Frank Setzler to further their careers by disseminating film, artwork, and cultural objects from remote Arnhem Land colleagues and audiences in both Australia and the USA.[14] Arnhem Land was fertile ground for researchers, and the Australian anthropologists Ronald and Catherine Berndt, who had also been forging their careers in Arnhem Land, felt threatened by the prospect of the Expedition treading on their 'turf'. Ronald Berndt remarked in a letter to the superintendent of the Methodist mission at Warruwi, Alf Ellison, that his department of Anthropology at the University of Sydney considered the Expedition:

> mainly a publicity stunt, and a prelude to opening up Arnhem Land for tourists—and consequently the eventual closing of mission stations or the degradation of them to the status of dude ranches ... However, there does not seem to be much we can do, as it is sponsored by the Dept. of Information and Australia needs U.S. dollars.[15]

Of course, the Expedition's leader, ethnologist Charles Mountford, stated the aims of his team in more aspiring terms: to 'increase... knowledge of the natural history and the Aborigines of Arnhem Land'.[16] Mountford and his team wanted to understand how the Aborigines 'lived off the land',[17] and indeed, the Expedition broke new ground by researching Indigenous culture and the environment of Arnhem Land for the first time within various disciplines, including archaeology, mammalogy, ichthyology, botany, ornithology, and nutrition. Mountford was particularly interested in Aboriginal art of Arnhem Land and collected 'several hundred' bark paintings to go along with the thousands of plant and animal specimens that other members of the Expedition collected.[18] As Thomas has observed, for Mountford the success of the Expedition would be measured 'not in terms of new theories or ideas, but in numbers of specimens'.[19]

The darker side of the Expedition's penchant for collecting things included Frank Setzler's removal of human remains from various sites near Groote and nearby islands, the Gove Peninsula, Milingimbi, and at Injalak Hill in Gunbalanya (see Figure 3.1).[20] Thomas, who has thoroughly researched this unofficial but significant chapter of the Arnhem Land Expedition, concludes:

> the number of bones collected from such a range of sites makes it plain that for Setzler, and to a lesser extent [anthropologist Frederick] McCarthy, the collection of human remains was a major part of the work conducted in Arnhem Land.[21]

Figure 3.1 AASEAL members at base camp in Gunbalanya (Oenpelli), 1948. Frank Setzler is pictured at the far right of photo, with Injalak Hill in the background, from where bones were stolen. Photo: Howell Walker, National Geographic magazine, cited in Thomas and Neale, ed., *Exploring the Legacy*, 52.

Thomas' theory as to why Mountford allowed the thefts to occur under his watch—in spite of the fact that bone collection was never mooted as part of the Expedition's activities or approved by the Australian Government,[22] and in spite of Mountford's prior experience with Aboriginal people, which would have taught him that it was wrong to disturb or remove human remains—centres on the question of how the 'spoils' of the Expedition would be divided up between the Australian leader and his American deputy:

> Mountford, who had no interest in physical anthropology, was prepared to let Setzler collect bones, hopeful that the acquisition of these trophies would lessen his requirement for the types of object—particularly the bark paintings—that Mountford so coveted.[23]

In spite of Setzler's efforts to conceal the theft from his Bininj/Arrarrkpi guides at the time,[24] an Iwaidjan story documented by Bruce Birch about an American 'clever man' (Expedition mammalogist David Johnson) reveals an awareness at least among some Bininj/Arrarrkpi that bones were stolen during this time and taken to the USA.[25] Exactly where they were stolen and where they ended up was certainly a mystery to many Bininj/Arrarrkpi at Gunbalanya, until the discovery of remains at the Smithsonian Institution by visiting Australian scholar Sally May in 2001.[26] Digitised footage originally shot by Howell Walker of the *National Geographic* provided further evidence of the theft, with one macabre sequence showing Setzler venturing into the caves at Injalak (suspiciously, without the Bininj/Arrarrkpi guides who led him there in the first place) and 'discovering' skulls and bones in the crevices, pulling them out, rearranging them, and placing them in the ammunition boxes.[27]

Where did the spirits go?

The weeks leading up to the reburial ceremony at Gunbalanya in 2011 were an anxious time for both Bininj/Arrarrkpi and Balanda involved in the process of bringing the bones home. Negotiations over the repatriation had taken over ten years and involved senior levels of the Australian Government lobbying the Smithsonian Institution in America on behalf of traditional owners to hand over all of the bones from their collection. A number of Balanda were therefore also eager to see that the bones were given a proper reburial and that care was taken to properly identify and transport the bones back from the various institutions where they had been stored to Gunbalanya.[28] For many Bininj/Arrarrkpi, the period between a person's death and their burial can be an anxious time, during which certain phenomena, particularly sickness, may be attributed to the actions of the deceased spirit. Added to this anxiety was uncertainty around the identity of these people whose *kun-marre-mok* (K: remains)[29] had been stolen, anger over their removal, and unease over the fact that these people had been away from their traditional country for so long. In many ways, the ceremony would be like any other contemporary funeral held in western Arnhem Land. However, a number of factors made it unique: the deceased were not known to anyone alive today; a large number had to be buried at once—the remains of some 60 individuals—and they were being buried for a second time.[30] For some, the imminent repatriation also raised significant questions about the past: 'why were these bones taken away in the first place?', 'who gave permission?', and 'who was responsible?'

Together with the ancestral bones stolen from Gunbalanya as part of AASEAL,[31] others stolen over a number of years by anthropologists and archaeologists from various sites near Gunbalanya in Mirarr and Manilakarr clan country—including Malakananja, Red Lily Billabong, Arrkuluk Hill, and Injalak Hill—were returned in the same ceremony. The earliest theft dates from Baldwin Spencer's visit in 1913, and the most recent dates from archaeologist Carmel Schrire's fieldwork in 1964. By 1948, the practice of grave robbing was well over 100 years old. Colonisers collected the remains of non-Europeans throughout the 19th and early 20th centuries in an attempt to 'prove' the racial inferiority of the colonised and justify the colonial project.[32] In Setzler's country of the United States, the stealing of bones had been institutionalised since the late 1880s and encouraged by the government, which offered money for Native American skulls. The Smithsonian Institution's United States National Museum (today called the National Museum of Natural History) collected human remains from all around the world, alongside other collections of exotic animals. Indeed, it was not until the 1980s that the rights of physical anthropologists and science to continue collecting bones came under scrutiny in the face of protests for the rights of the dead and their descendants.[33] Many museums are still reluctant to repatriate bones for fear of losing their collections, including the Smithsonian, who resisted requests for the return of all of the remains taken from Arnhem Land for many years before finally agreeing in 2009.[34]

After viewing footage of Setzler taking the bones from Arrkuluk Hill, Nayinggul and other Bininj such as Nagurrgurrba were particularly upset about the lack of respect shown to traditional owners at the time, in taking the bones without permission, and to the dead, in 'playing around' with their bones, as Nayinggul described Setzler's actions. Prior to the reburial ceremony, Martin Thomas was making a film with Nayinggul about the return of the bones to Gunbalanya, and asked him whether he believed the spirits of the people were taken when the bones were removed all those years ago:

> Thank you for asking that! That's what I thought first, when I heard that was happening—these people were taken away. And I thought, OK, how about them [the deceased] and their spirits? Where would that ends up or go to? What would happen to it? Where would the spirits go?[35]

Nayinggul's unresolved questions stem from Bininj/Arrarrkpi beliefs about the inseparability of body and spirit, and what scholars of northern Australian Aboriginal cultures have called the 'life cycle' or 'existence cycle' of the spirit.[36] This is the understanding that a person's spirit emerges from a specific totemic Dreaming site that is associated with fertility.[37] The spirit then enters the mother's womb and takes up residence in the human body. When Bininj/Arrarrkpi die, the deceased spirit remains attached to its body and to the places where it lived. Rituals accompanied by singing and dancing cajole the deceased spirit to return to its ancestral country. Reabsorbed in the landscape, as Marett writes, the deceased spirit is 'able to hear human voices, smell human presences, respond to human footprints', and may enter the womb of another person where it will start the life cycle once more.[38] From a Bininj/Arrarrkpi perspective, when the *kun-marre-mok* were stolen from their resting place in the past, the spirits were 'kidnapped' along with them, and the journey that a deceased person's spirit takes was fundamentally disrupted.[39] For Nayinggul and others, it was difficult to say exactly what happened to the spirits when the *kun-marre-mok* were not residing in their traditional country.

A number of scholars examining mortuary rites in Aboriginal society have highlighted the important function of song and dance in funeral ceremonies.[40] For example, Marett discusses the idea of liminality in the ceremonial performance of *wangga* by Marri Tjevin people of the Daly region, which functions to bring the living together with the spirits of the deceased (*maruy*), who are intimate with the song and dance repertoires that they passed down when they were alive:

> By joining with their Walakandha ancestors, through singing their songs, playing didjeridu, dancing their dances, painting the marks of Walakandha [ancestral spirits] on their bodies, and witnessing the production of their ceremonial forms, the living participants draw close to and interpenetrate with the dead. It is within this context that the spirits of the deceased are released from their attachments to the living and are freed to join the ancestral dead.[41]

Amid the uncertainty and anxiety at Gunbalanya surrounding the fate of the spirits that had gone missing, songmen were called upon by Nayinggul and other traditional owners, to help sing them home. What was certain was that bringing them home would put an end to all of the speculation and the worry on the part of the living about the dead.

You came a long way

For Bininj/Arrarrkpi of western Arnhem Land, indeed for many Indigenous people, the spirits of their ancestors have agency; they can see and hear the living, particularly when addressed in their own language that they had spoken in life. As Michael Walsh writes, this relationship between spirits and their languages extends to the places the spirits inhabit, and is thought to continue even after languages are lost, affecting the way that people interact with particular places in the country that traditionally belonged to language groups that no longer have any living speakers:

> In Aboriginal Australia, at least some small portion of an Indigenous language is seen as necessary for access to places [...] Particularly for places of special significance it is felt that access to such a place can be gained only when there is someone who can speak to the spirits that inhabit that place. And the "place" will understand only the language of the land-owning group in whose territory that place resides.[42]

The day before the burial, Nayinggul entered a tender dialogue with the spirits of the bones as they were brought out for the first time in preparation for burial. He addressed them in Mengerrdji—considered to be a 'remnant' language[43]—as *Ulkuwem* (Mjd: elders). His daughter, Connie Nayinggul, later explained to me that he was speaking in particular to the *na-kordang* (K: 'clever' men or sorcerers) among them, whom he did not want to upset during the burial process, lest they put curses on the living and make them sick. Connie helped me to translate her father's words:

> *Nu merreken Kunbarlanj.*[44] *Nu merreken Kunbarlanj [...] Ngarna-yam Nayinggul. Miya nge memme miya nu. Ulkuwem memek kuk. Nu merreken. Emerr bele::::::nj nu merreken. Emerr belenj nu merreken.*
> You belong to Gunbalanya.[45] You belong to Gunbalanya. I'm a new person called Nayinggul. You and I, we are friends. You top people, we love you. You belong here. You came a lo::::::ng way. You belong here.[46]

Nayinggul spoke slowly, clearly, and tenderly—the way one would speak to one's elders or to children. His stretching out of the final vowel of the word *belenj* seemed to imply the long journey that the bones had taken to America and back. He was reassuring them that they were home, after a long and potentially disorienting journey, and after the years they had spent in a store room listening to the foreign accents of Americans.

Each gesture of Nayinggul's was instructional and aimed to show both the local and wider audience of Bininj/Arrarrkpi and Balanda how traditional funeral ceremonies in this part of the country are carried out, and the significance of having ancestors back in their traditional country. Present alongside Bininj for these the preparations were Bill Ivory, Martin Thomas, and I, as well as Fairfax

Press photographer Glenn Campbell and the film crew.[47] The Bininj group in charge of preparing for the ceremony under Nayinggul's instruction consisted of families of the traditional owners of Gunbalanya, as well as other community leaders such as Nadjamerrek and Isaiah Nagurrgurrba. The previous day, Ivory, Thomas, and I accompanied them to an area a short drive from the township of Gunbalanya, where they collected paperbark and string from wattle trees. Nayinggul's daughters then laid out the paperbark for wrapping the bones and later stripped, soaked, and dried the string for tying up the paperbark bundles. Because of the sensitivity around the presence of the bones, Ivory, Thomas, and I anticipated that Nayinggul would want the preparation to occur behind closed doors. However, Nayinggul instructed the paperbark to be laid out on the ground outside the GBM's quarters, and for the bones to be brought out from their storage, removed from their boxes, ritually rubbed in ochre, and wrapped in full view of everyone.

In carrying out the ochre ritual, the men took a large red stone and rubbed it on a block of concrete, adding water to the ochre to create a richly coloured paint. Together with the women, they slowly, delicately, and methodically rubbed the paint into every crevice of the *kun-marre-mok*—the eye sockets of each skull, even the teeth. By rubbing ochre from Country into their bones, Nadjamerrek explained, they were helping to 'cool' the ancestral spirits. This ritual lasted several hours, after which the ochred bones were tied up in bundles of paperbark with string. Nayinggul sat in his wheelchair and watched over the proceedings, encouraging them to keep going. He instructed the film-makers and photographer, and occasionally, he would call Thomas or me over to bring him a cup of tea or help him fetch a cigarette from his bag (his fragility meant that he was unable to perform simple tasks without assistance). The sight of the bones laid out in the open was somewhat confronting for me personally; I had never seen human bones and skulls before, and although none of us knew who they were, through this ritual (along with the assembling of the bones carried out by Webb), they had clearly become subjects, rather than objects as they had previously been treated. The ritual also produced a calm mood over the group. By the end, the initial uncertainty and nervousness on the faces of the men gave way to smiles as they joked and conversed freely with each other in Kunwinjku and with Balanda in English.

Thus far, I had witnessed Bininj communicating with their ancestors through their language (Mengerrdji), their country (the red ochre), and their touch (handling and rubbing the bones in ochre). Yet, the most emotionally powerful and highly communicative act would occur during the final stages of the ceremony, with the performance of *kun-borrk/manyardi*. Up until this point, I had been concentrating on the practical challenges of the ceremony: navigating a sandy track in a four-wheel drive loaded with Bininj during a trip to collect the paperbark, or coordinating and transporting a public address system from Darwin in preparation for the speeches. On the day of the ceremony, I offered to transport the bundled *kun-marre-mok* in the back of my ute from the GBM's quarters to the grave site. The funeral procession began, and I drove behind at walking pace with Jacob Nayinggul's son Alfred Nayinggul in the ute, with the emergency lights flashing (another Arnhem Land funeral ceremony performance convention, signalling the transportation of the deceased, that I would learn that day). We reached the gravesite and I got out, opened the tray of the ute, and stood back as the men of the traditional owner families took the bones. When they did this, the dancers and singers came together around them and guided them towards the grave. Standing back and taking in the music and dance for the first time, I suddenly understood what was happening: the living were singing to the ancestors of the bones and interacting with them through the dance. This expression was so powerful, I found myself (along with others in the crowd) moved to tears.

Orienting them home

From the moment the boxes containing *kun-marre-mok* of people from Yirrkala, Groote Eylandt, and Gunbalanya journeyed home from America, their spirits had been, as Thomas put it, transported on a 'current of song'.[48] Traditional owners representing these three communities had previously gone to Washington in 2010 and performed a ceremony to accompany the bones home. Aware that the deceased were from different areas of Arnhem Land, each with their own languages and songs, they had come to an agreement that the late Joe Gumbula (representing the Yolŋu of northeast Arnhem Land) would sing his *manikay* on behalf of them all, accompanied on clapsticks by Thomas Amagula (Groote Eylandt). Gunbalanya traditional owner Victor Gummurdul accompanied the men for the ceremony, although he did not accompany the singing.[49] The reburial ceremony at Gunbalanya in 2011 represented the 'final leg' of the journey home for the spirits that had been taken from that area. In spite of the unusual set of circumstances, the bones were given the same reception that a recently deceased person might receive; the ceremony, in which mourners accompany the deceased to the grave while performing *kun-borrk* and *manyardi*, functioned much like any other funeral ceremony in western Arnhem Land. In the following section, I outline the stages of the funeral ceremony (roughly five), consisting of different performances of *kun-borrk* and *manyardi*—summarised in Table 3.1—interspersed with speeches from the traditional owners and the Anglican Diocese ministers (Table 3.1).

Table 3.1 Summary of *kun-borrk/manyardi* song items performed for a reburial ceremony, Gunbalanya, 2011. The table shows song item and corresponding DOI link, song ID(s), the rhythmic mode sequence of the songs, tempo of songs (in beats per minute), and the ceremonial action that took place alongside the performance

Song item/ Recording	DOI	Song/s	Rhythmic Mode	BPM	Ceremonial Action
20110719-MT_v0367_01.mp4	https://dx.doi.org/10.26278/1B6V-NM85	MP14 ('old')	4a (moderate even); Coda 2a (slow even, final 7 counts)	118/80	**Mirrijpu** performers lead procession from GBM's quarters towards Arrkuluk camp
20110719-MT_v0369_01.mp4	https://dx.doi.org/10.26278/W71M-BT88	MP06 *kiwken*	4a (moderate even); IS 4c (moderate uneven [♩♪♪♩♪♪♩♪♩]); Coda 2a (slow even)	128/93	
20110719-MT_v0370_01.mp4	https://dx.doi.org/10.26278/2931-ZF31	MP06	4a; IS 4c; Coda 2a	128/82	
20110719-MT_v0371_01.mp4	https://dx.doi.org/10.26278/2JCN-8R72	KB18	2a (slow even)	90	**Karrbarda** performers take over as procession enters burial ground, leading them towards the grave
20110719-MT_v0373_01.mp4; 20110719-MT_v0374_01.mp4; 20110719-MT_v0375_01.mp4	https://dx.doi.org/10.26278/AEG8-CD29; https://dx.doi.org/10.26278/0FC1-6D87; https://dx.doi.org/10.26278/CVW-JE29	KB01 (x4)	5b (fast doubled); Coda 5g (fast interspersed with fast doubled) ♪♪♪♪♪♪♪♪ ♫♫ ♫♫♫♫ ♫♫♫♫ ♪♪♪♪𝄽	268	
20110719-MT_v0379_01.mp4; 20110719-MT_v0380_01.mp4	https://dx.doi.org/10.26278/8B5M-QY15; https://dx.doi.org/10.26278/8SY7-ZE74	KB06 (x2)	2a	81	
20110719-MT_v0385_01.mp4	https://dx.doi.org/10.26278/RAZH-9C22	KB01 (x3)	5b; Coda 5g	277	After Nakodjok's speech, **Karrbarda** performers continue singing as the traditional owners place bones in the grave

(*Continued*)

84 'You Belong to Gunbalanya': A reburial ceremony

Table 3.1 (Continued)

Song item/Recording	DOI	Song/s	Rhythmic Mode	BPM	Ceremonial Action
20110719-MT_v0385_01.mp4	https://dx.doi.org/10.26278/RAZH-9C22	KB06/ KB14	2a 2a; IS 4a; Coda 4b [♩♪♩]	85 39/109/103	**Karrbarda** perform *ngalbadjan* (mother song) as the final bundles are placed in the grave
20110719-MT_v0394_01.mp4; 20110719-MT_v0395_01.mp4; 20110719-MT_v0396_01.mp4	https://dx.doi.org/10.26278/F93Y-BB59; https://dx.doi.org/10.26278/XZQH-5050; https://dx.doi.org/10.26278/AMBA-8X51	IL35 (x3)	4a; IS 4f (moderate uneven) [♩♪♩♪♩♪♩♪♩♪♩]; Coda 4f	122	**Inyjalarrku** perform their goodbye as bobcat works to cover the bones in dirt
20110719-MT_v0398_01.mp4; 20110719-MT_v0399_01.mp4; 20110719-MT_v0400_01.mp4	https://dx.doi.org/10.26278/XN8H-9F58; https://dx.doi.org/10.26278/YECE-PX87; https://dx.doi.org/10.26278/HV87-5666	IL47 (x3)	4a; IS 4f [♩♪♩♪♩♪♩♪♩♪♩]; Coda 4f	117	
20110719-MT_v0402_01.mp4	https://dx.doi.org/10.26278/NXDC-AH68	IL48	4a; IS 4f [♩♪♩♪♩♪♩♪♩♪♩]; Coda 4f	117	
20110719-MT_v0403_01.mp4; 20110719-RB_01_01_IL49.wav; 20110719-RB_01_02_IL49.wav; 20110719-RB_01_03_IL49.wav	https://dx.doi.org/10.26278/7R22-T391; https://dx.doi.org/10.26278/00QN-FV06; https://dx.doi.org/10.26278/0KEW-8E16; https://dx.doi.org/10.26278/K4PY-TR11	IL49 (x3)	3a (slow moderate) and 2b (slow uneven) [♩♪♩]	100/80 96/98	

(Continued)

Table 3.1 (Continued)

Song item/Recording	DOI	Song/s	Rhythmic Mode	BPM	Ceremonial Action
20110719-RB_01_04_IL49_IL50.wav	https://dx.doi.org/10.26278/TP1R-EJ58	IL49/IL50 'nigi no. 1'	3a, 2a 2a, 2c (slow doubled uneven) [♩♪,♬♪,♩♩ ♬♬♪]	98/60	Gulamuwu performs **Inyjalarrku** *nigi* and giant dance to say *bobo*
20110719-RB_02_01_MP06.wav	https://dx.doi.org/10.26278/RAHF-2B71	MP06	4a; IS 4c [♩♩♩♩♪♪♪♪♪♪♪]; Coda 2a	124/88	Nangamu continues performing **Mirrijpu**
20110719-RB_03_01.wav	https://dx.doi.org/10.26278/TMDM-B471	MP06	4a; IS 4c [♩♩♩♩♪♪♪♪♪♪♪]; Coda 2a	125/85	
20110719-RB_04_01_MP06.wav	https://dx.doi.org/10.26278/Z9KA-Q618	MP06	4a; IS 4c [♩♩♩♩♪♪♪♪♪♪♪]; Coda 2a	125/85	
20110719-RB_04_02_MP14.wav	https://dx.doi.org/10.26278/Y49P-5K83	MP14	4a; Coda 2a	121/90	
20110719-RB_04_03_MP14.wav	https://dx.doi.org/10.26278/S1KS-1K60	MP14	4a; Coda 2a	120/84	
20110719-RB_04_04_MP14.wav	https://dx.doi.org/10.26278/J1ND-P402	MP14	4a; Coda 2a	119/82	
20110719-RB_04_05_MP19.wav	https://dx.doi.org/10.26278/PS4X-RY82	MP19	4a; IS 4c [♩♩♩♩♪♪♪♪♪♪♪]; Coda 2a	125/84	
20110719-RB_04_06_MP19_MP04.wav	https://dx.doi.org/10.26278/KXKQ-X317	MP19/MP04	4a; IS 4c [♩♩♩♩♪♪♪♪♪♪♪]; Coda 2a/ 2a; (ends with final *bobo*)	124/82/87	Nangamu performs **Mirrijpu** 'morning star' song joined to *nigi* after final dirt is placed on grave
20110719-MT_v0442_01.mp4	https://dx.doi.org/10.26278/HPWY-FA30	MP06	4a; IS 4c [♩♩♩♩♪♪♪♪♪♪♪]; Coda 2a	123/82	Back at Injalak Arts and Crafts, Nangamu performs **Mirrijpu** *kiwken* and *nigi* for smoking ceremony
20110719-MT_v0443_01.mp4	https://dx.doi.org/10.26278/JNNT-D255	MP06/MP04	4a; IS 4c [♩♩♩♩♪♪♪♪♪♪♪]; Coda 2a/ 2a (ends with *bobo*)	122/90	

The procession

The first stage was a procession to accompany the bones and mourners to the grave site. In western Arnhem Land, the funeral procession occurs when the body of the deceased is accompanied from the home to the morgue, or vice versa. This movement is usually accompanied with song. The Mirrijpu singers, headed by Solomon Nangamu, Russell Agalara, and accompanied on the didjeridu by Alfred Gawaraidji, led the procession from the GBM's quarters where the bones had been stored and wrapped, south through Middle Camp and past Arrkuluk Camp to the grave site, situated in between Arrkuluk and Injalak hills (see Support Material Figure 3.ii). Nayinggul was at the centre of the procession, wheeled by Thomas and flanked by Donna Nadjamerrek and then NT Government Minister for Arnhem Malarndirri McCarthy and then Member of Parliament for Arafura Marion Scrymgour, while other members of the community and tourists walked behind. Having invited the local and national press (the event was reported in the Council newspaper and Fairfax media, as well as the ABC's *7:30* programme),[50] Nayinggul and others were keen to show a united front to the public.

Nangamu and Agalara sang two different songs (MP14 and MP06) in moderate even rhythmic mode (4a) as the group slowly walked to the site (see Table 3.1). They performed one song (MP06) called *kiwken* (M: 'boss')—which Nangamu later explained is a song that he opens his performances with—followed by another song (MP14) that Nangamu regards as one of the 'older' songs in the song-set. The procession paused when it reached the road to the grave site and the Karrbarda (K: long yam) singers Shane and Geoffrey Nabageyo took over the singing, with Nangamu accompanying them this time on didjeridu. I later asked Nangamu why the leading of the singing changed at this particular point in time. His answer related to the way that singing *kun-borrk/manyardi* songs from a particular country is understood to help carry the spirit through that country, and how the orientation of the bones was mapped out on a micro level through the performance at Gunbalanya:

SN: I'm from the saltwater country, I was born there. So when the bones arrived here, I came and collected the bones, and I took it and gave it to all the stone [country] mob, from this country. I passed it on to them, them mob now, them take it and bury it.

RB: Right, OK. So you're carrying the bones in, through song, right?

SN: From the sea.[51]

Of course, neither Nangamu nor any other performers physically handled the bones at any point. Rather, Nangamu's performance of Mirrijpu songs from the GBM's quarters enacted the 'collection' of the bones (and their spirits), which had travelled south across the Pacific Ocean from the United States of America. As a *kurrula* songman representing the saltwater country to the north of

Gunbalanya, Nangamu brought them in first, from the direction of his country. Then, once they reached the burial ground and were facing the stone country between Arrkuluk and Injalak hills, it was time for them to be accompanied by *wardde-ken* (K: stone country) songs.

Dancing them into the grave

The next phase of the performance involved both the *daluk* (K: women) and *bininj* (K: men) of the Karrbarda group, dancing the spirits into the grave (expressed in Kunwinjku as *ngarri-mulilma*).[52] As they entered the burial ground, the Karrbarda group performed a slow tempo song (KB18, rhythmic mode 2a), for the *daluk* to dance to. When *daluk* dance to Karrbarda songs, they sway their arms from side to side and walk with each beat of the clapstick beat, or stay on one spot with their heads bowed, swivelling the right foot in and out, which is anchored to the ground. This subtle movement represents walking and carrying the yam.[53] The *bininj* then came together in a circle and gave an initiating dance call, prompting the beginning of song (KB01) in fast doubled rhythmic mode (5b), where the clapsticks beat in double-time (watch **AVEx_3.1**). Eric Mardday, another one of the main singers for the Karrbarda (who was not present during this occasion), described this dance sequence in Kunwinjku as: '*kabirri-marren wanjh kabirri-melme kabirri-karung karrbarda*' (they sing out and then they dance; they're digging the long yam).[54] Once the song reached its Coda **[00:25]**, they lifted one foot high in the air and brought it down deftly into the dirt with the clapstick beat, at the same time lifting the elbows from side to side. With each repetition of the song, they continued coming in to a circle, calling out and then spreading out again, eventually leading the procession towards the pit. The *daluk* lined up on the southern side of the grave, in front of Jacob Nayinggul and the two grave pits, and danced at the same time as the men.[55]

AVEx_3.1 https://dx.doi.org/10.26278/MQ8R-7P72

Both *daluk* and *bininj* had covered their bodies in *delek* (K: white ochre), which the men apply by mixing the ochre with water and dipping ironbark branches into the liquid, using the branches to flick the *delek* over their arms, legs, torso, and back. (In Kunwinjku, this is expressed as '*karri-bedjekmerren delek*': 'we flick ourselves with white ochre'.) The *bininj* wore nagas and headbands from red cloth; the colour red symbolising their affinity to the stone country (*kurrula* dancers normally use nagas made from blue cloth symbolising the sea).

Next, Nayinggul instructed the group of men who were involved in the preparation of the bones—led by Alfred Nayinggul and Victor Gummurdul—to take the boxes containing bones wrapped in paperbark and place them next to the burial pits. Those containing bones that had belonged to *daluk* or *wurdurd* (K: children) were placed next to one pit, while those belonging to *bininj* were placed next to the other, 'just like when we're camping', Nayinggul explained.[56] As they did this, the Karrbarda singers switched back to a slower tempo song (KB06).[57] The men wiped their hands under their armpits and onto the boxes; a ritual that is performed in order to make an object 'familiar' to a place, so as no harm will come to them.[58] As the point of interment drew closer, it was as if the objective was for Bininj/Arrarrkpi to give the spirits an overdose of the senses—to make them hear the *kun-borrk* that they are familiar with, feel the vibration in the ground from the stamping of the Karrbarda dancers, and smell the sweat of their countrymen. All of this was orchestrated to ensure that the spirits stay with the bones, and stay in their country, from where they may continue to look after the living.[59]

In western Arnhem Land, it is common practice at funeral ceremonies for speeches to be held while everyone is assembled around the grave. On this occasion, four traditional owners representing the clans of Gunbalanya gave speeches acknowledging the clans and languages of the ancestors whose *kun-marre-mok* they were burying. Nayinggul spoke first in Kunwinjku, explaining that he didn't personally know who these people were who had been taken away, but that he can speak the languages of their country: '*Mengerrdju nga-wokdi, Kakadju nga-wokdi [...] Bugurnidja nga-wokdi*' (I speak Mengerrdji, I speak Gaagadju, I speak Bugurnidja).[60] In this way, Nayinggul was reassuring the majority Kunwinjku-speaking crowd about his earlier communication with the bones, and the fact that he was the intermediary that could welcome the spirits of the country home again. In their speeches, traditional owners Yvonne Gumurdul and Julie Narndal also acknowledged (in English and Kunwinjku respectively) the ancestors of the three language groups of Gunbalanya—Mengerrdji, Erre, and Urningangk.[61] Alfred Nayinggul then spoke in Kunwinjku about the journey that the bones had taken before arriving in Gunbalanya and the role he had played in going to America to lobby to bring these *ngandjak* (K: body parts) back.

During this part of the ceremony where the mourners gather next to the grave, a relative or kin of the deceased may deliver a monologue, in which some form of responsibility or portion of blame is laid on someone or something, for the death of the deceased. Nayinggul's final speech—in English because it was intended for both Balanda and Bininj/Arrarrkpi ears—was in this vein, but more measured and conciliatory than others I would later witness during my fieldwork. He conveyed the regret, sadness, and hurt on behalf of the community over the fact that the bones had been taken without Bininj/Arrarrkpi knowledge or permission, before offering a way forward:

> My father and his uncle didn't say 'yes'. No formal meeting was taken in those days... But good [that] they're back, and I can now—second generation—I can now bury them. But I feel sorry that they were stolen. Stealing is no bloody good to everybody. We should leave stealing and live together, black and white, live together in a beautiful country like this, no mucking around stealing or whatever.[62]

After the speeches, the Karrbarda singers started up again, this time with a fast tempo song (KB01). The dancers seemed to focus and move with greater intensity this time, as if lifting and encouraging the delivery of the spirits into the grave. With Alfred and others clapping with encouragement along to the clapstick beat, the men of the traditional owner families jumped down into the graves and started receiving the paperbark bundles of bones, placing them in the bottom of the pit. Each bundle was marked with an arrow indicating the direction of the head of the deceased, helping the traditional owners to lie them down with heads facing Arrkuluk Hill, the direction of their clan country where many had originally been taken.

Saying 'bobo'

As the final bundles were transferred into the ground, the Karrbarda singers returned once more to the slower tempo song (KB06) before transitioning into the 'mother song' (KB14) of the song-set, called the *ngalbadjan* in Kunwinjku,[63] and *nigi* in Mawng. The *ngalbadjan/nigi* is often the final song that *kun-borrk/manyardi* songmen perform, in order to conclude their part of the performance. In most song-sets, it is recognisable by the fact that it has the slowest tempo of all of the songs—roughly half that of other slow rhythmic mode songs in the song-set.[64] It is also rarely performed as a stand-alone song; on this occasion, it was joined onto the penultimate song that the singers decided to sing (KB06), with the continual accompaniment of the didjeridu and clapstick beat. Like other songs in slow rhythmic mode, the *ngalbadjan/nigi* features *daluk* dancing, as Mardday explains:

> that *ngalbadjan*, like Karrbarda mother, and *bu* last part, that's only for *daluk*, *kabirri-borrkke*, and plus that singer, *kabirri-yawan*, *ka-bonj*. All the dancers, *kabirri-borrkke* all that *yawok*, *man-yawok*, like young ones *karrbarda*, *na-yowok* [?]. All the dancers *borrkke* [?] *ngalbadjan djal* singer and *daluk*.[65]
>
> That mother, like [mother song belonging to the Karrbarda song-set], for the last part it's only for the women to dance to and the singer [to sing].

90 *'You Belong to Gunbalanya': A reburial ceremony*

All the dancers, they search for it [the yam], and it's just him [singing]. All the dancers dance that 'cheeky yam', the young yam. The dancers that dance for the mother song are just the singer and the women.

In the context of funeral ceremonies, the mother song is performed at key moments of transition: when the deceased is transferred from the *mutika* (Kr: motorcar) to the plane (to go to an outstation or morgue), from the *mutika* to the funeral bough shelter, or from the bough shelter to the grave. It expresses *bobo* (goodbye), from the mourners to the deceased, and from Bininj/Arrarrkpi to their ancestors so that they return with the spirit of the deceased to the spirit world. This change or transition in the spirit's orientation is marked in the music and the dance by alteration and interchange. For the Karrbarda mother song (KB14), a shift in the tempo of the clapstick beat occurs halfway through the song, when the time signature changes from compound (12/8) to simple time (4/4) (listen to **AVEx_3.2**). In measure 6 of Support Material Figure 3.iii, the clapstick beat falls on the crotchet beat rather than every second dotted crotchet, which has the effect of tripling the tempo. This alteration between the slower clapstick sections and faster sections builds a sense of surging and driving forward, then pulling back again, as the singers return to the original time signature.[66]

AVEx_3.2 https://dx.doi.org/10.26278/KSAV-N217

As discussed in Chapter 2, most *kun-borrk/manyardi* songs end with a Coda that consists of open vowels sung on the tonic, before the vocal and didjeridu parts 'cut out', leaving two or three solitary strikes of the clapstick beat to finish (the clapstick terminating pattern). For elicited recording sessions in particular, the performers usually stay quiet and pause after the last clapstick beat as they 'listen out' for signs of the ancestors completing their musical phrase. Support Material Figures 3.iv and 3.v illustrate the final Coda sections of both Karrbarda (KB14) and Inyjalarrku (IL50) respectively.

After the clapstick terminating pattern of the last song, singers mark the end (and often bookmark the beginning) of their session by singing a phrase of vocables, which sounds a little like a call or chant as the first vocable is unmetered. This has been described to me by western Arnhem Land songmen as final *bobo/* goodbye. Other mourners/dancers who are not part of the singing group also join in and sing this final *bobo*. I recorded different versions for both *wardde-ken* and *kurrula* song repertoires. The *wardde-ken* version, performed on this occasion at the end of the Karrbarda mother song (KB14), consists of an open vowel 'o' sung on the tonic, followed by a closed vowel sung on the flattened 7th of the scale, accompanied by three more clapstick beats (see Support Material Figure 3.vi). The *kurrula* version, performed at the end of the Mirrijpu mother song (MP04) for example, stays on the tonic throughout and has the same unmetered open 'o' vowel followed by vocables, which suggest a 4/4 metre [O::::::: o-oh-o-oh, o-oh-o-oh] accompanied by a ♩ ♩ 𝄾 pattern in the clapsticks on the second and fourth of the metred vocables (see Support Material Figure 3.vii; listen to **AVEx_3.3**). The singers and dancers form a line together facing the same direction, and with one outstretched arm, palm facing up, they raise and lower their arm so that it falls on the clapstick beat.

AVEx_3.3 https://dx.doi.org/10.26278/MGFC-VK27

This final *bobo* is very similar to early descriptions by Warner—also cited and discussed in McIntosh—of a mortuary ceremony belonging to the Wurramu song cycle of northeast Arnhem Land, which was performed when the mast of a Macassan boat had broken, or a man was about to die. Warner writes that during the funeral 'two or more men pick up the dead body and move it up and down as though they were lifting a mast. The chorus sings "oh-a-ha-la" while the mast is laid down. When it is picked up again they sing:

> O-o-o-o-o-a-ha-la!
> A-ha-la
> A-ha-la!'[67]

McIntosh notes that after the mission period at Elcho Island, people no longer practised lifting the body, and that in the contemporary period, the coffin is either lifted or moved as though it were a mast, or men 'simply mimic the actions of lifting the body'.[68]

Each of these examples leads us back to Marett's idea about the living '[drawing] close to and [interpenetrating] with the dead' through the performance.[69] Particularities in the music suggest a dialogue between the living and the deceased spirit, through unusual alterations in tempi within the *ngalbadjan/nigi* song reserved for the end of the performance; the Coda with its special clapstick terminating pattern, and finally through the *bobo* chant that occurs after the interment, when a particular group's singing and dancing comes to an end.

Covering the grave

Once all of the bundles were resting in the pit, many of the mourners began slowly leaving the burial ground to go back to the Arts Centre for the barbecue, while others stayed to cover the grave and for the Christian part of the ceremony. The ministers gave a sermon, and the Reverend Lois Nadjamerrek gave a speech in which she thanked God for bringing back the bones, before following up with a song that she had written for the occasion performed by the church choir in Kunwinjku. The song was unaccompanied and had a hymnal-like melody. Once the song was over, traditional owners and other men took their shovels and began filling in the grave.[70] Under instructions from Jacob Nayinggul, they took the boxes that the bones had been transported in and set them alight, in keeping with funeral rites whereby the belongings of the deceased are burned and their homes or dwellings smoked after death. Once more, the didjeridu started up and the *kurrula* singers took over, led by James Gulamuwu singing Inyjalarrku, backed by Russell Agalara and Solomon Nangamu with Alfred Gawaraidji on didjeridu. Gulamuwu began with three songs (IL35) in moderate even rhythmic mode (see Table 3.1) before evolving to the *nigi* (mother song) for the Inyjalarrku song-set (song IL19). At this point, Gulamuwu took his shirt off and stood up with the rest of the performance group to sing. Carrying the clapsticks in each hand (while Nangamu and Agalara kept time), he raised his arms and waved them above his head, almost in the same manner that the *daluk* imitate carrying the Karrbarda (watch **AVEx_3.4**). I later learned that this was a version of what is known as the 'giant' dance—a special dance which accompanies *nulatparlilil* (slow tempo) songs—that Gulamuwu learned from his father. Accompanying a section of uneven clapstick beating (rhythmic mode 2c, represented in measures 5–9 in Figure 3.2), Gulamuwu extended his arms out from his chest in the direction of the grave and pulled them back in with each clapstick beat, holding his hands out and then to his chest on the pause of the beat.

AVEx_3.4 https://dx.doi.org/10.26278/VRJ9-TS69

As the song progressed, Gulamuwu edged closer to the grave, as if to attain a more direct line of communication through the dance with the bones which now lay covered in dirt. Throughout all of this, a bobcat noisily and efficiently finished the job of filling in the grave; its diligent operator was quite possibly oblivious to the send-off the *manyardi* performers were giving to the deceased. With the bobcat having finished off the work and Gulamuwu having given his send-off, Nangamu then took over and sang farewell with his own *manyardi*.

©James Gulamuwu

94 'You Belong to Gunbalanya': A reburial ceremony

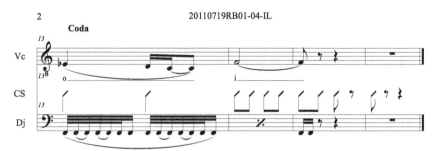

Figure 3.2 Music Transcription of Inyjalarrku *Nigi* no. 1, song IL50 (AVEx_3.4). Transcription by Reuben Brown.

Once again, he performed the two songs he had opened with in the procession (*kiwken* MP06 and MP14), before finishing with an old song he called the 'morning star' (MP19), conceived by his father, which was joined on to the mother song of the Mirrijpu song-set (MP04; see Table 3.1).

Smoking and cutting ties

The final stage of the ceremony involved a smoking ceremony, in which ironbark branches were set alight in a drum until they began to smoke. The smoke was then waved over every object and person that had come into contact with the deceased. This included my *mutika*, along with another hire vehicle that had carried the bones. All of the Balanda and Bininj/Arrarrkpi that had taken part in the preparations for the ceremony were also asked to come forward and be cleansed with the smoke, while at the same time, Nayinggul's children mixed red ochre with water and rubbed it all over our arms, from the hands up to the elbows. This action, which Nangamu described in English as 'cutting', was done to give the mourners a layer of protection from any other spirits that may want to linger without invitation, and as a sign to the living that we had been appropriately cleansed after going near the bones. Only opposite patrimoieties must rub ochre onto one another; *duwa* painted *yirridjdja*, while *yirridjdja* painted *duwa*. During this ritual (watch **AVEx_3.5**), Nangamu and Agalara again stood and sang Mirrijpu song MP06 followed by the mother song [00:30] once more MP04, with Gawaraidji accompanying on the *mako*, while Nayinggul shouted instructions over the top of the music to his children to 'hurry up' and get on with the smoking ceremony. Finally, Nayinggul instructed that the camera and sound crew, along with their camera, be ritually smoked.[71]

AVEx_3.5 https://dx.doi.org/10.26278/V6D2-ED20

Conclusion: *kun-borrk/manyardi* as repatriation

The significance of the reburial ceremony at Gunbalanya in 2011 was about so much more than the physical act of repatriating human remains to their place of origin. It was important for Bininj/Arrarrkpi not so much to re-*possess* the bones of their ancestors, as to re*locate* the spirits of their ancestors with the bones, back to the country in which they were born, so as not to further disrupt the powerful relationship between the spirits and the places in which they ought to dwell. As I learned personally through the preparation for the reburial, this relationship is of immeasurable importance to the living. Nangamu reflected after the ceremony that he had felt the spirits of the bones 'lifting' him while he was singing, while Jimmy Kalarriya similarly drew attention to the presence of the spirits during the preparation for the ceremony:

> They're happy. They bin go back for all the born here. But *yim-bekka* [you sense it, here] look, spirit, they're here already. They're happy [in] this country here.[72]

While the original theft of people's ancestors had left many bewildered, upset, and feeling sorry for their ancestors, Bininj also gained some things, perhaps unexpectedly, from the process of repatriation. Ceremonial leader Jacob Nayinggul was able to pass on his knowledge through instructing his family, younger Bininj, and even Balanda like me about different aspects of Bininj culture, language, and ceremony.[73] The younger generations also learned from Nayinggul how to bury their elders in the culturally appropriate way. At one point during his speech, Nayinggul addressed the children specifically, reminding them that 'we'll be here burying one another one day'.[74] Nayinggul and other traditional owners also understood the broader implications of the event. By opening up the ceremony to the public and inviting politicians and the media, they made a statement on behalf of Bininj/Arrarrkpi and also other Indigenous people, about the importance of having ancestral remains returned to their traditional country and communities.

Because of the logistical challenges of returning bones that had been taken from different places at different times to different institutions, the ceremony brought together clans and language groups from around Arnhem Land, and provided an opportunity for Bininj and Balanda organisations of Gunbalanya/ Jabiru region to work together and share resources. The reconciliatory tone of the ceremony was underscored with Nayinggul's open invitation that everyone join him after the ceremony for a barbecue followed by a beer at 'the Club' (Gunbalanya Sports and Social Club) in the afternoon. For Bininj/Arrarrkpi, the occasion raised important questions about the past that were relevant to the way in which they thought about the continuation of their cultural traditions: why and how did we allow Balanda to come and take these bones without our permission, and how will we ensure that it doesn't happen again? What sort of ceremony should we give for people who lived in the country where we now live and spoke the traditional languages of this country? How important is it that we hold onto these languages and songs that communicate with the country?

The performance of *kun-borrk/manyardi* at the ceremony at Gunbalanya, coming after the performance of *manikay* in Washington when the bones were collected from the Smithsonian, functioned to 'carry' the spirits of the *kun-marre-mok* from their place of storage in the United States back to their original resting places. Together with Nayinggul's address to the spirits in their language of Mengerrdji, the carefully constructed performance of *kun-borrk/manyardi* enabled Bininj/Arrarrkpi to properly say *bobo*. The *ngalbadjan/nigi* or 'mother song' in particular, performed by singers of both *wardde-ken* and *kurrula* song repertories, was the enactment of a final handover between the living and the dead. This demonstrated just how important Aboriginal song traditions are to the repatriation process: it was only by singing the songs of their ancestors and dancing the dances passed down from previous generations that Bininj/Arrarrkpi and Balanda could come to terms with the theft, make their peace with what had happened, and begin the process of moving on.

Notes

1. Ivory, "Kunmanggur, Legend and Leadership."
2. See Baldwin Spencer's documentation of funeral ceremonies by Gaagadju-speaking people at Gunbalanya in the early 20th century. Baldwin Spencer, *Native Tribes of the Northern Territory of Australia* (London: MacMillan, 1914), 242–50; Spencer, *Kakadu People*, 143–45.
3. See Margaret Clunies Ross and Stephen A. Wild, "Formal Performance: The Relations of Music, Text and Dance in Arnhem Land Clan Songs," *Ethnomusicology* 28, no. 2 (1984): 210. The ceremony is depicted in the film *Waiting for Harry*, where a funeral takes place east of Maningrida, and in L. R. Hiatt, *Kinship and Conflict: A Study of an Aboriginal Community in Northern Arnhem Land* (Canberra: A.N.U. Press, 1965), 53–60. Anthropologist Les Hiatt, the narrator and 'brother' of the *djungkay* for the ceremony, explains that after the bones are placed in the *lorrkkon* and as the hollowed log is erected, 'the souls of the deceased leave the community to

join the dead under the sea'. Kim McKenzie, *Waiting for Harry* (Canberra: Australian Institute of Aboriginal Studies, 1980), videorecording.
4 According to a report on the remains from Washington compiled by Steve Webb, some of the remains belonged to a child aged 11–12 years. It is likely that the bones belonged to people who were born and died in the 20th century. Steven Webb, "Survey of remains in the Northern Territory Museum repatriated from the Smithsonian Museum, Washington" (unpublished report, Bond University, 2011).
5 Kalarriya is referring to the old people who spoke those languages. 'Finished' is used here as a euphemism for 'dead', as Thomas notes in his article: Thomas, "Because it's Your Country," 1.
6 [Jimmy Kalarriya, RB2-20110717-MT_v0287_JNXX.mp4, https://dx.doi.org/10.26278/XV1W-9S88, 00:04:57–00:05:20].
7 The Northern Land Council was established in 1976 (with the creation of the Land Rights Act in the Northern Territory) to enable traditional owners and Aboriginal people living on Aboriginal land to negotiate with mining and other interests on their lands and decide how the profits should be used. Funeral ceremonies are one of the cultural events that receive financial support from the NLC. Museum Victoria was the organisation responsible for repatriating the Baldwin Spencer collection of remains.
8 My partner Rachel Orzech spent many hours preparing food for the guests. Students from Flinders University accompanying Sally May also helped operate the barbeques and serve the food to hundreds of guests after the burial.
9 See Thomas, "Turning Subjects into Objects and Objects into Subjects."
10 For an overview of the literature on this topic, see Cressida Fforde, Jane Hubert and Paul Turnbull, ed., *The Dead and Their Possessions: Repatriation in Principle, Policy, and Practice* (New York: Routledge, 2004); Paul Turnbull and Michael Pickering, ed., *The Long Way Home: The Meanings and Values of Repatriation* (New York: Berghahn, 2010).
11 The repatriation of Native American human remains and sacred objects is discussed in the context of US legislation in Joe Watkins, "Artefactual Awareness: Spiro Mounds, Grave Goods and Politics," in *The Dead and Their Possessions: Repatriation in Principle, Policy, and Practice*, ed. Cressida Fforde, Jane Hubert and Paul Turnbull (New York: Routledge, 2004), 152; Roger Anyon and Russell Thornton, "Implementing Repatriation in the United States: Issues Raised and Lessons Learned," in *The Dead and Their Possessions: Repatriation in Principle, Policy, and Practice*, ed. Cressida Fforde, Jane Hubert and Paul Turnbull (New York: Routledge, 2004), 197; C. Timothy McKeown, "Considering Repatriation as an Option: The National Museum of the American Indian Act (NMAIA) & the Native American Graves Protection and Repatriation Act (NAGPRA)," in *Utimut: Past Heritage—Future Partnerships: Discussions on Repatriation in the 21st Century*, ed. Mille Gabriel and Jens Dahl (Copenhagen: Danish Ministry of Foreign Affairs and Greenland National Museum & Archives, 2008): 134–147. For the Australian context, see Turnbull and Pickering, *The Long Way Home: The Meanings and Values of Repatriation*.
12 Charles P. Mountford, "Records of the American-Australian Scientific Expedition to Arnhem Land," *Art, Myth and Symbolism* 1 (1956): xxii.
13 See Kim Beazley, "Nation Building or Cold War: Political Settings for the Arnhem Land Expedition," in *Exploring the Legacy of the 1948 Arnhem Land Expedition*, ed. Martin Thomas and Margo Neale (Canberra: ANU E Press, 2011), 55; Mountford, "Records of the American-Australian Scientific Expedition to Arnhem Land," ix.
14 Mountford was known to share Indigenous materials he collected with artists both at home and in the USA—see Haskins' discussion of his influence on choreographer Beth Dean for example. Victoria Haskins, "Beth Dean and the Transnational

Circulation of Aboriginal Dance Culture: Gender, Authority and C.P. Mountford," in *Circulating Cultures: Exchanges of Australian Indigenous Music, Dance and Media*, ed. Amanda Harris (Canberra: ANU Press, 2014). Fellow Expedition member Frederick McCarthy also understood Mountford's motivations for collecting bark paintings in Arnhem Land as 'for the purpose of exhibitions & lectures in the U.S.' Frederick McCarthy, Diary 4, 1948, 1 August, MS3513/14/4, AIATSIS.
15 Ronald M. Berndt, Letter to Alf Ellison, 15 January 1948, Item 4.3.6. NTRS 38, Location 142/2/4, Northern Territory Archives.
16 Mountford, recorded in Colin Simpson, "Expedition to Arnhem Land," ABC Radio documentary (1948), ABC Radio Archives 83/CD/1239.
17 C.P. Mountford, "Letter to Gilbert Grosvenor", Setzler Files, Box 7, Folder 4, Arnhem Land Correspondence 1948–1949, Folder 1 of 2, National Anthropological Archives, Washington, DC.
18 See Mountford, "Records of the American-Australian Scientific Expedition to Arnhem Land," xxx.
19 Thomas, "Expedition as Time Capsule," 16.
20 See 'List of Specimens Collected by F. M. Setzler, Australia', 1948, Arnhem Land Expedition, RU 305, Accession File 178294, Smithsonian Institution, Washington, DC, cited in Thomas, "Turning Subjects into Objects and Objects into Subjects," 149.
21 Thomas, "Turning Subjects into Objects and Objects into Subjects," 149.
22 See Thomas, "Expedition as Time Capsule," 21.
23 Thomas, "Turning Subjects into Objects and Objects into Subjects," 151.
24 Setzler was careful in 1948 to discreetly place the bones in ammunition boxes, which he whisked away on the final day of the Expedition's stay. Frank M. Setzler, Diaries 1948, Box 14, Frank Maryl Setzler Papers 1927–1960, National Anthropological Archives, Suitland, MD, cited in Martin Thomas, "'Because It's Your Country': The Repatriation of Human Remains from the Smithsonian Institution to an Aboriginal Community in West Arnhem Land," *Life Writing* 12, no. 2 (2015): 8.
25 See Birch, "The American Clever Man (Marrkijbu Burdan Merika)," 335–36.
26 See Sally May et al., "'You Write it Down and Bring it Back … That's What we Want'—Revisiting the 1948 Removal of Human Remains from Gunbalanya (Oenpelli), Australia," in *Indigenous Archaeologies: Decolonising Theory and Practice*, ed. Claire Smith and H. Martin Wobst (London: Routledge, 2005): 104.
27 Discussed further in Thomas, "Turning Subjects into Objects and Objects into Subjects."
28 Some of those involved in assisting with the repatriation included Anthony Murphy of IAC, Lindy Allen from Museums Victoria, and Lori Richardson (Department of the Prime Minister and Cabinet), as well as others from the Commonwealth Repatriation Program who facilitated the repatriations and travel of traditional owners to the Smithsonian from 2008.
29 [Jimmy Kalarriya, RB2-20110717-MT_v0287_JNXX.mp4, https://dx.doi.org/10.26278/XV1W-9S88, 05:28–06:14].
30 Another account of the challenges of repatriating ancestral remains to their country is presented in Des Kootji Raymond, "Wrap Me up in Paperbark" (Sydney: Macumba Media Enterprises, 1999), videorecording.
31 Frank Setzler and Fred McCarthy also stole bones from Groote Eylandt, Milingimbi, and the Gove Peninsula. Frederick McCarthy, Field notes, Groote Eylandt, Diary 2, Entry for 4 June 1948, Winchelsea Island, AIATSIS, Canberra, 31–32.
32 Andrew Gulliford dates the beginning of this practice to the publication of physical anthropologist Samuel Morton's 1823 study that came to the conclusion that Indian skulls had slightly smaller cranium size in comparison to Caucasian skulls

and that this correlated with intellectual inferiority. Collecting skulls then became a 'hobby of gentleman', as 'the supposed link between, skulls, brain capacity, intelligence, and race led to the wholesale looting of thousands of Indian burials and a brisk, purportedly scientific trade'. Andrew Gulliford, "Bones of Contention: The Repatriation of Native American Human Remains," *The Public Historian* 18, no. 4 (1996): 122.
33 Ibid., 123.
34 See Margo Neale, "Epilogue: Sifting the Silence," in *Exploring the Legacy of the 1948 Arnhem Land Expedition*, ed. Martin Thomas and Margot Neale (Canberra: ANU E Press, 2011), 433.
35 [Jacob Nayinggul, 20110717-MT_v0141_JNXX.mp4, https://dx.doi.org/10.26278/B1NP-2822, 00:02:29–00:03:23].
36 Ronald M. Berndt, *Australian Aboriginal Religion* (Leiden: E.J. Brill, 1974), 25; Howard Morphy, *Journey to the Crocodile's Nest: An Accompanying Monograph to the Film* Madarrpa Funeral at Gurka'wuy (Canberra: Australian Institute of Aboriginal Studies, 1984), 32; Marett, "Ghostly Voices," 24.
37 Marett, "Ghostly Voices," 24.
38 Ibid., 24–25.
39 For further discussion, see Thomas, "'Because it's Your Country'", 14–15.
40 Some earlier studies include Ronald Berndt's overview of mortuary rituals in northern Australia: Berndt, *Australian Aboriginal Religion*, 23–31. See also Spencer's description of mortuary ceremonies of Gaagadju at Oenpelli in western Arnhem Land: Baldwin Spencer, *Native Tribes of the Northern Territory of Australia* (London: MacMillan, 1914). Morphy, Reid, and Warner give accounts of Yolŋu funeral ceremonies in eastern Arnhem Land: Morphy, *Journey to the Crocodile's Nest*; Janice Reid, "A Time to Live, a Time to Grieve: Patterns and Processes of Mourning among the Yolngu of Australia," *Culture, Medicine and Psychiatry* 3, no. 4 (1979): 319–346; W. Lloyd Warner, *A Black Civilization: A Social Study of an Australian Tribe*, rev. ed. (Gloucester, MA: P. Smith, 1969). More recent perspectives on contemporary attitudes to death in Aboriginal Australia are discussed in Katie Glaskin et al., ed., *Mortality, Mourning and Mortuary Practices in Indigenous Australia* (Surrey: Ashgate, 2008).
41 Marett, *Songs, Dreamings, Ghosts*, 31.
42 Michael Walsh, "Will Indigenous Languages Survive?" *Annual Review of Anthropology* 34 (2005): 307.
43 Birch, Dictionary of Erre, Mengerrdji and Urningangk, 6.
44 'Kunbarlanj' is the Mengerrdji name for 'Kunbarlanja'.
45 In the dictionary of Erre, Mengerrdji, and Urningangk, a similar word *merrekenk* is listed as the Mengerrdji noun 'camp'. Birch, *Dictionary of Erre, Mengerrdji and Urningangk*.
46 [Jacob Nayinggul, 20110718-MT_v0182_JNXX.mp4, https://dx.doi.org/10.26278/8KCP-YK62, 00:04:39.700–00:05:32.450]. This translation is provided by Connie Nayinggul, who is one of the few people who can understand her father's language. With no fluent speakers of Mengerrdji alive today, it is difficult to cross-check translations such as these for accuracy.
47 Campbell's photos of the event can be viewed online. See Lindsay Murdoch, "Repatriated Aboriginal remains are buried," *Sydney Morning Herald*, 20 July 2011, http://www.smh.com.au/photogallery/national/repatriated-aboriginal-remains-are-reburied-20110719-1hn0t.html?aggregate=&selectedImage=0
48 Thomas, "Because It's Your Country," 18.
49 See Thomas, "Expedition as Time Capsule," 21–22.

100   *'You Belong to Gunbalanya': A reburial ceremony*

50   Lindsay Murdoch, "Stolen Spirits Brought Home to be at Rest," *Sydney Morning Herald*, 19 July 2011, http://www.smh.com.au/national/stolen-spirits-brought-home-to-be-at-rest-20110719-1hnbv.html; Genevieve Hussey, "Celebrated Homecoming," *7:30 Report Northern Territory*, aired 30 July 2011, on ABC.
51   [Solomon Nangamu, 20110825-RB_01.wav, https://dx.doi.org/10.26278/HQWK-4E25, 00:08:19–00:09:24].
52   Joey Nganjmirra, personal communication, July 2011. In Kunwinjku, *ngarri* is the first person plural exclusive.
53   [Eric Mardday, 20130913-RB_01.wav, https://dx.doi.org/10.26278/RA1S-DG08, 00:06:36.892–00:06:45.392].
54   [Eric Mardday, 20130913-RB_01.wav, https://dx.doi.org/10.26278/RA1S-DG08, 00:06:30.742–00:06:36.242].
55   See 20110719-MT_v0375_01.mp4, https://dx.doi.org/10.26278/8CVW-JE29, Table 3.1.
56   [Jacob Nayinggul, 20110719-MT_v0380_01.mp4, https://dx.doi.org/10.26278/8SY7-ZE74, 00:03:26.850–00:03:27.970].
57   See 20110719-MT_v0380_01.mp4, https://dx.doi.org/10.26278/8SY7-ZE74, Table 3.1.
58   This is expressed through the Kunwinjku verb *-ngenmang* (to put scent from the axilla on an object). Murray Garde, personal communication, 2011.
59   Jacob Nayinggul, in conversation with Martin Thomas, July 2011.
60   [Jacob Nayinggul, 20110719-MT_v0380_01.mp4, https://dx.doi.org/10.26278/8SY7-ZE74, 00:02:10.420-00:02:17.610]. Nayinggul was a close friend of 'Big Bill' Neidji, one of the last recorded speakers of Gaagadju. Refer to map of languages, Figure 1.1, Chapter 1. Bugurnidja is related to the Umbugarla language. The "last speaker" Evans documented for this language was Butcher Knight. See Mark Harvey, *A Grammar of Gaaudju* (Berlin & New York: Mouton de Gruyter, 2002), 14; Nicholas Evans, "The Last Speaker Is Dead—Long Live the Last Speaker!" in *Linguistic Fieldwork*, ed. Martha Ratliff and Paul Newman (Cambridge & New York: Cambridge University Press, 2001), 273–74.
61   20110717-MT_v0382_JNXX.mp4, https://dx.doi.org/10.26278/48RM-7M18
62   [Jacob Nayinggul, 20110719-MT_v0383_01.mp4, https://dx.doi.org/10.26278/C1W0-4G68, 00:05:49–00:08:05].
63   See Moyle's discussion of Kurri recording. Alice M. Moyle, *Songs from the Northern Territory Companion Booklet for Five 12 inch LP Discs (Cat No. I.A.S M-001/5)* (Canberra: Australian Institute of Aboriginal Studies, 1967).
64   For example, the tempo of Karrbarda songs in slow rhythmic mode was roughly 81–85 bpm, whereas for the mother song, the tempo was 39 bpm (see Table 3.1 and Support Material Appendix iii).
65   [Eric Mardday, 20130913-RB_01.wav, https://dx.doi.org/10.26278/RA1S-DG08, 00:37:21.800–00:37:52.900].
66   This idea of the songs 'pulling' both the physical and spiritual elements is significant to *junba*, as explored by Treloyn. Treloyn, "Songs that Pull," 154. Although there are a number of differences between the song context of *junba* and *kun-borrk/manyardi*, the principle of the music activating or having a motivating effect on the metaphysical is common to both Top End genres.
67   Warner, A Black Civilisation, 420.
68   Ian S. McIntosh, "Islam and Australia's Aborigines? A Perspective from North-East Arnhem Land," *Journal of Religious History* 20, no. 1 (1996), 59.
69   Marett, *Songs, Dreamings, Ghosts*, 31.
70   [20110719-MT_v0394_01.mp4, https://dx.doi.org/10.26278/F93Y-BB59; and 20110719-MT_v0395_01.mp4, https://dx.doi.org/10.26278/XZQH-5050].
71   20110717-MT_v0445_JNXX.mp4, https://dx.doi.org/10.26278/Y65X-HG76

72 [Jimmy Kalarriya, RB2-20110717-MT_v0287_JNXX.mp4, https://dx.doi.org/10.26278/XV1W-9S88, 00:06:14–00:06:42].
73 Conversations with Kalarriya, Nadjamerrek, Mardday, Nangamu, and others after the event helped them to reflect on aspects of the ceremony and share their knowledge with me and others.
74 [Jacob Nayinggul, 20110719-MT_v0383_01.mp4, https://dx.doi.org/10.26278/C1W0-4G68, 00:05:49–00:08:05].

4 'It's a Secret, For You'
A Mamurrng ceremony

A sensory overload

'Hold on!' I shout to my partner Rachel, after we hit a wave that almost sends us flying over the side of the tin boat. She grips the edge of the boat, and I check to see whether the recording gear at my feet is still dry. Another series of waves sends us up in the air, and we land heavily on our backsides. We look at each other and start laughing, knowing that our bodies are now at the whim of the ocean as our boat skips along the waves. The sky is clear and blue, and out on the ocean, we are exposed to the harsh sunlight, which sparkles as it catches on the water. Back at Gunbalanya where we have come from, the surrounding rocks are baking and the wetlands drying out to a crust, as the hot weather of the dry season continues to scorch the earth, with no rain in sight. But out here, the sea breeze provides welcome relief from the harsh build-up of heat. Seated next to me at the front of the boat is my *yabok* (K: sister) Rhonda, who ordinarily lives at the remote outstation of Kabulwarnamayo with our *karrang* (K: mother), but has come along to accompany me for this important occasion. Rhonda has travelled all over the plateau country on the mainland, but she tells me that this is her first time in a boat. She too has one firm grip on the rope at the end of the boat and the other on a small bag of belongings that she has taken with her for the trip. Down the back of the boat next to the outboard motor sit Harold Warrabin and the owner and driver of the boat, who surveys the coastline as we track from Sandy Creek around the point, and wait for the southern tip of Goulburn Island to come into view. Over the roar of the motor and the rushing wind, Warrabin stands up and starts telling us something, pointing towards an unusual rocky outcrop on the mainland, covered in white ochre. The bright turquoise colour of the shallow Arafura Sea contrasts against the *delek* (K: white ochre) of the rock formations. He tells us that this is a site where two ancestral beings who had been travelling from eastern Arnhem Land got stuck, and turned into clay. Over to the north, we see Sims Island, and in the distance, we can now see Fletcher Point—the southern tip of Goulburn Island (refer to Support Material Figure 2.2). As we slow down and cruise in towards the island, the boat steadies once more and I glimpse

DOI: 10.4324/9781003216339-5

the familiar sight of a flat horizontal elevated shoreline with savannah woodland. Trees are perched right on the edge of the cliff, which drops down to the beach, exposing the layers of topsoil and clay; it looks almost as though someone has taken a giant spade and dug out the crust of earth above the sea level.

We arrive at Warruwi and settle down with the rest of the visiting group into our accommodation at the old medical centre, which looks out over Martpalk Bay to the point of Wigu. After unpacking, I sit on the front verandah and close my eyes, allowing that strong sea breeze to pass over me, ventilating my clothing, and cooling my hair and face. Jenny and David Manmurulu come over and greet the visitors, happy to see that we have all arrived safely on the island. They have been preparing for the ceremony and have with them several balls of brightly coloured lambswool that Linda Barwick and Allan Marett had sent them. They take a thread of blue yarn and measure my waist, torso, and head with it. Jenny takes this measured length of wool and loops it around one toe, continuing to loop it until it is thick with many strands of wool. She does the same with another length. Taking these two loops of wool between both toes, she binds them together with red wool to form a winglike pattern. They explain that this design is based on the flying fox and test it out on me by crossing it over and looping it through my arms so that it sits over my shoulders, joined at the back and crossed over at the front. David has made a headband for me from another colour of wool, which fits snugly. They explain that I will be wearing these decorative pieces the following day when they give me the *mamurrng*, but I can't have them now.

That evening, we are invited to come and listen to the Inyjalarrku ensemble give a performance as a 'warm-up' for the main event the next day. With the sun going down, we head over to the main hall where a ceremony ground has been pre-prepared with sand, and a tarpaulin rolled out for the singers and didjeridu player to sit on. David Manmurulu invites me to sit with them and introduces me to his two sons Renfred (the youngest) and Rupert (the second eldest) who lead the singing. The other dancers—Stanley Gameraidj, Brendan Marrgam, and Roderick Lee—and didjeridu player Shannon Lee, introduce themselves, speaking to me in Kunwinjku. Brendan Marrgam introduces himself 'properly' in a Bininj/Arrarrkpi sense, giving me his skin name (Nakodjok), country (Gumardir River, near the 'second crossing' from Gunbalanya), and clan affiliation (na-Djalama). This is the first time I have had the chance to sit down with the Inyjalarrku group and hear them, and I am struck by the incredible power and unity of their singing, the complexity of the clapstick beating, and the tricky changes in tempo. I clap along to the beat but find myself frequently caught off guard as it slows down or speeds up midway through a verse. As the clapstick beat gets faster, the dancers respond by rising to their feet and dancing, taking a shirt or a pair of thongs in their hands, and converting them into dance props. They have a bucket of *delek* on hand which they pass around, slapping the white clay over their arms and legs. Their synchronicity tells me that they know these songs intimately. I notice how the music and their dancing have transformed their mood to one of exhilaration; they crack jokes with one another, laugh, and call others over to join in the dance. Sitting with the ensemble, a warm sensation comes over me as the vibrations of the didjeridu are felt in my stomach, while at the same time, I am energised by the higher frequency sounds of the singing and the piercing sound of the clapstick beat.

The following afternoon, we receive the word that the Mamurrng will begin soon, and start to gather outside the local hall once more. The families of the dancers start to arrive with their children, and position themselves away from the ceremony ground as they ready themselves for the performance. The women wrap blue cloth around their waists to create a skirt. They mix ochre and water, rubbing the white paste into one another's skin in a pattern of rings across the arms and legs, and a diagonal stripe across the chest. The men gather in another area with more cloth, ripping it up and converting it into skirts and loincloths. They slap the *delek* over their skin with ironbark branches as they crack jokes with one another. Jenny Manmurulu brings me over to where the women are preparing, and I take my shirt off so that she can put the Mamurrng flying fox outfit around my shoulders. My *karrang* (the kin mother of Donna and Rhonda Nadjamerrek) Rosemary Urabadi makes two more woollen armlets for me to wear and fastens them above my elbows. My partner Rachel has a headband of the same colour to wear, while the rest of my Bininj family wear different coloured headbands too: we are like colour-coded Mamurrng recipients. Jenny sends me over to the men for further preparations. I feel like a little kid who is being fussed over by his relatives, unsure exactly of what is going on, just following instructions. The *bininj* dancers help me to put on a naga in the privacy of the back of the hall after seeing me struggle to fasten it around my waist without slipping. When I return, Jenny's instruction is for me to cover my body in red ochre. She takes a red stone and bottle of water and gets started on my arms and torso, and then Roderick helps out, rubbing it into my face, arms, and legs (Figure 4.1). I enjoy this feeling of ochre on skin: it feels cool and calming, like a protective layer. It's a simple act, this rubbing of earth into the body, and yet profoundly symbolic and affecting: I cannot help but feel literally connected to and part of the surrounding Country. Holding layers of the country on our skin, we are all just about ready to start, and I go over and sit with the rest of the recipient party to wait for the Mamurrng.

It's late in the evening now, and the sun has gone down. We have just witnessed an hour or so of spectacular dancing and singing, led by the old man Charlie Mangulda—haunting melodies from Amurdak people of the mainland. The *mamurrng* has been laid at my feet and taken back again, and now, the Inyjalarrku group are singing. Sitting next to me this whole time, Donna is a reassuring presence, clapping along and enjoying the music with her young daughters, one of whom films the ceremony on her mobile phone. Jenny Manmurulu and the other *warramumpik* (M: women) keep a steady hold on the beat of the clapsticks. They sway their torsos and arms in sync with the rhythm that seems to have taken hold of them, lifting a hand subtly to their heads and pausing with it there as the clapsticks skip a beat, before resuming their swaying once again as the beat continues.

'It's a Secret, For You': A Mamurrng ceremony   105

Figure 4.1 Roderick Lee helps to cover Reuben Brown in red ochre in preparation for the Mamurrng. Photograph by Martin Thomas.

Without warning, a ghostly figure covered in white clay emerges from behind the singing ensemble through the dancers in front, and strides over to me, stepping with the beat of the clapsticks. He has a sad look in his eyes, and fixes his gaze on me, then away to the distance, then back at me. It is almost as though he is looking through me. Taking the *mamurrng* between his teeth, he stretches his arms out towards me and brings them back into his chest, as though he were drawing me in and pushing me away. I recognise these movements from James Gulamuwu's performance at the reburial ceremony in Gunbalanya (Chapter 3). The clapstick beating gets louder as the ensemble edges closer to us, and the dancers continue their shouts of 'agh!' and 'yi!' over the top of the music. My skin is tingling. The *warramumpik* form a line, now standing over us, and we are hit with a wall of beautiful solid sound and flicks of sand from moving feet, as the Inyjalarrku singers move into the final *nigi* song. As the song comes to a climax, the ghostly figure reaches down and releases the *mamurrng* at my feet, just as the last solitary clapstick beat rings out. He moves back into line with the dancers, and they all hold one arm out, showing me the palms of their hands. 'Oh::::::' 'oh-oh-oh-oh, oh-oh-oh-oh' they sing, raising their arms up and down. They are saying *bobo*. Responding to their own farewell, but in a quieter tone now, the dancers and the audience let out a collective cry of appreciation. The performers come over to us and one by one, offer a shake of hands.

***

In previous chapters, I examined how songmen shape their performances to reflect and reinforce connections between participants, their ancestors, and traditional country. Here, our attention turns to an event which reflects something of the multiclan and multilingual character of western Arnhem Land communities: a ceremony which is underpinned by a history of contact between Aboriginal people of western Arnhem Land and strangers from overseas (Macassan, Balanda, and Japanese),[1] as well as the tradition of clan exogamy and marrying outside of one's language group in Arnhem Land (which has brought together the various Kunwinjku, Kun-barlang, Iwaidja, and Yolŋu families living at Warruwi, where the ceremony in focus took place). The ceremony is called the Mamurrng and takes its name from a simple wooden pole decorated with brightly coloured tassels of wool, which is a central part of the performance, and is handed over from the hosts of the Mamurrng ceremony to the recipient and his or her family, at the end of the ceremony. Whilst the ceremony historically provided an opportunity for an exchange of goods, it has persisted, as Altman and others observe, as an institution providing an 'opportunity for social exchange between groups as a distinct marker of group identity and speciality'.[2] I argue that 'exchange' ceremonies continue to play an important role in the contemporary situation in Arnhem Land, as more Balanda come to permanently live and work in communities like Warruwi and Gunbalanya, and a variety of intercultural interactions take place on a daily basis between Aboriginal people and non-Aboriginal researchers, journalists, government representatives, tourists, and others.[3]

In this chapter, I describe the unique set of circumstances that led to a Mamurrng ceremony at Warruwi in 2012, and reflect on my experience as the recipient and focus of the performance. I explore the connections between the Mamurrng I received and other exchange ceremonies held for Balanda, including a Rom ceremony (a different regional name for the same type of exchange ceremony)[4] for photographer Axel Poignant in 1952. The Mamurrng ceremony is discussed in the context of the 'gift economy' traditional to Aboriginal Australia and other Indigenous societies, in which 'inalienable gifts' are exchanged, which retain a link to their donor, even once they are handed over.[5] An analysis of the performance of the ceremony is then presented in three parts, reflecting the main stages of the ceremony: the 'warm-up' performed by the hosts for the recipients prior to the main event; the 'handover' of the *mamurrng*; and the 'thanks' performed by the recipients. The performance analysis centres on the two main song-sets that led the ceremony—the Inyjalarrku (mermaid) song-set led by David Manmurulu and Yanajanak song-set led by Charlie Mangulda. Examining the dancing that accompanied the performance of both the Inyjalarrku and Yanajanak (stone country spirits) songs, I explore further the connection between rhythmic modes and movement in *manyardi*. Here, I expand on the contention that the singer's choice of songs (including the ordering and choice of rhythmic modes in which to perform songs) is informed by the ceremonial action. By tracing the journey of the *mamurrng* from its initiation, in which a lock of hair is taken from the recipient and woven into the *mamurrng*, through the different stages of the performance, culminating in its handover and aftermath, I demonstrate how the *mamurrng* pole becomes imbued with symbolic, social, and spiritual meaning for both the giver and the recipient.[6]

Mamurrng diplomacy with Balanda

In 1952, photographer Axel Poignant travelled to a place called Nagalarramba on the mouth of the Liverpool River on the north coast of Arnhem Land, opposite what is today the community of Maningrida. He arrived on a boat belonging to the Methodist mission at Goulburn Island, and was accompanied by two Mawng-speaking brothers, Lazarus Lamilami and George Winunguj, as well as a Ndjébbana-speaking man from the Nagalarramba area. These men acted as guides, translators, and negotiators for Poignant while he remained at Nagalarramba for six weeks, equipped with his journal, camera, many rolls of film, food rations, and tobacco. Various groups of Aboriginal people, including Burarra from the Blyth River estuary further east, visited during his stay, allowing him to document and participate in their daily life, building shelters and canoes, hunting wallaby and cooking fish in ground ovens, and preparing for ceremony. Towards the end of Poignant's stay, the Burarra group performed a ceremony they called a Rom, in which the group sang, danced, and presented a painted and decorated pole (the *Rom*), to Poignant, as a gift for his having come to photograph them. In return, the Goulburn Island men that accompanied Poignant performed their songs for the Burarra group. Figure 4.2 shows George Winunguj, the ceremony

Figure 4.2 George Winunguj performing a Rom ceremony for Axel Poignant in 1952. George Winunguj (centre), flanked by female and male dancers. Lazarus Lamilami, third from right, holds clapsticks and provides backup singing. Photograph by Axel Poignant, by permission of Roslyn Poignant. In Poignant and Poignant, *Encounter at Nagalarramba*, 141.

leader for Inyjalarrku (mermaid) song-set, performing as part of the Rom ceremony for Axel Poignant in 1952.

As Poignant's widow Roslyn has written, Axel Poignant's visit served to 'formalise the cross-cultural interaction taking place' and provided 'continuities both with a ceremonial way of relating to strangers in the past, and with later Rom ceremonies performed as rituals of diplomacy in Canberra'.[7] Roslyn Poignant developed the photos that Axel sent from the field, and returned decades later with copies of those photos to Maningrida in the 1990s, in order to meet relatives of those Aboriginal people who were present in 1952, and to document their reflections on the photos (chronicled in a book titled *Encounter at Nagalarramba*). Another Mamurrng ceremony was held for Peter Cooke, then senior art advisor for Maningrida Arts and Crafts, in 1981.[8] Anbarra people of North-Central Arnhem Land performed the Canberra ceremonies for the Australian Institute of Aboriginal Studies (now Australian Institute for Aboriginal and Torres Strait Islander Studies, AIATSIS) in Canberra in 1982, which preceded another Rom performance by the same group of people from Maningrida for the minister of Aboriginal Affairs in 1995.[9] Musicologist Steven Wild, who was central to organising the Rom in Canberra, explains how the Anbarra people were motivated to present the ceremony for a number of reasons:

> partly in recognition of the [role of AIATSIS] in documenting and preserving records of Anbarra culture, and in publishing several articles, books and records... It was a gesture of goodwill also to the people of Canberra [who were invited to the event], and since Arnhem Land Aborigines are well aware of the national role of Canberra it was a gesture to Australia as a whole... The ceremony was performed at the time of the annual meeting of the Institute's advisory committees and a meeting of the Council so that many researchers associated with the Institute could witness the proceedings.[10]

These documented ceremonies of exchange and diplomacy with Balanda all had a common purpose: to express goodwill on behalf of Aboriginal people of Arnhem Land towards the individuals (such as Axel Poignant) and institutions (such as AIATSIS) that interact with and represent them, and bring them into relationships of reciprocity and accountability. These ceremonies aim to maintain good relations into the future with Balanda who are in part responsible for interpreting, producing (through publications), and keeping (in archives) representations of Aboriginal culture produced by knowledge holders.

The Warruwi Mamurrng

Sixty years after George Winunguj led a performance of the Rom for Axel Poignant at Nagalarramba, a Mamurrng was performed at Goulburn Island to formalise another kind of intercultural interaction, this time between songmen and women of Goulburn and Croker Islands, Kunwinjku-speaking people from the community of Gunbalanya on the mainland, and a group of Balanda researchers (see Support Material Figure 4.i). The Mamurrng ceremony is thought to have originated from Kundjeyhmi- and Jawoyn-speaking groups of the stone country, southwest of Gunbalanya.[11] Today, it is performed predominantly at Goulburn and Croker Islands as well as Maningrida, for families all around Arnhem Land. (While Mamurrng ceremonies have taken place in and around Gunbalanya in the recent past, they were not performed during my time there in 2011–13). One of the reasons for this shift may be because of the prominence of western Arnhem Land song groups that reside in these communities, including the two groups that hosted this Mamurrng ceremony: Inyjalarrku (M: mermaid) and Yanajanak (stone country spirits). The Inyjalarrku song-set—which we encountered at Gunbalanya in Chapter 3 led by James Gulamuwu—was also led by Gulamuwu's brother David Manmurulu and his family at Goulburn Island. Manmurulu and Gulamuwu inherited the songs from their father George Winunguj; however, many of the songs from Manmurulu's repertory also include songs that he received in dreams after his father died.[12] Similarly, the Yanajanak song-set led by Charlie Mangulda from Croker Island is made up of songs Mangulda inherited from his grandfather in addition to Mangulda's dream-conceived songs. Yanajanak is unique in that it straddles *wardde-ken/kurrula*, as a song-set from the stone country (the Murgenella region inland from the Cobourg Peninsula) which is associated with Amurdak, a language belonging to the 'saltwater' Iwaidjan family. Another participant in the 2012 ceremony at Goulburn Island with a connection to the Rom ceremony some 60 years earlier was a film-maker and nephew of Axel Poignant, Gus Berger, who came to Warruwi and helped to document the ceremony.

The Warruwi Mamurrng had been initiated a year earlier in 2011 during the Annual Symposium for Indigenous Music and Dance in Darwin.[13] The circumstances of its inception bear some similarities with earlier Rom ceremonies mentioned above, in that it was an attempt to find common ground and strengthen relations between Indigenous and non-Indigenous people from various communities and institutions with shared research interests around Aboriginal song and language. On the first day of the symposium in Darwin, Isaiah Nagurrgurrba from Gunbalanya and historian Martin Thomas presented a Bininj perspective on the story of Frank Setzler taking human remains from Injalak Hill in 1948. With the permission of Gunbalanya traditional owner Jacob Nayinggul, Nagurrgurrba and Thomas presented archival footage of Setzler removing the bones, as well as contemporary footage of Bininj burying the bones once more in the 2011 ceremony (discussed in Chapter 3). The footage and discussion of deceased ancestors caused anxiety and upset some of the Aboriginal groups attending the symposium. A smoking ceremony was carried out that evening by representatives from Gunbalanya, along with Charlie Mangulda and Archie Brown (another songman living at Croker Island), to cleanse the area and the attendees of any spirits that might have lingered as a result of the film being shown. The following day, Charlie Mangulda and Archie Brown suggested to Allan Marett that a Mamurrng be held in order to reconcile for the upset that had been caused the previous day, and to formally acknowledge the relationship between researchers and ceremony holders.[14] Marett discussed the idea with David Manmurulu and Charlie Mangulda, who offered to host the ceremony.

To initiate a Mamurrng ceremony, a lock of hair from the youngest person in the family of the receiving group may be given to the host group, who, in accepting the lock of hair, accept the invitation to hold a Mamurrng. The lock of hair is eventually woven onto the centre of the *mamurrng* pole with beeswax and string, where it hangs alongside brightly coloured tassels of wool. In this instance, I was the youngest member of the receiving group. Ordinarily, the recipient might be a small child from a different language group belonging to a distant clan, although, as with Axel Poignant's *Rom*, the recipients can also be adults. Nevertheless, I was aware of my 'childlike' status, both in the 'Balanda world' of academia where I was just starting out with my PhD studies and in the 'Bininj/Arrarrkpi world' where I was only just beginning to learn about *kun-borrk/manyardi* and other aspects of Aboriginal life. I was happy to play along with the role of the naïve child, keeping myself deliberately uninformed about the ceremony so as to maximise the surprise once the performance took place. Most Bininj/Arrarrkpi that I spoke to emphasised the element of surprise around the *mamurrng,* which serves to heighten the sense of anticipation once it is gradually revealed in performance. Russell Agalara explained to me that 'they're going to give you some gift', and Nangamu added: 'it's a secret, for you'.[15] Connie Nayinggul (daughter of Jacob Nayinggul) similarly stressed that the recipient must not know about the preparations that are made for the Mamurrng:

> Mamurrng's different; it's open [public ceremony] for everyone. Mamurrng means you'll give it to someone and he'll hand it over back. Probably what they do normally is, see that girl walking around? If you say: 'I want her to go in Mamurrng, because I know the families' [then] cut her hair, wrap it up and send it over—that's Mamurrng. So what they going to do, they're going to make something as a present the year before. They'll contact you. So they coming over for that Mamurrng, so you gotta start doing something like collecting all the Bininj in each area to be standing there and waiting for this main one… You can't tell her [where] that hair went—that's secret. She's gotta see what's going to happen. My father done it once, one of our brothers went to Bringken tribe[16]—we had it at Mikkinj Valley. So he sent his [Connie's brother's] hair to Bringken tribe. So they came there and the old man had to buy, like, blanket for gift—good things. And we had a good day. They were really expert old people, but nowadays you won't see them now, they're gone.[17]

The Mamurrng Connie Nayinggul refers to was held for her brother Alfred Nayinggul and his family (Namanilakarr clan) at Mikkinj Valley near Gunbalanya, and was given by people of the Daly region. Usually, the givers of the Mamurrng travel to the country of the recipients in order to give the ceremony. The Warruwi

Mamurrng in 2012 was therefore a little different in that, for practical reasons, it was held in the country of the givers of the Mamurrng.

The Mamurrng ceremony is predominantly a western Arnhem Land ceremony, and whilst it is different to the circumcision ceremonies of eastern and central Arnhem Land, it similarly signals some kind of transition or milestone in the social life of the recipient. Lazarus Lamilami describes how the Mamurrng ceremonies he attended would mark a significant occasion for the young child/recipient, such as their first hunt: 'when a boy or a girl finds something like a tortoise or some animal for the first time, or if he spears his first bird'. The parent would then take something from the bird or animal, put it onto wax, and tie it with string and send it on to the giving group along with an invitation to come for the ceremony and receive gifts.[18] For me, the 'milestone' was that this was the first time I had attended the Symposium for Aboriginal Music and Dance, during which I met other scholars and songmen such as Mangulda, Brown, and Manmurulu and other Indigenous ceremony holders from all around the country, and listened to them speak about and perform their song traditions. At the end of the symposium, Marett formally presented a lock of my hair to Manmurulu and Mangulda, and it was agreed that the ceremony would take place the following year on Croker or Goulburn Islands. Whereas the initial idea was to include all the attendees of the symposium in the ceremony, the challenges of scheduling a date when everyone could travel, and the costs associated with attending an event on a remote island, necessitated that the visiting party was scaled down. In attendance were primarily members of the ARC 'Intercultural Inquiry' project (DP1096897), which supported the ceremony by funding the transport and accommodation for the visiting group, as well as buying materials and catering for the ceremony, and providing payments to performers.

The Mamurrng performance is usually oriented around the recipient, who sits at the centre to receive the *mamurrng*, surrounded by family members who form part of the receiving group. Other members of the community (not related to the family or performing with the song group hosting the Mamurrng) usually gather to watch and encourage the performers (see Figure 4.3). For my Mamurrng, the receiving group included my partner, Rachel Orzech, who, along with other members of the visiting group, helped to prepare food for the ceremony. My primary supervisor Linda Barwick and her husband Allan Marett sat alongside me to receive the *mamurrng*, and stood in as my 'Balanda parents'. Also part of the receiving group were members of the Bininj family into which I was adopted at Gunbalanya, including two of my *yabok* (K: sisters), Donna and Rhonda Nadjamerrek, and Donna's daughters. My 'Bininj mother'—Donna's mother—was unable to make the long trip from Kabulwarnamayo to attend. Instead, Robert Djorlom† and his wife Rosemary Urabadi, both residents of Goulburn Island and relatives of Donna's, whom she calls *ngabba* and *karrang* (K: father and mother), sat alongside us as our parents (see Figure 4.3). Another important figure in the ceremony was Solomon Nangamu, who accompanied the 'Bininj family' and me from Gunbalanya, and joined his Mawng countrymen to perform the gift of the *mamurrng*.

112 *'It's a Secret, For You': A Mamurrng ceremony*

Figure 4.3 Recipients of the Warruwi Mamurrng in 2012. Front row (left to right): Esther Djorlom, Bruce Birch (standing), Rosemary Urabadi (*karrang*/mother of recipient), Rhonda Nadjamerrek (*yabok*/sister of the recipient), Reuben Brown, Amanda Harris, Donna Nadjamerrek (*yabok*), Rachel Orzech, Linda Barwick, Allan Marett. Background: Archie Brown and Johnny Namayiwa (seated).[19] Photograph by Martin Thomas.

Exchanging inalienable gifts

The Mamurrng ceremony involved many transactions, plans, and negotiations over a period of 12 months. Amanda Harris (Research Associate for the ARC project) coordinated logistics and catering for the ceremony, ordering extra food to be brought out on the barge that arrives fortnightly at Warruwi and stocks the local supermarket. Along with Martin Thomas and his partner Béatrice Bijon, I helped to transport visitors from Gunbalanya to Sandy Creek for the ceremony, while Kevin Pamurrulpa and Rodney Mardbinda provided transportation by boat from Sandy Creek to Warruwi. Volunteers, including partners of the researchers, assisted in a large-scale barbecue operation on both nights of the ceremony that fed all of the participants and others in the community, while key ceremony leaders, singers, dancers, and boat drivers were all paid in cash for their performance or duties. In return, the Manmurulus organised all of the dancers and singers to come and stage the performance, which was filmed and recorded by researchers Bruce Birch and Isabel O'Keeffe, and film-maker Gus Berger for the mutual benefit of researchers and the community.

Both the host and recipient groups derive much pleasure from listening to different songs connected to different languages and watching dances that they may not ordinarily get to see. Les Hiatt observes that one of the 'less tangible, but perhaps no less important', functions of what he terms 'rituals of diplomacy' in Arnhem Land 'is the enjoyment derived from travelling to unfamiliar places and seeing new faces. We should not think that tourism is merely an epiphenomenon of industrial capitalism'.[20] Performing one's songs and dances not only marks one's identity but also provides an event around which people can socialise, have fun, and meet people from another group. Both Hiatt and Berndt suggest that relationships and marriage bestowals between groups have historically played an important role in these ceremonies.[21] Lazarus Lamilami characterises the Mamurrng ceremony as an opportunity to visit relatives in a neighbouring community and to revisit a place. When the message is sent with the lock of hair to initiate a Mamurrng, he says, 'it's just like an excuse to have a dance... people like to see the dances that other people do and they like to invite a lot of people'.[22]

The final handover of the *mamurrng* on behalf of the givers is an emotional stage of the ceremony—akin to the final stage of the burial ceremony in which people say *bobo* to the deceased. Indeed, the same musical passage performed at the interment of a funeral ceremony accompanies this final handover, and this association is likely to trigger similar emotional responses of grief. Speaking at an AIATSIS conference in Canberra, Jenny Manmurulu commented that people feel sad to say goodbye to the *mamurrng* and that they sometimes cry for relatives who have passed away in the period since the lock of hair was first given.[23] It is almost as though the *mamurrng* were Bininj/Arrarrkpi, or kin.

Stages of the Warruwi Mamurrng

Based on my discussions with Bininj/Arrarrkpi about the Mamurrng ceremony, and on the literature on exchange ceremonies in Arnhem Land, we can say that while these ceremonies vary locally, enacting the particular songs, dances, and rituals of different language groups, they follow three broad phases.[24] The first phase involves a request to hold a ceremony, which, once agreed upon, is formalised by a ritual involving the handing over of a token of significance (a child's lock of hair or first spear; a turtle shell, bird feather, etc.). The second phase involves preparations for the ceremony, wherein the group giving the ceremony makes arrangements to bring dancers in for the ceremony, and prepares the carefully decorated gift (*rom* pole, *mamurrng*, etc.), usually with the token intertwined. The receiving group also prepares gifts to bring—typically food, bedding, and other consumer goods.[25] The third and final phase occurs at least a year later, when the givers perform a ceremony which culminates in the revealing and eventual handing over of the prized gift. This third phase—the main ceremony—is the focus of my analysis and can be broken down further into three stages: firstly, the hosts perform for their guests at the dance ground until they feel sufficiently 'warmed up', and the recipient party is ready for the exchange to happen. Secondly, the main gift is handed over through an elaborate 'teasing' performance involving all song groups from the 'giving' party. Thirdly, at the end of the ceremonial handover, the recipient group exchanges their gifts as thanks and may also perform as part of this exchange. Altogether, the ceremony may last several days, depending on how many song groups are involved, and how long the recipients stay until both groups feel satisfied. At Warruwi in 2012, the Mamurrng ceremony took place over two nights, mainly because Charlie Mangulda and Archie Brown, two of the main instigators and leaders of the ceremony, had to return to Croker Island. The following sections analyse the three stages of the Warruwi Mamurrng, examining the songs and dances that were performed, and their function within the ceremony.

Warming up

The first evening's performance was a warm-up and opportunity for the main hosts of the Mamurrng—the Inyjalarrku group—to come together and practise the songs and dancing that would be performed the following evening as part of the main event: the handover ceremony. (As we will explore in Chapter 5, funeral ceremonies in western Arnhem Land have a similar warm-up period lasting a number of days, during which the visiting dance groups perform until everybody has arrived and the main ritual action can take place.) The performance was also carried out for the giving group to 'introduce' us to their song-set. As discussed earlier, David Manmurulu invited me to sit with him and his sons Rupert and Renfred Manmurulu, and together with Shannon Lee on didjeridu, they performed 14 songs over a period of an hour, predominantly in fast even (5a) and fast doubled (5b) rhythmic modes, accompanied with dancing by Brendan Marrgam, Stanley Gameraidj, Roderick Lee, and Shannon Lee. Inyjalarrku songs are characterised by numerous, frequent changes of tempo and distinct rhythmic modes (such as 2c and 2d). The overall tempo of the performance followed a similar trajectory observed in other performances: songs with slow tempo sections (rhythmic mode 2a) were performed to begin with, building to fast tempo songs with doubled clapstick beating (rhythmic mode 5b), before a return to slow tempo songs at the end of the performance (see Support Material Figure 4.ii). The singers demonstrated remarkable musicianship and knowledge of the songs, by singing and beating in unison throughout the complex changes in rhythmic mode, while the dancers demonstrated their intimate knowledge of the song-set in following the clapstick beat closely with their movement.

Whilst most *kun-borrk/manyardi* songs typically feature changes in rhythmic mode during the Instrumental Section and the Coda, Inyjalarrku songs may change rhythmic mode in the Introduction and the Verse,[26] and commonly alternate between three and four tempi within one song. This variation in tempo and rhythmic mode became more pronounced as the performance went along. It reached a climax with the final song IL05 (listen to **AVEx_4.1**)—known as the 'tricky one' and frequently requested by younger dancers—which had a baffling five changes of rhythmic mode in three tempo bands—fast, moderate, and slow.

AVex_4.1 https://dx.doi.org/10.26278/M0DA-KV14

Guide to listening: [00:05] 5a (fast even), [00:20] 4a (moderate even), [00:30] 5a; [00:40] IS 5e [♩♩♩♩ ♩ ♩♩♩♩ ♩]; [00:46] Coda 4d [♩ ♩ ♩ ♩ ♩ ♩♩♩ ♩ ♩ ♩ ♩], [00:54] 2b [♩ ♩ ♩ ♩ ♩ ♩ ♩], [00:58] 2d [♩♩♩♩♩♩♩♩] [01:04] 2a [♩♩♩♩]

This song is one of the 'old' songs from Manmurulu's repertory and features what *manyardi* singers refer to as a 'turnaround' rhythmic mode pattern **[00:58]** (rhythmic mode 2d) associated with the Inyjalarrku song-set, which features four even beats in slow tempo (rhythmic mode 2a) followed by six beats in moderate tempo (which I have interpreted as a 'doubled' beating pattern of the previous slow tempo); two quick beats; two more beats returning to the moderate/slow-doubled tempo; and then four even beats in slow tempo (2a). The unusual rapid alternation of tempi and surprise 'added' quick beats is said to have been produced as a result of the musical interplay between songmen and didjeridu players of previous generations, who liked to challenge one another to keep time. The lead singer would try to trick the didjeridu player and second singer by changing the tempo or adding beats to the rhythm in the Coda and Instrumental Sections (we will explore further examples of this interplay in Chapter 6, examining songs recorded in 1948 at Gunbalanya).

Further analysis of the song structure and changes in rhythmic mode in the first two Inyjalarrku songs that were performed during this warm-up performance (IL01, Figure 2.3; and IL02, Table 4.1) helps us to understand how the singers, didjeridu player, and dancers keep track of such changes in rhythmic mode. Both IL01 and IL02 have a similar song structure: an Introduction (Text Phrase A), followed by the Verse (made up of Text Phrases B and C repeated two or three times); an Instrumental Section; and a Coda. As outlined in Figure 2.3 in Chapter 2, repeats of the Verse are separated by a metrical unit of clapstick beating or an Instrumental Section, and the number of repeats varies depending on the performance context. The lead singer can add or leave out a verse repeat spontaneously, elongating the song if the dancing is going well, or terminating the song if the dancers need a rest. Both IL01 and IL02 also have virtually the same melody and song text; what distinguishes these songs is the difference in rhythmic mode, and where this difference occurs.

Whereas IL01 is predominantly in fast even rhythmic mode 5a [♩♩♩♩], and features sections of slow tempo beating (2a) in the middle of the first Text Phrase of the Verse (and at the Coda where we would expect it), IL02 is predominantly in fast doubled rhythmic mode 5b [♫♫♫♫], which is established halfway through the Text Phrase in the Introduction (watch **AVEx_4.2** and listen to **AVEx_4.3**).

Table 4.1 Musical structure of Inyjalarrku song IL02 (AVEx_4.3)

Song structure	Inst	Introduction		Verse			Instrumental section			Verse			Coda		
Text Phrase		A		A	B	C	vocables			A	B	C	A		
Clapstick beats/ Metre	4 $\frac{4}{4}$	8	4		20	16	♩♪♪ $\frac{6}{8}$	6 ♩♪♪ $\frac{6}{8}$	8 $\frac{4}{4}$		20	16	4 $\frac{6}{8}$	8 $\frac{4}{4}$	4	3
Rhythmic mode	5a			5b			5f			5b			5e	5a	5b	5a
Tempo	123			283			128			285				128	280	130*

'It's a Secret, For You': A Mamurrng ceremony 117

AVEx_4.2 https://dx.doi.org/10.26278/WB4Z-YS67

AVEx 4.3 https://dx.doi.org/10.26278/E4FT-EH66

Guide to listening: [**0:01**] Introduction, [**0:10**] Text Phrase B, [**0:19**] Text Phrase C, [**0:26**] Instrumental Section, [**0:36**] Verse repeat, [**0:52**] Coda *Final two tempo readings not accurate because of small BPM sample size.

We might assume that the singers keep time by counting the number of clapstick beats (for both songs, each Verse consists of two Text Phrases of either 16 or 20 clapstick beats, and each Instrumental Section and Coda similarly consists of 16 or 20 beats of the clapsticks). However, lead singer Rupert Manmurulu informed me that this is not the case. Instead, the singers know when to change rhythmic mode based on the Text Phrase in the vocal part. The lead singer's choice to sing either a high or low melodic sequence in the Introduction also gives the rest of the ensemble a clue as to which rhythmic mode/version of the song will be performed (i.e. fast even or fast doubled). In the Instrumental Sections and Coda of both songs, where the dancers come together to stamp the ground and listen out for the 'gapped' beating, the beating changes from groups of four to a group of six (rhythmic mode 5e [♪ ♩ ♩ ♩ ♪ ♩ ♪]). Looking at the tempi in Figure 2.3 and Table 4.1, we can see evidence of 'absolute tempo'—temporal stability and accuracy—in the way singers perform the tempi to match the rhythmic mode.[27] In IL01, the fast tempo ranged between 119 and 120 bpm, while the slow tempo started at 85 bpm and finished at 86 bpm. Similarly, in IL02, the fast tempo started at 123 bpm and remained around 128 bpm, while the fast doubled rhythmic mode remained around 283 bpm.

Handing over

The handover of the *mamurrng* on the second evening at Warruwi was in fact enacted three times, first by male dancers who were accompanied by Yanajanak songs, then by both male and female dancers accompanied by Inyjalarrku songs, and finally by David Manmurulu, who performed the handover as the *yumparrparr* (M: giant spirit). The movement that accompanied the Mamurrng ceremony could be characterised as an elaborate and extended 'tease'. With each change of song, the dancers would advance towards the recipients, moving in a tight cluster. Eventually, a dancer would break out and reveal the *mamurrng* to the recipient group, offering a closer look at the prize, before retreating back into the cluster, concealing it again, and handing it to someone else (see Ceremonial Action column, Support Material Figure 4.iii). This game of 'reveal-and-conceal' continued until the dancers finally stood over the recipient group, and laid the *mamurrng* at my feet. However, just as the *mamurrng* had been handed over (and I thought the performance might be finished), they took it back again, and the process started all over again.

First, the Yanajanak group, led by Charlie Mangulda and Harrison Cooper, performed a total of 11 song items and six individual songs. Two main rhythmic modes underpinned the songs. Songs YJ01, YJ02, YJ05, and YJ06 were predominantly in fast doubled suspended rhythmic mode 5b[var] [♫♫♫♫], which the 'second singer' Harrison Cooper would beat, while Mangulda beat an even rhythm on the clapstick.[28] During the Coda at the end of the song when the tempo slows down, Cooper would beat an inverted version of this rhythm (rhythmic mode 3c [♪. ♪. ♪.]), while Mangulda maintained an even beat, before the two came together for the final two beats. The Instrumental Sections of these Yanajanak songs were characterised by a change of rhythm in the didjeridu pattern (roughly, from ♫♫♪. ♫♫♪. to ♪♫♪ ♪. ♫♫♪). This pattern mirrored the clapstick rhythm and cued a change in the clapstick to fast even (5a [♩♩♩♩]), which in turn cued an accentuating dance call on the third beat. The second prominent rhythmic mode was fast uneven quadruple rhythmic mode 5c [♩♩♩𝄾]. Song YJ03 began in this mode and returned to rhythmic mode 3c [♫] in the Instrumental Sections and in the third and fourth repeat of the verse (see Support Material Figure 4.iii).

The Yanajanak group (seated) started their performance with a warm-up song (YJ01) accompanied by the same group of female dancers positioned adjacent to the ceremony ground. They were far enough away so that the recipients could just hear the action but could not see it clearly. Then, the singing group and male dancers took their position right up the back of the dance ground to perform the next song. For the entirety of the Mamurrng ceremony, the singing group (consisting of the lead singers, backup singers, didjeridu player, and someone who holds up the didjeridu) stood in a cluster and traversed the ceremony ground towards the recipient group, as the dancers lead out in front and present the *Mamurrng*. This arrangement was similar to the stage in a funeral ceremony when singers accompany mourners into the bough shelter and move to the grave for the interring of the body (Chapter 3). At the beginning of each song, the male dancers huddled around the singers, facing inwards. As the didjeridu began and the singers started to sing the first Text Phrase of the song, the dancers held their arms to the singers and gave an 'initiating call' to start the dance phrase. They called out 'argh!' twice, slapped their thighs, or clapped their hands and then gave a high-pitched elongated call 'yi::::::!' Then, they unfolded from the huddle and spread out in the direction of the audience, preparing for the stamping phrase in the Instrumental Section. In the Instrumental Section (on beat 3) and in the Coda (on the final beat of the song), the dancers gave another short accentuating dance call, which was different from the other kinds of dance calls that I had previously heard performed at Gunbalanya. For this call, the dancers clapped their hands or slapped their thighs, at the same time yelling '*kudda, yi::::::!*', as they turned their backs and retreated into a huddle.

In contrast to the outwardly driven style of the male dancers (with their dance calls, knee lifts, and sand flicks), the movement of the women was subtle and internal; with each clapstick beat, they dipped their cupped hands, palms facing upwards, from left to centre and right to centre, as if drawing the letter 'W' in the air. They formed a tight group and lined up on either side of the singers. As soon as the clapstick beat began, they started their arm movements, while stepping on the spot in time with the main clapstick beat. As the singers began the Instrumental Section, the women raised their arm movements from chest to shoulder height, and back down again as the next Verse commenced. At the Coda as the clapstick beat slowed, their hand movements followed, until the final beat rang out (coinciding with the men's final dance call described above) and they let their arms drop away, as though letting go of the rhythm they had been holding.

A change in song and rhythmic mode signalled a change of mood and a new development in the performance (refer to Support Material Figure 4.iii). For example, when rhythmic mode 5c (♩♩♩ ♩) was introduced for the first time (song YJ03),[29] the male dancers moved out from their tight huddle with their backs facing us, stepping three times and pausing on the gapped beat, building a sense of anticipation. Eventually when they turned around, Rupert Manmurulu was holding the *mamurrng* in his hand—the first glimpse of it that we had seen. Manmurulu led the male dancers closer to us, dancing with the *mamurrng* held outstretched in front of him, tilting it one way and another, and following its direction with his body, as though it were leading him. He then returned to the group, and they gave another 'initiating call' as the next dancer emerged with the *mamurrng*, coming forward and presenting it to the recipients (see Figure 4.4; watch **AVEx_4.4**). Then, with the introduction of song YJ04 and a return to rhythmic mode 3c [♫. ♫. ♫.], the women split into two groups, flanking the men as the ensemble advanced on the recipients. Roy Mangirryang presented the *mamurrng* once more, this time placing it at our feet at the end of the song.[30] Afterwards, Rupert Manmurulu explained to me that the *mamurrng* had been passed around to each dancer in an order that related to their traditional country so that the dance roughly traced its journey from the stone country (Gunbalanya) to the saltwater country (Goulburn Island).

'It's a Secret, For You': A Mamurrng ceremony

AVEx_4.4 https://dx.doi.org/10.26278/5D2S-0D84

Figure 4.4 Roy Mangirryang presents the *mamurrng* and stamps the ground during the Instrumental Section of YJ03 (AVEx_4.4). From left to right, Stanley Gameraidj, Jason Brown, Harrison Cooper, and Charlie Mangulda (singing and playing clapsticks), and Isaac Galaminda, Roy Mangirryang, Solomon Nangamu, Maurice Gawayaku, and Rupert Manmurulu. Photograph by Martin Thomas.

After the first handover, with the sun fading, the dancers returned from a break with more urgency to their dancing, which was reflected in the tempo of the songs (see YJ05 and YJ06 in Support Material Figure 4.iii). Once more, the women flanked the men, and with Charlie Mangulda leading them in song, the group converged on the recipients to take back the *mamurrng*.

With the *mamurrng* retaken, the Inyjalarrku group took over the singing, led by David and Rupert Manmurulu. They performed seven songs including four individual songs (two of which were the same as those they had rehearsed the night before). In keeping with other ceremonial performances, the overall tempo followed a slow-fast-slow trajectory, with a period of high-energy dancing in the middle section to accompany songs in fast doubled rhythmic mode (5b). During this period, the audience around us became very boisterous, encouraging the men to perform for them elaborate stamping phrases, yelling out 'action, action!' and showing their appreciation when Stanley Gameraidj, Brendan Marrgam, and other dancers responded by breaking away from the ensemble and dancing towards the audience. As with the Yanajanak performance, the dancers started far away and edged closer to the recipients with each song until handing over the *mamurrng* (see Support Material Figure 4.iv). When it was the turn of the women to hand over the *mamurrng*, their movements intensified, and they began swinging their arms more freely from side to side to the beat of the clapstick. As each of the dancers took the *mamurrng* and came forward to present it, Rupert Manmurulu kept an eye on the action from behind them, and Jenny Manmurulu instructed him to keep singing, calling out 'one more!' This resulted in a very long version of the *Nigi* No. 1 (IL50) that involved six repeats of the verse.[31] The women placed the *mamurrng* down a second time at my feet and quickly took it back again, returning to the back of the ceremony ground once more.

At this point, it is worth emphasising the spontaneity that characterised the performance, and the moments of release that balanced the moments of intensity and focus. While I have attempted to show how the ceremonial action is structured and guided by the rhythmic modes and song choice, the performers always maintain a degree of agency within this structure, and the boundaries that delineate the ceremonial action from the audience-related action are porous so that events 'outside' of the performance may occasionally intrude upon the ceremonial action 'inside' the dance ground. For example, at several crucial points during the handover, some dogs wandered onto the ceremony ground and almost tripped up the dancers, who were forced to shoo them away. During one particularly memorable moment, the dancers gave a loud slap as part of their initiating dance call, at which point one of the dogs, positioned right in the centre of the ceremony ground, responded by letting out a yelp. Similarly, participation in the dancing and singing was somewhat fluid: Solomon Nangamu joined the Yanajanak singers to accompany them on the didjeridu halfway through their 'set', while Russell Agalara started the ceremony as an audience member looking on at the action and recording it on his mobile phone, before he and others joined in with the dancers once the Inyjalarrku group took over. David Manmurulu also moved in and out of the ceremony ground, directing and stage-managing the action. His instructions to the singers ensured that the performance was running to schedule (afterwards, he and Jenny lamented that the dancers had arrived a little late so they had to hurry things up); he also managed the handover of the *mamurrng* by secretly giving it to the dancers, and then arranging it in front of the recipients once it had been handed over, ensuring that it had been correctly laid out.

The elaborate 'tease' culminated with one final act of theatre. David Manmurulu, who had inconspicuously disappeared while the women were up front dancing and handing over the *mamurrng*, re-emerged from the shadows at the back of the ceremony ground through the middle of the group of singers, covered from head to toe in *delek* as the *yumparrparr* (M: giant). In Mawng mythology, the *yumparrparr* are giant spirits which sometimes take the form of a shooting star. Associated with the Nginji song-set, but also performed as part of the Inyjalarrku song-set, they are represented with either yellow and white ochre on each half of the body (split down the middle) or all white, as on this occasion.[32] David Manmurulu learned the dance of the *yumparrparr* from his father George Winunguj and has since taught it to his son Rupert Manmurulu, who continues to perform it on special occasions. Semi-crouched, he strode as the *yumparrparr* towards the recipients midway through the song (IL06),[33] swaying his loping arms and cocking his head from side to side, and accentuating the sense of the gravity to his movement. He then stopped on the spot, and, to the beat of the clapsticks, extended both arms out and pulled them in to his chest, as if reaching out to make a connection. (The movement was of course very similar to the dance that James Gulamuwu—brother of David Manmurulu—gave by the grave at the reburial ceremony in Gunbalanya, Chapter 3). Manmurulu held one arm out to us and rotated his hand (was it a refusal? A wave 'goodbye'?). Then for a brief moment, the *yumparrparr* held out his arms, and he looked at us directly. His eyes looked sad and his face somewhat anguished. As the rhythmic mode shifted once more to slow even beating (rhythmic mode 2a) and the singers began singing the 'farewell' *Nigi* song ('No. 2' IL19), the *yumparrparr* took the *mamurrng* in his hand and was joined in dance by the women, who echoed his swaying movements, swinging their arms outwards from the hip, and raising one arm to their head on the third beat of rhythmic mode 2c. Meanwhile, the men surrounded the *mamurrng* and clapped along to the beat. The y*umparrparr* took the *mamurrng* between his mouth, waving to us once more before placing it down one final time at my feet. To complete the handover, the women formed a line at the front of the ceremony ground, with Manmurulu in the middle, and performed one final song to say *bobo* (IL06; Watch **AVEx_4.5**).

AVEx_4.5 https://dx.doi.org/10.26278/JT96-6A04

Saying 'thanks'

With the handover complete, the final phase of the ceremony provided a counterbalance with a lighter, more reflective mood, as the recipients and other participants took part in exchanging various songs as 'thanks'. At times, the mood turned to hilarity, as children and Balanda got involved in the dancing, and adults played around for their amusement. The Inyjalarrku group performed two more fast doubled songs (IL02) which the younger girls from Warruwi and Gunbalanya—including Donna Nadjamerrek's daughters—joined in and danced too.[34] Solomon Nangamu and Russell Agalara then invited the recipients to sit with them as they sang Mirrijpu, with Rupert Manmurulu and Harrison Cooper accompanying on the didjeridu. Prior to the ceremony, Nangamu had told me that he would 'accompany' me to Warruwi for the Mamurrng, to show me the places where he grew up on Goulburn Island, and to 'help' me with the ceremony. Nangamu's gesture, first in joining with the Yanajanak and Inyjalarrku group, and then singing his own songs for us, showed his appreciation of the relationship that we had established since meeting at Gunbalanya.

The first song Nangamu and Agalara performed was MP06, followed by MP26 first in slow and then in fast doubled rhythmic modes. The didjeridu used to accompany Mirrijpu was the same instrument that had been used for all of the performances that evening and had a fundamental tone of F sharp, a tone above the didjeridu in E that belonged to Nangamu and Agalara, used at Gunbalanya. This difference meant that the vocal melody sat in the higher end of Nangamu's vocal range, giving the performance a more intense quality. From my position sitting amongst the group, this was a chance to simply enjoy listening to the songs that I already felt familiar with, and to clap along without the concern of analysing or recording the performance. Other members of our team also appreciated having such an intimate performance staged for them, during which they could sit in the same circle as the singers and closely observe and listen to the songs.

As a thank you to all the Bininj/Arrarrkpi who staged the performance for the recipients—particularly the Manmurulus who were central in organising the ceremony—Allan Marett performed two *wangga* songs from two different repertories (Barrtjap and Walakandha *wangga*).[35] He had been given permission to perform in ceremony by songmen Kenny Burrenjuck and Frank Dumoo.[36] Marett was accompanied on the didjeridu by David Manmurulu, Nangamu, and Roderick Lee, while Linda Barwick led the dancing for the women, with Jenny Manmurulu beside her and the younger girls following. This performance stirred the interest of the audience and created a buzz at the ceremony ground. Not only was it unusual for two Balanda to be performing an Aboriginal song tradition so expertly, but it was also amusing to see *manyardi* dancers attempting to dance to (the less familiar) *wangga* songs. In the absence of an expert male dance leader from the Daly region, Rupert Manmurulu, Marrgam, Warrabin, and others got up and led the dancing, provoking laughter as they exaggerated their movements and attempted to pause at the right moment and follow the rhythmic modes, sometimes misjudging the beat.

The first song Marett performed was the Walakandha song 'Truwu' in Marri Tjevin language.[37] With the local singers sitting around and listening intently, Marett started the song with no clapstick beating ('unmeasured' rhythmic mode 1), building suspense before the commencement of rhythmic mode 5b[var] [♫♫♫♫] in the Instrumental Section. At this point, the singers joined Marett and began to clap along, before an uneven rhythmic pattern not common among *manyardi* song-sets [♫♩ ♫♩♩𝄾] threw some out of sync with the clapping. They showed their appreciation of Marett's singing and leading of the song by calling out as he completed the Instrumental Section and continued with another verse. Meanwhile, the contrasting style of Barwick's dancing was also a source of amusement for local Bininj/Arrarrkpi, many of whom filmed the performance on their mobile phones. Barwick held her arms high with fists clenched as she danced, twisting and swinging vigorously during the Instrumental Sections accompanying the faster clapstick beating. Marett then performed a song in Batjamalh language called 'Bangany-nyung Ngaya'[38]— the same song he had performed at the Symposium in Darwin in 2011 when the Mamurrng was initiated. This song was in fast uneven quadruple rhythmic mode 5c (♩♩♩𝄾), similar to the Yanajanak songs performed earlier in the evening. With various people volunteering to accompany him on the didjeridu, Marett repeated the song four times, until they were able to finish the accompanying didjeridu rhythm at the right moment in the Coda, and the song came out correctly (Watch **AVEx_4.6**).

AVEx_4.6 https://dx.doi.org/10.26278/GMRE-7Z37

Conclusion: *kun-borrk/manyardi* as belonging

The analysis I have presented, focussing in particular on the function of different rhythmic modes performed during the three stages of the Mamurrng ceremony, gives further weight to the argument that rhythmic modes underpin the ceremonial action and help to distinguish the 'aural identity' of different song-sets.[39] Underneath a dynamic soundtrack of sand flicking, dogs yelping, thighs slapping, babies crying, and onlookers calling out, it was the didjeridu rhythm, clapstick beat, and singing of the Text Phrase that drove changes in the action of the Warruwi Mamurrng, and helped to imbue the *mamurrng* with meaning as an object that embodies Arrarrkpi relationality. Key ceremonial leaders—singers Charlie Mangulda and David Manmurulu and dance leaders Jenny Manmurulu, Brendan Marrgam, and Stanley Gameraidj—made certain choices which steered the ceremony in a particular direction, while the dancers and participants were allowed a degree of agency and spontaneity in the way that they followed this directive. The casual observer may conclude that the more flamboyant men's style of dancing, with its stamping, jumping, twisting, and turning, plays a more important role in the ceremony when contrasted with the more subtle style of the women's dancing. However, after closer inspection of the relationship between the movement and the musical elements of the song, I would argue that the male and female styles of dancing are complementary: while the men embody the external aspect of the song—following the vocal line and Text Phrase in particular, the women embody the internal aspect of the song—carrying the rhythm and the melody through their arm movements.

In the context of an intercultural encounter such as the Mamurrng ceremony, rhythmic modes also function as a kind of universally understood musical language: regardless of their familiarity with the repertory, both the men and women dancers were able to participate in Marett's performance of *wangga* because they recognised the rhythmic modes and the way they functioned within the song. One of the enduring strengths of the Mamurrng ceremony as a form of Aboriginal diplomacy is the way it caters for the diversity of Aboriginal expression and identity. The gift-giving performance is a statement of sovereignty and a way of presenting something essential about one's culture for another group. It is particularly thrilling for the spectators to see dancing that they may not normally get to see and listen to songmen who they would not normally hear perform. Like other ceremonial occasions, the Mamurrng provides an opportunity for songmen and dancers to share their craft (by playing didjeridu for another group or dancing to their songs, for example) and for the younger generation to learn different songs and dances from regions outside of their own.

The value of the *mamurrng* lies not in its material worth as a decorated pole, but what it represents as an inalienable gift given in a ceremony of exchange which has its origins in gift economies. From the perspective of the recipient, the initial cutting of my hair seemed an oddity. However, unbeknown to the recipient, the lock of hair takes on a new meaning through various transactions, starting from the time that it is sent over to another group and accepted as an invitation to hold a ceremony. It undergoes another transformation when it is embedded into the *mamurrng* pole with beeswax, string, and wool (important ceremonial materials of symbolic significance) and becomes the centrepiece of the performance. The transformed lock of hair is then finally handed back to its original owner through an elaborate tease, designed to overwhelm the senses and subvert the expectations of the recipient. This entire process helps the recipient understand that he or she is a small but essential part of a bigger network of people and cultures. By the end of my Mamurrng ceremony at Warruwi, in which the *mamurrng* had been sung by both the Yanajanak and Inyjalarrku groups and passed from one dancer to the next, it carried with it a kind of 'essence' of the country and people these songs embodied. It was not just a material gift, but a symbol of *being* Bininj/Arrarrkpi.

Aboriginal people in western Arnhem Land continue to live in multilingual, multiclan communities, and interact with Balanda through work and social environments. Capitalist-based transactions—often centred on the exploitation of mineral resources—have come to characterise the communities in which they live.[40] In this environment, the Mamurrng exchange ceremony, premised on goodwill, trust, mutual respect, and reciprocity, continues to play an important role on a number of levels. On a regional level, it reinforces kinship networks that exist across different language groups such as Kunwinjku and Mawng and families living in neighbouring communities such as Warruwi and Gunbalanya. For Aboriginal people working with non-Aboriginal researchers or partners from other organisations, the Mamurrng offers a way of formalising respectful relationships and bringing research and partnership aims into line with Bininj/Arrarrkpi protocols and ways of operating. The Warruwi Mamurrng was a uniquely Bininj/Arrarrkpi ceremonial response to a modern dilemma, born out of a situation involving both Indigenous and non-Indigenous research collaborators. Through the process of staging the ceremony, relationships between researchers and their collaborators in the Warruwi and Gunbalanya communities were strengthened.

By receiving the gift of the *mamurrng*, I personally felt that I was not only made welcome in Bininj/Arrarrkpi society, but also given a place within that society (formalised through the dance in which my hair was passed from Bininj of the stone country to Arrarrkpi of the saltwater country). Observing Marett performing *wangga* songs that he had been entrusted with to sing in ceremonial contexts, and reflecting on the overjoyed response to his performance by people at Warruwi, I was also reminded how Balanda can participate in ceremonial exchange in culturally meaningful and appropriate ways: it is through ceremony that we find our place among others and our sense of belonging.[41]

Notes

1 Berndt suggests 'exchange' ceremonies of Arnhem Land are unique to northern Australia and have grown out of a history of 'alien' contact and trade. Berndt, "Ceremonial Exchange," 156.

2 Jon Altman, "Maradjiri and Mamurrng: Ad Borsboom and Me," in *Cultural Styles of Knowledge Transmission: Essays in Honour of Ad Borsboom*, ed. J. Kommers and E. Venbrux (Amsterdam: Aksant Academic Publishers, 2008), 15.

3 Garde similarly suggests that at Maningrida, these ceremonies emphasise 'maintaining alliances of amity between groups who in some cases are living ... in closer contact with each other than they have in the past'. Murray Garde, "From a Distance: Aboriginal Music in the Maningrida Community and on Their Internet Site," *Perfect Beat: Pacific Journal of Research into Contemporary Music and Popular Culture* 4, no. 1 (1998): 5.

4 Other names for exchange ceremonies in Arnhem Land include Rom, Marrajiri, Barnumbirr (for Burarra, Djinang, and Wurlaki groups), or Middjarn (Kunabidji, Kun-barlang, Nakkara groups). Ibid., 5–6. See also Adrianus Petrus Borsboom, "Maradjiri: A Modern Ritual Complex in Arnhem Land, North Australia" (PhD thesis, Katholieke Universiteit Nijmegen, Nijmegen, 1978).

5 Keen, Aboriginal Economy and Society, 4.
6 Similar observations about the Mamurrng are presented in Corn and Garde. Aaron D.S. Corn, "Burr-Gi Wargugu ngu-Ninya Rrawa: Expressions of Ancestry and Country in Songs by the Letterstick Band," *Musicology Australia* 25, no. 1 (2002): 87; Garde, "The Language of *Kun-borrk*," 62.
7 Roslyn Poignant and Axel Poignant, *Encounter at Nagalarramba* (Canberra: National Library of Australia, 1996), 4.
8 See Altman, "Maradjiri and Mamurrng," 17.
9 See Stephen Wild and L.R. Hiatt, eds., *Rom: An Aboriginal Ritual of Diplomacy* (Canberra: Australian Institute of Aboriginal Studies, 1986).
10 Ibid., xi–xii.
11 Berndt, "Ceremonial Exchange," 160.
12 Discussed further in Isabel Anne O'Keeffe, "Multilingual *Manyardi/Kun-borrk*: Manifestations of Multilingualism in the Classical Song Traditions of Western Arnhem Land" (PhD Thesis, University of Melbourne, 2016).
13 The symposium was attended by Indigenous groups from around the country who continue to practise their song traditions, and convened by a group of researchers who have worked with these groups over a number of years, including musicologists Allan Marett and Linda Barwick.
14 The Mamurrng ceremony was at the forefront of participants' minds, as Barwick, Birch, Archie Brown, Mangulda, and Manmurulu had given a presentation about another Mamurrng performed at Croker Island.
15 [Connie Nayinggul, 20110825-RB_03.wav, https://dx.doi.org/10.26278/C9CB-9Y54, 04:22–04:39].
16 'Bringken' and 'Wagaitj' are terms that Bininj use to describe people of the Daly region.
17 Connie Nayinggul [20111108-RB_01_edit.wav, https://dx.doi.org/10.26278/SEE1-D409, 02:26:50].
18 Lamilami, *Lamilami Speaks*, 181.
19 Bruce Birch is a linguist who was present at the inception of the Mamurrng in 2011 in Darwin, and has worked with Charlie Mangulda and Archie Brown on Iwaidja language. Also attending the ceremony was Isabel O'Keeffe, a linguist musicologist who has worked primarily with the Manmurulu family and Kun-barlang speakers at Warruwi.
20 Wild and Hiatt, eds., *Rom: An Aboriginal Ritual of Diplomacy*, 11.
21 Ibid.; Berndt, "Ceremonial Exchange," 162.
22 Lamilami, *Lamilami Speaks*, 183.
23 Reuben Brown et al., "Continuing the History of Cultural Exchange in Arnhem Land: A Mamurrng Ceremony at Warruwi, Goulburn Island, August 2012" (paper presented at Breaking Barriers in Indigenous Research and Thinking: AIATSIS 50th Anniversary Conference, Canberra, 26–28 March 2014).
24 Compare with Ronald Berndt's survey of ceremonial exchange in western Arnhem Land in the late 1940s, based largely on his experiences at Gunbalanya. Berndt, "Ceremonial Exchange," 160.
25 See Garde, "The Language of *Kun-borrk*," 62–63.
26 Refer to recordings 20120810_11-IO_01_04_IL.wav, https://dx.doi.org/10.26278/WPZH-5K96; and 20120810_11-IO_01_05_IL.wav, https://dx.doi.org/10.26278/C7M0-YB54 (song IL04).
27 See Freya Bailes and Linda Barwick, "Absolute Tempo in Multiple Performances of Aboriginal Songs: Analyzing Recordings of Djanba 12 and Djanba 14," *Music Perception* 28, no. 5 (2011): 473–490.

28 This is a common rhythmic mode among many *wangga* repertories, but less common among western Arnhem Land song-sets.
29 [20120811IOv01-04, https://dx.doi.org/10.26278/V54M-AE24, 00:05:15–00:07:22].
30 [20120811IOv01-07, https://dx.doi.org/10.26278/V54M-AE24, 00:12:18–00:14:13].
31 [20120811IOv01-13, https://dx.doi.org/10.26278/V54M-AE24 00:23:32–00:25:54]. Refer also to Gulamuwu's version of the song, discussed in Chapter 3.
32 See O'Keeffe, "Multilingual *manyardi/kunborrk*", 298.
33 [20120811IOv01-17-IL06_IL07, https://dx.doi.org/10.26278/V54M-AE24 00:29:24.900–00:32:13.500].
34 [20120811IOv01-19-IL02, https://dx.doi.org/10.26278/V54M-AE24, 00:37:08.600–00:38:11.800].
35 See "Bangany-nyung Ngaya" and "Truwu," Chapters 4 and 8 in Marett, Barwick and Ford, *For the Sake of a Song*.
36 Ibid., 13.
37 For another version of this song, see recording Mar88-39-s02, in Marett, *Songs, Dreamings, Ghosts*. For further analysis, see Marett, Barwick, and Ford, *For the Sake of a Song*, 307–08.
38 See also recording Moy68-05-s05 in Marett, *Songs, Dreamings, Ghosts*. For further analysis, see Marett, Barwick, and Ford, *For the Sake of a Song*, 102–03.
39 Marett, Barwick and Ford, *For the Sake of a Song*, 47; Barwick, "Tempo bands"; Peter Toner, "When the Echoes Have Gone: A Yolngu Musical Anthropology" (PhD thesis, Australian National University, Canberra, 2001), 82–100; Gregory D. Anderson, "Striking a Balance: Limited Variability in Performances of a Clan Song Series from Arnhem Land," in *The Essence of Singing and the Substance of Song: Recent Responses to the Aboriginal Performing Arts and Other Essays in Honour of Catherine Ellis*, ed. Linda Barwick, Allan Marett and Guy Tunstill, Oceania Monographs 46 (Sydney: University of Sydney, 1995): 13–25.
40 For example, the multinational mining company ERA operating Ranger uranium mine in Jabiru until its closure in 2021; companies operating the bauxite and aluminium mines of Nhulunbuy and the Gove Peninsula, and many other foreign multinationals who hold exploration leases for minerals all over Arnhem Land.
41 The *mamurrng* ceremony pole given to me by members of the Warruwi community is on display in the foyer of the Sydney Conservatorium of Music.

5 'That Spirit Changed My Voice'

A funeral ceremony for Nakodjok

Nakodjok returns

The family had waited a long time for this. Their father had passed away some six months earlier, in the middle of the wet season in the Top End of the Northern Territory, and his body had been held in a morgue in Katherine all this time. Now that the dry season had begun and the water levels along the rivers and floodplains had receded, some of the remote dirt roads through Arnhem Land were once again open. The family's outstation on their ancestral country at Mikkinj Valley was now accessible via a road that ran east from Gunbalanya, and then west around the other side of the Arnhem Land escarpment, and preparations to bury their father on his country could begin in earnest. The burial had been planned for August, but with more deaths in the community of Gunbalanya creating a backlog of funerals and limiting space in the local morgue, the date was brought forward. In late June, the body of the late Jacob Nayinggul, or Nakodjok Namanilakarr as he was referred to post-mortem,[1] was finally returned to the family in a charter plane from Katherine to Gunbalanya.

Under instructions from the family, all work in the community finished for the day at 2:30 pm. Bininj/Arrarrkpi and Balanda gathered outside the house where Nakodjok had lived during the last part of his life, waiting in the sweat-inducing afternoon sun. There in the front yard, Nakodjok used to sit in his wheelchair, smoking a cigarette, waiting for his next appointment with members of community, family, researchers, and other visitors. Now the yard was occupied by his extended family, who sat with their children in the shade of tents. A tub of *delek* was passed around for those who wished to paint their arms, legs, face, and hair. At one end of the yard, further away from the tents, a visiting *bunggurl* group from Maningrida led by singer Stanley Djalarra Rankin sat under a tree singing to keep his hosts—the family of Nakodjok—company. I saw my chance to go inside the house and pay my respects to the family, and asked one of Nakodjok's grandchildren: '*Ka-mak bu ngam-rengimen*?' ('Is it OK if I go inside?'). He replied, '*Mah, ka-mak*' ('OK, that's fine') and led me through the house into a dark bedroom, where I found Nakodjok's daughters sitting around

DOI: 10.4324/9781003216339-6

the coffin, with their heads lowered and hands resting on the polished wood that encased their father.

One of Nakodjok's daughters, Connie, acknowledged me with a nod as I came in. Like many of Nakodjok's children, Connie took a leading role in the community, particularly around cultural matters. Like her father, she was generous about sharing Bininj knowledge with outsiders, and sought to bring the various elements of the Gunbalanya community together by including them in cultural practices, such as gathering, preparing, and cooking food in the traditional way. Now she was covered in *delek*; her voice hoarse from an earlier display of public grief at the airstrip in Gunbalanya upon the return of Nakodjok's body. She spoke quietly and determinedly, informing me of the funeral arrangements, and asking if I could pass on the invitation to some other Balanda researchers who had worked with Nakodjok in recent times. She pointed out Nakodjok's black cowboy hat hanging proudly on the wall. Once a symbol of his affiliation with stockmen, it had now become a sort of cult fashion item among the grandchildren, who wore their own hats as a sign of respect for Nakodjok. Connie then pointed out a gold plate at the head of the coffin, etched with Nakodjok's name. To an outsider, this detail, along with the large framed photograph of Nakodjok wearing his iconic hat that was later displayed during the funeral service at Gunbalanya church, seemed to sit awkwardly with hitherto common Bininj/Arrarrkpi practices of avoiding the name, image, or other aspects of the deceased during the period of mourning. Yet, it also indicated an adaptation of avoidance practices in the face of changes to the media and social media landscape and the incorporation of Judaeo-Christian traditions by Bininj/Arrarrkpi, ever since they had moved from the bush to live among the missionaries in the early 20th century, the era into which Nakodjok was born.[2]

I said *bobo* to the daughters and stepped back outside into the blinding sun. Soon the *bininj* (K: men; men and boys) went inside the house to collect the coffin. This was when the Karrbarda group started up, first with the blowing of the *mako*, then with fast beating of the clapsticks, providing the tempo for the didjeridu and a cue for the men to begin dancing. The men came together for the initiating dance call, shouting 'oh, argh', slapping their thighs twice before pointing their fingers to the sky, and calling 'yi!' The 'dance captain' of the group, Joey Nganjmirra, took off his shirt and wrapped it around each fist, pulling it tight in the middle.[3] At the end of the verse, they danced towards the coffin and began the 'stamping phrase', lifting their knees high in the air and kicking up the sand with their feet to the beat of the clapstick, then pausing with the skipping of the beat. With each stamp, they gave an accentuating dance call that sounded like a hiss ('ssk ssk'), and Nganjmirra held the taut shirt out in front of him, rotating it at different angles to articulate the movement. Then, the sound of the singing, didjeridu, and clapsticks and the flicking of sand were joined by a loud banging against the thin metal walls of the house, as the coffin was hoisted above the heads of the young men and taken out of the house away from the grieving daughters. Outside, other *daluk* (K: women; girls) joined in the wailing and crying, and onlookers shouted directions at the coffin-bearers, helping to steer the coffin from the narrow entrance of the house towards the back of the 'troopy'[4] that waited in the yard. Some *daluk* held rocks above their heads, threatening to strike themselves in a gesture of their uncontrollable grief, before *bininj* intervened and restrained them. As the sounds of grief grew to a crescendo, I reflected on how the display of emotion in this well-rehearsed ritual was as real as it was performative; the actions spontaneous yet also semi-staged.

Rising above the sounds of the bereaved, the Karrbarda singers slowed down the tempo of their clapstick beating and began singing a sweet melody, the notes of which were more elongated than before. Leading songman Eric Mardday kept singing, repeating another verse until the coffin had been securely placed inside the troopy and the rear doors swung shut. At this point, the wailing turned to sobbing, and the song came to a close. With emergency lights flashing, the vehicle slowly made its way out of the yard, around the corner and down the street to a small room at the back of the Gunbalanya health clinic known as the 'morgue house'. The family stayed close to the troopy, while the rest of us followed behind in quiet reflection. Once more Stanley Djalarra Rankin's *bunggurl* group took over, singing Nakodjok's casket out of the troopy and into the morgue. Connie then addressed everyone, thanking them for coming and confirming plans for a memorial service in Gunbalanya, followed by a burial ceremony out at Mikkinj Valley outstation in three weeks' time. 'Mah, bonj', she said ('Ok, that's it'). It was decided.

***

The description above of the movement of the deceased from his family home to the local morgue—reconstructed from field notes I took in Gunbalanya in western Arnhem Land in 2012—relates to just one of the many stages of the burial of Nakodjok involving song and dance. Each of these stages marked an aspect of the deceased's transition, in terms of both the body and the relationship between the deceased spirit and mourners. In this chapter, I show how song and dance express and mediate relationships between Aboriginal people, both living and deceased. I trace the diverse range of songs that were performed at various stages of transition for Nakodjok's funeral ceremony, which began in the community of Gunbalanya and ended at his outstation at Mikkinj Valley. By attending the funeral ceremony and performing songs for the families of the deceased, Bininj/Arrarrkpi and other Aboriginal people from around the region showed their respect for and their personal connection to the deceased, framing their performance as an acknowledgement of specific ties to kin and Country.

As discussed in Chapter 3, a number of scholars have remarked on the important role played by song and dance as part of mortuary rites both in this region and throughout Aboriginal society. Music not only directs the ritual action of the bereaved—as in the passage above where the Karrbarda songs cued the departure of the coffin and the outpouring of grief—it also influences and mediates interactions with the spirit world. Allan Marett describes how elements of the music and the dance in *wangga* reference both the ghostly and human worlds. By overlapping these elements in the performance of rag-burning (mortuary) ceremonies, the living are brought into a liminal space with the spirits, enabling the spirit of the deceased to exit the world of the living and enter the world of the ancestors who reside in the country.[5] Following on from Marett, I argue that the performance of *kun-borrk/manyardi* at funeral ceremonies in western Arnhem Land facilitates a kind of creative exchange between the living and the dead. In this exchange, songmen construct their performance partly for the benefit of spirits, while the spirits give them new songs in their dreams to perform for the occasion, and take part in—even influence—their ceremonial performance. This circulation of songs between the living and the dead is ultimately productive in sustaining the song tradition: as long as the living continue to please their ancestors by performing in ceremony the songs that were handed down to them, the possibility remains that they will receive new songs in the future, via spirit intervention in dreams.

This chapter details the role of funerals in Aboriginal society, and the influence of Christianity on contemporary funeral rites in western Arnhem Land. The performance analysis section discusses the diverse network of sociality represented in the funeral ceremony for Nakodjok, which brought together Aboriginal people from the Tiwi Islands and eastern Arnhem Land, as well as western Arnhem Land. I outline the different song traditions that were represented, as well as the sequence in which they were performed during the ceremony, and discuss how the music reflected the western Arnhem Land singers' relationship with the deceased. The second part of my analysis examines in closer detail a performance of Mirrijpu (M: seagull) at Mikkinj Valley on the penultimate evening of the funeral ceremony for Nakodjok, before his burial. Based on insights provided by Mirrijpu songmen Nangamu and Agalara—whom I accompanied to the burial—about the choices they made in ordering the songs, as well as my own analysis of changes in tempo and rhythmic mode, I discuss how the performance was constructed with an awareness of both the funeral mourners *and* the spirits of the deceased. Finally, I analyse two Mirrijpu songs: one an 'established' part of the repertory, having been inherited by the current songman, and the other a 'new' song that was conceived in a dream prior to Nakodjok's funeral, and performed specifically for the occasion. I show how 'new' songs share not only the same song words but also similar melodic material with older songs, and how this process pays homage to the songmen of previous generations who composed the songs while at the same time maintaining an aesthetic unity within the repertory which gives it its distinct aural identity.

Song and the life cycle

Funerals are an important feature of Aboriginal life in Australia. Aboriginal societies are kinship-based; in western Arnhem Land as in other areas of Australia, Bininj/Arrarrkpi are born into a particular skin group or subsection that gives everyone a relationship with one another, ensuring that no-one is a complete stranger.[6] When someone passes away, many people who are kin may come together at the funeral ceremony to play their part in assisting the bereaved and to express their own feelings of loss for the deceased.[7] In the dry season when roads are open and rivers passable, Bininj/Arrarrkpi may spend every second or third week travelling to nearby outstations and communities for funeral ceremonies of deceased kin. In Arnhem Land, ritual managers referred to as *djungkay* (K) help to coordinate the various stages of the funeral ceremony and arrange for various families to attend.

Funeral ceremonies are also a significant part of Aboriginal cultural and spiritual expression. Aboriginal cultures anticipate death; those who are elderly and are dying generally become the focus of community interest rather than being shut away, and mourning rituals take place over a long period of time, sometimes years.[8] As Morphy and Morphy suggest, the way that Aboriginal cultures deal with death is for many people a marker of their Aboriginality:

> All over Australia, it seems, and in very different colonial settings, the rituals surrounding death have become a constant theatre of life, where, in a relatively autonomous space indigenous values are affirmed and asserted, with greater or lesser degrees of consciousness, in contrast to those of the encapsulating society.[9]

As discussed in Chapter 3, throughout Arnhem Land an elaborate secondary burial ceremony called the *lorrkkon* traditionally took place some years after the initial burial. Isaiah Nagurrgurrba related to me that when it was time for the deceased to go into the *lorrkkon* coffin, elders would instruct a younger man to take a 'letter stick' with the message that the ceremony was ready, and that the 'postman' or carrier of the letter stick would run to neighbouring clan groups and take it to them. He would then return with the message of their arrival, and those organising the ceremony would go out hunting in preparation for the arrival of other mourners.[10] This ceremony represented the final departure of the spirit of the deceased from the world of the living. Over time, Aboriginal people of Arnhem Land have adapted their funeral ceremonies in the face of social changes such as the influence of missionaries who brought Christian beliefs and rituals, as well as adapting to various advances in technology. The *lorrkkon* ceremony met with the disapproval of missionaries, as they believed that bodies buried on 'consecrated' ground should not be disturbed.[11] The missionaries' deterrence, along with other factors including the loss of senior elders who held important knowledge about how to conduct *lorrkkon*, contributed to the demise of the *lorrkkon* in favour of a single, final burial.[12]

Contemporary funeral ceremonies in western Arnhem Land commonly incorporate a Christian service. This may involve a sermon and hymns as part of an earlier memorial service for the community in the church (if the deceased was well-known) and a separate sermon for the burial, as was the case for Nakodjok Nayinggul. In Baldwin Spencer's account of Bininj ceremonial life at Gunbalanya (then referred to as Oenpelli) in 1912, initial burials were held the day after someone passed away, and were not as prolonged as they can be today.[13] In the earlier part of the 20th century when missionaries established themselves in Arnhem Land, funerals were more frequently held at missions, settlements, or towns, whereas today, due to the availability of charter planes, ceremonies can be held at outstations and the deceased can be buried on their country.[14] This often means that ceremonies require significant pooling of money and resources to organise. Coordinating the travel of numerous family and kin from different communities to a remote location for the funeral presents logistical challenges. These days, the deceased may be flown to a central morgue in Darwin or Katherine and kept there for some months, and ceremonies may last several days or even weeks, while the family wait for relatives or important people from other areas of Arnhem Land to come and take their part in the funeral ceremony.[15]

Although mortuary rites vary across northern Australia, they have a common purpose, in addition to allowing for a process of grieving: to ensure that the spirit of the deceased no longer dwells among the living (potentially causing them trouble or danger), and is satisfied to leave, joining the ancestral dead and returning to its country.[16] In western Arnhem Land, after someone dies, Bininj/Arrarrkpi immediately take branches from the ironbark tree, place them in a metal drum, and set them alight, spreading the smoke through the dwellings where the deceased lived (their house and families' houses, the medical clinic, or the local art centre, for example). *Kun-borrk/manyardi* is performed as an accompaniment to this smoking ceremony, in order to drive away the spirit of the deceased from such places (which are left dormant for a period until the family are satisfied to return and use them again). Vehicles too are ceremonially smoked, and in some cases when a songman dies, his songs are performed and simultaneously smoked, before a period of dormancy during which they are not performed.[17]

As discussed previously in Chapter 3, songs play a vital role in the deceased spirit's transition out of the living world. Northeastern Arnhem Land mortuary rites involve the performance of ritual episodes or individual 'song series' according to a conceptual movement through the landscape, which takes the deceased spirit on a particular route to its ancestral country.[18] At Wadeye and Belyuen in the Daly region, *burnim-rag*[19] ceremonies involve driving the spirit away through the ritual burning of 'rags' belonging to the deceased (clothes, bedding, cooking, and hunting utensils and other prized possessions), in which the deceased spirit may have taken refuge.[20] Songs at funeral ceremonies in western Arnhem Land do not follow a broader narrative or specific journey as they do in northeastern Arnhem Land. However, similar principles relating to how the deceased spirit is oriented back to its country affect the presentation of different songs, depending on the origin and language affiliation of those songs. Dream-conceived songs in spirit language are particularly potent in the context of funeral ceremonies because they 'speak' exclusively to ancestral spirits who understand them. As Meiki Apted observes, by singing spirit language songs, 'spiritual faith and connection to country is asserted in a way that may not be possible with an ordinary spoken language'.[21] Perhaps because of their potency in funeral settings where an awareness of the spiritual is heightened, and because of the prominence of funeral ceremonies as the main occasions for the performance of *kun-borrk/manyardi* in western Arnhem Land, almost all western Arnhem Land song-sets recorded during my fieldwork were in spirit language (see Table 1.1, Chapter 1).

Coming together for Nakodjok

Whilst it is not unusual for a number of different song genres and repertoires to be represented at ceremonial occasions in western Arnhem Land—particularly at funerals[22]—the funeral ceremony for Nakodjok Nayinggul was unique, because it brought together such a diverse range of song traditions from all over the Top End. Altogether, seven different Aboriginal song groups performed at various stages of the ceremony (see Support Material Figure 5.i). Of equal prominence were the songs from adopted music genres that featured in the ceremony, including Christian hymns in Kunwinjku led by the local Reverend and sung by the congregation, as well as various Country and Western songs that were played through speakers on an mp3 player at Nakodjok's memorial service. The high level of participation from a diverse range of singers in the ceremony reflected not only Nakodjok's importance as a leader in his immediate community of Gunbalanya and western Arnhem Land, but also his kinship ties right across Arnhem Land and the Top End region.

The majority of the singers who performed at Nakodjok's ceremony were from western Arnhem Land, the region in which Nakodjok was born and where he spent most of his life. Many of the song repertoires performed were *manyardi* song-sets originating from Goulburn Island. This should not come as a surprise, given the family ties that exist between the two communities and the history of ceremonial exchange: Inyjalarrku was first recorded at Gunbalanya in 1963 by Alice Moyle, while Mawng singers were also recorded at Gunbalanya in 1948 by Colin Simpson (discussed in the following chapter). Today, numerous Mawng songmen who were born on Goulburn Island reside not only in the community of Warruwi (which, as we have seen in previous chapters, is arguably the centre of the western Arnhem Land song tradition) but also in other neighbouring communities, where they continue to perform the songs and receive new songs. One such example is the Inyjalarrku song-set, which was inherited by a number of singers including the late David Manmurulu (today led by sons Rupert and Renfred Manmurulu), his brother James Gulamuwu, and Tommy Madjalkaidj, residing in Warruwi, Gunbalanya, and Maningrida, respectively. Similarly, the Karrbarda song-set is performed by inheriting singers living on Croker Island

and Maningrida as well as Gunbalanya. As a *wardde-ken* song-set, it plays a central role in many funeral ceremonies held in Gunbalanya and surrounding stone country, and featured at the funeral for Nakodjok.

A number of songs from outside western Arnhem Land were also represented at the funeral ceremony, including patrilineal clan 'song series' from central and northeast Arnhem Land. Each clan performs a number of song subjects in a series that relate to different aspects of their ancestral stories.[23] Stanley Djalarra Rankin's songs belong to the Wurrkigandjarr clan group (also referred to as Marrangu Djinang). The songs are often referred to as 'Mewal songs' as they relate to the ancestral characters Mewal and Djambuwal who travelled together in Marrangu country.[24] The most prominent subject of their songs in this performance was the Wakwak (crow). These songs accompanied a dance that imitates the bird's movement and sound, in which the dancers circled and hopped as they moved towards the gravesite, calling out 'waak, waak!' Crows are associated with death in this region, and Wakwak songs are often performed during the final stages of burial.[25] Galpu clan *manikay* was also performed by the Gurruwiwi family and accompanied on the *bilma* (clapsticks) without didjeridu accompaniment by Gumatj clan singer Johnny Burrwanga, who was born in eastern Arnhem Land and married a Galpu clan woman. Burrwanga lives with other Galpu and Gumatj people who have long been resident at Warruwi, but who still maintain their *manikay* performance traditions by performing in western Arnhem Land.

Not only are these song series from central and northeast Arnhem Land different from those from western Arnhem Land in the way that they are inherited (through one's clan as opposed to individually), but they also sound different in a number of ways. Unlike western Arnhem Land songs, northeast Arnhem Land melodies do not necessarily take their pitch from the didjeridu, and both northeastern and central Arnhem Land songs feature didjeridu overtones that are absent from western Arnhem Land *mako* accompaniment. There are subtle differences in the layering of the musical texture too: whereas *kun-borrk/manyardi* begins with didjeridu accompaniment, followed by the beat of the clapstick and then the vocals, and ends with solitary beating of the clapsticks, *manikay/bunggurl* songs often begin with clapstick accompaniment and vocals then didjeridu, and finish with unaccompanied singing. Such characteristics make the geographic identity of the singers instantly recognisable to mourners in larger funeral ceremonies such as Nakodjok's, where different groups perform simultaneously, both during the day and in the evening.[26]

The last Aboriginal genre from outside Arnhem Land was Tiwi songs referred to by Nangamu as the Buffalo Dance. Genevieve Campbell suggests that while the dance is usually performed to Tiwi *Yoi* ('ceremony') songs by people with *Jarrangini* (Buffalo) Dreaming, it has Iwaidja origins, having been brought to Melville Island by Iwaidja people of western Arnhem Land.[27] The songs were performed unaccompanied (without clapsticks or didjeridu), and led by Wesley Kerinaiua, with Dean Rioli (celebrated Australian Rules Football League player) and Solomon Nangamu joining the dancing (Nangamu lived in Tiwi for a number of years and was invited to join the dancing as he was familiar with the songs). The dance took place next to the grave, after the coffin was put in the ground.[28] The melody of the song had a limited range, and the tempo gradually increased, culminating in a percussive slap of the body, followed by the distinctive response from the dance group: 'ah-eyah'.[29]

Of the Western musical genres performed, Reverend Lois Nadjamerrek and a small congregation of Kunwinjku Bininj sang Christian biblical hymns unaccompanied during the memorial service in the church at Gunbalanya, and as part of an open-air sermon by the gravesite at Mikkinj Valley, as the grave was being filled (see Table 5.1). Nadjamerrek led the service in both Kunwinjku and

Table 5.1 Summary of the main stages of the funeral ceremony for Nakodjok involving ritual song and dance

6 June 2012 Gunbalanya: transition to local morgue	28 June 2012 Gunbalanya: memorial service	29 June 2012 Mikkinj Valley: pre-interment	30 June 2012 Mikkinj Valley: interment and post-interment
Wurrkigandjarr clan sing *bunggurl* outside the home while family stays with coffin inside Nakodjok's house. **Karrbarda** dance body out of house and accompany procession of mourners to Gunbalanya morgue. **Wurrkigandjarr clan** then take over and sing Nakodjok inside the morgue	**Galpu clan** sing *manikay* accompanying procession from morgue to church. Upon arrival at church, **Mirrijpu** singers lead coffin and procession of mourners into church. Reverend Lois Nadjamerrek leads **Christian hymns in English** during service. **Country and Western** songs played over PA as local mourners farewell Nakodjok. **Inyjalarrku** is performed as the coffin is taken from church to airport and placed on a plane to Mikkinj Valley, where **Karrbarda** greets it.	**Mirrijpu, Djalarra Wurrkigandjarr clan,** and **Karrbarda** sing simultaneously after sundown while families cook dinner in separate camps. **Karrbarda** perform later in the evening, with children joining in dancing. **Mirrijpu** take over and continue to sing until early the next morning	**Mirrijpu, Inyjalarrku, and Karrbarda** lead groups of mourners into bough shelter to farewell Nakodjok. **Wurrkigandjarr clan** join them, and all groups dance outside bough shelter. **Karrbarda** 'mother song' leads Nakodjok into grave. **Buffalo Dance** performed beside the grave, followed by **Christian hymns in Kunwinjku.** After interment, **Wurrkigandjarr clan** and **Buffalo Dance** group remain for *kun-woning* (cleansing/washing ceremony), followed by smoking ceremony of Nakodjok's belongings and home at Mikkinj Valley

English, and composed one of the hymns in Kunwinjku. In addition, the family of Nakodjok requested three songs to be played at the end of the memorial service, as the mourners said goodbye to the coffin. The first song—'Gunbalanya' by Troy Cassar-Daly—pays homage to Nakodjok's country, with references to fishing for saratoga at Red Lily Billabong near the East Alligator River. Cassar-Daly is an Indigenous Country and Western Singer from New South Wales who travelled to the community and met Nakodjok, later dedicating the song to him. The second song—'We've Done us Proud' by Slim Dusty—is a nationalistic song about the progress of the Australian nation. Slim Dusty's music is well known in many Aboriginal communities in the Top End where he toured and performed throughout his career.[30] The song resonates with the history of this area, in particular the Bininj-owned cattle station at Gunbalanya ('I built the fences to hold the cattle'/I worked the land'). Sentiments about uniting people together for a common good ('side by side, hand in hand') also reflect Nakodjok's achievements as a key negotiator between Balanda and Bininj during his work for the Northern Land Council and as a board member of the joint-managed Kakadu National Park. The third song—'Blue Ridge Mountains' by African-American singer Charlie Pride—was, according to Nakodjok's son Alfred Nayinggul, a favourite of Nakodjok's because it reminded him of the landscape of his country. Nayinggul recalled his father sitting outside at Mikkinj Valley outstation, listening to the song on the record player while taking in the surrounding escarpment. These three songs indicate how Country and Western music in particular has come to be emblematic of Aboriginal experience and identification with the land,[31] and how popular music genres have been incorporated into the Bininj/Arrarrkpi worldview, taking on meanings that are locally specific.

The sequence in which the song repertories were performed (outlined in Table 5.1) was partly determined by practical factors (such as who could attend the ceremonies at Gunbalanya and Mikkinj Valley), and partly negotiated by the parties involved so that certain song repertories could be emphasised at certain stages of the ceremony. Many Balanda and Bininj/Arrarrkpi mourners who were unable to attend the burial at Mikkinj—including the *manikay* and *manyardi* singers resident at Warruwi—were given the opportunity to farewell the deceased after the memorial service at Gunbalanya. A number of people from the community and local organisations were asked by the family to speak about Nakodjok at the service.[32] The memorial service at Gunbalanya included Christian prayers and readings from the bible conducted largely in English; a eulogy, hymns, and Country and Western songs. In this sense, it was a more Balanda-oriented service that complemented the ceremony at Mikkinj Valley, with its focus on Bininj/Arrarrkpi rituals. This seemed fitting, given the bicultural world that Nakodjok had occupied.

Those groups who did not go on to Mikkinj accompanied Nakodjok from the morgue to the church for the service, including the Galpu clan, who performed *manikay* without didjeridu accompaniment, as well as David and Rupert

'That Spirit Changed My Voice': A funeral ceremony for Nakodjok 139

Manmurulu who performed Inyjalarrku as Nakodjok's coffin was taken from the church and placed into a troopy, before it was transported by plane to Mikkinj Valley. Rupert Manmurulu led the singing of the Inyjalarrku *nigi* song, before David Manmurulu performed the *yumparrparr* (M: giant spirit) dance. As discussed in previous chapters, this dance is marked by the fact that it is performed to a slow-moderate tempo, normally reserved for women's dancing (presumably as a spirit, the *yumparrparr* breaks gendered conventions of *kun-borrk/manyardi* dance observed by Bininj/Arrarrkpi). Manmurulu performed the dance of the *yumparrparr* as the coffin was carried away, extending his arms out towards it and drawing his arms into his chest, as if letting go, before waving 'goodbye' to Nakodjok.[33]

The Karrbarda and Wurrkigandjarr groups stayed with the family of the deceased, many of whom did not attend the memorial service at Gunbalanya but awaited Nakodjok at Mikkinj Valley inside the bough shelter constructed for his coffin. Bough shelters are usually made of stringybark branches and leaves, providing shade for the mourners. The shelter where the coffin is kept is an enclosed structure (see Figure 5.1), sometimes covered in red or yellow cloth, according to the patrimoiety of the deceased (Nakodjok's *duwa* moiety was represented with red cloth). The *daluk* members of the family stay inside the shelter beside the coffin until the burial. In the evening at Mikkinj Valley, the Karrbarda, Wurrkigandjarr, and Mirrijpu groups performed next to the shelter in order to keep the family company through the night. On the morning of the interment, Inyjalarrku singer

Figure 5.1 Photo of the construction of a bough shelter or 'shade' for the body of Nakodjok at Mikkinj Valley outstation. Photograph by Reuben Brown.

140 *'That Spirit Changed My Voice': A funeral ceremony for Nakodjok*

Tommy Madjalkaidj joined them, performing 'old' Inyjalarrku songs as well as 'new' dream-composed songs named Marrawiwi (M: salmon). Some of these newly conceived songs were performed for the first time in honour of the spirit of the deceased. Together, the four song groups took turns accompanying groups of mourners, including their own kin, into the bough shelter to visit Nakodjok one final time. Significantly, the Karrbarda group—representing *wardde-ken* people—performed the *ngalbadjan* (K: mother song) as the body was interred, in order to carry Nakodjok's spirit away at the final moment. As the grave was being filled in, the opportunity arose for any other groups to pay their respects to the deceased, and the Tiwi group obliged, performing their Buffalo Dance for Nakodjok. A Christian sermon and Kunwinjku hymns followed, concluding with a ritual in which the mourners throw a handful of dirt into the grave as a final goodbye.

Paying respects through song

A number of significant connections between the living and deceased were enacted and highlighted through these performances at Nakodjok's funeral ceremony. As *manikay* scholar Peter Toner suggests, the choice to perform, as well as the sequence of the performance—which is decided among not only the singers but also other senior members of different patrifilial groups—is a highly social and political act in Arnhem Land ceremonies:

> Yolŋu musical performances are events in which complex social identities are expressed, negotiated, constructed, and re-constructed; they are occasions during which a great deal of the work of Yolŋu sociality gets done at a number of different levels.[34]

Even the performance of Kunwinjku hymns, which came after a sermon delivered by Reverend Lois Nadjamerrek in which she mentioned Nakodjok's baptism and first marriage that had taken place at the Gunbalanya church,[35] articulated his relationship to the local congregation and to God.

Underpinning many of the social connections between the mourners and the deceased are cultural practices of clan exogamy (marriage outside one's own clan) and marriage agreements.[36] The large representation of *kurrula* song-sets at Nakodjok's funeral reflected not only the prevalence of *manyardi* in western Arnhem Land, but also Nakodjok's connection to Mawng-speaking families through his mother, Priscilla, who was *kurrula* (from the saltwater). Priscilla's father was *wardde-ken* (from the stone country) and helped resolve a dispute between the Gunbalanya and Goulburn Island communities. As thanks he was promised a Mawng woman for marriage.[37] This connection (between *wardde-ken* and *kurrula* people) was maintained when Priscilla made a pre-birth marriage agreement with the uncle of Tommy Madjalkaidj that Nakodjok would marry Tommy (if he were a woman) or one of his sisters. Although the marriage didn't

'That Spirit Changed My Voice': A funeral ceremony for Nakodjok 141

eventuate because Nakodjok was too young when the potential spouses were of the right age, Madjalkaidj and Nakodjok recognised the fact that they were in an affinal relationship, and would refer to each other as brother-in-law. Madjalkaidj continued to recognise this relationship (marked by a degree of physical avoidance) during his performance at the ceremony, accompanying the mourners to the edge of the bough shelter with his Marrawiwi songs, but remaining outside while they went in. The Tiwi performance was given by family groups who were connected through two members of Nakodjok's family who shared ownership of his country at Mikkinj Valley. They were taken away as children and sent first to Channel Island (a former Leprosarium where leprosy sufferers were sent to live in isolation) and then to Bathurst Island, where they had grown up. (Government policies of removal affecting generations of stolen Aboriginal children created a situation in which family ties are often spread far and wide.)[38]

At the same time that performances highlight or emphasise connections between the mourners and the deceased, they also reinforce connections among the living, in particular through the rituals that are performed for the family of the deceased to guide them through the grieving process. On the evening before Nakodjok's burial, Mirrijpu singers Solomon Nangamu and Russell Agalara came together with didjeridu player Alfred Gawaraidji, and the Karrbarda singers led by Eric Mardday, to take it in turns singing throughout the evening and into the next morning. Positioning themselves close to the family of the deceased inside the main bough shelter, they performed a mixture of moderate and fast tempo songs, encouraging the children to get up and join in the dance. The mood was high and the atmosphere jovial; the boisterous children kept themselves entertained by watching the adults, including Madjalkaidj, dancing to the songs, and through their own attempts to dance. As Agalara explained, part of the purpose of singing and dancing at funerals is to keep the emotions of the bereaved in check so that they can not only mourn but also feel supported. Explaining why they sing and dance, and its effect on the mourners, Agalara used the idiomatic Mawng expression *arnamawu kumpil*, which translates roughly as: 'they get a strong feeling in their chests':[39]

> [By singing], we respect and we connect with their families among them... being close to them[40] [we] lift their feelings a bit... they have sadness in their emotions and we... *arnamawu kumpil* means we have to be there for them to express their emotions and balance it.[41]

Again on the morning of the burial, all of the song groups performed fast tempo songs, with Joey Nganjmirra and Russell Agalara taking turns playing the role of 'dance captain', helping the children to put on their nagas and cover themselves in *delek*, and instructing those children from Tiwi or elsewhere who were unfamiliar with *kun-borrk/manyardi* how to dance to the various clapstick patterns. Funeral events therefore not only help the bereaved and their relatives to grieve, but also provide a natural setting for the intergenerational transmission of song and dance traditions, by bringing these different family groups together to perform their song traditions and articulate their language/clan identities in the process.

Intervening spirits

The extent to which performances in funeral ceremonies are constructed in order to reflect these connections between the living and the deceased became clear through discussions with Mirrijpu songmen Nangamu and Agalara about how they ordered the songs during the performance they gave the evening before the burial. Thus far, we have established that there is no strict ordering of songs in western Arnhem Land, and that song order varies from one performance to the next depending on the occasion (Chapters 3 and 4). We have observed a general pattern in the overall tempo of a performance, whereby songmen start singing at a slow to moderate tempo and build to songs in a fast tempo, before returning to a slow tempo at the end of the performance. This pattern also characterised Nangamu and Agalara's performance of Mirrijpu at Mikkinj Valley, which began with songs predominantly in moderate even rhythmic mode (4a) before graduating to a faster tempo, including a string of fast doubled rhythmic mode songs (5b) in the middle section for the men and young boys to practise dancing to, before returning to moderate tempo songs (4a/3a), finishing with the *nigi/ngalbadjan*.

We have also observed the way that songmen repeat a song until they feel it has been performed the 'right way', with the correct tempo, clapstick rhythm, and singing of the song text. When repeating songs (marked 'R' in the song column of Table 5.2), the singers often made fine adjustments to the tempo (usually, a couple of beats per minute slower) in their attempts to perform it accurately. In order to 'follow the track' of their ancestors (as Nangamu put it),[42] a song was often performed first in a slow or moderate rhythmic mode, before it was restated in fast rhythmic mode (for example, song MP25 in Table 5.2). As with previous performances, once they found the right tempo, the songmen were able to stick with it, in spite of pauses in the singing and changes to the song (see tempi for song items 20120628_02-RB_09_12_MP26.wav[43] to 20120628_02-RB_09_17_MP22.wav[44] and 20120628_02-RB_09_21_MP17.wav[45] to 20120628_02-RB_09_23_MP06.wav;[46] Table 5.2).

In determining how a performance is put together, western Arnhem Land songmen also consider the familiarity of a particular song, for both the living and the deceased. By attending the ceremony, Nangamu stated that he wanted to show his respect for the important role that Nakodjok had played as a ceremony leader. Beforehand, Nangamu told me that he intended to perform three songs for the first time, including two songs (songs MP21 and MP22 in Figure 5.2) that had been given to him as a gift by the spirit of Nakodjok not

Table 5.2 Summary of Mirrijpu song items performed by Solomon Nangamu and Russell Agalara at Mikkinj Valley for Nakodjok funeral ceremony

Song item	DOI	Song	Song text association	Rhythmic mode	BPM
20120628_02-RB_03_01_MP 06.wav	https://dx.doi.org/10.26278/BAEF-FG23	MP06	Kiwken (M: boss)	4a (moderate even); IS 4c (mod. uneven triple) [♩♩♪]; Coda 4c and 2a (slow even)	124/77
20120628_02-RB_04_01_MP 19.wav	https://dx.doi.org/10.26278/C340-QV80	MP19	Bobo: bininj (K: farewell: men)	4a; IS 4c [♩♩♪]; Coda 4c and 2a	122/77
20120628_02-RB_05_01_MP 18.wav	https://dx.doi.org/10.26278/VCY6-2Z19	MP18	Bobo: daluk (K: farewell: women)	4a; Coda 2a	116/80
20120628_02-RB_06_01_MP 18.wav	https://dx.doi.org/10.26278/89X8-E947	MP18 (R)	Bobo: daluk (K: farewell: women)	4a; Coda 2a	117/75
20120628_02-RB_07_01_MP 18.wav	https://dx.doi.org/10.26278/TRJ3-PX49	MP18 (R)	Bobo: daluk (K: farewell: women)	4a; Coda 2a	116/80
20120628_02-RB_07_02_MP 21.wav	https://dx.doi.org/10.26278/YWX4-PK75	MP21	Mamme (K: food; tucker)	5b (fast doubled even); Coda 3e (slow moderate uneven sextuple) [♩♩♩♪♪♪], 2a	250/110/80
20120628_02-RB_07_03_MP 21.wav	https://dx.doi.org/10.26278/QAN5-1F45	MP21 (R)	Mamme (K: food; tucker)	5b; Coda 3e [♩♪♪♩♪], 2a	244/105/83
20120628_02-RB_07_04_MP 24.wav	https://dx.doi.org/10.26278/A2JP-7B26	MP24	Ngaya (M: 'daughter')	4a; Coda 2b [♩♪♩♪], 2a	117/76
20120628_02-RB_07_05_MP 24.wav	https://dx.doi.org/10.26278/Z9WQ-JA30	MP24 (R)	Ngaya (M: 'daughter')	4a; Coda 2b [♩♪♩♪], 2a	118/81

Marrawiwi and Karrbarda groups perform before Mirrijpu group takes over again

20120628_02-RB_09_03_MP 25.wav	https://dx.doi.org/10.26278/S7D2-ZD07	MP25	Warramumpik (M: love song)	4a; IS 4c [♩♩♪]; Coda 4c and 2a	122/81
20120628_02-RB_09_04_MP 25.wav	https://dx.doi.org/10.26278/5IDA-S560	MP25 (R)	Warramumpik (M: love song)	4a; IS 4c [♩♩♪]; Coda 4c and 2a	120/81
20120628_02-RB_09_05_MP 25.wav	https://dx.doi.org/10.26278/RRW7-ZQ53	MP25 (R)	Warramumpik mulatparlangkat (M: love song, fast RM)	5b; IS 4c [♩♩♪]; Coda 4c and 2a	264/134/89
20120628_02-RB_09_06_MP 21.wav	https://dx.doi.org/10.26278/0780-6C83	MP21	Mamme (K: food; tucker)	5b; Coda 3e [♩♩♩♪♪♪], 2a	260/125/90
20120628_02-RB_09_07_MP 18.wav	https://dx.doi.org/10.26278/QBVC-BP79	MP18	Ngapawurru (M: respect)	4a; Coda 2a	119/84

(Continued)

Table 5.2 (Continued)

Song item	DOI	Song	Song text association	Rhythmic mode	BPM
20120628_02-RB_09_08_MP06.wav	https://dx.doi.org/10.26278/9DV1-6F11	MP06	*Kiwken* (M: boss)	4a; IS 4c [♩♩ ♪]; Coda 4c and 2a	123/81
20120628_02-RB_09_09_MP26_MP06_MP26.wav	https://dx.doi.org/10.26278/2DDD-JM79	MP26	'Going down'	4a; IS 4c [♩♩ ♪]; Coda 4c and 2a	122/80
20120628_02-RB_09_10_MP26.wav	https://dx.doi.org/10.26278/ZX3M-TD66	MP26 (R)	'Going down'	4a; IS 4c [♩♩ ♪]; Coda 4c and 2a	124/80
20120628_02-RB_09_11_MP26.wav	https://dx.doi.org/10.26278/C5H1-QZ87	MP26 (R)	'Going down'	4a; IS 4c [♩♩ ♪]; Coda 4c and 2a	122/80
20120628_02-RB_09_12_MP26.wav	https://dx.doi.org/10.26278/Y3XF-RH12	MP26 (R)	'Going down'	4a; IS 4c [♩♩ ♪]; Coda 4c and 2a	123/77
20120628_02-RB_09_13_MP14.wav	https://dx.doi.org/10.26278/PAC9-BR52	MP14	*Bobo* (K: farewell)	4a; Coda 2a	118/82
20120628_02-RB_09_14_MP14.wav	https://dx.doi.org/10.26278/ZW7R-G748	MP14 (R)	*Bobo* (K: farewell)	4a; Coda 2a	119/80
20120628_02-RB_09_15_MP22.wav	https://dx.doi.org/10.26278/9DG6-EX28	MP22	'Gift' song	4a; Coda 2b [♩ ♪ ♪], 2a	123/95/84
20120628_02-RB_09_16_MP22.wav	https://dx.doi.org/10.26278/SCQY-3S28	MP22 (R)	'Gift' song	4a; Coda 2b [♩ ♪ ♪], 2a	120/97/81
20120628_02-RB_09_17_MP22.wav	https://dx.doi.org/10.26278/GAKA-1V19	MP22 (R)	'Gift' song	4a; Coda 2b [♩ ♪ ♪], 2a	120/104/83
20120628_02-RB_09_18_MP27.wav	https://dx.doi.org/10.26278/7DCY-FT93	MP27	*Bobo* (farewell)	3a (slow moderate even)	95
20120628_02-RB_09_19_MP28.wav	https://dx.doi.org/10.26278/GN66-N838	MP28	'Going down'	3a (slow moderate even followed by 3b (slow moderate doubled); IS/Coda 3a	98/200
20120628_02-RB_09_20_MP28.wav	https://dx.doi.org/10.26278/ZTVB-XJ49	MP28 (R)	'Going down'	3a/3b; IS/Coda 3a	96/198
20120628_02-RB_09_21_MP17.wav	https://dx.doi.org/10.26278/ZPPX-Y191	MP17	*Mamme* (K: tucker)	4a	121
20120628_02-RB_09_22_MP06.wav	https://dx.doi.org/10.26278/3SXN-BS94	MP06	*Kiwken* (M: boss)	4a; IS 4c [♩♩ ♪]; Coda 4c and 2a	121/82
20120628_02-RB_09_23_MP06.wav	https://dx.doi.org/10.26278/R92P-CS53	MP06 (R)	*Kiwken* (M: boss)	4a; IS 4c [♩♩ ♪]; Coda 4c and 2a	121/82

Key to table: (R) indicates a repeated song; recently conceived songs shaded grey.

'That Spirit Changed My Voice': A funeral ceremony for Nakodjok 145

long after the 'old man' had passed away. On a social level, the debut of these newly gifted songs on such an important occasion would have generated interest among Bininj/Arrarrkpi who were already familiar with Mirrijpu songs, and would be listening to the 'new' songs for the first time. On a political level, as mentioned earlier, it would have further demonstrated the singer's affiliation with the song-set and the country connected to it. One might therefore expect Nangamu to have opened his performance with one of these songs. Instead, following precedents set down by his own Manangkardi ancestors, he performed a number of 'old' songs first, building up to the 'new' material that was intended for both his immediate audience and the deceased spirit of Nakodjok. So as not to stray too far 'off track', towards the end of the session, Nangamu returned once more to the old songs from *korroko*, which would be familiar to his ancestors (see recordings 20120628_02-RB_09_18_MP27.wav[47] to 20120628_02-RB_09_23_MP06.wav[48] in Figure 5.2, which are marked by a slow moderate tempo).

A further consideration for Nangamu was the way in which the performance environment calls for certain songs which have particular associations for him. For example, a number of the songs he performed were what he calls *bobo* (goodbye or 'farewell') songs, which he 'brings out' for funeral ceremonies in particular (see recordings 20120628_02-RB_04_01_MP19.wav[49] through to 20120628_02-RB_07_01_MP18.wav;[50] Figure 5.2). Song MP27, for example, is a '*bobo*' song Nangamu performed at the funeral of his older brother in 2007; he explained to me that 'if one of my family passes away, I sing that song'.[51] Other associations given to songs included *warramumpik* (M: 'love songs',[52] a reference to another subcategory of *kun-borrk/manyardi* song-sets), songs that he associates with a spiritual return to his country, translated into English as 'going down' songs, and songs associated with all of the kinds of *manme* (K: food or 'tucker') found at particular sites in his country of North Goulburn Island. At times, the choice to perform a song from one of these categories related what was going on around the singer, such as when Nangamu noticed people cooking their dinner on the fire, and returned to song MP21, a *manme* song (recording 20120628_02-RB_09_06_MP21.wav;[53] Figure 5.2). Tellingly, the song Nangamu calls *kiwken* (M: boss)—MP06—features frequently here (and in recordings of all performance events discussed in previous chapters). It is usually the song that Nangamu opens his performance with and returns to throughout (at Mikkinj Valley, he returned to the song midway through the performance and again at the end). Finally, there is the *ngaya* (M: daughter)[54] song—MP24—which often precedes and joins onto the final *nigi* (mother) song. Later, in the early hours of the morning, Nangamu and Agalara sang the *ngaya* together with the *nigi*, to finish their performance.[55]

Finally, some further comments by Nangamu and Agalara listening back on the recordings revealed the extent to which the spirit world is understood as affecting the outcome of the performance. On one occasion (recording

20120628_02-RB_09_09_MP26_MP23_MP06_MP26.wav[56]), Nangamu began singing one song (MP26) before unintentionally switching mid-song to another 'old' song from *korroko* (MP23), and then returning again to the first song. At the completion of the song, all of the performers laughed at Nangamu's apparent disorientation, and in the discussion that followed, Nangamu remarked 'that spirit bin grab me by the throat and he changed my voice!' In yet another example of spirit intervention, Agalara attributed his ability to sing songs with Solomon from *korroko* that he was familiar with but had not previously performed in ceremony, to the assistance of the spirit of his grandfather through whom he first learned to sing Mirrijpu:[57]

> He [Nangamu] connects me onto that group [of] songs [from *korroko*] what my granddad [sings]... he connects to me, when he sings it's sort of like a computer goes in my brain and I twist my tongue and start singing with him.[58]

Agalara's comments recall once more Marett's observation about the ability of song to open up a space between the spirit and living worlds. It appears ancestral and deceased spirits not only influence the way songs are ordered, but can also intervene in the middle of songs and lead the songman in the direction of another song, or take momentary control of his voice; the same way that a computer gamer might control a virtual avatar!

Circulating songs

Finally, the connection between the living and the ancestral spirits is renewed through the composition of 'new' dream-conceived songs, in which the words, melodic, and rhythmic material from 'old' songs (considered to belong to the ancestors) are recirculated and refashioned into a distinctly new song that is nonetheless recognisable as belonging to the other songs in the repertory. (This explains why songmen often describe recent dream-conceived songs as 'new, but old' or 'still the same one [as others in the song-set]').[59] The following passage analyses two songs—one 'old' (MP18) and one 'new' dream-conceived song (MP21) performed on the evening before the burial. The most obvious difference between these songs is the rhythmic mode: MP18 is performed predominantly in moderate even rhythmic mode in 3/4 time, whereas MP21 is performed in fast doubled rhythmic mode in 4/4 time. Another difference is the melodic mode: MP18 is in a major mode, whereas MP21 is in a Mixolydian mode (most songs in the Mirrijpu song-set are in Dorian and Aeolian modes).[60] Another unusual feature of the 'new' dream-composed song is the high degree of syncopation in the vocal rhythm, which is a feature of some songs that are performed in fast doubled rhythmic mode.

In spite of these differences, a number of musical elements mark the 'new' song MP21 as belonging to the Mirrijpu song-set, most notably the song text of the verses, which include the words '(iny)alatpa(rla)/latparta'. Particular melodic sequences are also recognisable from the 'older' Mirrijpu song MP18: the first is a descending sequence of the scale degrees 8-7-6-5 (see light shaded boxes in Figures 5.2 and 5.3), and the second is a descending sequence on the scale degrees 4-3-2-1 (see dark shaded boxes in Figures 5.2 and 5.3). Thirdly, the triplet rhythm that appears in MP18 set to the song text 'lart-pa-ya' re-emerges in the third line (bar 13) of MP21 (this time realised as 'lat-pa-da'). Indeed, when taken together, the 'new' dream-composed song MP21 can be seen as taking elements of the 'old' MP18 and inverting them: whereas MP18 begins with the song text ('alardparla) and ends with vocables ('ay-ay' 'na' etc.), MP21 begins with vocables ('na-na na-ya') and ends with the inverted song text ('lat-pa-da-ya'). Similarly, MP21 starts with the same 4-3-2-1 melodic sequence that MP18 finishes with, before moving to the 8-7-6-5 melodic sequence that MP18 started with (listen to **AVEx_5.1** and **AVEx_5.2**).

AVEx_5.1 https://dx.doi.org/10.26278/92ND-QM77

Figure 5.2 Excerpt from vocal part of 'old' Mirrijpu song MP18 (AVEx_5.1).[61]

AVEx_5.2 https://dx.doi.org/10.26278/18ZM-0431

148 'That Spirit Changed My Voice': A funeral ceremony for Nakodjok

Figure 5.3 Music transcription of vocal part excerpt of 'new' Mirrijpu dream-composed song MP21 (AVEx_5.2).[62]

Nangamu's decision to juxtapose these songs, performing the 'new' song after the 'old' (see song item listing in Table 5.2), was a way of highlighting the link between them. Through the performance, connections are made between the music of the living and that of the dead not only through song and tempo choice, but also through the text, melody, and rhythm, which reference shared aesthetic elements from the songs of past songmen and their ancestors.

Conclusion: *kun-borrk/manyardi* as a conduit

Funeral ceremonies in western Arnhem Land continue to serve as the primary occasions in which relationships between different clan and cultural groups are acknowledged through ritual performance. The funeral ceremony for Nakodjok brought together people from all over the region who came to pay their respects and express their particular relationship with the deceased by performing their own song traditions. The diversity of music represented at this event points to the way songs express different linguistic, cultural, and geographic identities and relationships. It also showed the role of funerals in providing an event in which these connections and differences can be played out, and the region's rich song traditions can be maintained.

Nakodjok's funeral ceremony highlighted both change and continuity/adaptation, with the incorporation of Christian rituals and non-Aboriginal music genres alongside Bininj/Arrarrkpi mortuary rites and song traditions, and with

'That Spirit Changed My Voice': A funeral ceremony for Nakodjok   149

the charter plane playing an essential role in transporting the body to and from regional and local morgues, and facilitating the participation of distant kin in the ceremony. At the same time, it was underpinned by Bininj/Arrarrkpi traditions: the focus of the ceremonial action was centred on the transition of the deceased spirit from the living to ancestral worlds, as it was eventually carried home to its traditional country through the performance of the 'mother song'. *Kun-borrk/manyardi* song repertoires and dances, with their access to the ancestral world and its language, were key to ensuring such a transition was managed.

The performance at Mikkinj Valley demonstrated the different ways in which *kun-borrk/manyardi* singers show their respect for, and their ongoing relationship with, the ancestors, and for the songs they have inherited. This was done firstly, by reserving the performance of these 'new' songs for the occasion of the funeral ceremony, when spirits familiar to them (Agalara's grandfather, for example) and the spirit of the deceased (Nakodjok) are likely to hear their performance, and secondly, by endeavouring to perform the songs and dances handed down to them in a way that respects the artistic integrity of previous songmen: setting the songs to particular rhythmic modes, and aligning songs to match the mood of the mourners around them, and to help balance their emotions. The compositional process of western Arnhem Land songs, in which melodic sequences of 'old' songs are recirculated and refashioned into 'new' compositions, represents an exchange of creative ideas between the living and their ancestral spirits, who are the source of the musical material.

Importantly, these songs help Bininj/Arrarrkpi not only to deal with death and say goodbye to their deceased relatives, but also to maintain some kind of relationship with the memory and spirit of the deceased. For Agalara, the Mirrijpu songs he sings are his connection to his grandfather, and as long as he feels that his grandfather's spirit is with him, he will continue to perform the Mirrijpu songs at funeral ceremonies, and pass them on to the next generation: 'That relates to the family… it doesn't matter where we go, the song is always there'.[63]

Having examined contemporary exchanges of *kun-borrk/manyardi* in western Arnhem Land, in the next chapter we will turn to a historic exchange in 1948.

Notes

1. Throughout this chapter, I refer to the deceased (who we were introduced to as the leader of the reburial ceremony in Chapter 3), as Nakodjok Nayinggul, or just Nakodjok, reflecting his name and status at the time of mourning. *Nakodjok* means a male (Kunwinjku noun class prefix *na-*) belonging to the *kodjok* subsection (in the kinship system of western Arnhem Land), while *Namanilakarr* means a male of the *Manilakarr* clan group.
2. The practice of displaying a photo of the deceased at the funeral service is also common among Yolŋu of eastern Arnhem Land. See Jennifer Deger, "Imprinting on the Heart: Photography and Contemporary Yolngu Mournings," *Visual Anthropology* 21, no. 4 (2008): 292–309.

3 'Dance captain' is the English word used by Eric Mardday to describe the leader of the male dancers for the Karrbarda song-set. [Eric Mardday, 20130913-RB_01.wav, https://dx.doi.org/10.26278/RA1S-DG08, 00:06:36.892–00:06:45.392].
4 The Toyota Land Cruiser is a four-wheel drive vehicle that can seat up to 11 passengers, ubiquitous throughout remote Aboriginal Australia, and commonly referred to as a 'troop carrier' or 'troopy'. In western Arnhem Land, these *mutika* (vehicles) are used frequently for the transportation of the deceased, after which they are ceremonially smoked and streaked with red ochre.
5 Marett, "Ghostly Voices," 24–25.
6 For an overview of systems of kinship in Aboriginal Australia, see Keen, *Knowledge and Secrecy in an Aboriginal Religion*, 174–209. For western Arnhem Land kinship terms, see Khaki Marrala, *Kindi Ngamin Nuwung? What Do I Call you? A Guide to Kinship and Address* (Jabiru: Iwaidja Inyman and West Arnhem Shire Council, 2008).
7 See Myrna Tonkinson, "Solidarity in Shared Loss: Death-Related Observances Among the Martu of the Western Desert," in *Mortality, Mourning and Mortuary Practices in Indigenous Australia*, ed. Katie Glaskin et al. (Surrey: Ashgate, 2008): 37–54.
8 Morphy, *Journey to the Crocodile's Nest*, 37.
9 Howard Morphy and Frances Morphy, "Afterword: Demography and Destiny," in *Mortality, Mourning and Mortuary Practices in Indigenous Australia*, ed. Katie Glaskin et al. (Surrey: Ashgate, 2008), 210–11.
10 Isaiah Nagurrgurrba, in conversation with the author, Gunbalanya, 17 August 2011.
11 See Morphy, *Journey to the Crocodile's Nest*, 44–45.
12 Reid observes that *lorrkkon* is no longer widely practised in northeast Arnhem Land. Reid, "A Time to Live, a Time to Grieve," 328.
13 Spencer, *Native Tribes of the Northern Territory*, 240. Spencer spent time with Gaagadju speakers who are no longer the dominant group in Gunbalanya.
14 For further discussion about the significance of burial on Country, see Deborah Bird Rose, *Dingo Makes us Human: Life and Land in an Australian Aboriginal Culture* (Cambridge: Cambridge University Press, 2009), 73.
15 See McKenzie, *Waiting for Harry*.
16 Cf. earlier discussions of the "life cycle," Chapters 1 and 3.
17 Linda Barwick et al., "West Arnhem Land Song Project Data Collection," Endangered Language Archive, https://elar.soas.ac.uk/Collection/MPI1013566
18 See Fiona Magowan, *Melodies of Mourning: Music and Emotion in Northern Australia* (Crawley: UWA Press, 2007); Peter Toner, "Tropes of Longing and Belonging: Nostalgia and Musical Instruments in Northeast Arnhem Land," *Yearbook for Traditional Music* 37 (2005): 4.
19 As Marett explains, this is the Aboriginal English word for the ceremony, which does not have a proper noun in Marri Tjevin, the language spoken by *wangga* groups at Wadeye. At Belyuen, Batjamalh speakers call the ceremony *kapuk*, which means 'wash' or 'bathe', referring to the purification ritual at the end of the ceremony (also practised in western Arnhem Land). Marett, *Songs, Dreamings, Ghosts*, 60–61.
20 Marett, "Ghostly Voices," 25–26; Marett, *Songs, Dreamings, Ghosts*, 31.
21 Meiki Elizabeth Apted, "Songs from the Inyjalarrku: The Use of a Non-Translatable Spirit Language in a Song Set from North-West Arnhem Land, Australia," *Australian Journal of Linguistics* 30, no. 1 (2010): 101.
22 Funeral ceremonies that I attended in and around Gunbalanya during my fieldwork commonly featured two or three song-sets by singers either residing in the region of the deceased or visiting from outside the region, usually from central Arnhem Land or the Daly region.

23 Ross and Wild, "Formal Performance," 209. Toner, "Tropes of Longing and Belonging," 4.
24 For an extended performance of Stanley Djalarra Rankin and others singing and dancing these songs on their country of Gulerri, see: "Wakwak: A Wurrkigandjarr Performance", Batchelor Institute for Indigenous Tertiary Education, 2015, https://ictv.com.au/video/item/3125, accessed 1 September 2021.
25 Ross and Wild, "Formal Performance," 213. Borsboom suggests that the crow is somewhat ambiguous: not only is it associated with death (gathering around dead animals and humans) but also with life (eating berries and other fruits). Thus, its ritual significance marks 'the link that exists between life and death in Aboriginal philosophy'. Adrianus Petrus Borsboom, "Yolngu Ways of Knowing Country" (paper presented at *Barks, Birds and Billabongs* symposium, Canberra, 2009), http://www.nma.gov.au/audio/detail/yolngu-ways-of-knowing-country-insights-from-the-1948-expedition-to-arnhem-land. For a detailed account of the Wurrkigandjarr song cycle and Wakwak dance, see also Borsboom, "Maradjiri," 106–13.
26 See Barwick, "Musical Form and Style in Murriny Patha Djanba Songs at Wadeye," 349; Marett, Barwick and Ford, *For the Sake of a Song*, 63.
27 See Genevieve Campbell, "Ngarukuruwala—We Sing: The Songs of the Tiwi Islands, Northern Australia" (PhD thesis, University of Sydney, 2013), 47–48. This western Arnhem Land connection would also have made the performance of these songs significant for the occasion of Nakodjok's funeral ceremony.
28 Similar dances were photographed and described by Baldwin Spencer when he travelled to Melville Island in 1911. Spencer, *Native Tribes of the Northern Territory*, 237.
29 For further discussion, see Campbell, "Ngarukuruwala—We Sing," 35.
30 Jon Fitzgerald and Philip Hayward, "At the Confluence: Slim Dusty and Australian Country Music," in *Outback and Urban: Australian Country Music*, ed. Philip Hayward (Gympie: AICM Press, 2003), 43.
31 See Clinton Walker, *Buried Country: The Story of Aboriginal Country Music* (Sydney: Pluto Press, 2000).
32 For a Kunwinjku and English transcription of the eulogy given on behalf of Nakodjok's family, see Murray Garde, "Nakodjok Namanilakarr," Bininj Kunwok blog, 27 June 2012, https://bininjkunwok.org.au/nakodjok-namanilakarr
33 This interpretation was informed by discussions with David Manmurulu, personal communication, Warruwi, 3 November 2012.
34 Toner, "Tropes of Longing and Belonging," 5–6.
35 See Book of Births, Deaths and Marriages, 1950–1965, Box 6, Location 75/5/4, Northern Territory Archives.
36 See Barwick and Marett, "Snapshots of Musical Life," 364–65.
37 Alfred Nayinggul, personal communication, 16 November 2012.
38 See Ronald Wilson, Bringing Them Home: Report of the National Inquiry into the Separation of Aboriginal and Torres Strait Islander Children from their Families (Sydney: Human Rights and Equal Opportunity Commission, 1997).
39 This translation was assisted by Ruth Singer, who observes that the phrase is similar to an expression such as 'break (someone's) heart' in English. In this example, a transitive prefix is missing which would provide a clearer meaning of the expression. Ruth Singer, personal communication, 25 February 2013.
40 By singing next to the bough shelter.
41 Russell Agalara, Reuben Brown and Solomon Nangamu, "That Spirit Changed My Voice: The Performance of *Kun-borrk* at a Funeral Ceremony in Mikkinj Valley, Western Arnhem Land" (paper presented at Musicological Society of Australia Annual Conference, Canberra, 2012).
42 Solomon Nangamu, personal communication, 25 November 2012.
43 https://dx.doi.org/10.26278/Y3XF-RH12

44 https://dx.doi.org/10.26278/GAKA-1V19
45 https://dx.doi.org/10.26278/ZPPX-Y191
46 https://dx.doi.org/10.26278/R92P-CS53
47 https://dx.doi.org/10.26278/7DCY-FT93
48 https://dx.doi.org/10.26278/R92P-CS53
49 https://dx.doi.org/10.26278/C340-QV80
50 https://dx.doi.org/10.26278/TRJ3-PX49
51 Solomon Nangamu, personal communication, 25 November 2012.
52 Also the Mawng word for 'woman'.
53 https://dx.doi.org/10.26278/0780-6C83
54 Nangamu translated this term as 'daughter'; however, it may also refer to any child, from the perspective of the mother.
55 Note that the last group of moderate-slow songs, including the *ngaya* and *nigi*, are not represented in Table 5.2, as they were not recorded.
56 https://dx.doi.org/10.26278/2DDD-JM79
57 Refer to song inheritance for Mirrijpu song-set, Figure 2.3, Chapter 2.
58 Agalara, Brown and Nangamu, "That Spirit Changed My Voice."
59 For similar discussion in relation to northeast Arnhem Land *manikay*, see Steven Knopoff, "Yuta Manikay: Juxtaposition of Ancestral and Contemporary Elements in the Performance of Yolngu Clan Songs," *Yearbook for Traditional Music* 24 (1992); Peter Toner, "Ideology, Influence and Innovation: The Impact of Macassan Contact on Yolngu Music," *Perfect Beat: Pacific Journal of Research into Contemporary Music and Popular Culture* 5, no. 1 (2000): 35–37.
60 See Appendix 4.3 in Brown, "Following Footsteps."
61 [20120628_02-RB_06_01_MP18.wav, https://dx.doi.org/10.26278/89X8-E947].
62 [20120628_02-RB_07_02_MP21.wav, https://dx.doi.org/10.26278/YWX4-PK75].
63 Agalara, Brown and Nangamu, "That Spirit Changed My Voice."

6 'I'll Tell You This Corroboree Song'

An intercultural exchange in 1948

Playing it back

In October 1948, at the end of a hot dry season in western Arnhem Land, journalist Colin Simpson of the Australian Broadcasting Commission and technician Ray Giles visited the Aboriginal mission of Oenpelli to record the events of the American-Australian Scientific Expedition to Arnhem Land for a radio feature titled *Expedition to Arnhem Land*. Expedition leader C.P. Mountford had had ambitions to record Aboriginal song and to study 'music in secular and ceremonial life'.[1] However, this aim was not fully realised, in part not only because of equipment failure at the first camp of Groote Eylandt but also because of a lack of expertise in music among the science-focussed Expedition team.[2] Luckily, a small sample of the rich and varied song traditions of the region during this time was captured by Simpson and Giles on their wire recorder, and later archived to acetate disc before being converted to tape, from which it was recently digitised.[3] In total, Simpson and Giles recorded just 11 public-genre songs at Gunbalanya.[4] Yet, it is likely that they witnessed many more performances of *kun-borrk/manyardi* and other public-genre songs during their stay.

The first time I played back the recordings at Gunbalanya in 2011, more than 60 years after they had been made, I sat with Jimmy Kalarriya, Don Namundja, and Isaiah Nagurrgurrba in the screen printing room of Injalak Arts and Crafts Centre. The two elders, Kalarriya and Namundja, were living at Gunbalanya in 1948, and remembered the Expedition's visit. Now, they sat as close as they could to the large computer screen, eagerly watching and listening to the playback of the media files, while the sounds of a staple gun and hair drier punctuated our discussion, as other artists printed t-shirts for the upcoming Stone Country Festival at Gunbalanya. As I paused and reviewed the audio and video playback for these two old men, Nagurrgurrba helped to pause and review the conversation, translating their commentary into English for me, and my questions back into Kunwinjku for them, while posing questions of his own in Kunwinjku and relaying the answers back to me in English. (Later, as I began to speak a little bit of Kunwinjku, Kalarriya would encourage my language learning by conversing with me almost entirely in his language.)[5] Kalarriya and Namundja relished the

DOI: 10.4324/9781003216339-7

opportunity that the playback afforded to elucidate the relationship of the old people in the recordings with the people alive today. Seen through Kalarriya's and Namundja's eyes, once anonymous 'Stone Age' people of Arnhem Land (as they had once been presented to the world by the likes of Mountford)[6] were now Bininj/Arrarrkpi subjects with specific kin relationships to everyone seated in that screen printing room. While watching National Geographic footage of Bininj/Arrarrkpi shooting buffalo for example (AVEx_6.1), Nagurrgurrba asked Kalarriya and Namundja about the identity of the men in the film. Kalarriya not only identified them, but also explained their relationship to Nagurrgurrba, using *kun-derbi* kin terms which encode triangular relations:[7]

IN: *Nani wardi ngurribenkukna?*
 Try and recognise all these people?
 [RB pauses playback at 01:19 as JK identifies Jonathan Marangurra]
JK: Daughter one *nuye ngadburrung ngalbali ngundimanjmeng. Nakorddo nawu ngane danginj*[8]
 This man of *Nakorddo Ngalbali* clan name is my brother [to IN using *kun-derbi* term: brother to me and maternal grandfather to you]

Kalarriya was one of the spriteliest, most engaging, and independent men I met at Gunbalanya. This was despite his physical limitations: he could not walk, suffered from a lung condition, and was missing joints on the fingers of one of his hands as a result of leprosy when he was a young man. Kalarriya's small stature belied the attention he could command, owing to both his standing as a senior cultural elder and his high penetrating voice, which could project far beyond the space that he occupied. He could always be spotted riding around town on his electric wheelchair—or 'cord-runner' as it was locally known—with his six dogs orbiting him, as he made the daily commute from his home in Arrkuluk camp to Injalak Arts and Crafts Centre. Here, Kalarriya's bark paintings featured prominently in the gallery, depicting aspects of ceremonial law and Bininj culture and mythology. Not only did painting provide him and his family with an important source of income, but it also allowed him to pass on his knowledge to younger generations of Bininj through the process of producing the painting, and to the broader community through exhibitions of his artworks organised by IAC.

Kalarriya was born 'in the bush' near the Mankorlord area of central Arnhem Land, and like other Bininj from the plateau country, he first came in with his family to the mission at Oenpelli and would go back and forth for rations of flour, sugar, and tea:

We bin all come in here—two my mother, and all of my brother—Oenpelli.[9] We bin touch... flour, sugar and smoke, we bin start here...we bin taste [it] long time you know.[10] 'Oh, good tucker' we reckon—white man tucker. But same sugarbag—bush honey—we bin using long time. And yam...[11]

I'll Tell You This Corroboree Song': An intercultural exchange in 1948 155

Although some of the Balanda tucker made some people sick, they could go back to the bush to fish, hunt, and collect bush honey and yam as they had always done, while taking advantage of the availability of sugar and tobacco which required less work to collect compared with traditional bush foods:

> Sugarbag, you cut him, cut axe, hard work, and you climb up and cut 'em. And even yam, you crack 'im, you get 'im. But Balanda [tucker], more easy one.[12]

Kalarriya grew up on the mission before he went and worked for a buffalo shooting contractor at Pine Creek and Canon Hill, southwest of Oenpelli. During this time, he learned to ride horseback, and got his English name—Jimmy—from the Balanda who employed him. Kalarriya was also 'travelling everywhere'—as *kakkawarr* (K: ceremonial messenger) for the regional men's initiation ceremony, bringing participants from Beswick, Bulman, and 'sunrise' (eastern Arnhem Land) to the ceremony.[13] World War Two afforded work for Aboriginal people in places such as Darwin, Adelaide River, and Larrimah, where they worked as stockmen and drovers or were recruited to the Armed Forces.[14]

That morning of the first playback, we listened through each of the 11 songs recorded by Simpson, originally from ABC Radio Archives disc MA24 (referred to hereafter as the 'Simpson recordings'),[15] and viewed 17 short silent colour films (non-restricted), shot for the National Geographic Society by Howell Walker (referred to hereafter as 'NGS footage'),[16] as well as photos taken by Setzler at Gunbalanya in 1948. Such was Kalarriya's knowledge of the songs that he recognised their origin immediately on first hearing. With the help of Namundja and the other artists, he also identified many of the Bininj/Arrarrkpi in the films and photographs, and gave Kunwinjku names for the places where the films had been taken.

On my laptop, I selected tracks from the Simpson recordings from an iTunes library, where I entered song information, such as the names of the singers and the category, language, and genre of the songs. The distinctive crackling sound of the record needle on acetate disc—captured during the conversion to tape[17]—heralded the start of each recording, along with an archive identification: 'cut one'; 'cut two', etc. Then, the music did its own announcing, beginning with the muffled sound of the didjeridu, followed by the regular beat of the clapsticks and singing in Bininj Kunwok, telling us that this was western Arnhem Land *kun-borrk*. As soon as the singer began singing the first cut, Kalarriya's body froze and his eyes fixed on the computer screen. After some moments, he nodded to himself, and told us that we were listening to his *ngadjadj*—his uncle—Namunurr:

> *Nakohbanj ngadjadj manekke wayihwayini.* Weyirra *kunyed. Oh! Yoh, nungka.* [To Isaiah Nagurrgurrba] *ngorrkbelhwarreeh. Yoh,* Weyirra *kunred. Manekke wanjh wayihwayini, nakohbanj ngadjadj Mukudu nganehyaw. 1948 bu wanjh ngane yahwurdni ngaye nani ngane-yawurdni ngadburrung*

nadjalama [Mukudu]. *Bu* second World War Two. *Birri dulubuleni* Darwin. *Kunukka wanjh ngarri-yahyawurdni*.[18]

That old man singing is my uncle—born at Weyirra (North Goulburn Island). Oh! Yes, that's him! [To Nagurrgurrba] [*kun-derbi* term] My uncle and your nephew. Yes, his country was North Goulburn Island. This song was sung by that old man who is uncle to me and Mukudu [Kalarriya's brother]. Back in 1948, me and him were little boys—my brother of Djalama clan [Mukudu]. During the Second World War, when they were fighting in Darwin. During that time we were little kids.[19]

When the singing on the recording came to an end and the sound of the crackle faded out, Kalarriya called out in appreciation, cocked his head to one side, and made a 'tut-tut' sound in an expression of affection for his uncle. Namunurr's song had been used to aurally set the scene in the opening soundtrack to Simpson's radio feature *Expedition to Arnhem Land*—first broadcast over ABC airwaves in late 1948.[20] The song is not attributed to Namunurr in the radio programme, or in Simpson's book *Adam in Ochre*, or in the ABC Radio Archives. Yet for Kalarriya, this unidentified track—this 'cut one'—was indelibly linked to the memory of his uncle. Like other Arrarrkpi songmen living in Gunbalanya today such as Nangamu, Namunurr spoke Kunwinjku, but was born on North Goulburn Island, and spoke the languages of the 'saltwater country', including his traditional language of Manangkardi, as well as Marrku/Malwakardi and Mawng.[21] For Kalarriya, not only was this song linked to the memory of Namunurr at Gunbalanya, but it was also linked to the time when he was only a young boy, during the Second World War when the Japanese bombed Darwin harbour in 1942, some six years before the Expedition's visit.[22]

With each playback session, more details began to emerge, as connections between the past and the present were made, and a broader picture of Bininj/Arrarrkpi life in Gunbalanya during '1948 time' started to crystallise. On one occasion, I sat with Kalarriya outside Injalak Arts and Crafts Centre, facing the town of Gunbalanya, with Injalak Hill behind us. With my laptop on my knees and some portable speakers in Kalarriya's lap—the volume turned up to maximum—we began listening to the songs. He pointed towards Banyan camp on the northern side of town and explained how all the '*arrapujpa* (M: beautiful) singermen' from Goulburn and Croker Islands would come together with singers from Gunbalanya to sing under the tamarind tree, where the 'single men's cottage' now stands. I wondered whether this was one of the locations where Simpson and Giles had recorded at Oenpelli? Tamarind trees can be found all over western Arnhem Land—originally planted at various sites along the saltwater country where the Macassans camped during their yearly voyages, such as Wigu Point on Goulburn Island.[23] Kalarriya explained that during this time, he still lived in Mankorlord, and would stay at a place called Mibarndal when he came to Oenpelli mission, near the ceremony ground at Arrkuluk Hill (where the reburial ceremony described in Chapter 3 took place):

'I'll Tell You This Corroboree Song': An intercultural exchange in 1948 157

Birri-wayini-wirrinj dabbarrabbolk nawu birri-dorrobeng kurinangarri-ye-di kuni ngarri-wernh-Mibarndal. Kaluk bolkimme missionary marnbom Mr Cook my brother, *[sic] Karri derrehkeng ngadberre konda, but ngad ngarri [?]* missionary time *Mibarndal[a?] Manmi-nakeb-kali-yidi-yo-wurrme-ngadi-yoy.* Missionary time. *And birri-rey dabbarrabbolk birrim-rey two island an birri-wayini ngadberre, kun-borrk.*[24]

They sang here, those old people, where you are sitting. We[25] [lived in Mibarndal in those days?]. Missionaries—Mr Cook my [classificatory] brother built here, [before we moved here?] [but in those days we slept further out and came in for food?] And the old people from the two islands sang our songs, *kun-borrk*.

The ability to store large data on a portable external hard drive and play it on the screen of a laptop in the field allowed assisted Bininj/Arrarrkpi to 'repatriate' these recordings, in a quite literal sense. Many playback sessions were held in the locations where the recordings and photos had originally been captured, allowing us to retrace the footsteps of Bininj/Arrarrkpi in the recordings. Isaiah Nagurrgurrba was intimate with the galleries and burial places of Injalak Hill, and took a keen interest in the intercultural history at Gunbalanya, in particular, the episode of Setzler's theft of bones from Injalak in 1948. Together with the late artist Nabulanj Namok Allan Nadjamerrek, he took colleague and ARC Research Associate Amanda Harris and me up the hill so that we could see the places that Setzler visited in 1948. Nagurrgurrba had examined in forensic detail Frank Setzler's black and white photographs[26] (referred to hereafter as 'Setzler photographs') and the NGS footage of Setzler taking human remains.[27] We carried the photos up on my laptop, and Nagurrgurrba pointed out the exact location from where the bones were likely to have been removed. On another occasion, Kalarriya arranged a playback session with Nagurrgurrba, his brother Mukudu, and other members of his family, at an old mission era shed in Arrkuluk camp—near Mibarndal where they had listened to the songs in their childhood. Some of those present at this playback session had previously worked on buffalo skinning camps. As they watched footage of Bininj/Arrarrkpi skinning buffalo at a place they identified as *Ukenj* near Red Lily Billabong, they commented on how hard a job it was in those days to lift the enormous buffalo hide, carry it into the water, and then lay it out to dry to be salted, as depicted in the film (watch **AVEx_6.1**).

AVex_6.1 https://dx.doi.org/10.26278/691D-C745

158 *'I'll Tell You This Corroboree Song': An intercultural exchange in 1948*

Kalarriya enjoyed listening to the Simpson recordings in particular. He listened intently, and I would pause the playback to ask him questions about the song, or to elicit the song text. He would speak for a little while; then, after a few minutes he would say, "one more *yi-kurrmeng, Balang*, and *ngarre-bekkan*" (K: "play one more song, Balang,[28] and let's [you and I] listen to it"). Sometimes, one of his hands seemed to involuntarily circle to the rhythm of the didjeridu and clapsticks, and he would start singing along. He would ask me to replay the songs most familiar to him—*wardde-ken* songs were his first preference, followed by *kurrula,* and then the songs from the Daly.[29] For some songs, he requested that I repeat the playback several times, in order for him to pick out the words of the song text. I had the feeling that the performers were right there with him and that he was 'tuning in' to the song, reliving the experience of some past performance.

Just as the recording could evoke for someone like Kalarriya the particular social, cultural, and performative context in which it was originally made, it could also be reframed, recontextualised, and reinterpreted, depending on where, when, how, and for whom it was played. After adding Simpson's recordings to the iTunes music library at Gunbalanya, I observed that some of the Injalak artists selected songs to add to their own personal music playlist (alongside a diverse range of popular music, from Bob Marley to AC/DC), which they listened to while they worked. Once more, the artists generally chose songs that belonged to *wardde-ken* song-sets—particularly those in Kunwinjku—that were the most familiar to them. At the Stone Country Festival at Gunbalanya in 2011 and again in 2012 (see Chapter 7), I helped facilitate a playback of the NGS footage at Gunbalanya, which was projected on a screen behind the performers, cross-fading back and forth with a live feed of the performance on stage.

The effect of the projection was interesting and unpredictable, depending on the way that the film lined up with the action on stage. At times, people in the crowd called out and cheered as they recognised their ancestors in the footage, collecting lily roots at Red Lily Billabong, making fire with a stick the traditional way, or shooting buffalo and digging for turtle on the floodplains. They pointed towards the actual location of the place shown in the film, as they recognised it on the screen. The footage often fitted the sentiment of the live music, as various bands sang about their ancestral country, and in the case of the Wildflower Band (based in Gunbalanya and the nearby outstation of Mamadawerre), about their affection for Gunbalanya. At other times—as when the footage showed mammalogist David Johnson dissecting and stuffing a spotted quoll—the response was one of bemusement and intrigue.

The playback of the 1948 recordings immediately became a device that elders such as Kalarriya could use to teach younger generations. During earlier playback sessions (see Support Material Figure 6.i), grandchildren of Kalarriya spontaneously dropped by, curious to know what he was watching or listening to. He would explain to them for as long as he could hold their attention. In November 2011, I accompanied Kalarriya and Nagurrgurrba for a one-off visit to Jabiru Youth Centre with manager Joel Saint-Clare so that they could speak to Bininj students attending the *An-gare ga-dokme* (G: 'Culture First') programme

'I'll Tell You This Corroboree Song': An intercultural exchange in 1948   159

at the local school. The class consisted of Bininj students living in and around Jabiru and outstations in Kakadu National Park. Kalarriya spoke to the children in their ancestral language of Kundjeyhmi, explained to each of them their relationship to him through their family, and then spoke about what life was like during the missionary time depicted in the films. The session involved playing back the films and some of the recordings, followed by questions from the students. Initially shy, they soon gained confidence to ask Kalarriya and Nagurrgurrba about what life was like *korroko*. At the end of the session, the Balanda teacher commented that he had never before seen the students so attentive and focussed.

Thomas has observed that for the Expedition, 'science must not only be done, but seen to be done by as large an audience as possible'.[30] Watching the NGS footage during these playback sessions, I observed a general formula to the film-making. First, Bininj/Arrarrkpi would be shown going about their daily business (collecting food, hunting, making fire, etc.). Then, the camera would zoom in on the 'prize' (fish, turtle, fire, etc.), followed by some rather gratuitous staged close-ups of Bininj/Arrarrkpi smiling for the camera, as if to fit a simplistic narrative for a Balanda audience. For example, in one of the films,[31] a young woman—identified as the mother of another contemporary artist and tour guide Thompson Nganjmirra—appears with nutritionist Margaret McArthur and three other *yawkyawk* (K: girls) at an area known as *kulukang*, where the Club at Gunbalanya now stands. Demonstrating for the camera how Bininj/Arrarrkpi collect the red bush apple (K: *man-djarduk*), she first throws a stick into a branch of the tree to try and knock it down, and then climbs up the trunk and plucks the fruit herself, resting on a branch. From her position up in the tree, she holds out the fruit for the NGS camera below, then the film cuts to a shot of the collected fruit on the ground, followed by the *yawkyawk* sitting neatly in a row, consuming the fruit and giving some rather forced smiles for the camera. This 'smiling with fruit' take is then reshot several times over (watch **AVEx_6.2**).

AVex_6.2 https://dx.doi.org/10.26278/8PXR-C641

Although the staged nature of some of these recordings gives the NGS footage an awkward look and feel at times, in some ways the fact that the film is silent lends it a degree of authenticity; it is almost as though in the absence of a narrative or emotionally manipulative musical soundtrack, the Balanda film-maker's intentions are laid bare. Watching the footage in silence, I liked to imagine the confusing intercultural exchange that might have taken place between the film-maker and Bininj/Arrarrkpi subjects, as they attempted to stage the action and get the 'right' take. Of course, the Expedition's recordings were never intended

160 'I'll Tell You This Corroboree Song': An intercultural exchange in 1948

to be viewed this way; to be made sense of by the Bininj/Arrarrkpi communities that helped produce them.[32] Yet once returned to Gunbalanya and played back to people like Kalarriya, Namundja, Nagurrgurrba, and current-day songmen with specialist knowledge, they had become recontextualised and re-embedded, both within Bininj/Arrarrkpi society and within the landscape.

***

Having described the repatriation and playback of the songs and media in Gunbalanya—a performance event in itself which can conjure memory, and act as a vehicle for passing on knowledge—the second part of this chapter reconstructs the performance events that led to Simpson and Giles' recordings at Gunbalanya, based on both the written accounts of Balanda who were there in 1948, and insights provided by Bininj/Arrarrkpi during the playback sessions. In doing so, it draws on recent research by scholars such as Barwick, Birch, Garde, McIntosh, and Thomas,[33] providing a perspective on the events of the Expedition that acknowledges the role of Aboriginal people such as Larry Marawana who helped the Expedition to negotiate the cultural landscape of Arnhem Land, but were not acknowledged in the official records.[34]

The third section of this chapter builds on Barwick and Marett's analysis of Colin Simpson's recordings from 1948 in Oenpelli. Barwick and Marett suggest that Simpson's recordings can be considered 'aural snapshots' which represent 'partial record[s] constrained by the time, place and means of [their] capture',[35] divorced of the complex performance tradition to which they belong. In particular, they examine the *kapuk* (rag-burning) ceremony recorded by Simpson at Delissaville the same year, and trace the continuity of this performance with others subsequently recorded by the authors in later years, and performed by the descendants of those Simpson recorded.[36] My analysis of the public recordings from Gunbalanya—informed by cultural elders and current songmen who were familiar with both the musical and literary language of the songs—details the diverse repertories recorded, and draws similarities to songs that are still performed. The songs were a source of great pride and interest for current-day songmen, whose own cultural practice was validated through the process of listening to their relatives' song-making from this period.[37] Simpson and Giles encountered a diverse song tradition in 1948 that included music not only from Gunbalanya but also from Goulburn and Croker Islands, and further afield to the Daly region. Today, these groups continue to visit and perform their songs at Gunbalanya. Considering these findings, I argue that the exercise of returning archival media not only shone new light on old recordings; it revealed the agency of Bininj/Arrarrkpi in helping to curate the songs that were recorded for the broader public and for future generations to hear.

Reconstructing the exchange

Music was a regular part of Bininj/Arrarrkpi social life in 1948 and was never far from the experience of the Expedition members during their time at Gunbalanya

'I'll Tell You This Corroboree Song': An intercultural exchange in 1948 161

and surrounds. The diaries of nutritionist Margaret McArthur, cook John Bray, ichthyologist Bob Miller, secretary Bessie Mountford, and anthropologist Fred McCarthy all make mention of corroboree—or 'singsong' as some called it—as an almost daily occurrence. As Amanda Harris writes:

> The auditory experiences they wrote about fell into three categories: hearing Aboriginal music drifting from nearby camps after dark; on rare occasions, gramophone music or shortwave radio bringing familiar culture from afar; and camp songs that were a spontaneous feature of many an evening's entertainment in the bush.[38]

Harris suggests that for John Bray in particular, the experience of listening to the music of the Gumardir River people each night—while accompanying nutritionist Margaret McArthur outside of Gunbalanya at a place called Kunnanj (Fish Creek)—changed the way he heard Aboriginal music, and gave him a deeper perspective of Aboriginal culture.[39] In his diary entries during this period,[40] Bray describes the 'charming songs with varying rhythms'[41] of men's didjeridu and clapstick-accompanied song, and expresses feeling comforted while listening to their music by the light of the full moon.[42] Bray's impressions highlight the role that *kun-borrk/manyardi* played in facilitating the exchange taking place between the visitors and their hosts. Listening to *kun-borrk* at Kunnanj enabled Bray to feel less estranged in the foreign cultural environment he found himself in. For Bininj/Arrarrkpi, Bray's involvement in their social rituals would have also helped to normalise the 'research' taking place on their country, which required them to interact and cooperate with strangers from outside their broader kinship network.

The decision as to which song repertories and songs would be suitable to record for public distribution was evidently something that was negotiated amongst the Aboriginal songmen who were present at Gunbalanya during Simpson and Giles' stay. As Simpson explains in *Adam in Ochre*, the singers were made aware of the fact that the recording would be broadcast nationally on the ABC,[43] and they had the opportunity to listen back and discuss the recordings, and even to rerecord those songs that they were not happy with (see Figure 6.1). As I discuss later in this chapter, with this knowledge, the singers ensured a cross-section of different repertories from all over the Top End was captured on the wire recorder.[44]

So who exactly was present during these recordings, and in what context did they occur? By triangulating notes from the Expedition members' diaries,[45] Colin Simpson's (non-chronological) account in *Adam in Ochre*, and information gained from playback sessions about the songs with contemporary consultants, we can sketch a rough outline of the sequence of events during Simpson and Giles' stay at Gunbalanya, and tentatively place Simpson's recordings and the NGA footage within this timeline of events (see Support Material Figure 6.ii). Soon after arriving at Gunbalanya on 15 October 1948, Simpson and Giles took part in a buffalo shooting and skinning excursion to Red Lily Billabong. Approximately half of the musical recordings ('MA24 Cuts 1–6') appear to have been made over two evenings during this trip: on 17 October, when Bessie Mountford writes of Simpson

162 *'I'll Tell You This Corroboree Song': An intercultural exchange in 1948*

Figure 6.1 Larry Marawana and group listening to recordings of *kun-borrk/manyardi* made at Red Lily billabong, Gunbalanya, 1948. Clockwise from left: Larry Marawana, unidentified man, Djambunuwa, Ray Giles, Colin Simpson and Tommy Madjalkaidj. Photograpah by Howell Walker. NLA MS5253, Box 99, Bag B, by permission of the National Library of Australia.

and Giles recording Aboriginal men singing 'with drone pipe and stick'[46] and on 18 October, when she describes falling asleep to the sound of [Bill] Harney talking, the Aboriginal men 'singing and playing their instruments', and 'scurrying creatures'.[47] Red Lily is situated in Manilakarr clan country on the floodplains west of Gunbalanya, close to the Arnhem Land escarpment. Simpson describes the area in which he camped in 1948 in the following way: 'east of our camp at Red Lily the sandstone rose in a great cliff, flanked by a craggy hill of sparse bush tangled between big outcrops of fretted grey rock'.[48] Walker also filmed at Red Lily, possibly nearby their camp.[49] Today, one passes by Red Lily Billabong on the road to Gunbalanya, about six kilometres after crossing the East Alligator

I'll Tell You This Corroboree Song': An intercultural exchange in 1948 163

River and entering into Arnhem Land. During their four-day stay at Red Lily, Simpson, Giles, and Howell Walker accompanied the group of buffalo shooters to various locations further from the camp to conduct buffalo hunts. Simpson describes one of these locations as 'about 15 miles from Gunbalanya... under a big milkwood tree in a clump of shade near a waterhole on the edge of the plain'. This is likely the place known to Bininj as *Ukenj*, identified in the NGS films R03R04-O-4 and R03R04-O-16.[50]

Those who partook in the Red Lily excursion included Simpson and Giles, Bessie Mountford and Charles Mountford ('Monty'), Bill Harney, Howell Walker, and two buffalo hunters employed by the Oenpelli mission: Len Hillier and Aub Dunkley. The identity of the Bininj/Arrarrkpi participants is less certain: Simpson's records make mention of several men, women, and children at Red Lily, most prominently his interpreter and guide 'Larry' Marawana, who was Simpson's main interlocutor and translator. Their interaction is captured in 'Cut 7', where Marawana gives an explanation for one of the songs, and again in 'Cut 8', where he identifies himself as the singer of the previous 'Cut 7', along with didjeridu player 'Tommy' Madjalkaidj (after whom Inyjalarrku singer Nangarridj Tommy Madjalkaidj is named).[51] Marawana was present during most of the recordings, helping to convey information to Simpson and Giles about the origins of the various song-sets that were recorded. For example, Simpson writes on another occasion 'when Marawana told me they were ready to start I held the mike to him and he said into it that they would sing a song of the blue tongued lizard totem of the Gunwinggu tribe'.[52] This most likely refers to 'Cut 10', which Jimmy Kalarriya identified as belonging to the Kurri (K: blue tongue lizard) song-set, sung by Manilakarr clansman Philip Nayuku of Nangarridj subsection (and brother of Nakodjok Jacob Nayinggul's father, Olamatta).[53]

Other Bininj/Arrarrkpi participants mentioned by Simpson include 'Paddy', 'John', his wife 'Millie', and some 'young boys', as well as 'Naalbrit'.[54] The man Simpson referred to as 'Paddy' may have been singer 'Paddy Bull' of Nangarridj subsection, while 'John' is likely to be Jonathan Nakorddo Marangurra of Nawamud subsection, identified by Jimmy Kalarriya as the figure with ammunition around his waist in NGS footage R01R02-O-04; 'Naalbrit' is possibly a mishearing of 'Namarrabundja' of Nangarridj subsection, who Namarnyilk identified as the man standing next to Jonathan Marangurra in the same footage (see Support Material Figure 6.iii). Kalarriya also identified his uncle Nabulanj Joseph Gameraidj as another of the men involved in the buffalo shooting party (see Support Material Figure 6.iv). Kalarriya explained that like many Bininj, Kamarradj had come to Gunbalanya for work in the buffalo industry from his traditional country of Nabarlek, situated further east.

As a consequence of the introduction of Timorese water buffalo to earlier settlements in western Arnhem Land, the feral buffalo population multiplied and spread south from the Cobourg Peninsula across the wetlands and savannah woodlands, as well as spreading over Melville island, numbering in the tens of thousands by the last decade of the nineteenth century.⁵⁵ From the 1890s, a number of buffalo shooting camps were established during the dry season around the East Alligator region, where the buffalo would be shot and their hides skinned in preparation to be sold. Bininj/Arrarrkpi were paid per buffalo hide, drawing on traditional skills to hunt and skin the buffalo, then salt and preserve the hide. While the pay was minimal, the work was local and seasonal which suited many people, and the leftover meat (which couldn't be sold because there was no refrigeration at the time) could be taken home and shared among families.⁵⁶ Buffalo shooter Paddy Cahill bought a pastoral lease for a cattle station at Oenpelli in 1910, which he managed for over a decade, continuing to employ people through the buffalo trade, as well as producing butter and maintaining a vegetable garden. Although some Kunwinjku Bininj at Gunbalanya resented Cahill's authority,⁵⁷ and administrators in Darwin judged his agricultural pursuits as commercially unsuccessful, Mulvaney argues that they overlooked:

> the positive contribution that local self-sufficiency, a nourishing diet and better health made to the welfare of the indigenous community. [Oenpelli cattle station] also provided the labour force with training in white [people's] pursuits, and several men were in paid employment throughout Cahill's tenure.⁵⁸

Another buffalo shooter and major employer of Bininj/Arrarrkpi in western Arnhem Land during this time was Joe Cooper, who lived on Melville Island and established a saw mill at Malay Bay on the Cobourg Peninsula. People from Croker Island and the mainland would come and work at the mill, cutting cypress pine and milling the timber with a saw driven by donkeys and horses, and continuing to collect *trepang* to sell.⁵⁹ Cooper married an Iwaidja woman, and their son, Reuben Cooper, later took over the mill.⁶⁰

The Bininj/Arrarrkpi who accompanied Balanda to Red Lily would have had experience working navigating both the country and the expectations of Balanda from their experience in the buffalo industry. They were not merely passive subjects in the documentation of the Expedition's work, but active producers of it. Simpson also recalls how 'John' and 'Millie' went to rather elaborate lengths— wading out into crocodile-infested water—to assist him and Giles in recording the sound of birds taking off in flight from the billabong.⁶¹

Further references in Simpson's written account give us more clues as to the chronology of events and how these events relate to the audio and visual recordings. Referring to 'Cut 6' (which Marawana identifies as belonging to the Kunbarlang song-set at the start of the recording), Simpson comments: 'John had a didjeridoo propped on one extended foot and to the drone of it Marawana was singing a goonbarlung [*sic*] song as he sat cross-legged, beating the rhythm on two sticks'.⁶² Whereas Simpson identifies Marawana as the singer, during playback Kalarriya identified Balir Balir and/or Bilinyarra as the singers. Listening to the recording, we can hear that there is clearly more than one singer and that the vocal timbre of the main singer is higher and lighter compared with the *Kolobarr* song ('Cut 7') which we know Marawana alone was recorded singing. This suggests that Marawana may have in fact played 'back up' singer to Balir Balir and/or Bilinyarra for this recording of the Kunbarlang song. Elsewhere, Simpson makes reference to 'some of the youths we had with us at Red Lily' who were 'good with the didjeridoo, too, and one night we decided to record some of their campfire songs'.[63] This undoubtedly refers to 'Cuts 11 and 12', which appear to be sung by children. Current-day songmen identified these songs as originating from Goulburn Island, suggesting that the young singers may have been relatives of John and Millie from Goulburn Island.

Although it does not follow chronologically in the ABC Archives, the other half of the recordings ('MA24 Cuts 1-4' and possibly 'Cut 5') appear to have been made back at Oenpelli mission after the Red Lily excursion. Simpson reports that Marawana arranged a corroboree at a place where Aboriginal people camped in 'gunyahs [aboriginal bush huts] of galvanised iron'[64]—possibly the place identified by Kalarriya as Mibarndal. These recordings include songs not only from Gunbalanya, but also from Goulburn Island, Croker Island, and the Daly region (Simpson makes no mention of people from the Daly or Croker Island partaking in the trip to Red Lily, which gives greater plausibility to the suggestion that these songs were recorded back at Oenpelli). As has been noted by other scholars, word of the Expedition's presence in Arnhem Land spread throughout the region, bringing various Aboriginal groups into contact with both Aboriginal and non-Aboriginal people who were taking part in the event.[65] For example, Bessie Mountford notes in her diary on Thursday 7 October 1948 that three Aboriginal men from Croker Island arrived in Oenpelli from a timber camp (Reuben Cooper's saw mill on the Cobourg Peninsula) to buy horses.[66] It is possible that these were the same Croker Island men recorded by Simpson and Giles ('MA24 Cuts 2 and 5') back at Gunbalanya.

Many of the songs that Simpson, Giles, and other Expedition members heard during their stay at Gunbalanya were not recorded on wire, including songs in the *kun-borrk/manyardi* genre composed 'spontaneously', reflecting on 'everyday' events, which are less common today. Simpson describes one such song that was composed by 'Paddy' (likely Paddy Bull, see Table 6.1) on the way back to their camp at Red Lily in the back of the truck carrying buffalo skins. The song reflected on their buffalo hunting excursion, during which buffalo were hunted, shot, and skinned, and the hides were loaded onto the truck and taken to a waterhole where the Aboriginal men washed and salted them (see Support Material Figure 6.iv). Simpson recalls the song text, presumably with the assistance of Marawana in translating from Kunwinjku into English:

> Just before the sunset they went out to shoot
> The truck stood out in the plain
> The shooters on their horses chased the buffaloes towards us,
> They shot them as they came out on the plain.[67]

166   *'I'll Tell You This Corroboree Song': An intercultural exchange in 1948*

This song text appears typical of such 'spontaneously composed' songs in the western Arnhem *kun-borrk* genre—a minimalist and evocative description of an event, suspended in time; the narrator seemingly removed from the action taking place. The text would possibly have been set to an ABCB musical form, and presumably would finish with some kind of vocables or didjeridu mouth sounds. The ambiguity of the song text is also a familiar convention of *kun-borrk/manyardi* and *jurtbirrk* songs: in this case, it is not immediately clear who is the agent and subject of the action ('they', 'them', 'us'). On the other hand, this ambiguity may also have been the result of certain specificities of the original text—presumably in Kunwinjku language—getting 'lost' in the translation to English.[68]

Curating the record of *kun-borrk/manyardi* in 1948

Born in 1913, Marawana was 35 when the Expedition came through Gunbalanya. (Sadly, just five years later in 1953, Marawana died suddenly—the cause of his death recorded as 'unknown'.)[69] Known to Bininj/Arrarrkpi by his skin name Nakodjok, he belonged to the Wurrik clan and was born in the Nimbuwa region near Gunbalanya, and would therefore have had authority to 'guide' the Expedition through country around Gunbalanya. Articulate in English, Kunwinjku, and presumably other Bininj Kunwok languages, Marawana was one of those figures (like Gerald Blitner, the Expedition's guide on Groote Eylandt)[70] who were central to the Expedition's fieldwork—introducing them to the right Aboriginal people, and negotiating with traditional owners around the movements and activities of the Expedition. At both Red Lily and Oenpelli mission, Larry Marawana played a crucial role in orchestrating the corroboree and curating the songs to record, as well as providing contextual information for the songs and ensuring that proper performances were given. Simpson recalls how midway through a song, Marawana stopped playing the didjeridu, and requested politely that Simpson start the recording again, because he had played the 'wrong note':[71]

> We solemnly ran back the wire. After some preliminary tuning up they began again. When it finished we played it back and Marawana, the conscientious artist, listened intently. I looked at him for his approval, and he nodded gravely and said, "orright, that one." Then he added, "thank you." The white people of Australia were not going to hear him blow a wrong note on the didjeridoo, which the white people of Australia would never have heard on the air before.[72]

Writer Allan Marshall, who encountered Marawana at Oenpelli in 1946 a couple of years before the Expedition's visit, describes in his book *Ourselves Writ Strange* how Marawana approached him having learned of his interest in

I'll Tell You This Corroboree Song': An intercultural exchange in 1948 167

Aboriginal culture, telling him: "I know all Old People [K: *kobah-kohbanj*] stories. My father, he tell them to me. I tell them to you".[73] Marawana honed his skills representing Bininj/Arrarrkpi mythology and storytelling in the English language during his exchanges with Marshall. Marshall describes how Marawana carefully rehearsed the stories he would tell to Marshall for the payment of tobacco, which Marshall in turn transcribed:

> He viewed the production of my note-book with an increase in the rate of his breathing and finally there came a time when, with a protective flutter of his hand, he conveyed his desire that I refrain from recording his words until he had first practised and perfected his part. "No I just say it today. Tomorrer—feel good then. You write it tomorrer, eh? I tell it tomorrer, 'nother time."[74]

Whereas the official Expedition records do not acknowledge the important curatorial and diplomatic work that go-betweens and cultural brokers such as Marawana did, Simpson seems to have been more attuned to it. Like Marshall, he was trained as a journalist and storyteller, and was therefore interested in 'real life' narratives. His status as a reporter and outsider to the Expedition team also gave him a degree of freedom from the internal hierarchy of other Expedition members: unlike others, he did not have to conform to what Expedition leader Mountford wanted.[75] In *Adam in Ochre,* Simpson offers some insight into the challenging position in which people like Marawana were at times placed, as they attempted to meet the expectations of Balanda and assist them with their work, while navigating the Bininj/Arrarrkpi social space of Gunbalanya, which was inhabited by multiple clans living together with different modes of operation:

> One day at Oenpelli, he [Marawana] offered to arrange a corroboree for me. That night we took the recording gear up to the camp near the mission where the natives lived, most of them in gunyahs of galvanised iron. We waited for the corroboree and nothing happened and I said testily to Marawana that we couldn't wait all night. He harangued the people. They laughed at him. It was painful to watch. Eventually they gave a few songs—but not until they had let us see that they did not dance whenever our "Larry" called the tune.[76]

Although he was arguably more attuned to the Bininj/Arrarrkpi social world around him than others writing during this period, even Simpson was at times unaware of the cultural information offered to him by his guide. A recorded exchange between Simpson and Marawana reveals for me a possible disjunction between an emphasis by Bininj/Arrarrkpi on the uniqueness of their oral and performance traditions on the one hand, and the focus of the European outsiders on more material aspects of Bininj/Arrarrkpi culture—rock art, hunting and gathering, etc. In this exchange, Marawana begins by telling Simpson the name of the song-set he performed:

168 *'I'll Tell You This Corroboree Song': An intercultural exchange in 1948*

Marawana: Ah, I tell you this corroboree song, we callim Kolobarr. An we don't using it for, like a boomerang, and for... we never using-a boomerangs...

Kolobarr means 'big red' kangaroo in Kunwinjku and also refers to the name of a song-set in a special genre called *morrdjdjanjno* (discussed later in this chapter).[77] Marawana is most likely referring to the fact that songs are played with clapsticks, rather than boomerangs, as in Central Australia (watch **AVEx_6.3**, in which Marawana appears to demonstrate playing with boomerang clapsticks).[78]

AVex_6.3 https://dx.doi.org/10.26278/QQAC-8J21

Perhaps having rehearsed some of the material for the recording earlier, Simpson knows that *kolobarr* means 'kangaroo', and jumps in (so to speak) with another question. However, he possibly mistakes Marawana's comment as referring to the way Bininj/Arrarrkpi *hunt* the *kolobarr*, rather than the way that they *sing* the Kolobarr [song-set]:

Simpson: What do you hunt this kangaroo with?
Marawana: Oh, we hunt the kangaroo with the shovel spear...
Simpson: Yes?
Marawana: ...and the stone spear
Simpson: Mmm.
Marawana: —that's all we can do
Simpson: ...and this is a song from the kangaroo corroboree of the Kunwinjku people?
Marawana: ...yeah, and we call this Kolobarr[79]

These glimpses of Marawana's interaction with Simpson tell us something of the way in which he was attempting to educate Balanda about Bininj/Arrarrkpi cultural traditions—a role he appeared to enjoy, in spite of the challenges he shouldered in helping to carry out much of the negotiating work of the Expedition. Such interactions also make it clear that Simpson's recordings were not just random 'fragments', but carefully curated samples (or 'snapshots' as Barwick and Marett have called them) chosen in order to reflect something of the richness of the song traditions of Bininj/Arrarrkpi and neighbouring Aboriginal groups during this time.

I'll Tell You This Corroboree Song': An intercultural exchange in 1948 169

Diversity of song in 1948

Barwick and Marett's preliminary research into the origins of Simpson's 1948 recordings at Gunbalanya, based on information provided by Iwaidja informants, found that many of the songs recorded in 1948 originated from outside Gunbalanya.[80] Similarly, Bininj/Arrarrkpi respondents at Gunbalanya and Warruwi confirmed the mixed origins of the songs, which included both *wardde-ken* 'stone country' songs and *kurrula* 'saltwater' songs from Croker and Goulburn Islands, as well as some *wangga* songs from the Daly region, previously identified by Iwaidja respondents as 'Jawoyn sweetheart' songs.[81] Mawng elder Rosemary Urabadi and Inyjalarrku singer Renfred Manmurulu commented that Bininj/Arrarrkpi used to travel to other communities in October around the time that the Expedition visited Gunbalanya and that Marawana likely sent out a message stick about the Expedition's visit to those singers at Goulburn Island, who came and camped at Gunbalanya and recorded their songs.[82] Table 6.1 (see also Support Material Figure 6.v) locates the origins of the song repertories recorded at Gunbalanya in 1948 in relation to Aboriginal languages in the Top End, showing how the songs originated not only from neighbouring language groups around Gunbalanya but also from further afield, including Iwaidja and Marrku speakers to the north and Batjamalh speakers to the west.

Many of the singers from the 1948 recordings were born in the country surrounding Gunbalanya, and were related to traditional owner families living at Gunbalanya today, such as the Gumurdul and Nayinggul families. Wurrik clansman Larry Marawana was identified by Kalarriya as the grandfather of Gabby Gumurdul, a traditional owner of Gunbalanya. Nakangkila Frank Djendjorr Namornkodj, identified as the singer of songs 'Cut 9' and 'Cut 10', was also of Mirarr clan—a traditional owner of the country near Madjinbardi outstation. Connie Nayinggul remembered how Frank used to sing 'love songs' about his wife, for the entertainment of his daughters and for the Nayinggul family, when they stayed at Madjinbardi.[83] Kalarriya recalled how Frank would sing under the tamarind tree at the single men's cottage in Gunbalanya, and recited another of his songs.[84] Frank was Nangarradjku moiety, and would sing with another man, Nangarridj Namanilakarr Philip Nayuku, of opposite (na-Mardku) moiety. Nayuku was a 'father' of Jacob Nayinggul.[85] Similarly, Nangarridj 'Paddy Bull'—identified as the singer of 'Cut 2'—was a Djok clansman from country near Gunbalanya and was the father of Priscilla, Jacob Nayinggul's mother.[86] He would sing with 'Ilarri', an Iwaidja speaker from Croker Island, who Alice Moyle recorded in 1962.[87] Bob Balir Balir and his brother Bilinyarra—identified as the singers of the song belonging to the Kunbarlang song-set ('Cut 6')—were also Kunwinjku people of the Djalama clan.

Other songmen living at Gunbalanya in 1948 were born elsewhere in the region. Among them was Nakangila Tommy Madjalkaidj (senior), who plays the didjeridu on 'Cut 7'. Madjalkaidj was a Mawng speaker who came from the Mandjurngudj clan, whose traditional country is located along the coast

Table 6.1 Summary of recordings at Gunbalanya in 1948, showing the song origin, song-set, language, conception, and details of recording[88]

Recording	Song origin	Song-set	Language	Song conception	Singer/s
MA24 Cut 1	Saltwater	Nganaru	Spirit language associated with Manangkardi	Dream-conceived	Nabulanj Billy Namunurr from *Weyirra* (North Goulburn Island)
MA24 Cut 2	Stone country love song	Itpyitpy?	Kunwinjku, Kun-barlang (and Mawng?)	Probably spontaneous	Nangarridj Paddy Bull (Djok clan) and Nangarridj Ilarri (Iwaidja speaker from Croker Island)
MA24 Cut 3&4	*Wangga* (Daly region)	Possibly Lambudju	Batjamalh	Dream-conceived	Mun.gi (adopted father of Bobby Lane) or Billy Mandji
MA24 Cut 5	Saltwater (*kurrula*)	Saltwater Fish	Spirit language assoc. with Iwaidja & Marrku	Dream-conceived	Unidentified Nadanek (Iwaidja) clansman of Nabulanj subsection from Croker Island (possibly Jackie Brown)
MA24 Cut 6	Saltwater love song	Kun-barlang	Kun-barlang, Mawng, and Kunwinjku	Probably spontaneous	Balir Balir and Bilinyarra (Djalama clan), possibly John Marangurra (Goulburn Island) on didjeridu
MA24 Cut 7&8	Stone country	Kolobarr (male antilopine wallaroo)	*Morrdjdjanjno* esoteric language	Unknown	Nakodjok Larry Marawana (Wurrik clan), Nakangkila Tommy Madjalkaidj (Namandurngudj) on didjeridu
MA24 Cut 9&10	Stone country	Kurri	Spirit language assoc. with Kunwinjku	Unknown	Nakangkila Frank Djendjorr Namornkodj (Mirrar clan) and Nangarridj Philip Nayuku
MA24 Cut 11	Saltwater (*kurrula*)	Kurrula (saltwater)	Possibly spirit language assoc. with Mawng/Iwaidja	Dream-conceived	Unidentified children from Croker Island
MA24 Cut 12	Saltwater (*kurrula*)	Marrwakara (goanna)	Spirit language mixed with Mawng/ Manangkardi	Dream-conceived	Unidentified singers from Goulburn Island

Key to table: *kurrula* songs are shaded light grey; stone country *wardde-ken* songs are shaded dark grey; *wangga* (Daly) songs are unshaded.

opposite Goulburn Island. As discussed earlier, the singer of 'Cut 1', Jimmy Kalarriya's uncle Nabulanj Namunurr, was from North Goulburn Island and spoke Mawng, Manangkardi, and Marrku languages, as well as Kunwinjku. Whilst Kalarriya was certain of the identities of *wardde-ken* singers, his memory of the *kurrula* singers was a little less clear, owing to the fact that they were further removed from his immediate kin. He remembered the singer of Cut 5—a Saltwater Fish song associated with Iwaidja and Marrku people—was also a Nabulanj whom he called uncle: a Nadanek clansman from Croker Island. Kalarriya and current-day Mawng songmen also recognised 'Cuts 11 and 12' as *kurrula* songs, and Solomon Nangamu identified 'Cut 12' as belonging to the Marrwakara (goanna) song-set from Goulburn Island. Mawng ceremony leaders identified the singers of 'Cut 11' as young children from Croker Island, and explained how their generation learned to sing when they were very young. (Whilst there are some places in western Arnhem Land such as Croker and Goulburn Island where children continue to learn at a very young age, they reflected that this was no longer common practice at Gunbalanya.) Finally, Kalarriya identified the singer on 'Cut 3' and 'Cut 4' as Billy Mandji, whom he remembered used to live nearby in Arrkuluk camp with other 'Wogatij mob' from Belyuen (see Table 6.1). Barwick and Marett have also traced this song—identified as part of the Lambudju repertory in Batjamalh language—to another singer named Mun.gi.[89]

Song texts recorded in 1948

Not only are the 1948 songs diverse in origin, but they are also diverse in *nature*—the manner in which they were conceived or composed, the social context of their performance, the musical style, and the song texts—four of which I will discuss in detail here. Half of the recordings are dream-conceived songs in spirit language, or in spirit language mixed with ordinary language. Because the 1948 singers are no longer around to provide interpretations for these spirit language songs, it is of course difficult to work up an entirely accurate transcription of the song texts, although the song-sets were recognisable to present-day ceremony leaders from western Arnhem Land. For example, the singer for 'Cut 1' was identified first by Kalarriya as Billy Namunurr (father of the present owner of the song, Billy Nawaloinjba), and the Manmurulu family at Goulburn Island later identified the song-set as Nganaru.[90] Certain words in the song text such as *lanme* and *artpa(ta)* also appear in Inyjalarrku and Mirrijpu song texts respectively, suggesting a connection with Mawng and Manangkardi spirit languages (see Support Material Figure 6.vi; listen to **AVEx_6.4**).

AVex_6.4 https://dx.doi.org/10.26278/RMWW-VD47

Similarly, the Marrwakara song 'Cut 12'—while not identifiable among the previously recorded Marrwakara songs that Harold Warrabin sings with Solomon Nangamu (Chapter 2)—contains Mawng and Manangkardi spirit language words such as *lanma* and *kamalinya*, found in other Marrwakara songs.[91] The structure of the song is AABCCB, where Phrase A of the song text is sung to the rhythm of two crotchets followed by four quavers; Phrase B is a combination of vocables sung to a crotchet rhythm and *kamalinya*, and Phrase C is an inversion of the song text and rhythm in Phrase A (see Support Material Figure 6.vii; listen to **AVEx_6.5**).

AVex_6.5 https://dx.doi.org/10.26278/CSRB-HF79

Another category of non-translatable language songs represented in the 1948 recordings is the *morrdjdjanjno* genre song called *kolobarr* (K: 'big red kangaroo'), performed by Larry Marawana. *Morrdjdjanjno* songs from the central Arnhem Land region were once performed as part of animal 'increase' rituals, and differ from *kun-borrk* songs in that, while performed by men, they are not individually owned, or clan-owned like eastern Arnhem Land *manikay* and central Arnhem Land *bunggurl*, but are handed down as 'open domain' songs.[92] Usually, *morrdjdjanjno* songs are performed unaccompanied; however, on this recording we hear didjeridu accompaniment with overblown notes (or 'hoots') played over the vowel sounds ('ii' 'aa' and 'u') in the vocables section—the style of didjeridu playing associated with eastern and central Arnhem Land rather than western Arnhem Land. Kalarriya, who was one of the last men to sing these songs, explained that the song originally came from Djalawarrurru people from the Roper River region (where this style of didjeridu playing is common) who are 'all finished' now, and that it made its way into western Arnhem Land after it was passed on to Kunwinjku people at Gunbalanya.[93] Murray Garde has written of a performance of *morrdjdjanjno* songs by Kalarriya, which came about while visiting a particular site on the sandstone plateau owned by Kundedjnjenghmi people, associated with the hunting of kangaroos. The performance involved singing a different song for each species of macropods, after which Kalarriya would discuss the words

'I'll Tell You This Corroboree Song': An intercultural exchange in 1948 173

in the song and give a story that explained an aspect of the kangaroo species: 'their movements, their behaviour, the scats they leave as evidence of their presence and more esoteric aspects of their relationship with humans'.[94] The song performed by Larry Marawana would therefore have been one of many, and the performance would have led to an explanation of the song text by the singer, and in this way would have been used for the passing down of specific cultural knowledge. The Kolobarr song text is made up of different words of esoteric meaning set to compound duple time ($\S$), while the clapsticks beat a syncopated rhythm in simple quadruple time ($\frac{1}{4}$). Perhaps because it is in an esoteric language, the words of the Kolobarr song appear to be somewhat interchangeable; there are no clear 'phrases' to the song text, which is made up of phrases of three or four words with five or six syllables strung together in multiple combinations. The first half of the text, transcribed by Murray Garde and Lewis Naborlhborlh—who sings the song today—is shown in Support Material Figure 6.viii (listen to **AVEx_6.6**).

AVex_6.6 https://dx.doi.org/10.26278/J01N-6S87

Unlike most of the songs performed today in western Arnhem Land, a number of songs recorded in 1948 were in 'ordinary' languages. One of these includes a *wangga* song in Batjamalh language, about the return of a ghost (see Support Material Figure 6.ix; listen to **AVEx_6.7**).

AVex_6.7 https://dx.doi.org/10.26278/A47F-Z684

There is some uncertainty over the identity of the singer of this particular song. Kalarriya identified the singer as Billy Mandji, who he says lived in Gunbalanya during this period. According to Barwick and Marett, Mandji migrated to Belyuen in the 1940s (before he came to stay in Gunbalanya) and was involved in the pastoral industry, and 'for this reason recordings of him and his songs turn up over a widespread area'.[95] However, Mandji was not known for singing in Batjamalh language,[96] and Barwick and Marett identified the song text as belonging to a repertory associated with Bobby Lambudju Lane. Lambudju was born in

1941 so he would have been too young to sing the songs in 1948; however, his adopted father, Nym Mun.gi, performed the songs during this time, having been entrusted with the songs originally composed by Lane's father before he died.[97] The confusion over the singer's identity also centres around the style of vocable singing in this song recorded by Simpson in 1948, which characterises Mun.gi's style (evidenced from recordings made by Alice Moyle of his son performing with Lane in 1959) and Mandji's style (also recorded by Moyle).[98]

The other two ordinary language songs are stone country 'love songs' about everyday events, composed spontaneously rather than received in a dream. Both Jimmy Kalarriya and Connie Nayinggul were familiar with these songs and recited the words back for me during playback sessions (Item ID 20110818 and 20111108 respectively; see Support Material Figure 6.i). This assisted me in a transcription of the song texts (Tables 6.2 and 6.3), which I was later able to work up into a possible English translation, with the aid of Murray Garde and Isabel O'Keeffe. One feature of these love songs is their multilingual song texts, which 'code-switch' from one language to another, sometimes within one phrase of the song. For example, 'Cut 2' (see Table 6.2)—identified as an Itpiyitpi (grasshopper) song by Paddy Bull—begins in Kunwinjku (Phrase A), followed by a phrase that Connie Nayinggul identified as Mengerrdji (Phrase A, highlighted), then a switch to Kun-barlang (Phrase B, highlighted), and back to Kunwinjku (listen to **AVEx_6.8**):

AVex_6.8 https://dx.doi.org/10.26278/FESP-P266

This text is typical of *kun-borrk* love songs, in that it evokes more questions than it provides answers: Who lit the fire? Who is being referred to in the first person dual pronominal prefix *ngarr* ('you and me')? Is it the singer and the listener, or some other subjects? Who is the female subject looking for, and where or what is Urrkarra? As Garde suggests, the deliberate opacity of the 'text' of these songs invites multiple layers of meaning, and much of the entertainment value is derived from speculating about the meaning of the song.[99] Connie Nayinggul, who remembered the song from her childhood, explained some of these ambiguities. For example, the lighting of a fire is in this case an act to create a smoke signal from one group inviting another group to join them. These groups are on either side of Urrkarra, a 'main river' north of Gunbalanya, which borders two clan estates. As Kalarriya explained, in crossing the river, the subject is therefore attempting to go over and find a woman (euphemistically referred to as 'cheeky yam'), who might be interested in having an affair:

Table 6.2 Music transcription of Itpiyitpi song, MA24 Cut 2 (AVEx_6.8)

Didj						(x8)
Clapstick						(x8)
Syllabic						(x8)
Phrase A	kunak	birri-wurlhkeng		ngarr-ra-	winj/yinj	(x8)
Gloss	fire	3pl-light [a fire]-P		1-du-INC	go-IRR	
Trans.	As they lit the fire			you and me, we should go		

Phrase B	(ng)a marne-m-	dukbe[?]	nga-marne-	yimeng (na-)	ngale	ka-yawan
	1sg-BEN	DIREC[?]	1sg-BEN-	ask for name	what	3s-search for
	I'll talk to her	[and ask?]		who is she looking for		

Phrase C	abba,	nga-djowkkemeninj	Urrkarra	man-yawok	kandi-woyi	
	Interj.	1sg–wade across water IRR	Urrkarra	cheeky yam	some–3>12-give. IRR	
	Well then, I should cross over Urrkarra			they should give us some cheeky yam[100]		

JK: '*Birri wurrlkeng. An manekke [?] namekke Bininj yi-yimeng ngaldjowk-kemeninj 'kandi-woyi' narren Urrkarra manyawud [manyawok?] yimeng kumekke nga-bolknayo ngamed.*

'They lit [the fire]'. And that one refers to people you know who waded across Urrkarra, 'them giving to us', look for a relationship [from clanspeople on the other side], saying 'I'm just looking for some long yam over there'.[101]

Garde similarly suggests that Text Phrase B can be interpreted as meaning: "I'll talk to her and ask which man she is after".[102] The entire meaning of the song text is therefore dependent on one's cultural understanding, as well as the knowledge, revealed through performance, about who is singing, who is listening, and where this story is taking place, because this provides the context for the relationship that is being discussed in the song.

'Cut 6' (see Table 6.3), which belongs to the Kunbarlang song-set (although it is not part of the current repertory of songs that continue to be performed today as part of the Karrbarda song-set), seems to similarly capture the anticipation and

Table 6.3 Music transcription of Kunbarlang song, MA24 Cut 6 (AVEx_6.9)

Didj	♫♫ ♫♫		♫♫ ♫♫	
Clapstick	♪♪		♪♪	
Syllabic	♫♫ ♪		♪ ♩	
Phrase A	Ring(no)? kingmi Ring ? Ring [he bought?]		kanwong/kanj-wunj 3FUT-give.NP [gave to a woman?]/S/he will give it	

	♫♫ ♫♫	♫♫ ♫♫	♫♫ ♫♫
	♪♪	♪♪	♪♪
	♫♫ ♪	♫♫ ♪	♫♫ ♪
Phrase B	Baleh [ka]kodjyime What 3s-think what is s/he thinking,	ngan(e)-yime nuk 1du-excl-tell-interj.maybe maybe we two (excl) should tell him/her	bolkwarrewong loc. ruin-P s/he's spoiled it

	♫♫ ♫♫	♫♫ ♫♫	♫♫ ♫♫
	♪♪	♪♪	♪♪
	♪ ♫♫	♫♫ ♪	♫♫ ♩
Phrase C	ka-warre nuk, ka 3s bad DUB (dubitative) R s/he might be bad/unsound	-warre nuk, ka	-warre nuk

speculation surrounding an arranged meeting. The song text is very similar to a Kunbarlang song attributed to a Mayali singer transcribed by Elkin (see Support Material Appendix v). The version recorded in 1948 (Table 6.3) appears to begin in Kun-barlang language (Phrase A, highlighted) before switching to Kunwinjku (Phrase B) and ending in Kun-barlang again (Phrase C, highlighted),[103] perhaps reflecting two states of consciousness, or the subject's dialogue with another interlocutor in another language (listen to **AVEx_6.9**). Again, a tentative translation was worked up with assistance from O'Keeffe for Kun-barlang and Garde for Kunwinjku, taking into account Elkin's transcription.

AVex_6.9 https://dx.doi.org/10.26278/1MQ3-B996

The songs recorded in 1948—particularly those *wardde-ken* songs that originated from the stone country—were remembered well not just by older people

I'll Tell You This Corroboree Song': An intercultural exchange in 1948 177

like Jimmy Kalarriya, but also by members of younger generations such as Connie Nayinggul, who had heard the songs performed at Gunbalanya when they were children in the 1970s and 1980s. While the individual songs recorded in 1948 are no longer performed today, some of the repertories such as Marrwakara and Kunbarlang continue to be performed with a different set of songs from those that existed over 60 years ago. This is not surprising, given that certain songs 'pass away' with the songmen that composed them, and can be replaced by other new songs composed by the singer who takes on the repertory. The playback sessions sparked interest in reviving some of the songs, in particular the 'love songs' in Kunwinjku by composers such as Paddy Bull and Frank Djendjorr originating from Gunbalanya. Bininj/Arrarrkpi reflected on the way that the songs contribute to the passing down of knowledge specific to their language and culture. Connie Nayinggul expressed her desire to obtain any other recordings of *wardde-ken* repertories such as Kurri (K: blue tongue lizard) and Manyawko (K: box tree) that might exist, in the hope that younger male relatives of those old singers might relearn their own songs and 'bring it back' into their musical repertoire:

> Yoh, we should get together them boys, instead of all the time singing [just] Karrbarda.... they can sing their own [songs] and learn the dance. Same like if you want to be John Travolta or whatever... If you [RB] find [any recordings of] Kurri [Blue Tongue lizard song-set] and Manyawko [unknown Kunwinjku song-set], bring it back and we can show these young people, because some of them they know how to sing Manyawko but they forgot, all them little words.[104]

Connie Nayinggul's comments once more reinforce the importance of archival recordings to the descendants of those singers who originally recorded them. The unique musical qualities and specialised language (i.e. 'little words') contained in the 1948 songs are highly valued as an important learning resource for the maintenance of these performance traditions and endangered or dormant/ extinct languages like Kun-barlang and Mengerrdji.

Continuity and change

Analysis of the rhythmic modes that feature in the 1948 Gunbalanya recordings (summarised in Support Material Figure 6.xi) informed by contemporary singers' knowledge of the songs revealed a great deal of continuity in the song practice from 1948 to today. 'Cuts 3&4' feature the unmeasured rhythmic mode 1 during verses of the song—in which the singer sings only to the accompaniment of the didjeridu and there is an absence of clapstick beat. This mode is common in *wangga* repertories but is seldom found in western Arnhem Land songs, identifying this song as originating from the Daly region (the song also features rhythmic mode 5b [var] (♫) in the Instrumental Sections; another common mode in *wangga* repertories). Many of the songs ('Cuts 5, 11, and 12')

178   *'I'll Tell You This Corroboree Song': An intercultural exchange in 1948*

feature the fast doubled even rhythmic mode 5b, which is usually accompanied by male dancing in the *kun-borrk/manyardi* tradition. Goulburn Island songmen were able to identify Cuts 6, 9, and 10 as *kurrula* repertories in part because they recognised the prominent moderate even rhythmic mode (4a), and the convention whereby the tempo slows in the Coda before the terminating pattern (compare with my analysis of Mirrijpu songs in previous chapters). The fast uneven sextuple rhythmic mode 5e [♩♩♩𝄾♩𝄾] in 'Cut 12' has also been observed in contemporary songs (refer to my analysis of Inyjalarrku song IL01 in Chapter 4).

Significantly, one of the *wardde-ken* Kurri songs by Frank Djendjorr and/or Philip Nayuku ('Cut 10') has three changes of rhythmic mode in three tempo bands (moderate, slow, and fast). The song begins in moderate tempo (120 bpm) with even clapstick beating (rhythmic mode 4a). Text Phrase A (Support Material Figure 6.xii) is set to a syncopated rhythm in 3/4 time over 6 beats, repeated three times (18 beats in total). Text Phrase A is then repeated again, this time set to a slightly varied melodic phrase, before a section with no vocals lasting 20 clapstick beats leads to an extended Instrumental Section where the tempo slows to 59 bpm. In this section, the singer sings Text Phrase B to a different melody set to a repeated rhythm.

The singers then return to a faster tempo (130 bpm) in the Coda, which alternates between even clapstick beating (rhythmic mode 5a) and suspended beating (rhythmic mode 5b [var] ♫),[105] before the song finishes with the standard clapstick terminating pattern (♩♩𝄾). Table 6.4 shows where the changes in rhythmic mode occur within the song (listen to **AVEx_6.10**).

AVex_6.10 https://dx.doi.org/10.26278/RWNX-MR02

Several clues suggest that the extended Instrumental Section in this recording is in fact the *ngalbadjan/nigi* song of this song-set.[106] Firstly, the slow tempo of 59 bpm is normally only reserved for the *ngalbadjan/nigi* (compare for example with IL50 discussed in Chapter 4). Secondly, the 'bridging' section of 20 beats with no singing appears to 'join' the first part/song together with the *ngalbadjan/nigi* (as with other *nigi/ngalbadjan* songs previously analysed). Thirdly, as we have observed of other *kun-borrk/manyardi* song-sets, vocables on an open vowel such as 'o' or 'i' are usually sung during Instrumental Sections in the song, whereas in this case, we have a short, repeated phrase (Text Phrase B). And finally, the slow Instrumental Section/*Nigi* is repeated three times, extending the duration of the song to over four minutes. This is another characteristic of *nigi* songs, which are often double the length of other songs in the set.

I'll Tell You This Corroboree Song': An intercultural exchange in 1948   179

Table 6.4 Changes in rhythmic mode in Kurri song by Frank Djendjorr/Philip Nayuku, MA24 Cut 10 (AVEx_6.10)

				Repeat x3					
Song structure	Verse		Bridge	Instrumental section (x2) or *Nigi* (mother song)?			Coda		
Text Phrase	A (x3)	A² (x3)			B				
Clapstick beats/	18 (6x3)	18 (6x3)	18 +2	4	8+9+8	4	12	20	2
Metre	$\frac{3}{4}$	$\frac{3}{4}$	$\frac{3}{4}$ $\frac{2}{4}$	$\frac{2}{4}$	$\frac{2}{4}+\frac{3}{4}+\frac{2}{4}$	$\frac{2}{4}$	$\frac{4}{4}$	$\frac{4}{4}$	$\frac{2}{4}$
Rhythmic mode	4a			2a			5e	5b[var]	5e
Tempo (bpm)	← 120 →			← 59 →			← 130 →		

Due to their understanding of the *kun-borrk/manyardi* song tradition, current Mawng songmen Solomon Nangamu, Russell Agalara, Johnny Namayiwa, and others were able to interpret not only the genre and song-set of the recordings, but also the musical interactions between performers recorded by Simpson in 1948. For example, while listening to the end part of the *kurrula* Saltwater Fish song by Iwaidja songmen ('Cut 5'), they were amused to hear a particular passage in the music, and requested that I play back the end part of the song again. During this passage, the lead singer finishes singing and the didjeridu accompaniment cuts out, cueing the end of the didjeridu accompaniment and clapstick terminating pattern. Against expectations, the didjeridu part starts up once again, and the singer follows, continuing to beat the clapstick and singing one last vocable phrase on the tonic, before the song ends. The singers singled this out as significant because of the way it demonstrated a level of musical ingenuity and understanding between the singer and accompanist, in leading and following one another:

RA: The didjeridu [is] playing tricks on the clapstick
SN: But he still knows…
JN: Older people are very smart
RB: So he's pretending to finish but not quite finishing?
RA: Yeah, y'know like [when you're] playing guitar and your goin' to play a song?
SN: Like that lead, take over, lead. Like that singerman, so the didjeridu he blew all that tricks his part[107]

It is these aspects of the song tradition—the cueing, leading, and following between lead singer, backup singer, and didjeridu player; the unspoken recognition that a particular tempo signals a change in mood and a shift in the ceremonial action; the knowledge of the origins of another singer's songs, etc.—which make up the things that cannot be learned by simply memorising the melody or the song text, but must be observed and 'followed' over a period of time. These elements help to define the song tradition of *kun-borrk/manyardi*, and are clearly valued today, as they were in 1948.

Conclusion: *kun-borrk/manyardi*, then and now

As I reflected on the diversity of the 1948 recordings—12 songs that neatly showcase repertories from language groups all over the region of western Arnhem Land and beyond, representing different aspects of the song tradition in this area—I could not help but be reminded of the recording session with the Goulburn Island singers at Gunbalanya, in which they came to a collective decision to perform four songs from each of their repertories (Chapter 1). Just as Marawana and other Bininj/Arrarrkpi songmen had done with Simpson and Giles in 1948, they were facilitating and directing the intercultural encounter by making decisions as to which songs would be appropriate to record and discuss, and which songs would ultimately best represent their song tradition to a wider audience. The Expedition members' diaries and Simpson's written account suggest that Bininj/Arrarrkpi cultural brokers such as Marawana were instrumental in enabling the Expedition to carry out their work at Gunbalanya and that *kun-borrk/manyardi* was an important part of the cultural exchange between Bininj/Arrarrkpi and Balanda. It may have even helped to formalise relationships between the two groups. Over 60 years after Simpson and Giles' visit, this carefully curated record from 1948 was able to serve as a point for further interaction between Bininj/Arrarrkpi and Balanda when I played it back at Gunbalanya.

By playing back the 1948 media in the places where it had originated, and situating its contents within existing kinship networks, Bininj/Arrarrkpi showed how 'intangible' digital records are nevertheless understood as 'tangible' things that require re-embedding in the social and physical landscape. For Bininj/Arrarrkpi, it was not enough to know *who* is doing *what* in the record, but also to know *where* they are doing it, and their relationship to the listener/viewer. By taking Amanda Harris and me up into the caves of Injalak Hill to the place where Setzler stole ancestral bones and where other skeletons still lie, Isaiah Nagurrgurrba was able to reframe Setzler's black and white photographs within an ongoing practice of looking after ancestral spirits that still reside in Country. By repeating certain songs and reordering the material during playback, elders like Kalarriya were able to re-embed the songs in their memory and situate them within their experience. This triggered some emotional responses and stimulated discussion about what people were doing during this time, providing a platform for Kalarriya and Namundja to share their knowledge of this period. Kalarriya's death the following year in 2012 served to underscore the urgency of returning such culturally significant legacy recordings and media to those who can still interpret it so that future generations are able to make sense of it in a rich and meaningful way.

I'll Tell You This Corroboree Song': An intercultural exchange in 1948 181

The narrative that emerged from the reception of Simpson and Giles' fragmented recordings was one of musical diversity, reflecting the linguistic profile of western Arnhem Land. The traditional country of the listener and their personal experience determined the degree to which they were familiar with the song traditions of their neighbours. For example, current Mawng songmen recognised distinct musical characteristics in *kurrula* repertories, while Kunwinjku respondents were familiar with the words of *wardde-ken* songs. The fact that respondents were able to interpret such rich detail from these 'aural snapshots' some 60 years later is a testament to the way that the western Arnhem Land song tradition has been handed down in the intervening generations.

Clearly, the musical diversity of 1948 continues today, although in a different form. Of all of the repertories that were recorded in 1948, only two (Kun-barlang and Marrwakara) continue to be performed, and with different songs from those performed in 1948. Whereas in 1948 there was an even mix of spirit language songs and songs spontaneously composed in everyday language, this is no longer the case today, as most repertories I recorded are in spirit languages. A greater representation of *wardde-ken* songs from the stone country is also evident in 1948 compared with today; most of the song repertories performed at Gunbalanya now originate from Goulburn and Croker Islands. Comparing the musical characteristics of western Arnhem Land songs then and now, it is clear that the song tradition has maintained an aural identity that is unique to the region. And while the repatriation of these recordings may spark interest in their revival, new songs and repertories have also since sprung up in the place of old ones, demonstrating that the song tradition is resilient and adaptable in the face of change.

Just as they were doing in 1948, various singers from Croker and Goulburn Island and the Daly continue to travel to Gunbalanya and throughout the region to perform at funeral ceremonies, circumcision ceremonies, gift exchange ceremonies, and official community celebrations and events such as cultural festivals, and other informal settings. One thing that has changed since 1948 is the absence of western Arnhem Land songs as 'entertainment' around the campfire, and a reduction in songs composed spontaneously that reflect on everyday events. What sort of changes at Gunbalanya might have brought this about? And what other avenues for social interaction and 'music as entertainment' exist today? In the following chapter, I will consider these questions by examining the forms of musical expression at festivals that stand in as 'everyday entertainment' for Bininj/Arrarrkpi.

Notes

1. C. P. Mountford, Application to Chairman of the Research Committee, National Geographic Society, 5 March 1945, Correspondence 1945–49, vol. 1 1945–47, American/Australian Scientific Expedition to Arnhem Land 1948 Records, PRG 1218/17/4, Mountford-Sheard Collection, State Library of South Australia, Adelaide.
2. See Barwick and Marett, "Snapshots of Musical Life," 355; Linden Jones, "The Circle of Songs," 52–53.

3 See Martin Thomas, "The Crackle of the Wire: Media, Digitization, and the Voicing of Aboriginal Languages," in *Voice: Vocal Aesthetics in Digital Arts and Media*, ed. Norie Neumark, Ross Gibson and Theo Van Leeuwen (Cambridge, MA: MIT Press, 2010), 86.
4 Other songs recorded by Simpson and Giles of a restricted men's ceremony at Gunbalanya are not discussed here. See Garde, "The Forbidden Gaze."
5 Kalarriya was well practised at communicating with Balanda in a mixture of Northern Kriol and English, but was most comfortable speaking Kunwinjku and other dialects of Bininj Kunwok.
6 See the advertisement for Mountford's 1945 film and lecture tour of the United States, cited in Thomas, "Expedition as Time Capsule," 12. See also C. P. Mountford, "Exploring Stone Age Arnhem Land," *National Geographic Magazine* 96, no. 6 (1949): 778, cited in Thomas, "Turning Subjects into Objects and Objects into Subjects", 150.
7 For further explanation, see Garde, Culture, Interaction and Person Reference in an Australian Language, 95.
8 [Isaiah Nagurrgurrba and Jimmy Kalarriya, 20110802-RB_01_edit.wav, https://dx.doi.org/10.26278/TM2K-6V50, 00:54:13.000–00:54:23.700].
9 Here, Kalarriya is referring to his mother and her sister, who are both his classificatory mothers (K: *Karrang*).
10 'A long time ago' (K: *korroko*)—many Bininj of Kalarriya's generation cannot recall the exact year in which certain events took place, but refer instead to eras such as 'second world war time'.
11 Jimmy Kalarriya, interviewed by Martin Thomas, 13 and 16 May 2011 in Gunbalanya, N.T., National Library of Australia OH ORAL TRC 6311, nla.oh-vn5299380; [00:15:16–00:16:19].
12 Ibid., [00:22:59–00:23:22].
13 Ibid., [00:01:06–00:02:13].
14 Berndt and Berndt, *End of an Era*, 155.
15 For a description of the provenance of the recordings, see Barwick and Marett, "Snapshots of Musical Life."
16 For further discussion of the provenance of this footage and how it came to be digitised, see Harris, "Hidden for Sixty Years."
17 Thanks to Anthony Linden-Jones for pointing this out to me.
18 [Jimmy Kalarriya, 20110802-RB_01_edit.wav, https://dx.doi.org/10.26278/TM2K-6V50, 00:02:13.100–00:04:26.107].
19 Translation assisted by Andrew Manakgu.
20 Colin Simpson, "Expedition to Arnhem Land," radio feature, first broadcast 30 November 1948 (Sydney: Australian Broadcasting Commission, 1948). See Tony MacGregor's discussion of the way this recording is used in the radio feature—along with romantic descriptions in *Adam in Ochre*—to evoke a magical Eden-like scene at Oenpelli. Martin Thomas also makes the observation that the recording's juxtaposition with the pompous orchestral fanfare that proceeds it mirrors a 'shift from prewar to postwar mindset'. Tony MacGregor, "Birds on the Wire: Wild Sound, Informal Speech and the Emergence of the Radio Documentary," in *Exploring the Legacy of the 1948 Arnhem Land Expedition*, ed. Martin Thomas and Margot Neale (Canberra: ANU E Press, 2011), 10–13.
21 'Malwakardi' is a cognate name for Marrku. [Jimmy Kalarriya, 20120610-RB_v01.mp4, https://dx.doi.org/10.26278/27RB-ME58, 06:40–07:47].
22 For Kalarriya and others such as Isaiah Nagurrgurrba who took an interest in the history of Bininj at Gunbalanya, '1948' was often discussed as a historical reference point

that came to mean not necessarily the year 1948, but rather that period of time—in Kunwinjku, *korroko* or *kun-ware*—that was marked by the visit of AASEAL in 1948.
23 Johnny Namayiwa, personal communication, November 2013.
24 Jimmy Kalarriya, [20120610-RB_v01.mp4, https://dx.doi.org/10.26278/27RB-ME58, 00:09:26.800–00:10:06.000].
25 1p excl.
26 Originally archived at the Smithsonian Institution and National Anthropological Archives.
27 For further discussion, see Thomas, "Turning Subjects into Objects and Objects into Subjects."
28 Balang is another name for my skin name (Nangarridj).
29 Cf. observations about song order at Stone Country Festival, Figure 7.2, where a similar preference is demonstrated for songs to be performed in order of proximity to the traditional country in which the performance is held.
30 Thomas, "Expedition as Time Capsule," 18.
31 [R09R10-O-25, 01:57]. See Support Material Appendix ii.
32 For further discussion of their use in film, see Linden Jones, "The Circle of Songs."
33 See Thomas and Neale, ed. *Exploring the Legacy*.
34 See Mountford, "Records of the American-Australian Scientific Expedition to Arnhem Land."
35 Barwick and Marett, "Snapshots of Musical Life," 356.
36 Barwick and Marett, "Snapshots," 368–75.
37 For a related discussion about the impact of the repatriation of old recordings of Tiwi song on song-making, see Genevieve Campbell, "Song as Artefact: The Reclaiming of Song Recordings Empowering Indigenous Stakeholders—and the Recordings Themselves," in *Circulating Cultures: Exchanges of Australian Indigenous Music, Dance and Media*, ed. Amanda Harris (Canberra: ANU Press, 2014), 101–28.
38 Amanda Harris, "Hearing Aboriginal Music Making in Non-Indigenous Accounts of the Bush from the Mid-Twentieth Century," in *Circulating Cultures: Exchanges of Australian Indigenous Music, Dance and Media*, ed. Amanda Harris (Canberra: ANU Press, 2014), 75.
39 Ibid. Harris points out that Bray's earlier diary entries from the Expedition's period in Eastern Arnhem Land show less interest in the music around him, while his later entries at Kunnanj show an increasing understanding of the nuances of the different kinds of music he was hearing. John Bray, Diary, unpublished manuscript in private collection of Andrew Bray, 19 April 1948.
40 Bray, Diary, 13–18 October 1948.
41 Bray is likely referring here to the various rhythmic modes of *kun-borrk*. Ibid., 18 October 1948.
42 Ibid, 20 October 1948.
43 Colin Simpson, *Adam in Ochre: Inside Aboriginal Australia* (Sydney: Angus & Robertson, 1952), 67.
44 Of course, there may have been other factors that influenced the final collection of recordings: the amount of wire the recordists carried may have limited what they could record, and Simpson and Giles may also have been motivated to capture a number of different songs, in order to have a variety of material on which to draw for the ABC radio feature.
45 Bessie J. Mountford, Arnhem Land Expedition Diary No. 4, 1948, PRG 487/1/4, State Library of South Australia, Adelaide; Bessie J. Mountford, Arnhem Land Expedition Diary No. 5, 1948, PRG 487/1/5, State Library of South Australia, Adelaide; Bray, Diary; McCarthy, Diary 5, Yirrkala Diary No. 2 and Oenpelli, 1948.

46 Mountford, Arnhem Land Expedition Diary No. 4, 73.
47 Ibid., 74A.
48 Simpson, *Adam in Ochre*, 64.
49 See [R03R04-O-11, 0:39–59]. See Support Material Appendix ii.
50 Jimmy Kalarriya [20110802-RB_02_edit.wav, https://dx.doi.org/10.26278/CNKN-C338, 00:01:10.804–00:01:14.971].
51 Refer to Support Material Figure 1.ii.
52 Simpson, *Adam in Ochre*, 67.
53 Jimmy Kalarriya [20110802-RB_01_edit.wav, 38:46–39:10].
54 Simpson, *Adam in Ochre*, 29–39.
55 Mulvaney, *Paddy Cahill of Oenpelli*, 11.
56 Ibid.
57 Peter John Carroll, "The Old People Told Us: Verbal Art in Western Arnhem Land" (PhD thesis, University of Queensland, Brisbane, 1995), 12–13.
58 Mulvaney, *Paddy Cahill of Oenpelli*, 36–37.
59 Lamilami, *Lamilami Speaks*, 84.
60 Ibid; Poignant and Poignant, *Encounter at Nagalarramba*, 36.
61 Ibid., 69–71.
62 Ibid., 61. This song was used by composer Mirrie Hill as the theme for the film *Aborigines of the Seacoast*, and is referred to elsewhere as the "Winbalung Song" or "Gunbalang Sweetheart" song. See Linden Jones, "The Circle of Songs," 59–60.
63 Ibid., 67.
64 Simpson, *Adam in Ochre*, 68.
65 Barwick and Marett, "Snapshots of Musical Life," 365.
66 Mountford, Arnhem Land Expedition Diary No. 4, 7 October 1948, 40.
67 Simpson, *Adam in Ochre*, 39.
68 For variations on first person and third person pronouns, refer to pronominal prefixes in Bininj Kunwok in the Front Matter to this book.
69 Superintendent's diaries, CMS Australia Committee, Oenpelli, 1944–1981, NTRS 865/P1, Item 3, Box 1, Location 143/3/2, Northern Territory Archives; Register of burials, 1926–1978, NTRS 864, box 7, location 75/5/4, Northern Territory Archives.
70 See Thomas, "Unpacking the Testimony of Gerald Blitner."
71 Most likely, he meant that he had played the wrong rhythmic sequence for that particular song, since the didjeridu only has one 'note'.
72 Simpson, *Adam in Ochre*, 67.
73 Alan Marshall, *Ourselves Writ Strange* (Melbourne & London: Cheshire, 1948), 263.
74 Ibid., 265.
75 See Thomas' comments on the Expedition maintaining the hierarchy of the society it represents. Thomas, "Unpacking the Testimony of Gerald Blitner," 18.
76 Simpson, *Adam in Ochre*, 68. Marshall also writes of the difficulties Marawana faced among his own people in the role of go-between. See Marshall, *Ourselves Writ Strange*, 263.
77 See also Murray Garde, "Morrdjdjanjno Ngan-Marnbom Story Nakka, 'Songs That Turn Me into a Story Teller': The Morrdjdjanjno of Western Arnhem Land," *Australian Aboriginal Studies* 2 (2007): 35–45.
78 While helping to prepare the 1948 materials for playback in the field, Linda Barwick discovered an overlap between Walker's silent footage (R01R02-O-05) and Simpson's audio recordings (the beginning of 'Cut 7') and synced the two together (R01R02-O-05_audio). This enabled us to deduce what Marawana is discussing. See Support Material Appendix ii.
79 [Simpson MA24 Cut 7, 00:00:08.500–00:00:41.200].
80 Barwick and Marett, "Snapshots of Musical Life," 364.

'I'll Tell You This Corroboree Song': An intercultural exchange in 1948 185

81 Ibid.
82 Renfred Manmurulu, personal communication, Warruwi, 23 June 2022.
83 [Connie Nayinggul, 20111108-RB_01_edit.wav, https://dx.doi.org/10.26278/SEE1-D409, 00:17:15.300–00:20:13.300]. For an example, see Support Material Appendix v.
84 [Jimmy Kalarriya, 20120610-RB_v03.mp4, https://dx.doi.org/10.26278/YJQR-5W42, 00:08:56–00:10:53]. See Support Material Appendix v.
85 According to Kalarriya, Philip Nayuku was the brother of Jacob Nayinggul's father [Jimmy Kalarriya, 20110802-RB_01_edit.wav, https://dx.doi.org/10.26278/TM2K-6V50, 00:43:49–00:44:06].
86 [Connie Nayinggul, 20111108-RB_01_edit.wav, https://dx.doi.org/10.26278/SEE1-D409, 00:01:52.780–00:01:58.823].
87 Moyle, Songs from the Northern Territory Companion Booklet.
88 See recording session 1948SIMP in Support Material Appendix ii for further details.
89 In the orthography used for Batjamalh language, the full stop in the middle of the word indicates a syllable break between the two syllables 'Mun' and 'gi'.
90 David, Jenny, Rupert and Renfred Manmurulu, personal communication, 20 June 2016. Kalarriya also identified this song as belonging to the Marrwakani song-set [20110802-RB_01_edit.wav, https://dx.doi.org/10.26278/TM2K-6V50, 00:05:20.932–00:05:24.797]. A repertory of the same name inherited by Archie Brown and originally composed by Nabulanj Paddy Compass is in fact associated with Amurdak, and was recorded by Linda Barwick and Bruce Birch on 22 October 2004. Barwick et al., "West Arnhem Land Song Project Data Collection."
91 See song MK03 in Barwick, O'Keeffe and Singer, "Dilemmas in Interpretation," 52.
92 See Garde, "Morrdjdjanjno Ngan-Marnbom Story Nakka."
93 [Jimmy Kalarriya, 20120610-RB_v04.mp4, https://dx.doi.org/10.26278/3TJP-RN24, 00:08:42.500 - 00:09:11.800].
94 Garde, "Morrdjdjanjno Ngan-Marnbom Story Nakka," 36.
95 Marett, Barwick and Ford, *For the Sake of a Song*, 32.
96 His songs were in Emmi, Marri Tjevin, Mendhe, and ghost language. Ibid., 219.
97 Ibid., 239.
98 Moyle, Songs from the Northern Territory Companion Booklet.
99 Garde, "The Language of *Kun-borrk*," 84.
100 This yam is referred to in Aboriginal English as 'cheeky yam' because it has toxins, which need to be removed by leaching before eating. Garde, personal communication, 2011.
101 [Jimmy Kalarriya, 20120610-RB_v01.mp4, https://dx.doi.org/10.26278/27RB-ME58, 00:11:22.957–00:11:34.757].
102 Garde, personal communication, 2012.
103 It is not clear whether the final words *ka-warre-nuk* are in Kun-barlang or Kunwinjku. Garde offers the translation 's/he's spoiled it, it's no good' for Kunwinjku. According to Barwick and O'Keeffe, the Kun-barlang translation 'it might happen' fits with other songs of this kind. Barwick, Garde and O'Keeffe, personal communication, 29 August 2014. Another translation of this part of the text offered by Elkin is 'she might be wrong'. Elkin, "Arnhem Land Music," 74.
104 [Connie Nayinggul, 20111108-RB_01.wav, https://dx.doi.org/10.26278/6FPG-AD80, 00:09:31.961–00:09:44.230].
105 As well as featuring in *wangga* repertories, this rhythmic mode is prominent in Yanajanak songs of the stone country, discussed in Chapter 4.
106 I am yet to confirm this with research collaborators/current songmen.
107 [Solomon Nangamu, Russell Agalara, Johnny Namayiwa, and Reuben Brown (interviewer), 20110825-RB_03.wav, https://dx.doi.org/10.26278/C9CB-9Y54, 0:54:31.525–00:55:06.646].

7 'Join in and Dance'

Festivals and new forms of exchange

Exchanges on the dance ground

One warm and breezy evening in September 2013, I drove a troopy loaded with singers and dancers across the East Alligator River to their homes in Gunbalanya, after a performance of *kun-borrk/manyardi* at the Mahbilil Festival in Jabiru. We were recounting their performance, which had been jointly led by Solomon Nangamu, Russell Agalara, and Eric Mardday, alternating Mirrijpu and Karrbarda songs for an enthralled and generous audience. Having performed with one another at other ceremonies recently, the songmen switched seamlessly between song-sets and kept the momentum of the dancing going, with minimal gaps in-between song items. Earlier that evening, I had introduced the singers and dancers to the crowd of festival-goers, and on instructions from the group, I had encouraged the audience to join in the dancing. Most people had been a little reluctant at first, but eventually, two Japanese tourists got up and entered the dance ground—a large circle of sand set in front of the stage overlooking the lake of Jabiru.

The two dancing volunteers were young, athletic, and enthusiastic. Their movements were a little sporadic and heavy-footed at first, but with Karrbarda dance captain Joey Nganjmirra leading, they soon got the hang of the dance—listening for the clapstick beat and stamping at particular moments in the song. Watching the Bininj dancers, they began to lift their knees high in the air, leaping from side to side and moving their arms around in a way that resembled something from the martial arts. The tourists' unique take on *kun-borrk/manyardi* dancing did not go unnoticed by the singers, who were encouraging of their dancing and enjoying the spectacle, trying to keep their composure as they watched the dancing while leading the performance. In a break between the singing, Russell Agalara pulled out his mobile phone and filmed the two men dancing, capturing this rare moment of intercultural exchange for posterity. Now, travelling back home in the troopy to Gunbalanya, they were all in hysterics, replaying the video of 'those boys doing the Kung fu moves'. The singers shared the video with friends and family back in Gunbalanya and Goulburn Island, and still take pleasure in recalling the story with me.

Over at Gunbalanya, a palpable atmosphere of anticipation and an unusual flurry of activity characterised the period leading up to the Stone Country Festival. Ordinarily, the town would grow quiet by early afternoon, when most people have finished work before the sun sits high in the sky and temperatures reach their peak. In the days leading up to the festival, however, the clashing of drums and electric guitars started up early in the day and could still be heard down the main street well into the evening, along with the singing of choruses in Kunwinjku. The rehearsal space was an open-air shed, where young men queued to practise their set in the couple of hours that they had been allocated, before passing the equipment on to the next band. A couple of days before the festival, a stage crew from Darwin came to set up the rostrum and projector screen on the northern end of the oval. On the day of the festival, many of the young men would sweat it out competing in the football tournament, before jumping up on stage in the evening to perform with their band.

Prior to 2011, Gunbalanya's annual event had been called an 'Open Day', and was focussed around the Sports and Social Club, where the music tended towards rock 'n' roll favourites such as AC/DC rather than *kun-borrk/manyardi* or other Bininj music. Now, it was renamed the 'Stone Country Festival', reflecting Bininj ownership and curatorship over the event, with a focus on Bininj cultural activities (see Support Material Figure 7.i). Months before the first rebadged festival in 2011, I sat with the director of IAC, Lorna Martin, and then president of IAC Isaiah Nagurrgurrba, as they held meetings with traditional owners and community stakeholders to decide on logistics and programming for the festival. The evening's performances would be shifted from the Club to the more family-friendly environment of the oval. A dance ground for the performance of *kun-borrk/manyardi* would be prepared by the local artists who, for the first time, would build bough shelters for the audience and singers to sit under, like they have in funeral ceremonies. Bininj/Arrarrkpi council workers would bring in sand for the ceremony ground from a nearby gorge at Adjumalarl waterfall with a front-end loader. Events would run concurrently during the day, showcasing traditional arts and crafts such as spear-making and basket weaving, and a public forum called *Bim kunwok* (K: rock art stories) would be set up at the church where Injalak artists such as Joey Nganjmirra would tell stories explaining the meanings behind their paintings, and Bininj elders such as Kalarriya would talk about life growing up on Oenpelli mission.

Both in 2011 and in 2012, there was a great deal of interest and anticipation around the *kun-borrk/manyardi* ceremony, held in the afternoon of the festival. A large crowd of international visitors and locals would gather next to Injalak Arts and Crafts Centre, their cameras poised to capture the action set against the picturesque backdrop of Injalak Hill. Among the crowd were both Bininj/Arrarrkpi and Balanda based in Gunbalanya and Jabiru, and a wide variety of tourists, from those of retirement age travelling the country (referred to in Australia affectionately as 'grey nomads'), to families with children and young travellers from overseas. In 2011, they were welcomed by traditional owner Nakodjok Jacob

Nayinggul, who offered his encouragement to the dancers: 'have a good time and have a good go'. 'Emcee' Isaiah Nagurrgurrba then took up the microphone and introduced each of the dance groups to the audience. The 'host' group—the Karrbarda dancers—began the ceremony, with Eric Mardday and Geoffrey Nabageyo leading the singing. Ganbaladj Nabageyo led the women in the digging of the yam to the steady beat of the clapstick, before the *yawurrinj* joined in as the tempo became faster. They formed a huddle and called out together to start the dance. Nganjmirra led out in different directions around the large ground, facing the audience, before turning in and fixing his gaze on his fellow dancers. The audience was captivated by his poise and balance, as he moved in towards the group, stamped the ground deftly and rapidly, then crouched on one leg and called out once more with the rest of the group, pointing to the sky.

Skipping ahead to 2012, the host group Karrbarda opened proceedings as they had the year before. Now, it was time for the visiting group from Ramingining to take over, led by singer Bobby Bunungurr, with Michael Dawu (Support Material Figure 7.ii) and Frances Djulibing leading the dancing.[1] This group of performers are well known throughout Arnhem Land, having appeared on screen in a number of films. 'You seen that film *Ten Canoes*?' Dawu prompted the audience, referring to the 2006 film directed by Rolf De Heer and set in the Arafura swamp near Ramingining. '[That's] us mob, right here… I'm The Stranger [character] right now. Manjmak! Yoh! (*Great, yes!*)'.[2] He planted two poles in the centre of the ceremony ground, which became a focal point for the dance. The singing and didjeridu playing started up and the dancers skipped around the poles, lifting their knees high. To the sound of overblown notes on the didjeridu, they paused and extended an arm out to the singing ensemble, palms facing down. The stopping and starting of the didjeridu rhythm gave the music a halting quality. This was so unlike the steady didjeridu rhythms that characterise western Arnhem Land accompaniment that it marked this music as coming from *koyek* (K: east).

Singer Bobby Bunungurr addressed the crowd: 'audience… you see… my daughter [Frances Djulibing] Stand there [Bobby points to where Djulibing is standing]. All the girls, women, lined up, join in! You're welcome, this is a public [genre]!'[3] Dawu then walked around the perimeter of the dance ground, pointing out men in the crowd, commanding them: 'stand up, stand up!' Nagurrgurrba further encouraged the audience, quipping 'show us some moves—*larrk*!'[4] Gleefully and just a little sheepishly, the audience moved forward and lined up behind Dawu and Djulibing, according to gender. I left my recording gear running and got up with the rest of the male tourists to follow the dancers, crouching and pretending to hold rifles as the singers sang the verse of the song, then lunging forward and calling out with the overblown notes of the didjeridu, performing a dance that enacted a story from World War Two. Just as we started to get the hang of the actions, the song ended abruptly. The tourists resumed their places in the crowd once more, short of air from that burst of physical exertion, but feeling jovial about their attempts to dance to the music, which now seemed less alien than before.

Returning to the performance in 2011, and the final group to perform were the 'Goulburn Island mob', led by Johnny Namayiwa, with Solomon Nangamu and Alfred Gawaraidji taking turns to accompany on the didjeridu. The audience was again encouraged to join in, much to the delight of two young women wearing tie-dyed fabrics and fairy wings, who had been keenly watching the *daluk* from opposite the dance ground and swaying their own arms from side to side with the music. They rushed over excitedly and lined up beside the *daluk*, joining a dozen or so others, and prepared for the beginning of the next song. The didjeridu started up and Namayiwa began to beat a steady rhythm. Soon, all of the female tourists were dancing in unison with the *daluk*, with some enthusiastically moving their hips and arms to the beat. The more astute observers replicated the subtle turning in and out of the feet, while others lifted their knees, mimicking the men's style of dance, much to the amusement of the local Bininj (see Support Material Figure 7.iii).

Namayiwa shifted up a gear to a fast tempo song, and some *yawurrinj* from Goulburn and Croker Islands emerged from the crowd onto the dance ground. They demonstrated how to lead in, stamp, pause, and call Bininj/Arrarrkpi style. A young Balanda boy watched them closely and attempted to imitate their scooping and flicking the sand with their feet, frantically scraping his shoes back and forth in the sand. Some workers from the uranium mine dressed in high-visibility uniform joined in, their heavy boots proving somewhat of a burden in executing the knee lifts. From the audience, a local group of *daluk* looked on, laughing and cheering at the unusual sight of men marching and clomping their way around the dance ground. At the end of the song, with the guidance of Joey Nganjmirra and others from Minjilang and Warruwi, the men started to work together, coordinating their stamping with the beat and mimicking the oscillating arm movements of the *yawurrinj*.

Both in 2011 and 2012, as the sun went down the action would shift from the ceremony ground to the oval, where a boisterous crowd gathered, eager to see their relatives up on stage, and to dance to the energetic rhythms of the reggae and rock-inspired music. Many performers and audience members would check in first at the Club on the other end of town for some drinks, before wandering over to the oval. Although no longer the centre of the festival's activities, the Club remained a significant social meeting place, and its opening hours on Festival day would determine to a large extent the programming and duration of the *kun-borrk* performance. (The Club's opening time of 5:30 pm presented a tension for members of the community with alcohol dependency since *kun-borrk* is normally held in the late afternoon/evening). The atmosphere on the oval would be festive and jovial, with audience members singing along to songs that they had heard on the radio or listened to on their smartphones. They called out in appreciation whenever the performers announced particular songs and dedicated the songs to particular clan groups, and pointed in the direction of their homelands when the performers sang about these places.

190   *'Join in and Dance'*: *Festivals and new forms of exchange*

Certain conventions used by performers would be recognisable in any rock concert setting, for example, the configuration of the band members on the stage, and the way that the more flamboyant performers tilted their microphones skyward to sing, or struck masculine poses with their guitars. However, there were other aspects to these performances that marked them specifically as Bininj/Arrarrkpi concerts, for example, the inclusion of the didjeridu during Instrumental Sections with lead guitar, and the words of the songs, most of which would only be understood by the Kunwinjku and Mawng speakers who were jumping up and down to the music near the front of the stage, calling out, and singing along. Other elements further signalled the identity of the bands in more specific ways. For example, underneath their casual dress of jeans and t-shirts, Warruwi-based band Matter of Soul would paint themselves with *delek* in the same way used for *manyardi* ceremony when dancing to the Nginji/Ngili and Inyjalarrku songs: with white stripes across the forehead, arms, and legs (see Figure 7.1).

One of the highlights of the stage performance in 2011 was a band called Wildflower from Mamadawerre outstation in western Arnhem Land, led by three

Figure 7.1 Matter of Soul Band from Goulburn Island performing at the 2012 Stone Country Festival in Gunbalanya with *manyardi* ceremonial body paint. From left to right, Roderick Lee, Peter, Darren Narul, Russel Agalara, and Jay Galaminda. The video projected on the screen behind the performers is from the 1948 NGS footage at Gunbalanya, and depicts Larry Marawana's children examining a fish pulled from the billabong. Photograph by Reuben Brown.

frontwomen singing powerful choruses in Kunwinjku language, while the lead guitarist Dominic Narorrga gracefully led in the songs and filled Instrumental Sections between verses with catchy riffs. Wildflower Band are unique not only because they are talented musicians singing rock 'n' roll songs in Kunwinjku, but also because they embody new expressions of *daluk* participation and knowledge of the *bininj*-oriented domain of public song. While most bands draw on patrilineally inherited *kun-borrk* song traditions, Wildflower draw instead on matrilineally inherited knowledge, singing songs inspired by Dreaming stories passed down from their aunty Jill Nganjmirra. The lyrics frequently reference their clan country. For example, one song called 'Kabbari' pays homage to the ancestors that lived in that particular place (listen to **AVEx_7.1**):

AVex_7.1 https://wildflowerband.bandcamp.com/track/kabbari

Korroko Bininj birri-ni kunred Kabbari
Nawu kun-borrk birri-karrmi birri-borrkkeyi
Kaluk Bininj birrim-dolkkang nawu kakbibeh
(Chorus:) *Ahwurd Kabbari, Kabbari*
A long time ago people lived on this land Kabbari
They used to have ceremonies, singing and dancing at that place
Then some people came from the north
(Chorus:) My special place, Kabbari, Kabarri[5]

I had purchased Wildflower's album *Manginburru Bininj* at the start of my fieldwork, and played it many times during the four-hour trip along the Arnhem Highway from Darwin to Jabiru and Gunbalanya. I enjoyed listening to the Bininj Kunwok language, so clearly enunciated by the singers, and singing along to the lyrics in the booklet accompanying the album (with translations by Murray Garde). Now at Gunbalanya oval, I watched Wildflower performing a song called 'Gunbalanya', which was proving a hit with the local crowd. It tells of the creation story about an echidna and turtle that is linked to the formation of the three surrounding hills—Arrkuluk, Injalak, and Nimbabirr. Suddenly, I had the impulse to move closer and join with the crowd of Bininj/Arrarrkpi gathered at the front of the stage. Jammed in together, we jumped up and down to the beat, sang along to the chorus in Kunwinjku and English, called out, and pointed to the hill country surrounding us.

***

192 'Join in and Dance': Festivals and new forms of exchange

In previous chapters, I have described events that centre on the theme of exchange and intercultural encounter: a reburial ceremony, a Mamurrng ceremony, a funeral ceremony, and informal corroborees held for visiting parties. This chapter examines another significant event in western Arnhem Land involving intercultural exchange through the performance of *kun-borrk/manyardi*: the Indigenous music festival. Highly anticipated by locals and visitors each year, Indigenous cultural festivals in western Arnhem Land and beyond play a significant role in creating and maintaining a genuine dialogue between Indigenous and non-Indigenous people about what it means to live as Bininj/Arrarrkpi in contemporary Australia. Unlike other mainstream festivals, these community-run festivals reflect Bininj/Arrarrkpi concepts, themes, languages, and traditions which are understood and celebrated by local audiences. They rely on both Bininj/Arrarrkpi and Balanda participation and stewardship, and are dependent on local resources and customs as well as insecure council, regional, and federal funding. This chapter focusses on two festivals that I participated in—the Mahbilil Festival (Mahbilil) held in Jabiru, and the Stone Country Festival (SCF) held at Gunbalanya. *Mahbilil* is a Kundjeyhmi word that refers to the wind that blows late in the afternoon in late September when the festival is held, while the 'stone country' refers to the country around the Arnhem Land plateau belonging to (*wardde-ken*-identifying) Bininj.

As described in the opening passage of this chapter, festival participants are invited by ceremony leaders onto the dance ground during the daytime to engage directly with the song traditions of Arnhem Land, and to familiarise themselves with the sounds and aesthetics of Arnhem Land culture through participation rather than explanation. This experience contextualises for the audience performances of music in adopted musical styles that take place in the evening on the stage. Following the work of other scholars who have analysed popular music in the Top End, this chapter will show how the 'stage' music performed by bands at festivals draws on themes from a Bininj/Arrarrkpi worldview, and directly references known *kun-borrk/manyardi* repertories performed on the dance ground. In this sense, the contemporary music performed by local bands on the stage represents a continuation of, rather than a departure from, Indigenous song traditions. Both emphasise connection to Country and ancestors, as well as language and clan affiliations.

Following my analysis in previous chapters of the way that song order, tempo, and rhythmic mode relate to particular ceremonial occasions, I discuss the variety of different *kun-borrk/manyardi* groups that performed on the ceremony ground at the Mahbilil and Stone Country Festivals and analyse the songs that they selected to perform specifically for an international audience. Focussing on a performance by Milyarryarr singer Johnny Namayiwa, I show how changes in musical texture and rhythmic mode are exploited to build tension in the music and provide opportunities for virtuosic dance for an audience including tourists. The second part of the performance analysis examines how the various bands that performed on the stage at the Mahbilil and SCF drew inspiration from various *kun-borrk/manyardi* song-sets and other song traditions from the Top End. I analyse the way that a popular rock song called 'Long Grass Man' performed by the band 'The Northern Gentlemen' at the 2011 SCF draws on the *manyardi* repertoires of Mirrijpu and Marrwakara, and appeals to different audiences through the locally specific themes and languages. In this way, festival events have become a locus for song revival and renewal, attracting younger participants by giving them an opportunity to express themselves creatively, from the ceremony ground to the stage. The festival setting also enables Aboriginal ceremony leaders to engage younger generations in the performance traditions connected to their traditional country, helping to sustain their songs and keep their relationship to Country and their personal wellbeing strong and healthy.[6]

Indigenous cultural festivals in the contemporary era

In Arnhem Land and throughout Australia, cultural festivals are public occasions in which music and dance is front and centre as an expression of Australian Aboriginal and Torres Strait Islander culture and identity. Such events draw diverse participation from different Aboriginal and Torres Strait Islander communities, as well as non-Indigenous audiences. A number of annual, biennial, and triennial festivals celebrating Indigenous culture take place in various communities around Australia. These festivals are held both in major cities such as Melbourne (i.e. Indigenous Arts Festival), Sydney (i.e. Yabun, Dancerites), Adelaide (i.e. Spirit Festival), and Darwin (i.e. National Indigenous Music Awards), and in remote communities in Queensland (i.e. Laura Aboriginal Dance Festival), Western Australia (i.e. Mowanjum, KALACC festivals), and the Northern Territory (i.e. Walking With Spirits Festival at Beswick; Desert Mob at Alice Springs; Garma at Gulkula, etc.). The Mahbilil and Stone Country Festivals discussed in this chapter are just two of many festivals in Arnhem Land, including the Jamalak Festival at Warruwi, named after a ceremony associated with the Mamurrng, which involves the host group 'whacking' the visitors with *delek*;[7] the Gurruwiling Festival held at Ramingining, named after the solar eclipse that sometimes occurs very late in the dry season; the Yugul Mangi Festival at Ngukurr; and the Lurr'a Festival at Maningrida, which draws on the Middjarn ceremony and takes its name from the concept of saltwater and freshwater people coming together to share knowledge.[8] Further afield in northeast Arnhem Land at Gulkula in the Yolŋu homelands is the popular Garma ('open') Festival, which references the festival's focus on public ceremony and sharing of Yolŋu law.[9]

Typically, these festivals take place during the dry season when roads into Kakadu National Park and Arnhem Land become accessible, bringing international visitors to the area. The usual permit from the Northern Land Council to enter Aboriginal Land may be waived for the festival, and visitors usually camp in designated areas of the town during their stay. 'Traditional dancing' (*kun-borrk/manyardi/bunggurl*) is often the highlight of the 'cultural experience' for many festival-goers, and is programmed in the cool of the late afternoon after the sun has gone down. Ceremony leaders offer the audience a brief exegesis on the origin of the songs and dances and invite audience participation for particular dances. Other festival activities may include bark painting and weaving demonstrations and workshops, preparation and consumption of 'bush foods' such as buffalo, barramundi, and magpie geese cooked the traditional way in a ground oven, and other traditionally inspired activities such as spear-throwing and didjeridu competitions. The evening's entertainment generally features rock and reggae-inspired bands from around Arnhem Land and sometimes further afield such as Central and Western Australia, or even international acts. The boundaries between performer and audience can be blurred, as family members of the bands often get up on stage to dance along and join in the singing.

Historically, festivals have provided a forum for Bininj/Arrarrkpi and other Indigenous Australians not only to express their unique cultures but also to assert sovereignty over their country and to voice opinions and feelings concerning issues such as land rights, community services, health and safety, and maintaining traditional culture and language. Famously, Yolŋu elders from Yirrkala used the occasion of the Barunga Festival of 1988 to present to former Prime Minister Robert Hawke their 'Barunga Statement' calling on the government to recognise their continued ownership over traditional homelands.[10] Hawke received the petition on Yolŋu land and promised a treaty, but ultimately failed to deliver (as recounted in the Yothu Yindi song *Treaty*). The Garma festival has also repeatedly brought together a broad representation of the Indigenous Australian community including ceremony holders from different clans, as well as Indigenous policy-makers, politicians, academics, and local organisation leaders. This has provided an opportunity for stakeholders concerned about cultural maintenance and survival to discuss issues affecting their communities and to lobby for political support.[11]

Increasingly, music festivals have become the main occasions in which custodians can pass on their song and dance traditions to younger generations and revitalise and reclaim repertories and ceremony. For example, the Mowanjum Festival in the Kimberley region of Western Australia has become an event around which older generations have reintroduced songs and dances to younger people from archival recordings, and passed on vital cultural knowledge, in preparation for the performance of *junba* at the festival. Ethnomusicologist Sally Treloyn liaised with Mowanjum Art and Cultural Centre in the Kimberley and with local rangers to assist Ngarinyin/Wunambal elders and songmen to record, discuss, and pass on their *junba* repertories.[12] In this instance as elsewhere, it was not just the festival event, but the support in terms of resources and personnel provided by local organisations such as the Aboriginal Arts Centre and individual researchers such as Treloyn—that came together around the event to help elders and songmen in their efforts to teach the next generation and keep their tradition strong.

Fast one for bininj; slow one for daluk

The period of 2011–13 was an energising time for the public presentation of *kun-borrk/manyardi* and *bunggurl* in Jabiru and Gunbalanya at the Stone Country and Mahbilil Festivals. 'Traditional dance' gained elevated status in the programme of the 2011 SCF as part of the festival's focus on Bininj culture. Funding was allocated not only for local groups from Gunbalanya and western Arnhem Land to perform but also for visiting dance groups to take part. This included the Gurrumba Gurrumba clan singers and dancers, led by Roy Burnyila and Bobby Bunungurr from Ramingining, who participated in 2011 and 2012 respectively, as well as Mimih singers and dancers led by Crusoe Kurddal from Maningrida, who participated in 2012. The Gurrumba Gurrumba group in turn invited local groups from Gunbalanya to attend their local festival, Gurruwiling.[13] Nabarlek singers led by Terrah Guymala based in Gunbalanya and the outstation of Manmoyi (about 55 km south of Maningrida) also took part in the performance in 2012 (see Support Material Figure 7.b). Under the direction of Saint-Clare in previous years, the Mahbilil Festival at Jabiru had featured the Karrbarda dancers alongside dance groups from northeast Arnhem Land (where Saint-Clare had previously worked) such as David Dingala's *bunggurl* group from Groote Eylandt. With my involvement in 2011 and 2012 as 'cultural liaison' for the festival's *kun-borrk* programme, I facilitated Goulburn Island *manyardi* singers and dancers (Milyarryarr and Mirrijpu song-sets) to participate alongside Karrbarda (see Support Material Figure 7.iv). In this way, the festival programmes in both 2011 and 2012 at both SCF and Mahbilil reflected and reinforced pre-existing relationships of ceremonial exchange between groups living together at Gunbalanya, living within the region of Arnhem Land, and also from outside of the region.

Following conventions observed in previous chapters that examine performance events where multiple groups come together, the ordering of songs at the Mahbilil and Stone Country Festivals took into consideration the origins of the various song repertories.[14] Each performance was configured differently depending on which groups participated, and their proximity to the 'stone country' in which the festival took place. On each occasion, the Karrbarda group opened proceedings as the 'host' group, representing the songs of the stone country (in the absence of specific song-sets connected to Mengerrdji, Erre, Urningangk, Gaagadju, and Kundjeyhmi language groups, the traditional owners of Gunbalanya and Jabiru). Speaking on behalf of the Karrbarda group and Bininj Kunwok-speaking clans long resident at Gunbalanya and Jabiru, Isaiah Nagurrgurrba acknowledged and thanked the traditional owners. The second group to perform on three occasions were Goulburn Island singers representing *kurrula* or the saltwater country (Milyarryarr at Mahbilil 2011, Mirrijpu at SCF 2012 and Mahbilil 2013, and Marrawiwi at SCF 2012). Where 'visiting' groups from outside of western Arnhem Land also participated (for example, SCF 2011 and SCF 2012), they took over in the middle section of the ceremony, before handing back to a group from western Arnhem Land to conclude the performance (Milyarryarr at SCF 2011 and Nabarlek at SCF 2012). In this way, the performance sequence came full circle: starting from the 'home' country, venturing out, and then returning home once more. This was perhaps best illustrated at the SCF 2012, in which six groups participated in the order (in terms of communities represented by the song groups): Gunbalanya—Goulburn—Goulburn—Maningrida—Ramingining—Manmoyi/Gunbalanya (see Table 7.1 and Figure 7.2).

Because festivals attract a broader non-Indigenous audience compared with other public ceremonial occasions in western Arnhem Land, *kun-borrk/manyardi* songmen tend to perform more songs in fast rhythmic modes, which provide the opportunity for the *bininj* in particular to 'show their moves' for the audience (as Nagurrgurrba put it), while *daluk* are also encouraged to join in the dance.

Table 7.1 The ordering of song groups at the Stone Country Festival in 2011 and 2012 and Mahbilil Festival in 2011 and 2013[15]

SCF 2011 https://dx.doi.org/10.26278/WS37-Y814	**Mahbilil 2011** https://dx.doi.org/10.26278/HYVF-8B21	**SCF 2012** https://dx.doi.org/10.26278/N3RF-2E63	**Mahbilil 2013** https://dx.doi.org/10.26278/J648-H005
Karrbarda open with six song items (songs KB12, KB07, KB02)	**Karrbarda** open with two song items (KB01)	**Karrbarda** open with five song items (songs KB02, KB13)	**Karrbarda** open with eleven song items (songs KB02, KB07, KB10, KB17)
Gurrumba Gurrumba clan perform six song items (4 Magpie Geese; 2 Frog songs)	**Milyarryarr** follow with one song item (songs MR04 and MR05)	**Mirrijpu** follow with three song items (songs MP06 and MP04)	**Mirrijpu** join **Karrbarda**, singing four song items in combination (songs MP06, KB17, MP26, MP04)
Milyarryarr finish with four song items (songs MR04 and MR05)		**Marrawiwi** joins Mirrijpu group to perform one song item (MX01) **Mimih** group perform four song items (songs MY03, MY04, and MY02) **Gurrumba Gurrumba clan** perform four song items (Magpie Geese and War dance) **Nabarlek** group finish with four song items ('rock pigeon', NK01 'mandjandamed', NK07 'ngalkaldilhmiken', and 'barrk/black wallaroo')	

'Join in and Dance': Festivals and new forms of exchange   197

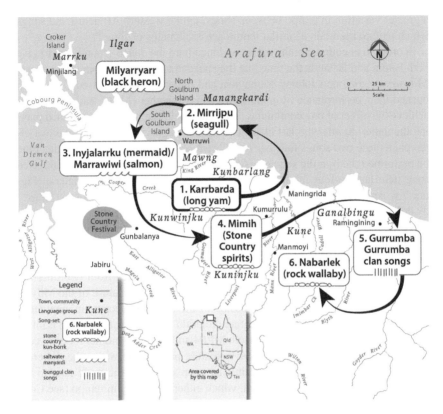

Figure 7.2 Map showing the order of ceremonial performance at the Stone Country Festival, 2012. Cartography © Brenda Thornley 2023.

Normally, we might expect a performance of *kun-borrk/manyardi* to start with a number of songs in slow rhythmic mode, after which the overall tempo gets faster before returning to a slow tempo at the end (marked by the slowest song, the *nigi/ngalbadjan*). An analysis of the songs performed at the SCF 2011 and their corresponding rhythmic modes and tempi illustrates a different trend (see Support Material Figure 7.v). While the Karrbarda group began and ended with a song in moderate rhythmic mode, the majority of their songs were performed in fast doubled rhythmic mode (5b). Similarly, the Milyarryarr group performed only songs in fast even (5a) and fast doubled rhythmic modes (5b/5g), and the overall tempo of their performance gradually became faster but did not slow at the end. Significantly, neither group performed the *ngalbadjan/nigi* song to finish their performance. The Gurrumba Gurrumba *bunggurl* (clan songs) from central Arnhem Land were shorter in duration and featured different rhythmic modes than those typically featured in western Arnhem Land songs (for example, unmeasured rhythmic mode [1] in which the singer sings without didjeridu or clapstick accompaniment). Overall, the *bunggurl* performance was characterised by a greater variation in tempo between songs, unlike western Arnhem Land songs which tend to maintain a similar tempo across changes of song.[16]

In order to encourage both women and men onto the dance ground, and to give both Bininj and Balanda the time that they needed to get up and join in the dance, Milyarryarr songman Johnny Namayiwa and didjeridu player Alfred Gawaraidji opened their performance by joining two songs together (MR05 and MR04). To achieve the effect of one continuous song, Gawaraidji immediately resumed playing the didjeridu after the last clapstick beat of the previous song. Namayiwa often pairs these two songs together in different combinations;[17] however, this time he performed them in the sequence MR05_MR04_MR05 to create one elongated song item lasting four minutes and 32 seconds (refer to Support Material Figure 7.v, song item 20110827_02-RB_07_26_MR05_MR04_MR05.wav, https://dx.doi.org/10.26278/HM05-D789).[18] One of these songs—MR04—features suspended clapstick beating in the Introduction, where the singer suspends clapstick accompaniment while singing the opening melodic section of the song, while the didjeridu accompaniment provides the metre. This is a feature of *wangga* in the Daly region, as Marett has analysed in relation to two songs from two different *wangga* repertories by Barrtjap and Burrenjuck.[19] Another feature of the Milyarryarr repertory is the extended suspension of the didjeridu accompaniment (Inyjalarrku and Karrbarda songs also feature didjeridu suspension, although it is much shorter, lasting one clapstick beat). Both MR04 and MR13—another recently conceived song in Namayiwa's song-set[20]—feature passages in which the didjeridu stops playing and the singer/s sustain/s an open vowel on the tonic note to the accompaniment of the clapstick beat, which either decreases in tempo (see Coda of MR05 in Table 7.2) or increases in tempo (see the Coda section in Table 7.3).

This change in tempo and in musical texture has the effect of building and releasing tension in the music, and corresponds to changes in rhythmic mode, which indicate the dance cues. In MR04, as the didjeridu stops and the clapstick beat increases in tempo, the dancers respond by coming together and moving in towards the singing ensemble as they perform the 'stamping and pausing' dance phrase. Once the singer 'lets go' of the note and the clapstick beat is terminated, the dancers call out on the final beat, and the tension is released as the didjeridu accompaniment returns.[21] Tables 7.2 and 7.3 analyse how the structural components of songs MR04 and MR05 correspond with the clapstick beat and changes in the rhythmic mode (listen to **AVEx_7.2** and follow the song structure transcript). The songs are structured in a similar way to other western Arnhem Land songs in a strophic form, with a repeated verse made up of two phrases of the song text, interspersed with sung vocables in the Instrumental Sections and the Coda. The rhythm is additive: various sections of the song are made up of clapstick beat groupings that are divisible by four for the most part, while the beat is also grouped into six during the Coda of both songs. Gapped rhythmic patterns in the clapstick beating function not only to synchronise the dance and punctuate the dance calls (marked with an *), but also to cue the shift from one rhythmic mode into another (i.e. from fast even to fast doubled beating in MR04 and from fast even to slow even beating in MR05).

'Join in and Dance': Festivals and new forms of exchange 199

AVex_7.2 https://dx.doi.org/10.26278/M1GM-5X70

Table 7.2 MR05 song structure and changes in rhythmic mode (AVEx_7.2)

Song structure	Intro	Verse				Instrumental section			Verse (repeat)		Coda			
Text Phrase		A	B (24 counts)			Vocables "oh, i____"			A	B	Vocables			
CS Beat Dance Call	None	16	16	8 ♪♫♩ *	12	16	♪♫♩ *	8	16	24	8 ♩♩♩♫♩♩	8 ♫♫♫♩♩ *		
Rhythmic mode		5a (with dance call rhythm)									2a/2e			
Tempo (bpm)		←———————— 130 ————————→								←slow rit.	←— 74 —→			
Didjeridu	←———————————————————————————————→										←————→			

Guide to listening: [0:16] Text Phrase A, [0:23] Text Phrase B, [0:52] Instrumental Section, [01:24] Coda.

Table 7.3 MR04 song structure and changes in rhythmic mode (AVEx_7.2).

Song structure	Intro	Verse				Instr. section	Verse (repeat)		Coda		
Text Phrase		A	B (8+6 counts)			Vocables "i"	A	B	Vocables "i"		
CS Beat Dance call	None	12 (counts)	10	+2 ♩♩♩♩♩♫♩♪ ♫♫♫♫♫ *		12	12	14 *	6	12	♩♩♩ *
Rhythmic mode		5b	5a/5c[var]		5b		5a/5c[var]	5b	5b	5a	
Tempo (bpm)		284 ←——→	136		286 ←————→		135	278	300		
Didjeridu	←————————————————————————————————————→										

Guide to listening: [0:42] Intro, [1:50] Text Phrase A, [1:56] Text Phrase B, [2:02] Instrumental Section, [2:18] Coda, [3:12] Repeat MR05.[22]

Figure 7.3 Toby Cooper from Croker Island dancing to rhythmic mode 5c in Milyarryarr song MR04 (AVEx_7.3). Photograph by David Mackenzie.

Figure 7.3 shows Toby Cooper from Croker Island dancing to Milyarryarr song MR04 and responding to the gapped rhythmic pattern [♩♩♩♩♩ ♪ ♩ ♩. ♪] (rhythmic mode 5c[var] in Table 7.3 MR04). Cooper anticipates the rhythmic mode (which is also mirrored in the vocal rhythm of Text Phrase B) by venturing away from the group of tourists behind him (who are learning the dance from another *bininj* dancer) and stamping for the first five beats, scooping the sand up with his feet as he goes. On the first rest beat, he pauses, then on the penultimate beat, he leaps, lifting both knees high up off the sand, and pivots his torso while in the air, before landing and calling out with the first doubled clapstick beat of rhythmic mode 5b (watch **AVEx_7.3**). In the background, the *daluk* dance with tourists and look on as Cooper executes his dance move. This sequence illustrates the way in which western Arnhem Land songmen joined together particular songs with passages of fast clapstick beating and contrasts in musical texture, in order to showcase the more virtuosic side of *kun-borrk/manyardi* for their audience of international visitors. The dancers responded by simultaneously instructing the tourists through their performance and also 'entertaining' the audience by demonstrating their athleticism combined with their particular knowledge of the songs and rhythmic modes.

AVex_7.3 https://dx.doi.org/10.26278/8183-4Q09

Taking kun-borrk/manyardi to the stage

The audience of international visitors and non-Indigenous locals may not have been fully aware of it, but the performances that took place on the main stage at the Stone Country and Mahbilil Festivals had much in common with the *kun-borrk/manyardi/bunggurl* performances that preceded them. Indeed, many of the singers who got up on stage to perform with their countrymen had earlier been singing and dancing on the ceremony ground. For example, at the SCF 2012, Crusoe Kurddal performed his Mimih song-set on the dance ground, and in the evening performed the same dances to the rock music of the Sunrize Band from Maningrida. Similarly, Mawng-speaking Arrarrkpi bands from Goulburn Island—Matter of Soul and Northern Gentlemen—featuring singers Solomon Nangamu, Harold Warrabin, and Russell Agalara, drew inspiration from *manyardi* song-sets Mirrijpu and Marrwakara. Nabarlek songmen, led by Terrah Guymala, performed at the SCF 2012 *kun-borrk* performance, and then on stage as the Nabarlek Band, where their ceremonial songs were reframed into different rock compositions. The Nabarlek song-set in particular has spawned a number of intergenerational musical formations. Members of the Nabarlek Band, including Stuart Guymala, Birdibob Watson, and Winston Naborlhborlh, first learned the ceremonial songs from Jimmy Kalarriya. The Rock Wallaby Band (a translation of the Bininj Kunwok word *nabarlek*) is made up of younger men from Manmoyi and led by Winston Naborlhborlh, who is also part of the Nawarddeken Band with Isaiah Nagurrgurrba. All three bands sing songs from the Nabarlek *kun-borrk* repertory. As Barwick et al. have shown, many Nabarlek Band songs typically pay homage to their *kun-borrk* origins by presenting the songs as they would be performed ceremonially with didjeridu and clapstick accompaniment, before 'reframing' the songs by setting them to different instrumentation (guitar, organ, piano, and drums) and by splicing lines of song text from different songs together, setting the text to new melodies, and changing the musical form of the song.[23]

This method of taking ancestral song traditions and reframing them in new ways for a contemporary audience was pioneered in the 1980s and 1990s by Yolŋu cultural leaders from eastern Arnhem Land who performed with bands such as Soft Sands and Yothu Yindi, and has since become the template for contemporary rock and reggae-inspired bands from western Arnhem Land.[24] As scholars of popular music from northeast Arnhem Land and the Daly region have argued, a primary motivation behind Indigenous clan-based rock bands is to use new musical mediums in order to reproduce Indigenous values and structures which '[point] local audiences "back to culture"'.[25] Stubington and Dunbar-Hall trace the Yolŋu ideology of *ganma* (mixing of opposites) in Yothu Yindi's music, through the presentation of musical material in their album *Tribal Voice*—where *manikay* melodies are heard first in their original form before they are set to rock music in the following track—and through the hit song 'Treaty', in which the song text alternates between Yolŋu Matha and English, and musical sections of rock are juxtaposed with *manikay*.[26] Expanding on this analysis,

Table 7.4 Summary of bands that performed at the Stone Country and Mahbilil Festivals in Gunbalanya and Jabiru in 2011 and 2012

Band/group	Origin	Language	Genre	Affiliated song-set/genre/inspiration	Festival
Mambali Band	Numbulwar	English/ Nunggubuyu	Rock	Central Arnhem Land *bunggurl*	SCF 2012
Nabarlek Band	Manmoyi/ Gunbalanya	Kunwinjku	Rock/ Reggae/Country	Nabarlek song-set, western Arnhem Land *kun-borrk*	Mahbilil 2012
Nawarddeken Band	Manmoyi/ Gunbalanya	Kunwinjku	Rock/ Reggae	Nabarlek song-set (*kun-borrk*); Nabarlek Band	Mahbilil 2012 SCF 2012
Rock Wallaby	Manmoyi/ Gunbalanya	Kunwinjku	Rock/ Reggae	Nabarlek song-set (*kun-borrk*); Nabarlek Band	SCF 2011, Mahbilil 2011&2012
West Arnhem Boss	Gunbalanya	English	Rock/ Hip hop	Bininj moral/social themes	Mahbilil 2011; SCF 2011
Wildflower Band	Mamadawerre/ Gunbalanya	Kunwinjku	Rock/ reggae	Bininj dreaming stories by Jill Nganjmirra	SCF 2011
Yugul Voice	Ngukurr	English	Hip hop/rock	Bininj moral/social themes	SCF 2012
Matter of Soul (MOS) Band	Warruwi	Mawng	Rock	Mirrijpu/Marrwakara/ Nginji/Ngiii/Injialarku song-sets (*manyardi*)	Mahbilil 2012 SCF 2011 SCF 2012
Northern Gentlemen	Warruwi	Mawng	Rock	Mirrijpu/Marrwakara song-sets (*manyardi*)	SCF 2012
Bininj Band	Croker Island Gunbalanya Maningrida Warruwi	Kunwinjku/ English	Pop/rock/ reggae	*Kun-borrk/manyardi*	Mahbilil 2011 and 2012
Sunrize Band	Maningrida Liverpool River	Burarra	Rock	Mimih song-set (*kun-borrk*)	SCF 2012
Sunset Liverpool River	Maningrida	Burarra/ Possibly Ndjébbana	Rock/ Reggae	Central Arnhem Land *bunggurl*	SCF 2012

(*Continued*)

'Join in and Dance': Festivals and new forms of exchange   203

Table 7.4 (Continued)

Band/group	Origin	Language	Genre	Affiliated song-set/genre/inspiration	Festival
Black Arm Band	(Indigenous) Australia	English/ Aboriginal languages	Various	Various Indigenous song traditions, languages, stories	Mahbilil 2012
New Generation	(Indigenous) Darwin	English	Rock	Unknown	SCF 2012
Reggae Dave (Dave Asera)	(Indigenous) Darwin	English	Reggae	Unknown	Mahbilil 2011
Tjupi Band	Papunya, Central Australia	Luritja/English	Reggae	Warumpi Band	SCF 2011
Young Guns	(Indigenous) Bagot, Darwin	English	Rock/pop	Unknown	Mahbilil 2011; SCF 2012
African Brothers	Africa	Unknown	African drum music	Unknown	Mahbilil 2012
Dream Voice	Possibly Democratic Republic of Congo	Unknown	Congo music	Possibly Soukous	Mahbilil 2011
Unknown	New Zealand	Maori	Haka	Traditional Maori dance	Mahbilil 2011
Jess Ribeiro and the Bone Collectors	(Balanda) Darwin	English	Country/folk	Unknown	Mahbilil 2012

Key to table: *wardde-ken* bands shaded grey; *kurrula* bands shaded light grey; mixed *wardde-ken/kurrula* bands shaded dark grey; other Indigenous Australian bands shaded light grey; and non-indigenous Australian and international bands unshaded.

Corn explains how Yothu Yindi experimented with Western music styles, while their music remained grounded in the principles of Yolŋu culture and law. This melding of traditions reflected 'in microcosm the ethos of biculturalism that [lead singer] Mandawuy [Yunupingu] sought to introduce into Yolŋu school curriculum',[27] and it demonstrated how 'durable traditional ideas could be contemporised for younger Yolŋu audiences, and successfully draw their attention away from competing Anglophonic entertainments'.[28] Alberto Furlan similarly explores how popular bands of Wadeye became 'instrumental in the preservation of indigenous culture', standing in as 'the contemporary counterpart of *Dhanba* [an Aboriginal song genre from the Daly region] and other traditional songs'.[29] Popular music from Wadeye aimed to educate young audiences by pointing to affiliations with traditional estates and a network of kinship relationships.[30]

Table 7.4 outlines the various bands and dance groups that performed on the stage at the Stone Country and Mahbilil Festivals in the period of 2011–13. The table shows the origins of the bands, the language of the songs, and a generic description for the genre that characterised each band's music, as well as the song-set or 'traditional' genre affiliated with the band or inspiration behind the band's songs, and the festival at which the band performed. The Stone Country Festival and Mahbilil Festival programmes overlapped in terms of both the *kun-borrk/manyardi* performance and the stage concert, because the festivals were held within a few weeks of one another and bands were often invited to perform at both events. The Stone Country Festival featured mainly 'local' (western Arnhem Land) bands and Indigenous bands such as Tjupi Band from Central Australia and New Generation and Young Guns from Darwin, while Mahbilil Festival featured more of an even mix of local bands, non-local Indigenous bands (Black Arm Band), non-Indigenous Darwin-based bands (Jess Ribeiro and the Bone Collectors), and international groups (African Brothers, Dream Voice, Maori dancers), perhaps reflecting the mix of the community at Jabiru, consisting of Bininj, Balanda, and a large number of transient international tourists.

Unlike in northeastern Arnhem Land, band participation in western Arnhem Land is not strictly based on clan membership; bands are loosely organised instead around language and family groups, sometimes located at particular outstation communities (although some band members are spread over the broader region of western Arnhem Land, such as the Bininj Band whose members are from Croker Island, Gunbalanya, Maningrida, and Warruwi). Performers nevertheless dedicate certain songs to countrymen in the audience and ancestors of their particular clan, i.e. Maningburru, Mayinjinaj, and Majakurdu. Because *kun-borrk/manyardi* song-sets are individually owned, some bands may be made up of musicians with connections to numerous *kun-borrk/manyardi* repertoires. Even when band members do not have specific patrilineally or matrilineally inherited *kun-borrk/manyardi* song repertoires, they may reference the song tradition either directly or indirectly through their music. Some contemporary Bininj singers such as Gunbalanya singer/composer Dallas Thompson, who performs with West Arnhem Boss and Yugul Voice, make no direct reference to *kun-borrk/*

manyardi, focussing instead on contemporary moral issues and problems—such as alcohol and drug abuse, and irresponsible driving—as the subject matter for their songs, and singing mainly in English rather than Aboriginal languages.[31]

An example of a rock song that proved popular with local Indigenous audiences at the festivals and that follows the 'template' of other Arnhem Land bands by continuing the *kun-borrk/manyardi* tradition in a contemporary format is 'Long Grass Man', performed by Matter of Soul (MOS) Band (SCF 2011) and also by The Northern Gentlemen (SCF 2012). (The 'long grass' refers to various areas of Darwin where predominantly Aboriginal homeless populations live in temporary shelters among the spear grass that grows very tall in the monsoon season.) 'Long Grass Man' was originally composed and recorded by Harold Warrabin and Solomon Nangamu in 2003, with members of both the Northern Gentlemen and MOS band at Warruwi, during a visit from music students studying at Charles Darwin University. It has since become something of an anthem for the 'long grass' community in Darwin, many of whom have left their Aboriginal communities to live in the city. In one of several versions of the song posted on YouTube,[32] 'long grassers' busking at Mindil Beach in front of the popular tourist market perform a spirited rendition with a reggae-inspired guitar vamp, demonstrating the way that the song has been adopted across a number of Indigenous language groups that live together in the long grass communities in Darwin.[33]

The 2003 recording (listen to **AVEx_7.4**) opens with Mirrijpu song MP06 sung by the late Solomon Ganawa with clapstick and didjeridu accompaniment, followed by an upbeat drum and electric guitar lead-in to the rock song **[0:49]**. This follows the convention discussed earlier with regard to Arnhem Land bands such as Soft Sands, Yothu Yindi, and Nabarlek Band, of acknowledging the 'source' of the musical inspiration for the song before expanding the song into the domain of the rock genre. Each verse of the song is sung in English, while the chorus is performed in Mawng and Manangkardi. The song text encapsulates the feeling of abandonment for an Aboriginal person who has left their homeland and is 'running' from some kind of trouble, eventually turning to the Indigenous community in Darwin (the 'long grass mob'). The chorus consists of the call-and-response, 'I'm a long grass man' [♫ ♩ ♩ ♩]. When performed at the festival, the audience join in with the response so that both singer and audience are encouraged to identify with the community of long grassers. In the second verse **[01:12]**, the subject of the singer/narrator changes from first person singular (I don't know where to go') to first person plural ('we don't know where to go'), further emphasising the inclusivity of the audience[34]:

AVex_7.4 https://dx.doi.org/10.26278/Z57Q-EN95

206 *'Join in and Dance': Festivals and new forms of exchange*

VERSE 1

It's been a long time

Since I left my home and my family

Bin running and thinking about my-self

Seasons come and seasons go

and I don't know where to go

so I pack up my swag and head into my long grass mob

CHORUS

I'm a long grass man   [response: I'm a long grass man]

I'm a lo:ong grass man   [response: I'm a long grass man]

People call me I'm a long grass man

VERSE 2

People come and people go

And we don't know where to go

And one and only

The ones that are the spirit of this land

Following a repeat of the chorus in English, the third **[01:59]** chorus is sung in Mawng. This could be interpreted as the singer/narrator's countrymen—other long grassers among the Darwin community originally from Goulburn Island—addressing him/her in their shared language, inviting the singer/narrator to join them ('come and sit here with me in the long grass'). The final chorus **[02:22]** addresses the subject's ancestral spirits in their language of Manangkardi:

MAWNG CHORUS

Ngawu kani Kutjanyjiga nga- wu

Come, sit down here

Ngawu kani Kutjanyjiga nga- wu

Come, sit down here

Ngawu Kutjanyjiga kani atpawani tuka Mirlak

Sit here together with me in the grass

'Join in and Dance': Festivals and new forms of exchange

kurrungmanyjiga   nuntirri   kani

Come, bring your grog here

kurrungmanyjiga   nuntirri   kani

Come, bring your grog here

Ngawu   Kutjanyjiga   kani   atpawani   tuka   Mirlak

Sit here together with me in the grass

MANANGKARDI CHORUS

Inyalatpa(rra)   lat**pa**-inyalat**pa**

Inyalatpa(rra)   lat**pa**-inyalat**pa**

Inyalat**pa**rra   lat**pa**rra   in**y**alat**pa**rra   Manangkardi

Again, the song pays homage to ancestral song traditions, by repeating the Mirrijpu/Marrwakara song word *inyalatpa* three times in one melodic sequence lasting eight beats (which is then repeated twice). In order to fit the words within the constraints of the rhythm, and to avoid enunciating two vowels at the boundaries of the repeated word, the singers replace the first syllable of the repeated word 'in' with the syllable 'rra' so that 'inyalatpa, inyalatpa, inyalatpa' becomes 'inyalatparralatparra-inyalatpa(rra)', with the stress of the beat (highlighted above in bold) falling on a different syllable each time. (This also suggests the high degree of flexibility of spirit language song words: we see this particular Manangkardi song word *inyalatpa* rendered in numerous ways—'inyalatpa-latpa-latpa-ye', 'alatparra inyalatparra' etc.—in order to fit the vocal rhythm of the song).[35] The singers finish the phrase of the final chorus with the word 'Manangkardi', which serves to identify the origin of these words to their audience of long grassers, speakers of other Aboriginal languages, and non-Aboriginal English speakers (to whom the language would be unrecognisable).[36]

In speaking to both broad and localised audiences with its use of English, Mawng, and spirit language Manangkardi, 'Long Grass Man' follows in the tradition of spontaneously composed *kun-borrk/manyardi* songs in multiple 'everyday' languages. The themes of the song also resonate with Aboriginal people in contemporary society who are living in 'two worlds', having either personally experienced a life of homelessness in the 'long grass', or who have family members and friends who are 'long grassers'.

Conclusion: new expressions for old songs

As events that are built around intercultural exchange on regional, national, and international levels, cultural festivals have been enthusiastically taken up by Bininj/Arrarrkpi of western Arnhem Land (as well as by other Indigenous Australians) as a contemporary extension of funeral and exchange ceremonies such as the Mamurrng. Although the action on the dance ground at these festivals constitutes faster and somewhat truncated versions of these other ceremonies, singers nevertheless borrow from the same inventory of songs and dances, and follow similar principles in the presentation of the songs, by considering the traditional country and languages associated with the songs in deciding the order in which various groups will perform. Just as Bininj/Arrarrkpi of western Arnhem Land and Yolŋu of eastern Arnhem Land have hosted Macassan and Balanda visitors in the past, nowadays at festival events they host French, Germans, Dutch, Chinese and Japanese, and other international visitors, as well as Indigenous and non-Indigenous Australians. Perhaps it was no coincidence that the dance ground where the ceremonial performance of *kun-borrk/manyardi* was held for the Stone Country Festival at Gunbalanya was located precisely at the same site of cross-cultural encounter which took place over 60 years ago, when visiting members of AASEAL pitched their tents overlooking the southern end of the billabong, between the ancient craggy hills of Arrkuluk to the west and Injalak to the east. The parallels are also striking between the role of Larry Marawana and 'emcee' Nagurrgurrba in acting as a cultural broker for the event and introducing the singers to the audience.

A key difference between the festival event and other Bininj/Arrarrkpi ceremonial occasions involving *kun-borrk/manyardi* is the very public nature of the forum and the extent to which it provides opportunities to engage with broader non-Indigenous audiences. As Phipps argues, Indigenous festivals are more than just acts of cultural 'revival and survival'; rather, they are 'significant, playful, and urgent acts of cultural politics'.[37] Events such as Mahbilil Festival and the

Stone Country Festival create opportunities for genuine intercultural learning, bringing Balanda who have an interest in Aboriginal culture—including those living in Aboriginal communities and towns such as Gunbalanya and Jabiru—together with Aboriginal artists and ceremony leaders, to participate in events which place Bininj/Arrarrkpi cultural values, languages, ideas, and lived realities at the fore. Much of this engagement takes place on the dance ground, where ceremony leaders such as Bunungurr, Djulibing, Kurddal, Gawaraidji, Guymala, Namayiwa, Nangamu, Mardday, and others invite audiences to join in and learn by actually *experiencing* the song tradition in its ceremonial setting. Because of the inherently flexible format of *kun-borrk/manyardi*, which caters for intergenerational participation, adult Balanda took on the role of Bininj/Arrarrkpi children as we attempted to follow the leaders of the dance. By connecting with the music—finding the patterns of the clapstick beat and allowing one's movements to follow them, while sweating under the heat of the sun and enjoying the feeling of sand between toes, the reverberations of the didjeridu and clapstick beat, and the frenzy of limbs and sand being tossed about—one had the feeling not only of working together with fellow dancers, but also of connecting with the surrounding Country.

By drawing in large audiences and local and international acts, festivals have become venues in which connections between clan and language groups are refreshed and reinstated, as well as sites for innovation of Bininj/Arrarrkpi artistic expression, including the *kun-borrk/manyardi* song tradition. The two songs that Namayiwa performed at the Stone Country Festival were in fact 'new' songs that he conceived in a dream not long before I met him in 2011. Performed in fast rhythmic modes, they complemented the predominantly moderate rhythmic mode songs that make up Namayiwa's inherited repertory of songs (passed on to him by Charlie Wardaga). In addition to generating new songs as part of *kun-borrk/manyardi* genres performed in the 'old way' for the ceremony ground, festivals also produce songs in the 'new' formats and genres for the stage. Drawing on foundational stories and inherited song traditions, western Arnhem Land bands have followed the Arnhem Land template by bringing these traditional elements into juxtaposition with contemporary musical expressions, in order to appeal to a broad audience of both Bininj/Arrarrkpi and Balanda dealing with various changes. This audience includes an itinerant population spread between outstations and towns such as Gunbalanya and Manmoyi, as well as cities such as Darwin, and a large proportion of younger Indigenous people living amongst a population that is ignorant of their lived experiences. By singing songs in their own languages and paying homage to their specific clan identities, younger Bininj/Arrarrkpi in particular are able to express their identity in an international but highly localised setting, and to challenge the stereotype of Aboriginality as it is often characterised by mainstream society.[38]

Because festivals encourage innovation, they play an increasingly important role in sustaining Bininj/Arrarrkpi performance traditions. Not only do such events raise the profile of *kun-borrk/manyardi* and educate the broader public about the diversity of other Aboriginal song genres from the Top End, but they also provide opportunities for ceremony leaders and elders to ensure that their numerous repertories of songs and dances continue to be passed down. But are festivals themselves sustainable? In spite of their popularity in the tourist calendar for the Top End and elsewhere in Australia, most festivals operate on modest budgets and rely on the resources and labour of local and visiting volunteers. As a consequence of the short-term and volatile nature of funding arrangements for community arts, the long-term sustainability of these festivals remains very much uncertain. Unfortunately, in the years after I finished my fieldwork at Gunbalanya (2014 and 2015), the Stone Country Festival at Gunbalanya did not run, partly because it lacked the funding and human resources to keep it going.

Notes

1 Singer Roy Burnyila led the group the year before in 2011.
2 Djulibing and Bunungurr also appeared in De Heer's 2014 film *Charlie's Country*, starring David Gulpilil.
3 [Bobby Bunungurr, 20120825-RB_05_edit.wav, https://dx.doi.org/10.26278/J0XD-TY87, 00:36:36.900–00:36:52.700].
4 K: 'not!; just kidding!' [Isaiah Nagurrgurrba, 20120825-RB_05_edit.wav, https://dx.doi.org/10.26278/J0XD-TY87, 00:37:38.100–00:37:45.600].
5 Wildflower, "Kabbari," recorded 2009, from the album *Manginburru Bininj*, Skinnyfish Music, 2009, compact disc.
6 Linda Barwick, Mary Laughren and Myfany Turpin, "Sustaining Women's Yawulyu/Awelye: Some Practitioners' and Learners' Perspectives," *Musicology Australia* 35, no. 2 (2013): 207.
7 Berndt, "Ceremonial Exchange," 162; Emma Sleath, "Island Festival Revives the Spirit of 'Jamalak'", Australian Broadcasting Corporation, 18 September 2013, http://www.abc.net.au/local/photos/2013/08/27/3835177.htm, accessed 9 April 2014.
8 Peter James Dawson and Noeletta McKenzie, "Inagurual Lurr'a Festival Comes to Maningrida," *West Arnhem Wire*, 31 October 2013, http://westarnhem.nt.gov.au/the-wire-news/2013/10/31/inagurual-lurra-festival-comes-to-maningrida, accessed January 2014.
9 See discussion in Aaron Corn, "Land, Song, Constitution: Exploring Expressions of Ancestral Agency, Intercultural Diplomacy and Family Legacy in the Music of Yothu Yindi with Mandawuy Yunupiŋu," *Popular Music* 29, no. 1 (2010): 85.
10 See Corn, "Land, Song, Constitution," 97.
11 At the 2002 Garma Festival, a forum on Indigenous Performance produced the "Garma Statement on Indigenous Music," calling for the recording and documentation of Indigenous song traditions as a matter of high priority and suggesting strategies to make archival recordings accessible to communities, such as the establishment of Indigenous Knowledge Centres with digital storage and retrieval systems where sound and digital records could be repatriated to communities (see "Garma Statement on Indigenous Music," National Recording Project for Indigenous Performance in Australia, 2002, http://www.aboriginalartists.com.au/NRP_statement.htm#statement). Since its inception, Garma has become a place where mainstream audiences and politicians come to listen to Indigenous perspectives on issues of Indigenous policy.

12 The "Sustaining *Junba* Project" involved a multifaceted approach including the management of a database for archival recordings at Mowanjum Art and Cultural Centre; conducting '*junba* camps' on traditional country led by elders and supported by Treloyn and the Cultural Centre, where children could prepare for ceremonial performance and learn the songs and dances; and training in producing multimedia, documenting songs, and managing the database of recordings. Treloyn and Emberly, "Sustaining Traditions," 165–69.

13 Singer Bobby Bunungurr and daughter Frances Djulibing also returned to Gunbalanya in subsequent years to learn screen printing techniques from artists at IAC.

14 Compare with my discussion of the performance of the Mamurrng at Goulburn Island (Chapter 4) in which the men enacted the journey from Gunbalanya to Warruwi by dancing the *mamurrng* in an order relating to their traditional country.

15 Details of the SCF 2011 recordings are provided in this chapter; for details of recordings from other festivals, see PARADISEC collection RB2, https://dx.doi.org/10.4225/72/56E97741DD607. No recordings were made of the performance at Mahbilil 2012; however, the song-set order mirrored that of 2013, with Karrbarda opening followed by Mirrijpu. The Stone Country Festival was not held between the period 2013–2021.

16 Further analysis of the use of rhythmic mode and tempo in Gurrumba Gurrumba clan songs did not fit within the scope of this study; however, future research might investigate whether similar differences are present in the presentation of songs for festival audiences compared with other ceremonial contexts.

17 Refer to previous recording sessions 20061018GUMR and 20070427MRMP, Support Material Appendix ii.

18 Such a long duration is unusual; most song items last between 1.5 and 2.5 minutes.

19 See Marett, *Songs, Dreamings, and Ghosts*, 164–69.

20 See recording session 20131106MR in Support Material Figure 1.e.

21 This build-up of tension created by 'cutting out' the underlying didjeridu accompaniment and increasing the clapstick beat tempo is perhaps similar to a 'bass drop' in electronic dance music, where a sudden minimisation of texture or an end to the pulsing bass rhythm leads to a build-up of texture as the music gets louder and louder and the tempo faster, before a climax point where the bass line is 'dropped' back in. In club music, this is orchestrated to coincide with an upsurge of energy, ecstasy, and movement on the dance floor.

22 For the repeat of MR05, the Introduction is shorter (eight counts) and there is only one instance of the Verse, Instrumental section, Verse repeat, and Coda.

23 Linda Barwick et al., "Bongolinj-Bongolinj and its Children: Collaborative Research on the Language, Music and History of a Songset from Northwest Arnhem Land," unpublished paper presented at Postgraduate Seminar, University of Oxford, 22 October 2009.

24 Corn, "Land, Song, Constitution," 100. Also see Aaron Corn, "'Djiliwirri Ganha Dhärranhana, Wänä Limurrungu': The Creative Foundations of a Yolŋu Popular Song," *Australasian Music Research* 7 (2002) 55–66; Corn, "Burr-Gi Wargugu nguNinya Rrawa," 65.

25 Corn, "Land, Song, Constitution," 100.

26 Jill Stubington and Peter Dunbar-Hall, "Yothu Yindi's 'Treaty': Ganma in Music," *Popular Music* 13, no. 3 (1994): 257.

27 Corn, "Land, Song, Constitution," 95.

28 Ibid., 100.

29 Furlan, "Songs of Continuity," 247. For an extensive discussion on the tripartite system of ceremonial reciprocity at Port Keats, which also saw a number of Marri Ngarr men creating a localised form of *kun-borrk*, see Marett, *Songs Dreamings, Ghosts*, 24–25.

30 Ibid., 250.
31 The more didactic rhetoric that characterises some of these songs is a direct result of the Northern Territory Government's Road Safety competition of 2012, which offered prizes for the best songs that contained particular government-sponsored messages such as 'never drink and drive'.
32 One video includes a version of the song by a Balanda singer 'Archer', who performs it with a Southern American accent, and says he first heard the song being performed at Elcho Island and the islands of the Torres Strait. "Archer—Long Grass Man (trad)", YouTube video, uploaded by user 'Si Jay Gould', 6 February 2012, https://www.youtube.com/watch?v=J2cRrs5YThk
33 "Mindil Beach LongGrassBand", YouTube video, uploaded by user 'adminwhereisthelove' on 30 October 2007, https://www.youtube.com/watch?v=7e_i57cXdzU
34 Transcribed from recording from the album titled "Best of Warruwi 2003" held at Martpalk Arts Centre, Warruwi.
35 See also Barwick, Birch, and Evans' discussion of the use of the epenthetic trill or flap in Jurtbirrk songs. Barwick, Birch and Evans, "Iwaidja Jurtbirrk songs."
36 The recorded version of the song ends with an Instrumental section and electric organ solo part. In live performance, the singers usually sing the words 'Manangkardi' a final time at the end of the song—once more signing off with a gesture to the ancestors.
37 Phipps, "Performances of Power," 237.
38 Tamisari suggests that Indigenous festivals give Yolŋu youth license to joke and (within limits) ridicule more serious meanings conveyed by ritual dance. She cites the Chooky Dancers' success with "Zorba the Greek Yolŋu style" as its ability to stage 'the anachronistic absurdity of white audiences' stereotypical representations'. Tamisari, "Dancing for Strangers," 66.

8 'We're All Family Now'

Understanding the exchange

A few months after the Mamurrng ceremony of 2012, I gave a co-presentation with members of our ARC research team and Bininj/Arrarrkpi collaborators Solomon Nangamu, Russell Agalara, Jay Galaminda, and the Manmurulu family (David, Jenny, and Rupert) at conferences and symposiums in Canberra (see Support Material Figure 8.i). We spoke about the significance of the Mamurrng, and the two groups performed songs from their Mirrijpu and Inyjalarrku song-sets for conference attendees, with Jenny Manmurulu, Linda Barwick, and Amanda Harris dancing to the songs. At the conference dinner after our presentation, Nangamu and Agalara took me aside to tell me that we were 'all family now' and that their songs, which we had recorded together in our travels to different locations for different performance occasions, would 'stay with [me] wherever [I] go'.[1] It was an acknowledgement of both my relationship with them and with their songs, which are bound up in further relationships with Bininj/Arrarrkpi and their ancestors who have carried on the songs.

Their comments recalled Agalara's reflections on the way he memorises and performs songs, by connecting with the spirit of his grandfather who taught him. Just as humans follow in the footsteps of their ancestors by performing *kun-borrk/manyardi*, spirits also follow humans wherever they travel, staying with the custodians of their songs. In this sense, Agalara and Nangamu were acknowledging the level of expertise I had gained, both through listening to them perform and talk about *kun-borrk/manyardi* and learning to dance to their songs, and through the process of tracing deeper meanings through interviews, transcriptions, and analysis. They were also reminding me that having undertaken this process, I now have my own responsibilities in helping to nurture the songs. These responsibilities relate to the recordings we have made together, and to the role I have undertaken in the field and in other public forums as a cultural liaison, helping Bininj/Arrarrkpi performers to navigate Balanda-centric environments and interactions, and communicating Bininj/Arrarrkpi perspectives about the significance of western Arnhem Land song to Balanda audiences. Through my fieldwork experience and through the process of writing this book, I've embarked on my own path, from which I now cannot turn back!

DOI: 10.4324/9781003216339-9

'We're All Family Now': Understanding the exchange 215

This book has shown that 'following footsteps' can be understood not only as a framework for the way that *kun-borrk/manyardi* operates in western Arnhem Land society, but also as a Bininj/Arrarrkpi methodology for re-embedding archival recordings and for processes of repatriation. This approach was to situate recordings of old songs that I first brought to Gunbalanya within the context of a larger regional song tradition (hence the subsequent recordings of new songs that we made), and to interpret historical photos and videos not necessarily in a linear way, but rather to link them to ongoing ceremonial performance events, kinship networks, and associations with Country.

In concluding the book, then, I reflect on the key themes that tie together the different performance events analysed in each of the chapters, and return to the question of what it means to follow in the footsteps of Bininj/Arrarrkpi ancestors and perform *kun-borrk/manyardi*. In responding to this question, I compare and analyse the performances discussed in each of the chapters and present a number of significant findings: that *kun-borrk/manyardi* not only reflects the diversity of the western Arnhem Land society in which it is situated, but actively fosters it; that the song tradition operates primarily through various modes of exchange; that innovation and adaptability are not only features of the song tradition but are the qualities that sustain it; and that Bininj/Arrarrkpi therefore continue to perform *kun-borrk/manyardi* as a way of negotiating and dealing with social change.

Tracing the footsteps of *kun-borrk/manyardi*

Through the performance analysis sections of the book, I have sought to highlight many of the foundational principles that songmen must consider, and the choices they must make in order to follow the 'footsteps' of ancestors before them, and respond through their performance to the action taking place in their immediate social environment. Some of these foundational principles can be considered 'contextualisation cues', because they give meaning to the performance and help to produce a sequence of songs that is desirable for both a human audience (mourners, dancers, tourists, etc.) and an audience of ancestral and deceased spirits, who may be listening in.[2] Alfred Nayinggul described the process of Bininj/Arrarrkpi learning these principles as being akin to the way that Balanda gain knowledge through the Western system by reading and writing academic literature:

> it's just [like you] doing all them *djurra* [K: academic papers, books, etc.]. We gotta do the same thing as well. You gotta check like if you're on the right track—right songline [i.e. song-set], right didjeridu player, and you gotta pick one [song] that *daluk* will dance properly, like, and [know] what they're singing about; [know] 'what's the song about'?[3]

Many of these considerations that Nayinggul alludes to—choice of song, rhythmic mode, tempo, the context of the song, and whether it fits the occasion, etc.—have

216 'We're All Family Now': Understanding the exchange

Table 8.1 Summary of considerations in the performance of *kun-borrk/manyardi* affecting song order, rhythmic mode, and tempo

Relevant chapter	Consideration	Effect on song order, rhythmic mode, tempo
2, 3, 4, 5, 7	Accompanying men's and women's dancing; responding to highs and lows in mood of group and to stages of ceremony	Performing songs in slow-moderate rhythmic mode to highlight and facilitate women's dancing/reflection/seriousness and songs in fast/fast doubled rhythmic mode to highlight and facilitate men's dancing/liveliness/comic relief
3, 4, 5, 6, 7	The origins of songs (*wardde-ken/kurrula*; Kunwinjku/Mawng; Ngurtikin/Mayinjinaj, etc.)	Curating performance to ensure equal representation of different song-sets and the people/country they represent; ordering songs so as to chart a path that starts (and ideally ends) in the traditional country where the performance takes place (i.e. host-visitor-host).
2, 3, 4, 5	The 'life cycle' (and the tides)	Overall tempo of performance characterised by slow-moderate-fast-slow
2, 5	Thematic associations of particular songs (in relation to humans and spirits)	Matching performance of songs to mood or activities of audience and identity of deceased; starting and ending performance with 'old' songs rather than 'newly conceived' songs
2, 3, 4, 5, 7	Achieving accurate tempo	Repetition of songs in performance until tempo is achieved; maintaining specific tempo during changes of song-set
2, 3, 4, 5, 6, 7	Saying *bobo* (goodbye)	Performing the *ngalbadjan/nigi* ('mother') song—with the slowest tempo—at the end of a stage in the ceremony

been analysed closely in this book. Table 8.1 summarises some of the main considerations for *kun-borrk/manyardi* performance, and the ways that ceremony leaders responded to these considerations through various performance events.

Treatment of rhythmic mode and song order

Many of these musical findings support and enrich our understanding of previous observations about the treatment of rhythmic mode and ordering of songs made by scholars in relation to western Arnhem Land song and neighbouring genres such as *wangga, lirrga*, and *manikay/bunggurl*. In particular, the analysis presented in this book, building on earlier work by Marett and others, confirms the ubiquity of rhythmic mode as a form of musical organisation throughout northern Australia. Marett, Barwick, and Ford have observed the way that *wangga* singers associate rhythmic modes with affect—i.e. fast rhythmic modes with a heightened, happy mood—and make choices about whether to sing certain songs in particular rhythmic modes through the association with dance: 'it is the association with dance (which can occur in both vocal and Instrumental Sections) that most strongly underpins the system of rhythmic modes'.[4] I have similarly shown how the choice of rhythmic mode helps to drive the action or the next stage of the ceremony, and also allows singers to respond to changes in mood among participants of the ceremony. When the group is ready to dance, and/or when the singers decide that they want to elevate the mood of the performance in order to 'balance' the emotions of funeral mourners, *nulatparlangkat* (M: fast, lively) songs in fast even or fast doubled rhythmic mode are introduced. Equally, when dancers are tired, or when the funeral mourners enter the bough shelter for one last time in order to say goodbye to the deceased, *nulatparlilil* (M: slow, reflective) songs are performed.[5] Occasionally, these rhythmic mode conventions are utilised or consciously subverted for powerful effect, such as when Inyjalarrku songmen dance the *Yumparrparr* 'giant' dance accompanied by a slower rhythmic mode elsewhere reserved for women to dance to (as analysed in Chapters 3–5). And when Bininj/Arrarrkpi are engaging with tourists at festivals, singers such as Namayiwa perform songs with fast rhythmic modes and multiple changes of rhythmic mode within the song, so as to provide opportunity for spectacular dancing and build-up/release of tension in the music.

As with other Aboriginal Australian genres, singers repeat songs until they feel that they have got it 'right'—i.e. no mistakes have been made: everyone is singing the right song text with the right melody in full voice, and the songman feels that the tempo is correct. As has also been observed of *lirrga*, tempi ranges in the clapstick remain remarkably stable throughout the different stages of a performance, to the extent that when singers alternate song-sets or introduce a new song, it is often performed at the exact same tempo as the last song (accurate to within two or three beats per minute), until the point where the overall tempo of the songs changes again.

Barwick, Birch, and Evans observe that singers consider the geographical symbolism of songs in constructing a performance (i.e. choosing *kurrula*/saltwater or *wardde-ken*/stone country songs), and map associated languages onto clan lands,[6] while scholars such as Magowan, Toner, and Morphy observe in their ethnographies of east Arnhem Land *manikay* (discussed in Chapter 5) that songs are ordered according to their origin in such a way as to trace particular journeys. In this book, I have observed how songmen similarly order their songs in order to enact the journey of spirits of stolen bones from the United States of America back to their traditional country, or to enact through dancing the journey of the *mamurrng* from Gunbalanya to Warruwi. In funeral ceremonies and festivals in which multiple groups perform from different regions, I have shown how songs are ordered in relation to the country of the deceased or host of the festival, beginning with the songs of traditional owners/deceased's estate, extending to the country farthest away, and returning to the country of the host.

Other findings presented in this book are new to the literature on western Arnhem Land song, and strengthen findings made by scholars of neighbouring genres in the Top End. For example, unlike *lirrga* and *junba*, where fast and slow songs that are thematically linked are often paired together,[7] we have seen in each of the performances analysed in this book how *kun-borrk/manyardi* singers perform a cluster of slow-tempo songs or fast-tempo songs, aiming to alternate or contrast song-sets that are thematically linked. The overall tempo

218 *'We're All Family Now': Understanding the exchange*

of the performance can be characterised as slow-fast-slow. This can be interpreted as a metaphor for the 'life cycle' of both the spirit (which is born into the country, grows up, then returns to its country to dwell as an ancestral spirit) and the body (babies crawl; adults walk and run; elders' movements slow down in the late stages of life). Another explanation that Mawng speakers prefer relates to the metaphor of the tide coming in and going out, or *weli* and *ningkaryak* in Mawng language, meaning 'low tide' and 'high tide'.[8] This accords with the poetics and cosmological significance of the tide which is a feature of *wangga* repertories. As Marett writes, for coastal people of the Daly, *wangga* articulates themes of death and reincarnation that 'is conceived poetically as the ebb and flow of the tides'.[9]

Another interesting finding relates to spirit language songs and the way that songmen such as Nangamu, in the absence of a clearly translatable song text, nevertheless assign particular semantic categories to specific songs, and relate these songs in performance to the mood of the audience or the identity of the deceased. For example, the Mirrijpu songs that usually open the performance are grouped together as 'opening songs', whereas songs that usually close the performance are called *bobo*, and the most prominent song (see MP06, Support Material Appendix iii) is called *kiwken* (M: boss). Performances never begin with 'newly conceived' songs. Rather, 'old' songs are introduced first in order to please the group's ancestors who may be listening to the performance. 'New' songs also tend to be performed in fast doubled rhythmic modes and feature in performance settings such as festivals where multiple groups perform abbreviated versions of their repertory and showcase virtuosic dancing. In contrast, older songs tend to be in slow rhythmic modes and feature at funeral ceremonies, where the duration of performances is longer and where there may be greater consideration for songs composed by deceased relatives.

Finally, no matter the occasion, all performances finish with the 'mother' song, which is performed in order to 'send off' a deceased spirit, or to say 'goodbye' to ancestors and ceremony participants.[10] It is left for last because it is considered the essence of the song-set (the other songs are considered its children). Sometimes, songmen call it the 'heavy' one,[11] referring to both its slow tempo and the emotional gravitas associated with it. As observed in Chapters 3 and 6, the mother song is also marked by the fact that the singers and didjeridu player will often stand up to perform and the main songman may dance.

Staying on the right track: cross-repertory/cross-event musical analysis

Relative weighting of different repertories within a performance

For each performance event examined in this book, there was a relatively even distribution of song items across song-sets. This reflects the principle that individual ceremony leaders work together and share the load in constructing a

Table 8.2 Number of song items and weighting of song-sets performed across events

	GG	IL (JG)	IL (DM)	KB	MK	MR	MP	MX	YJ
Ch. 2 Goulburn Island (2012)					18		37		
Ch. 3 Reburial ceremony (2011)		12		12			15		
Ch. 4 Mamurrng handover (2011)			10						11
Ch. 5 Nakodjok funeral (2012)				20			30	4	
Ch. 7 Stone Country Festival (2011)	6			7		8			

Key to song repertories: Gurrumba Gurrumba clan (GG), James Gulamuwu's Inyjalarrku (IL [JG]), David Manmurulu's Inyjalarrku (IL [DM]), Karrbarda (KB), Marrwakara (MK), Milyarryarr (MR), Mirrijpu (MP), Marrawiwi (MX), and Yanajanak (YJ).

ceremonial performance. Table 8.2 shows the relevant event and records the number of discrete song items (including repeats of the same song) by repertory for a given performance. The only instances where there was an uneven spread of song items relate to the performance of Marrwakara (MK) and Mirrijpu (MP) in Chapter 2 and Marrawiwi (MX), Mirrijpu (MP), and Karrbarda (KB) in Chapter 5. This can perhaps be explained by the fact that fewer individual songs make up these song-sets (two for Marrwakara and four for Marrawiwi, compared with 29 for Mirrijpu, 50 for Inyjalarrku, and 18 for Karrbarda).

Aural identity of repertories signalled through rhythmic mode

Further analysis of the distribution of rhythmic modes across song items belonging to a selection of different western Arnhem Land song-sets advanced the contention that rhythmic mode contributes to the 'aural identity' of a given song-set.[12] Based on an analysis (provided in full in Support Material Appendix iii) of songs drawn from fieldwork recordings analysed in the 'performance analysis' sections of the book, as well as a selection of legacy recordings of Mirrijpu, Karrbarda, and Milyarryarr songs (listed in PARADISEC collection RB2), I built up a rhythmic mode profile for certain song-sets. Support Material Figure 8.ii summarises rhythmic mode sequences for Mirrijpu songs, while Support Material Figure 8.iii summarises rhythmic mode sequences for Karrbarda songs.[13] This comparison shows differences and similarities between song-sets, and allows us to deduce what a 'typical' Mirrijpu or Karrbarda song might sound like. For example, Mirrijpu songs are most commonly in moderate even rhythmic mode (4a), which is established at the beginning of the song and is maintained throughout until the Coda, where the tempo slows (rhythmic mode 2a) and the clapsticks beat the terminating pattern of three beats without the vocal or didjeridu part. As a variation (the second most common sequence), the clapsticks beat an uneven pattern (rhythmic mode 4c) in the Instrumental Section and the Coda. For fast tempo songs, the most common rhythmic mode is fast doubled beating (5b), which continues throughout the song, or, as a variation, changes to a similar uneven beating pattern (rhythmic mode 5d) in the Instrumental Section and Coda, where the tempo slows (2a). In contrast, Karrbarda songs are more evenly distributed between slow moderate, moderate, and fast modes, and have less variation within these modes in terms of clapstick beating patterns (as well as changes in didjeridu rhythm).[14]

While both song-sets share similar or identical rhythmic mode sequences, there are also some sequences that are unique to a particular song-set. For example, many Karrbarda songs feature a brief stop or pause in the didjeridu accompaniment before the vocal phrase in the Coda, or (when in fast doubled tempo) a unique clapstick beating pattern combining even and doubled beating (rhythmic mode 5g). The Karrbarda *ngalbadjan* song also changes tempo from slow to moderate, in contrast to other Inyjalarrku and Mirrijpu *Nigi* songs, which maintain a slow tempo. Other rhythmic modes analysed in the book were found to be unique to particular repertories—for example, rhythmic mode 2c, which is a feature of the Inyjalarrku *Nigi* song (of which there are two versions, IL50 and IL07), and rhythmic modes 5c[var] and 3c[var], which feature in the Instrumental Sections and Codas of Milyarryarr songs.[15]

Preferred tempo bands

By collating tempo data from the rhythmic mode analysis of the same selection of western Arnhem Land songs, I compared tempo bands for rhythmic modes in each repertory (and in some instances, for different singers of the same repertory). Support Material Figure 8.iv shows the song-set name, the number of songs that were analysed in the song-set (with a breakdown of different singers of the same song-set), and the tempo bands—represented in beats per minute—for each of the different rhythmic modes featured in recordings.

Based on this analysis, I suggest that like *wangga*, *kun-borrk/manyardi* repertories similarly 'use slightly different absolute tempi for the various tempo bands'.[16] For example, whereas the tempo for Karrbarda songs in slow moderate rhythmic mode was between 96 and 100 bpm, for Mirrijpu it was between 102 and 125 bpm. Similarly, Mirrijpu songs in fast rhythmic mode were slightly faster (134–139 bpm) than Karrbarda (126–137 bpm). Whereas Inyjalarrku, Karrbarda, and Kurri repertories each performed the 'mother song' at a tempo of between 39 and 60 bpm, the Mirrijpu mother song was faster at 73–86 bpm.

Tempo bands also varied significantly between singers, suggesting that singers inheriting the same set of songs have particular ideas about the tempo at which to perform these songs. As a case study, I compared recordings of Mirrijpu song MP14 over a period of five years. For recordings made in 2007 shortly after previous songman Solomon Ganawa passed away, Nangamu performed the song at a tempo of around 110 bpm, which I suggest was close to Ganawa's preferred tempo. Later, in 2012 and 2013, after Nangamu had established himself as the lead singer for the repertory, he performed the same song at a tempo of around 120 bpm—his preferred tempo. Interestingly, at the performance at Goulburn Island[17] when Russell Agalara and Harold Warrabin took over leading a performance of the song, their tempo was between 102 and 109 bpm—close to Ganawa's (and possibly Agalara's grandfather's) preferred tempo (see Support Material Figure 8.v).

Cross-repertory tendency to sequence songs by rhythmic mode

Certain songs (but not all) can be performed either in a slow-moderate rhythmic mode sequence or alternatively in a fast rhythmic mode sequence (see Support Material Appendix iii). Often, the song is performed first in slow-moderate mode, before it is performed again in fast doubled rhythmic mode.[18] Significantly, in every contemporary event analysed in the book, ceremony leaders frequently performed together songs which had distinctly different melodies and texts, but which shared the same rhythmic mode sequence, demonstrating the importance of rhythmic mode as a consideration in the ordering of songs in ceremony.[19]

Diversity and flexibility

In spite of language loss in Arnhem Land and elsewhere in Australia, highly valued and linguistically diverse *kun-borrk/manyardi* song-sets continue to be performed in and around the communities of Gunbalanya and Warruwi in a variety of ceremonial contexts. New songs continue to be added to these repertories, and a new generation of singers is performing a number of these repertories in ceremony. *Kun-borrk/manyardi* has also evolved beyond the ceremony ground to the stage, where songs are reframed using different musical styles for diverse audiences. By deliberately maintaining and fostering diversity through ceremonial performance, *kun-borrk/manyardi* expresses different facets of people's identity. Depending on the performance context, songs can express connections to language/dialect groups and/or clan groups, affiliations to saltwater or stone country, and identification with other Aboriginal people from the region or from Australia, or with other Indigenous or 'Black' cultures from outside of Australia. The conscious juxtaposition of different songs in ceremonial performance serves to highlight these different aspects, while at the same time, the ceremonial action cannot move forward without different groups working together, emphasising social cohesion and harmony.

Musical variegation and multilingualism go together in western Arnhem Land, both stemming from a society that values difference. While there are no longer *kobah-kohbanj* around who can speak languages such as Manangkardi and Ilgar, their descendants still have their songs (Mirrijpu, Milyarryarr), which act as musical imprints of these ancestral languages that they are able to follow. Singing these songs, songmen such as Nangamu not only identify as Manangkardi, but also feel that they are speaking to their ancestors in their language. And whilst song-sets have their origins in specific languages and traditional country, their singers may frequently reside and perform elsewhere. Therefore, when considering how to repatriate legacy recordings, archive new recordings, and maintain access to recordings, a regional approach is necessary.[20]

Each of the chapters of this book has examined different combinations of dancers and singers coming together to perform, demonstrating the flexibility of *kun-borrk/manyardi* as a genre that can be adapted to many different scenarios. The spatial boundaries surrounding the performance and the social event are similarly flexible and porous, allowing for people to move in and out of the ceremony ground and the surrounding social space, and for ceremony leaders to 'stage-manage' the dancers from outside before stepping in to lead the performance when it is their turn to sing or dance. Depending on the event, the 'contextualisation cues' of the performance can stand for different things. For example, at the reburial ceremony, the performance of the 'mother song' expressed goodbye to the spirits of the bones that had been returned from Washington, whereas at the Mamurrng ceremony, the performance of the same song emphasised the letting go of the *mamurrng* pole and all that the object symbolised. In addition, there is the ceremonial function of the 'mother' song, as a way of closing proceedings and allowing the performers to say 'thank you' and 'goodbye' to their audience. The way in which people learn to dance to *kun-borrk/manyardi* is also flexible: emphasis is placed on finding one's own understanding of the music by joining in and 'having a go'. The Balanda who participated at festivals in Gunbalanya and Jabiru naturally found it challenging to anticipate the beat of the clapstick. Yet, as I discovered through the processes of participation and music analysis, the more familiar one is with the song repertories and their particular rhythmic modes, the easier it becomes to 'follow the footsteps' of the dance. Expert dancers perform with an awareness of particular songs gained after many years of listening to the songs, and rehearsing them until they can 'fix 'im proper'.

Comparing recordings of performance events from 1948 in Gunbalanya (Figure 6.3) with the corpus of songs derived from my fieldwork recorded some 60 years later (Figure 1.4), musical diversity emerges as a common factor. Many song-sets that featured in Simpson and Giles' recordings are no longer performed, suggesting significant attrition; yet a few have remained, and others still have emerged to take their place, suggesting regeneration of *kun-borrk/manyardi* songs over time. In particular, there are a greater number of spirit language song-sets performed at Gunbalanya today than appear in the 1948 snapshot. The reasons for this require further investigation; however, it could be inferred that the prominence of spirit language songs relates to their powerful role in funeral settings, which are the main occasions for *kun-borrk/manyardi* today (rather than informal settings, which have been the domain of 'spontaneously composed' songs in the past).

Modes of exchange

This book has contributed to a richer understanding of the agents and nature of exchange in Indigenous societies and in Indigenous and non-Indigenous relations. From the outset, the process of repatriating archival recordings to Gunbalanya was framed as an exchange: in return for bringing digital copies of culturally significant songs, Bininj/Arrarrkpi showed me how these songs fit into their social world, and, in doing so, offered me a place in it. By showing me how *kun-borrk/manyardi* operated in the contemporary situation, Nangamu and others were able shed light on older *kun-borrk/manyardi* recordings. Reflecting on the performance events analysed in this book, exchange has been shown to occur not only between Bininj/Arrarrkpi and Balanda, but also between language groups, between dancers and singers, between generations, and between the songman and didjeridu player during performance, as they decide on the song order and rhythmic mode. *Kun-borrk/manyardi* performance is characterised not merely by economic exchange of money or material goods, but also by intercultural (Mamurrng; festivals), spiritual or supernatural (funeral ceremonies), unconscious (Amartjitpalk performance), and artistic or creative forms of exchange (new songs gifted during funerals and in festival settings). These exchanges continue to innovate the song tradition and to sustain people's health and wellbeing, keeping them connected to family and Country. By giving to neighbouring language groups and sharing their songs with outsiders, Bininj/Arrarrkpi maintain relationships of reciprocity with others, based on respect for people's culture, language, and sovereignty over traditional country. This is important because it helps to counter dominant economic relationships in the region based on mining and the exploitation of resources, and helps to foster co-dependence and coexistence between diverse groups occupying multilingual and multicultural communities such as Gunbalanya and Warruwi.

By presenting the research data as a series of distinct performance events characterised by intercultural encounters of exchange, I have attempted to convey the 'complex whole' of *kun-borrk/manyardi* performance. To perform *kun-borrk/manyardi* is to exchange with the ongoing life force or power of the Dreaming, and to make connections to historical events, places, and people. Performing *kun-borrk/manyardi* is also a major part of looking after Country: by satisfying the spirits that live in the country through performance, Bininj/Arrarrkpi feel cared for while they live on ancestral country by the spirits of people who lived and died there, who first composed the songs, and who continue to give them musical inspiration for new songs in dreams. Certain conventions acknowledge this relationship, such as when songmen perform the clapstick terminating pattern in the Coda by slowing down the beat and striking two or three unaccompanied beats of the clapstick before listening out for the reverberations—signs of their ancestors completing the clapstick phrase of the song. Songmen also construct their performance partly for the benefit of spirits, and observe these spirits in return enhancing their vocal quality or aiding their memory in performance (Chapter 5).

Exchanges involving *kun-borrk/manyardi* can also be understood as political acts which shape Bininj/Arrarrkpi relations on local, national, and international levels. Exchange ceremonies such as the Mamurrng have been shown to be important acts of diplomacy between Aboriginal people and those institutions and individuals that represent them or are responsible for maintaining material and digital collections of cultural value (i.e. AIATSIS; our ARC research team). Performances at funeral ceremonies are also highly political in that they align certain singers and their families with the deceased, or make a public statement about one's connection to their clan estate or traditional country. Similarly, the international spotlight placed on Bininj/Arrarrkpi culture at public festivals allows certain groups to demonstrate their ongoing connection to traditional culture by performing their songs, and gain wider recognition of sovereignty over traditional lands.

Adaptability and innovation

Over time, the western Arnhem Land song tradition has remained dynamic and regenerative, rather than static. As examined elsewhere in relation to Marrwakara and Mirrijpu songs,[21] while certain aspects of the performance are 'fixed' (the song text, considerations for song order, rhythmic modes, and certain melodic sequences), other elements can be adapted or rearranged (ornamentation, vocal timbre, melody, adjustments in tempo) as repertories are passed on to new singers, and new songs are added. At the same time, this symbiotic relationship between humans and spirits, whereby singing songs *the right way* in ceremonial contexts begets new songs in dreams, ensures that regeneration is grounded in the principles that have been set out before. As a universally understood musical language, rhythmic modes also provide an adaptable and innovative framework: while each song repertory is characterised by distinct rhythmic modes, groups from across the Top End region that share rhythmic modes can all participate in ceremony by dancing to one another's songs. For example, at the Warruwi Mamurrng of 2012 when Marett performed *wangga* songs from the Daly region, Arrarrkpi were still able to dance to the songs by recognising the rhythmic modes, and could respond to the songs in a more light-hearted and less serious way than they might dance to their own repertories.

The adaptable and innovative nature of *kun-borrk/manyardi* has seen it used by Bininj/Arrarrkpi as a strategy for dealing with social change. In particular, it has played an important role in mediating relationships between Aboriginal groups and outsiders, from the annual voyages of the Macassans, to contact with

Balanda, Japanese, and others during the mission era, World War Two, and in 1948, and then after the resources boom with the permanent presence of Balanda in mining towns such as Jabiru. With different language groups living together permanently in communities such as Gunbalanya and Warruwi for the first time as a result of these changes, *kun-borrk/manyardi* has helped people to find their place (for example, Mawng songman Solomon Nangamu was relied upon to lead ceremonial events at Gunbalanya with the Karrbarda group because of a shortage of other song groups resident at Gunbalanya). In recent decades, cultural festivals have brought international audiences to western Arnhem Land and involved many Balanda, negotiating a new dialogue with the wider Australian and international public, based around Aboriginal culture and values. Popular bands from western Arnhem Land have carried on the song tradition in new directions, adapting their inherited song repertories into new musical expressions for the stage. While music genres such as rock and reggae remain popular with younger generations, this adaptation has not brought an end to the intergenerational transmission of *kun-borrk/manyardi*; rather, it has come to complement the western Arnhem Land song tradition. Many artists, such as Terrah Guymala of the Nabarlek Band, perform both on the ceremony ground and the festival stage, and continue to 'train up' the next generation to perform in both arenas, and to explore new styles of musical expression.[22]

A number of events demonstrated that in spite of changes resulting from technology and colonisation, and Balanda interference in Bininj/Arrarrkpi cultural practices, these cultural practices and responses remain fundamentally unaltered. The reburial ceremony chapter of this book demonstrated how 'intangible' aspects of culture—including language, song, and dance—have a vital role to play in responding to the tangible process of returning human remains taken from Country. Careful consideration was given to the ordering of songs and the direction of the dance, reflecting an awareness of the journey the remains had taken from Washington to Gunbalanya, while ceremony leader Nakodjok Jacob Nayinggul addressed spirits in the language of the country in order to reassure them that they were home. The process of returning digitised media from archives to Gunbalanya also showed how Bininj/Arrarrkpi make sense of these records by making them tangible, grounding them in the time, place, and social sphere to which they belong. Old recordings of *kun-borrk/manyardi* in particular had a profound effect on songmen because it made them remember those older people whose footsteps they follow—songmen such as Madjalkaidj senior, Marawana, Namunurr, and George Winunguj.

The path ahead

The death of elders and cultural experts such as Kalarriya and Nayinggul during my fieldwork period in western Arnhem Land was greeted with sadness and a great sense of loss, and it also underlined a bigger crisis. This crisis concerns the loss of diversity of human expression, as articulated through language, performance, knowledge, relationship to the environment, and other unique ways of 'being in the world'. This loss is felt not only by Bininj/Arrarrkpi in western Arnhem Land but also by Indigenous people around the world; indeed, it has been identified in the literature as a global problem affecting humanity itself.[23] The challenge for broader society is: how can we sustain the knowledge, traditions, and practices that have helped us to evolve on this planet over millennia so that they can continue to help us deal with large-scale problems that affect our global society and economy (such as climate change, environmental degradation, and species extinction)?

Through engagement with 'outsiders'—including researchers and other organisations—Bininj/Arrarrkpi in western Arnhem Land are already charting new pathways by working with new technologies and incorporating Western research methodologies alongside traditional practices, to resolve environmental and social challenges.[24] In a similar way, this book has shown how intergenerational transmission of knowledge, which is passed on through performance, remains particularly strong in scenarios of cultural exchange, where support is lent from 'outsiders'. In Chapter 7 for example, we learned how Bininj/Arrarrkpi songmen are engaging with younger generations and non-Aboriginal people in the broader community through the performance of *kun-borrk/manyardi* on the ceremony ground and the stage at cultural festivals, providing an opportunity to pass on knowledge about their song traditions to others. The success of this recruitment strategy undoubtedly relies on the survival of festivals such as Mahbilil and SCF. Likewise, government policies to 'close the gap' between Indigenous and non-Indigenous Australians in key measures such as health, education, employment, and incarceration require funding and Indigenous leadership to ensure events such as festivals continue to provide a genuine forum for intercultural exchange and close the gap in non-Indigenous *understanding* about Indigenous lived realities in the 21st century.

Through the ethnographic account, I have attempted to give the reader some insight into the role that Balanda can provide in bringing resources and assistance to performance events, and the benefits of engaging with the culture and the language of Bininj/Arrarrkpi. Given the social, political, economic, and spiritual benefits of *kun-borrk/manyardi* that I have outlined, it is vital that Balanda continue to engage with the song tradition either personally or through their own institutions, companies, professions, and public policies, in order to support younger people to 'follow in the footsteps' of their elders, and keep this performance tradition for future generations.[25]

Returning once more to the occasion of the recording session at Injalak Hill, it was revealing to observe the way in which the songmen helped one another in constructing and curating the performance. At one point, Gulamuwu struggled to remember the words to the song. Alfred Gawaraidji patiently restarted his didjeridu accompaniment, Solomon Nangamu respectfully sang along with Gulamuwu, helping him to remember the words, and Johnny Namayiwa quietly tapped along to the beat, helping him to find the right rhythmic modes and keep up with the tempo. The other singers could have taken over and led Gulamu-wu's songs themselves, such was their knowledge, but it was important that they helped him, as the owner of the songs, to remember through the act of performing. As Nangamu commented:

> They used to help each other, long time. Old people, they used to help each other. But we still help each other. Like Johnny's songs, James' songs, and my songs, we still all understand, all know that meaning.[26]

This participation of the group extends beyond the singers, to all those attending the performance event. It is acknowledged by the fact that the singers and didjeridu player will only ever attend a ceremony once they have been invited to someone's country to sing their songs in that ceremony:

JG: If someone want us…they'll call us, we have to go.
SN: We can't just go and please ourselves, no. We have to wait.
JG: Wait till they tell us or they come and pick us up: 'come on, we go' and all that. We can't just go, otherwise they turn around and say 'who told these people to come here and sing?'[27]

It is highly significant that in each of the performance events analysed in the book, not one involved the performance of just one song-set; all were characterised instead by multiple song-sets. This finding speaks to the significant aesthetic and social value given to pluralism and multilingualism in Aboriginal societies, a topic that has occupied anthropologists and linguists alike.[28] Throughout this book, Aboriginal music making emerges as an activity involving the collective memory, in which the surrounding environment—the time, place, company, mood, and occasion—plays as important a role as the music itself. Whilst songmen have their own distinct repertoires of songs, they rely on each other for didjeridu accompaniment and support in ceremony, and are required to be familiar with one another's songs in order to work together. Above all, it is when people come together—*daluk* and *bininj*, *kobah-kohbanj* and *yawurrinj/yawkyawk*, Bininj/Arrarrkpi and Balanda, Indigenous and non-Indigenous—particularly in the country where their ancestors performed the music in the past, that they are able to reactivate the spirits and regenerate the creative potential of *kun-borrk/manyardi*.

Notes

1 Solomon Nangamu and Russell Agalara, personal communication, 4 December 2012.
2 This finding is consistent with observations made by Treloyn of Scotty Martin's *junba* repertory, in which the pairing of slow/fast songs that share subject matter and lexical content 'has the overall effect of foregrounding the relationship between the

228   *'We're All Family Now': Understanding the exchange*

living performers, and the spirits… that they enact on the dance ground'. Treloyn, "'When Everybody There Together… then I Call that One'", 110.
3   [Alfred Nayinggul, 20121116-RB_01.wav, https://dx.doi.org/10.26278/CYG2-TP33, 00:22:24–00:22:51].
4   Marett, Barwick and Ford, *For the Sake of a Song*, 49.
5   See also discussion of role of tempo in Djanba in Freya Bailes and Linda Barwick, "Absolute Tempo", 485.
6   Barwick, Birch and Evans, "Iwaidja Jurtbirrk Songs", 29–30.
7   See Barwick's discussion of *lirrga* song order. Barwick, "Marri Ngarr Lirrga Songs," 13. Also see Treloyn's discussion of *junba* song order in relation to Western Desert and central Australian songs. Treloyn, "'When Everybody There Together… then I Call that One'", 116.
8   See [Solomon Nangamu, 20110825-RB_02.wav, https://dx.doi.org/10.26278/FA3X-VT77, 00:25:54–00:26:07]; [Jimmy Kalarriya, 20120610-RB_v05.mp4, https://dx.doi.org/10.26278/645C-Y746, 00:06:57.000–00:07:15.200].
9   Marett, Songs, Dreamings, Ghosts, 1–2.
10 Whilst the SCF 2011 performance analysed in Chapter 7 did not feature the *ngalbadjan/nigi*, another performance of Mirrijpu in the following year (SCF 2012) did include the *nigi*, although it was performed at an unusually moderate tempo of 96 bpm (consistent with my observation about the absence of slow tempo songs at festival events). My analysis of 'Cut 10' in Chapter 6 also suggests that Simpson and Giles recorded the 'mother' song of one of the Goulburn Island song-sets in 1948.
11 'Every time you hear the slow song … that's the heavy part' [Johnny Namayiwa, 20110825-RB_02.wav, https://dx.doi.org/10.26278/FA3X-VT77, 00:07:42–00:07:54].
12 See Marett, Barwick and Ford, *For the Sake of a Song*, 47; Barwick, "Tempo Bands"; Toner, "When the Echoes Have Gone," 82–100; Anderson, "Striking a Balance."
13 These repertoires were the most useful for comparison since they represented *warddeken* and *kurrula*-affiliated song-sets, and were heavily represented in the data.
14 Cf. discussion of rhythmic mode, Chapter 2, and Russell Agalara's comment characterising the didjeridu playing for Karrbarda as 'straight' compared with Mirrijpu, which is 'different-different'.
15 See Support Material Appendix iii.
16 Marett, Barwick and Ford, *For the Sake of a Song*, 58–59.
17 See Chapter 4 in Brown, "Following Footsteps."
18 See, for example, songs MP06 and MP26 discussed in Chapter 2 and song MP25 analysed in Chapter 5.
19 Refer to 20110719-MT_v0396_01.mp4 (https://dx.doi.org/10.26278/AMBA-8X51) to 20110719-MT_v0402_01.mp4 (https://dx.doi.org/10.26278/NXDC-AH68) and 20110719-RB_04_06_MP19_MP04.wav (https://dx.doi.org/10.26278/KXKQ-X317) to 20110719-MT_v0443_01.mp4 (https://dx.doi.org/10.26278/JNNT-D255) analysed in Chapter 3; 20121103-RB_01_07_MP22.wav (https://dx.doi.org/10.26278/YPP5-H083) to 20121103-RB_02_04_MP26.wav (https://dx.doi.org/10.26278/14S4-5C24), 20121103-RB_03_04_MP25.wav (https://dx.doi.org/10.26278/T6SK-S674) to 20121103-RB_03_15_MP26.wav (https://dx.doi.org/10.26278/F1ZE-NM822), and 20121103-RB_03_20_MP19.wav (https://dx.doi.org/10.26278/E1ND-AV691) to 20121103-RB_03_24_MP25.wav (https://dx.doi.org/10.26278/J1ST-CM91) analysed in Chapter 2; 20120810_11-IO_01_01_IL.wav (https://dx.doi.org/10.26278/EA3K-N793) to 20120810_11-IO_01_03_IL.wav (https://dx.doi.org/10.26278/TH21-CR28) analysed in Chapter 4; 20120628_02-RB_03_01_MP06.wav (https://dx.doi.org/10.26278/BAEF-FG23) to 20120628_02-RB_04_01_MP19.wav (https://dx.doi.org/10.26278/C340-QV80), 20120628_02-RB_09_08_MP06.wav (https://dx.doi.org/10.26278/9DV1-6F11)

to 20120628_02-RB_09_12_MP26.wav (https://dx.doi.org/10.26278/Y3XF-RH12), and 20120628_02-RB_09_18_MP27.wav (https://dx.doi.org/10.26278/7DCY-FT93) to 20120628_02-RB_09_19_MP28.wav(https://dx.doi.org/10.26278/GN66-N838)analysed in Chapter 5; and 20110827_02-RB_07_04_KB12_KB07.wav (https://dx.doi.org/10.26278/3763-NY50) to 20110827_02-RB_07_10_KB02.wav (https://dx.doi.org/10.26278/KG63-9Z66) analysed in Chapter 7.

20 This was also demonstrated in other scholars' experiences of repatriating digital recordings of *wangga*, *lirrga*, and *junba* song in the Daly and Kimberly regions. Treloyn and Emberly, "Sustaining Traditions," 167.
21 See Brown, "Following Footsteps," Chapter 4.
22 For their album *Malk* [skin], Saltwater Band also experimented with Latin American music styles.
23 For example, in the fields of anthropology, linguistics, and musicology: Wade Davis, *The Wayfinders: Why Ancient Wisdom Matters in the Modern World* (Crawley: UWA Publishing, 2010); Evans, *Dying Words*; Walsh, "Will Indigenous Languages Survive?"; Catherine Grant, *Music Endangerment: How Language Maintenance Can Help* (Oxford & New York: Oxford University Press, 2014); Allan Marett, "Vanishing Songs: How Musical Extinctions Threaten the Planet," *Ethnomusicology Forum* 19, no. 2 (2010).
24 For example, the work of Warddeken Land Management group, representing Bininj Kunwok–speaking clans of the Arnhem Land plateau region, together with assistance from scientists, rock art specialists, and other researchers, is helping people to live and work on their traditional lands. Their clan country is recognised as an Indigenous Protected Area, and the running of outstations within this area is supported in part by a carbon abatement programme—the West Arnhem Land Fire Abatement Project—which provides the group with income for the carbon that Warddeken rangers offset through traditional fire management. See http://www.environment.gov.au/indigenous/ipa/declared/warddeken.html
25 This might include financial, material, and/or moral support for festivals, funerals, diplomacy ceremonies, and funding for local art centres or other Aboriginal organisations to facilitate trips on Country led by elders and songmen, enabling younger people to return to their ancestral country, and using *kun-borrk/manyardi* performance as the setting for a broader Bininj/Arrarrkpi education.
26 [Solomon Nangamu, 20110903-RB_07.wav, https://dx.doi.org/10.26278/NWFE-VJ78, 00:06:07–00:06:31].
27 [James Gulamuwu and Solomon Nangamu, 20110903-RB_07.wav, https://dx.doi.org/10.26278/NWFE-VJ78, 00:14:10.087–00:14:30.528].
28 See, for example, Evans' and Sutton's examinations of the principles of variety and complementarity that underpin multilingualism and totemism in Aboriginal society. Nicholas Evans, "A Tale of Many Tongues: Documenting Polyglot Narrative in North Australian Oral Traditions," in *Indigenous Language and Social Identity: Papers in Honour of Michael Walsh*, ed. Brett Baker et al. (Canberra: Pacific Linguistics, 2010), 275–95; Peter Sutton, "Materialism, Sacred Myth, and Pluralism: Competing Theories of the Origin of Australian Languages," in *Scholar and Sceptic: Australian Aboriginal Studies in Honour of L.R. Hiatt*, ed. Francesca Merlan, John Morton and Alan Rumsey (Canberra: Aboriginal Studies Press, 1997), 239–41.

Epilogue
Returning the gift

It's *wurrkeng* (dry, cool) season in 2019, and I am returning to western Arnhem Land as I have done annually, this time with my partner and one-year-old son.[1] We turn off the Arnhem Highway to Gunbalanya and drive through Magela Creek on Mirarr clan country, emerging through paperbark swamp to a clear view of the escarpment. The Guluyambi (G: paperbark raft) *djang* (K: sacred site) towers above us, perched on the edge of the ancient sandstone cliffs. I stop the car and we get out to take in the escarpment and surrounding wetlands. I feel a sense of insignificance and awe, as well as weightlessness—like greeting an old friend.

At Gunbalanya, we reconnect with Donna and her family, who address my son in Kunwinjku using his skin name, Nakodjok. I pay a visit to the families of the late songmen James Gulamuwu and Eric Mardday, both of whom have since passed away, and give them USB sticks containing the audio recordings, photos, and videos of our interviews. We sit and listen to the songs and view the photos on my laptop, reminiscing about the events in the recordings and discussing the status of the Karrbarda and Inyjalarrku song-sets at Gunbalanya and in the region. *Kun-borrk* is performed less frequently these days at Gunbalanya compared with the period when we made the recordings, but there are several *yawurrinj* who are still singing and playing *mako*. Shaun Namarnyilk—grandson of Jimmy Kalarriya and a resident artist at Injalak Arts and Crafts—has collaborated with Isaiah Nagurrgurrba to compose *kun-borrk* about the story of the theft of bones from Injalak Hill in 1948 told in Kunwinjku from a Bininj perspective and to paint the story on bark. James Gulamuwu's son Theo Gulamuwu is also learning his father's songs and is overwhelmed to see photos and videos of his late father singing Inyjalarrku.

After saying goodbye to friends and adopted family in Gunbalanya and to my own family at Darwin airport, I met up with David, Jenny, Rupert and Renfred Manmurulu, and Solomon Nangamu who have flown in from Warruwi. Since my time carrying out fieldwork in western Arnhem Land, I have collaborated with Nangamu and the Manmurulus for a number of performances, including a Mamurrng ceremony in 2016 given to a Rak Mak Mak Marranunggu family

DOI: 10.4324/9781003216339-10

Epilogue: Returning the gift 231

Figure 9.1 Photo of the author with Solomon Nangamu, Lynize, Jamie Milpurr, Jenny Manmurulu, David Manmurulu, Rupert Manmurulu, and Renfred Manmurulu at Twin Hill Station after a Mamurrng ceremony, 2016. Photograph by Reuben Brown.

at Twin Hill station (see Figure 9.1). We travel this time by plane to Broome, Western Australia, and on to Derby by car for the annual Mowanjum community festival. The festival is one of the highlights of the Kimberley tourist calendar, featuring intergenerational performances of a diversity of *junba*—the result of community efforts in the past ten years in particular to revive dances and songs by teaching them to children on country, with the aid of archival recordings.[2]

As I discussed in Chapter 5, Ngarinyin/Worrora/Wunambal ceremony leaders including Matthew Denmbal Martin, Pansy Nulgit, and Rona Charles, and Mawng/Kunwinjku ceremony leaders had engaged in cultural exchange since the 2011 Symposium for Indigenous Music and Dance in Darwin around the beginning of my research (the events of which gave rise to the Warruwi Mamurrng in 2012), and had maintained connections in subsequent conferences and symposia that I took part in. Since 2017, the Manmurulu family and other young Mawng/Kunwinjku singers and dancers had travelled annually to Melbourne to share their songs, stories, and artistic practices of weaving and carving with a network of Indigenous artists from the southeast and beyond, including the Kimberley.[3] A new generation of *junba* singers and dancers including Folau

Umbagai, Johnny Divilli, and Pete O'Connor had found support and encouragement from the Manmurulus and Nangamu to perform *wangga* repertories originating from the Daly region known to all parties. The Kimberley group had invited the Warruwi group and me to bring *manyardi* to Mowanjum, and to help play *mako* for *wangga*. I had been able to facilitate this exchange with an Early Career Research Grant from the University.

Now at Mowanjum, we gather at sundown with the local children and practise *wangga, junba,* and *manyardi*. Jenny Manmurulu leads the women and girls, demonstrating how to dance to Inyjalarrku, Nginji, Nganaru and Mirrijpu. In the absence of other *yawurrinj* familiar with the repertories from Goulburn Island, I take on the role of 'dance captain' for the boys and men. (I share this role with expert dancer Pete O'Connor, who puts in a tireless effort wrangling the local children.) We teach the young boys the *manyardi*-style dance call and demonstrate how to follow the rhythmic modes for Inyjalarrku and Mirrijpu. On the evening of the public performance, Jenny Manmurulu helps to paint her husband David in half in white and half in yellow from head to toe as the *yumparrparr* (M: giant) for the final Inyjalarrku song. He emerges from the bough shelter with a dramatic effect to farewell an engrossed crowd of hundreds of tourists and locals.

After this exchange, a small contingent from the Kimberley and Goulburn Island groups travel on to Thailand with Treloyn and me for the International Council for Traditional Music World Conference. We present as part of a panel on the repatriation of archival recordings and Indigenous song practices, and perform in a concert with other groups from around the world where we are billed as the Wulanggu and Inyjalarrku group from Australia. We help one another with the accompanying dances, and with Rupert and Renfred's encouragement, I invite conference delegates and audience members to join in, follow my lead, and participate in the dance.

On the flight home, I reflect on my responsibility to the songs that I have learned and recorded, and to future singers and dancers. By helping to create opportunities for songmen to sing, women ceremony leaders to share their knowledge, *mako/arrawirr* players to play, and young men and women to dance, I intend to help pass on 'that thing' that *kobah-kobanj* handed down to songmen like Nangamu. Likewise, by supporting opportunities for the exchange of song and dance between Indigenous and non-Indigenous groups and individuals, I hope to be able to pass on my experience of *kun-borrk/manyardi* and return the gift that has been handed to me. It is through continual processes of renewal and exchange that *kun-borrk/manyardi* will be sustained and supported into the future.

Postscript: Inyjalarrku songman David Manmurulu passed away in 2021. This book is dedicated to his legacy and the legacy of other kun-borrk/manyardi ceremony leaders who have passed away. The Inyjalarrku songs have since been ceremonially smoked, and his sons Rupert Manmurulu, Renfred Manmurulu and Reuben Manmurulu continue singing, while Rupert Manmurulu carries on dancing the yumparrparr, and has dreamt new songs. A new generation of singers, arawirr (didjeridu) players and dancers taught by Rupert, Renfred and Jenny, also support them in ceremonial performance at Warruwi and abroad.

Notes

1 This trip would be the last opportunity to meet research collaborators in person for another three years after the COVID-19 pandemic, lockdowns and other factors reduced opportunities to travel between 2020–2022.
2 See Sally Treloyn, Matthew Dembal Martin and Rona Goonginda Charles, "Moving Songs: Repatriating Audiovisual Recordings of Aboriginal Australian Dance and Song (Kimberley Region, Northwestern Australia)," in *The Oxford Handbook of Musical Repatriation*, ed. Frank Gunderson, Robert C. Lancefield and Bret Woods (Oxford: Oxford University Press, 2019), 592.
3 Annual workshops and symposia focus on reclamation, diplomacy, and philosophies of Indigenous art practices, led by Yorta Yorta/Dja Dja Wurrung scholar and artist Tiriki Onus and ethnomusicologist Sally Treloyn, co-directors of the Research Unit for Indigenous Arts and Cultures at the University of Melbourne.

References

Archival sources

American/Australian Scientific Expedition to Arnhem Land 1948 Records, Mountford-Sheard Collection, State Library of South Australia, Adelaide.
Arnhem Land Expedition file 178294, Accession Files (Record Unit 305), Smithsonian Institution Archives, Washington DC.
Berndt, Ronald. Letter to Alf Ellison, 15 January 1948, Item 4.3.6. NTRS 38, Location 142/2/4, Northern Territory Archives.
Book of Births, Deaths and Marriages. 1950–65, Box 6, Location 75/5/4, Northern Territory Archives Centre, Darwin.
Bray, John. Diary, Unpublished Manuscript in Private Collection of Andrew Bray, 1948.
CMS Australia Committee, Superintendent's diaries, Oenpelli, 1944–81, NTRS 865/P1, Item 3, Box 1, Location 143/3/2, Northern Territory Archives.
List of Specimens Collected by F. M. Setzler, Australia. 1948, Arnhem Land Expedition, RU 305, Accession File 178294, Smithsonian Institution, Washington DC.
McCarthy, Frederick. Papers of Frederick David McCarthy, AIATSIS.
Mountford, Bessie J. Arnhem Land Expedition Diaries, State Library of South Australia, Adelaide.
Mountford, C. P. Application to Chairman of the Research Committee, National Geographic Society, 5 March 1945, Correspondence 1945–49, Vol. 1, 1945–47.
———. 28 January 1947, Letter to Gilbert Grosvenor, Setzler Files, Box 7, Folder 4, Arnhem Land Correspondence 1948–49, Folder 1 of 2, National Anthropological Archives, Washington, DC.
Register of burials, 1926–78, NTRS 864, Box 7, location 75/5/4, Northern Territory Archives Centre, Darwin.
Setzler, Frank. Photographs 1948, Lot 36, National Anthropological Archives, Smithsonian Institution, Washington, DC.
Setzler, Frank M. Diaries 1948, Box 14, Frank Maryl Setzler Papers 1927–60, National Anthropological Archives, Suitland MD.
Simpson, Colin. "Expedition to Arnhem Land", ABC Radio documentary, first broadcast 30 November 1948, ABC Radio Archives 83/CD/1239. Sydney: Australian Broadcasting Commission.
———. ABC Radio archives Disc MA24. Sydney: Australian Broadcasting Commission.

236 References

Walker, Howell (cine-photographer). Footage of the 1948 American Australian Expedition to Arnhem Land held in the National Geographic Society Film Archives, Washington, DC.

Published and other sources

Agalara, Russell, Reuben Brown, and Solomon Nangamu. "That Spirit Changed My Voice: The Performance of *Kun-borrk* at a Funeral Ceremony in Mikkinj Valley, Western Arnhem Land." Paper presented at the Musicological Society of Australia Annual Conference, Canberra, 2012.

Altman, Jon. "Maradjiri and Mamurrng: Ad Borsboom and Me." In *Cultural Styles of Knowledge Transmission: Essays in Honour of Ad Borsboom*, edited by Jean Kommers and Eric Venbrux, 13–18. Amsterdam: Aksant Academic Publishers, 2008.

Anderson, Gregory D. "Striking a Balance: Limited Variability in Performances of a Clan Song Series from Arnhem Land." In *The Essence of Singing and the Substance of Song: Recent Responses to the Aboriginal Performing Arts and Other Essays in Honour of Catherine Ellis*, edited by Linda Barwick, Allan Marett and Guy Tunstill, 13–25. Sydney: University of Sydney (Oceania Monograph 46), 1995.

Anyon, Roger, and Russell Thornton. "Implementing Repatriation in the United States: Issues Raised and Lessons Learned." In *The Dead and Their Possessions: Repatriation in Principle, Policy, and Practice*, edited by Cressida Fforde, Jane Hubert and Paul Turnbull. New York: Routledge, 2004: 190–198.

Apted, Meiki Elizabeth. "Songs from the Inyjalarrku: The Use of a Non-Translatable Spirit Language in a Song Set from North-West Arnhem Land, Australia." *Australian Journal of Linguistics* 30, no. 1 (2010): 93–103.

"Archer – Long Grass Man (trad)", YouTube video, uploaded by 'Si Jay Gould', 6 February 2012, https://www.youtube.com/watch?v=J2cRrs5YThk.

Bailes, Freya, and Linda Barwick. "Absolute Tempo in Multiple Performances of Aboriginal Songs: Analyzing Recordings of Djanba 12 and Djanba 14." *Music Perception* 28, no. 5 (2011): 473–90.

Barwick, Linda. "Central Australian Women's Ritual Music: Knowing through Analysis Versus Knowing through Performance." *Yearbook for Traditional Music* 22 (1990): 60–79.

———. "Marri Ngarr Lirrga Songs: A Musicological Analysis of Song Pairs in Performance." *Musicology Australia* 28 (2005): 1–25.

———. "Musical Form and Style in Murriny Patha Djanba Songs at Wadeye (Northern Territory, Australia)." In *Analytical and Cross-Cultural Studies in World Music*, edited by Michael Tenzer and John Roeder, 316–54. Oxford and New York: Oxford University Press, 2011.

———. "Performance, Aesthetics, Experience: Thoughts on Yawulyu Mungamunga Songs." In *Aesthetics and Experience in Music Performance*, edited by Elizabeth MacKinlay, Denis Collins and Samantha Owens, 1–18. Newcastle: Cambridge Scholars, 2005.

———. "Song as an Indigenous Art." In *The Oxford Companion to Aboriginal Art and Culture*, edited by M. Neale and S. Kleinert. Melbourne: Oxford University Press, 2000: 328–335.

———. "Tempo Bands, Metre and Rhythmic Mode in Marri Ngarr 'Church Lirrga' Songs." *Australasian Music Research* 7 (2002): 67–83.

———. "Unison and Disagreement in a Mixed Women's and Men's Performance (Ellis Collection, Oodnadatta 1966)." In *The Essence of Singing and the Substance of Song: Recent Responses to the Aboriginal Performing Arts and Other Essays in Honour of Catherine Ellis*, edited by Linda Barwick, Allan Marett and Guy Tunstill, 95–105. Sydney: University of Sydney (Oceania Monograph 46), 1995.

Barwick, Linda, Bruce Birch, and Nicholas Evans. "Iwaidja Jurtbirrk Songs: Bringing Language and Music Together." *Australian Aboriginal Studies*, 2 (2007): 6–34.

Barwick, Linda, Nicholas Evans, Murray Garde, Allan Marett with assistance from Isabel O'Keeffe, Ruth Singer and Bruce Birch. 'The West Arnhem Land Song Project Metadata Database, 2011–2015'. Funded by Hans Rousing Endangered Languages Project, http://elar.soas.ac.uk/deposit/0155.

Barwick, Linda, Mary Laughren, and Myfany Turpin. "Sustaining Women's Yawulyu/Awelye: Some Practitioners' and Learners' Perspectives." *Musicology Australia* 35, no. 2 (2013): 191–220.

Barwick, Linda, and Allan Marett. "Snapshots of Musical Life: The 1948 Recordings." In *Exploring the Legacy of the 1948 Arnhem Land Expedition*, edited by Martin Thomas and Margo Neale, 355–77. Canberra: Australian National University E Press, 2011.

———. "The West Arnhem Song Project—Linda Barwick." *SOAS radio* podcast, http://soasradio.org/content/western-arnhem-land-song-project-linda-barwick, updated 3 September 2013.

Barwick, Linda, Allan Marett, Murray Garde, and Nick Evans. "Bongolinj-Bongolinj and Its Children: Collaborative Research on the Language, Music and History of a Songset from Northwest Arnhem Land." Unpublished paper presented at Postgraduate Seminar, University of Oxford, 22 October 2009.

Barwick, Linda, Isabel O'Keeffe, and Ruth Singer. "Dilemmas in Interpretation: Contemporary Perspectives on Berndt's Goulburn Island Song Documentation." In *Little Paintings, Big Stories: Gossip Songs of Western Arnhem Land*, edited by John E. Stanton, 46–71. Nedlands: University of Western Australia Berndt Museum of Anthropology, 2013.

Bauman, Richard. "Verbal Art as Performance." *American Anthropologist* 77, no. 2 (1975): 290–311.

Bauman, Richard, and Charles L. Briggs. "Poetics and Performance as Critical Perspectives on Language and Social Life." *Annual Review of Anthropology* 19 (1990): 59–88.

Beazley, Kim. "Nation Building or Cold War: Political Settings for the Arnhem Land Expedition." In *Exploring the Legacy of the 1948 Arnhem Land Expedition*, edited by Martin Edward Thomas and Margo Neale, 55–73. Canberra: ANU E Press, 2011.

Bennett, Lou. "Black fulla, White fulla: Can There Be a Truly Balanced Collaboration?" In *Musical Collaboration between Indigenous and Non-indigenous People in Australia: Exchanges in the Third Space*, edited by Katelyn Barney. New York: Routledge, 2022: 9–23.

Berndt, Ronald M., ed. *Australian Aboriginal Art*. Sydney: Ure Smith, 1964.

———. *Australian Aboriginal Religion*. Leiden: E. J. Brill, 1974.

———. "Ceremonial Exchange in Western Arnhem Land." *Southwestern Journal of Anthropology* 7, no. 2 (1951): 156–76.

———. *Love Songs of Arnhem Land*. Melbourne: T. Nelson, 1976.

———. "Other Creatures in Human Guise and Vice Versa: A Dilemma in Understanding." In *Songs of Aboriginal Australia*, edited by Margaret Clunies Ross, Tamsin Donaldson and Stephen. A. Wild. Sydney: Sydney University Press, 1987: 169–193.

Berndt, Ronald M., and Catherine H. Berndt. *Arnhem Land: Its History and Its People*. Melbourne: Cheshire, 1954.

———. *End of an Era: Aboriginal Labour in the Northern Territory*. Canberra: Australian Institute of Aboriginal Studies, 1987.

———. *Man, Land & Myth in North Australia; the Gunwinggu People*. East Lansing: Michigan State University Press, 1970.

———. *Sexual Behavior in Western Arnhem Land*. New York: Viking Fund, 1951.

———. *The World of the First Australians, Aboriginal Traditional Life: Past and Present*. Canberra: Aboriginal Studies Press, 1999.

Birch, Bruce. *A First Dictionary of Erre, Mengerrdji and Urningangk: Three Languages from the Alligator Rivers Region of North Western Arnhem Land, Northern Territory, Australia*. Jabiru: Gundjeihmi Aboriginal Corporation, 2006.

———. "The American Clever Man (Marrkijbu Burdan Merika)." In *Exploring the Legacy of the 1948 Arnhem Land Expedition*, edited by M. Thomas and M. Neale. Canberra: ANU E Press, 2011: 313–336.

Borsboom, Adrianus Petrus. "Maradjiri: A Modern Ritual Complex in Arnhem Land, North Australqalia." PhD thesis, Katholieke Universiteit, 1978.

———. "Yolngu Ways of Knowing Country". Podcast of paper presented at *Barks, Birds and Billabongs* symposium, Canberra, 2009. http://www.nma.gov.au/audio/detail/yolngu-ways-of-knowing-country-insights-from-the-1948-expedition-to-arnhem-land.

Brandl, M., and M. Walsh. "Speakers of Many Tongues: Toward Understanding Multilingualism among Aboriginal Australians." *International Journal of the Sociology of Language* 36 (1982): 71–81.

Brown, Reuben, David Manmurulu, Jenny Manmurulu, Rupert Manmurulu, and Isabel O'Keeffe. "Continuing the History of Cultural Exchange in Arnhem Land: A Mamurrng Ceremony at Warruwi, Goulburn Island, August 2012." Paper presented at *Breaking Barriers in Indigenous Research and Thinking: AITSIS 50th Anniversary Conference*, Canberra, 2013.

Brown, Reuben, David Manmurulu, Jenny Manmurulu, Isabel O'Keeffe, and Ruth Singer. "Maintaining Song Traditions and Languages Together at Warruwi (western Arnhem Land)." In *Recirculating Songs: Revitalising the Singing Practices of Indigenous Australia*, edited by Jim Wafer and Myfany Turpin, 268–86. Canberra: Asia Pacific Linguistics, 2017.

Brown, Reuben and Solomon Nangamu. "'I'll show you that manyardi': Memory and lived experience in the performance of public ceremony in Western Arnhem Land." In *Music, Dance and the Archive*, edited by Amanda Harris, Linda Barwick and Jakelin Troy. Sydney: Sydney University Press, 2022: 15–38.

Campbell, Genevieve. "Ngarukuruwala–We Sing: The Songs of the Tiwi Islands, Northern Australia." PhD thesis, University of Sydney, 2013.

———. "Song as Artefact: The Reclaiming of Song Recordings Empowering Indigenous Stakeholders – and the Recordings Themselves." In *Circulating Cultures: Exchanges of Australian Indigenous Music, Dance and Media*, edited by Amanda Harris, 101–128. Canberra: ANU E Press, 2014.

Campbell, J. "Smallpox in Aboriginal Australia, the Early 1830s." *Historical Studies* no. 21 (1985): 336–58.

Campbell, Lauren. "A Sketch Grammar of Urningangk, Erre and Mengerrdji: The Giimbiyu Languages of Western Arnhem Land." Honours Thesis, Department of Linguistics and Applied Linguistics, the University of Melbourne, 2006.

Carroll, Peter. "Kunwinjku (Gunwinggu): A Language of Western Arnhem Land." Masters thesis, Australian National University, 1976.

———. "The Old People Told Us: Verbal Art in Western Arnhem Land." PhD thesis, the University of Queensland, 1995.

Chaloupka, George. *Journey in Time: The 50,000 Year Story of the Australian Aboriginal Rock Art of Arnhem Land.* Chatswood: Reed Books, 1993.

Chatwin, Bruce. *The Songlines.* London: Random House, 1988.

Christie, Michael. "Aboriginal Knowledge Traditions in Digital Environments." *Australian Journal of Indigenous Education* 34 (2005): 61–66.

Corn, Aaron. "Burr-Gi Wargugu Ngu-Ninya Rrawa: Expressions of Ancestry and Country in Songs by the Letterstick Band." *Musicology Australia* 25, no. 1 (2002): 76–101.

———. "'Djiliwirri Ganha Dhärranhana, Wänä Limurrungu': The Creative Foundations of a Yolŋu Popular Song." *Australasian Music Research* 7 (2002): 55–66.

———. "Dreamtime Wisdom, Modern-Time Vision: Tradition and Innovation in the Popular Band Movement of Arnhem Land, Australia." PhD thesis, University of Melbourne, 2002.

———. "Land, Song, Constitution: Exploring Expressions of Ancestral Agency, Intercultural Diplomacy and Family Legacy in the Music of Yothu Yindi with Mandawuy Yunupiŋu." *Popular Music* 29, no. 1 (2010): 81–102.

Curkpatrick, Samuel. *Singing Bones: Ancestral Creativity and Collaboration.* Indigenous Music of Australia series. Sydney: Sydney University Press, 2020.

Davis, Wade. *The Wayfinders: Why Ancient Wisdom Matters in the Modern World.* Crawley: UWA Publishing, 2010.

Deger, Jennifer. "Imprinting on the Heart: Photography and Contemporary Yolngu Mournings." *Visual Anthropology* 21 (2008): 292–309.

Elkin, A. P. *Arnhem Land: Authentic Australian Aboriginal Songs and Dances. The A. P. Elkin Collection* [compact disc]. Sydney: Larrikin, 1993

———. "Arnhem Land Music: Introduction." *Oceania* 24, no. 2 (1953): 81–109.

———. "Arnhem Land Music (continued)." *Oceania* 25, no. 1 (1954): 74–121.

———. *The Australian Aborigines: How to Understand Them.* 2nd ed. Sydney: Angus and Robertson, 1948.

Elkin, A. P., and Trevor A. Jones. *Arnhem Land Music (North Australia).* Oceania Monographs. Sydney: University of Sydney, 1956.

Ellis, Catherine J. *Aboriginal Music, Education for Living: Cross-Cultural Experiences from South Australia.* St. Lucia: University of Queensland Press, 1985.

Ellis, Catherine J., and Linda M. Barwick. "Musical Syntax and the Problem of Meaning in a Central Australian Songline." *Musicology Australia* 10, no. 1 (1987): 41–57.

Etherington, Steven, and Narelle Etherington. *Kunwinjku Kunwok: A Short Introduction to Kunwinjku Language and Society.* Kunbarlanja: The Kunwinjku Language Centre, 1994.

Evans, Nicholas. "A Tale of Many Tongues: Documenting Polyglot Narrative in North Australian Oral Traditions." In *Indigenous Language and Social Identity: Papers in*

Honour of Michael Walsh, edited by Brett Baker, Ilana Mushin Mark Harvey and Rod Gardner, 275–95. Canberra: Pacific Linguistics, 2010.

———. *Bininj Gun-wok: A Pan-Dialectal Grammar of Mayali, Kunwinjku and Kune*. 2 vols. Canberra: Pacific Linguistics, 2003.

———. *Dying Words: Endangered Languages and What They Have to Tell Us*. Chichester: Wiley-Blackwell, 2010.

———. "Macassan Loanwords in Top End Languages." *Australian Journal of Linguistics* 12, no. 1 (1992): 45–91.

———. "The Last Speaker Is Dead – Long Live the Last Speaker!." In *Linguistic Fieldwork*, edited by Martha Ratliff and Paul Newman. Cambridge; New York: Cambridge University Press, 2001: 250–281.

Evans, Nicholas and Hans-Jürgen Sasse, eds. *Problems of Polysynthesis*. Berlin: Akademie Verlag, 2002.

Fforde, Cressida, Jane Hubert, and Paul Turnbull, eds. *The Dead and Their Possessions: Repatriation in Principle, Policy, and Practice*. New York: Routledge, 2004.

Fitzgerald, Jon, and Philip Hayward. "At the Confluence: Slim Dusty and Australian Country Music." In *Outback and Urban: Australian Country Music*, edited by Philip Hayward, 29–54. Gympie: AICM Press, 2003.

Ford, Linda Payi. "The Indigenous Australian Knowledge Traditions: New Ways for Old Ceremonies – a Case Study of Aboriginal Final Mortuary Ceremonial Practices in the Northern Territory." *International Journal of Asia-Pacific Studies* 16, no. 2 (2020): 11–27.

Furlan, Alberto. "Songs of Continuity and Change: The Reproduction of Aboriginal Culture through Traditional and Popular Music." PhD thesis, University of Sydney, 2005.

Garde, Murray. "Bininj Gun-wok Blog Page." http://bininjgunwok.org.au.

———, ed. *Bininj Gunwok Talk about Health: Medical Terms and Vocabulary for Health Professionals*. Jabiru: Gundjeihmi Aboriginal Corporation, 2010.

———. *Culture, Interaction and Person Reference in an Australian Language: An Ethnography of Bininj Gunwok Communication*. Amsterdam: John Benjamins Publishing Company, 2013.

———. "From a Distance: Aboriginal Music in the Maningrida Community and on Their Internet Site." *Perfect Beat* 4, no. 1 (1998): 4–18.

———. "Morrdjdjanjno Ngan-Marnbom Story Nakka, 'Songs That Turn Me into a Story Teller': The Morrdjdjanjno of Western Arnhem Land." *Australian Aboriginal Studies* 2 (2007): 35–45.

———. "Nakodjok Namanilakarr, 27 June 2012." *Bininj Kunwok* blog page, https://bininjkunwok.org.au/nakodjok-namanilakarr, Accessed 19 July 2021.

———. "The Forbidden Gaze: The 1948 Wubarr Ceremony Performed for the American–Australian Scientific Expedition to Arnhem Land." In *Exploring the Legacy of the 1948 Arnhem Land Expedition*, edited by Martin Thomas and Margo Neale, 403–22. Canberra: ANU E Press, 2011.

———. "The Language of *Kun-borrk* in Western Arnhem Land." *Musicology Australia* 28 (2006): 59–89.

———. Warrurrumi Kun-borrk: Songs from Western Arnhem Land by Kevin Djimarr [CD booklet]. Sydney: Sydney University Press, 2007.

Geertz, Clifford. *Local Knowledge: Further Essays in Interpretive Anthropology*. New York: Basic Books, 1983.

Glaskin, Katie, Myrna Tonkinson, Yasmine Musharbash, and Victoria Burbank, eds. *Mortality, Mourning and Mortuary Practices in Indigenous Australia*. Surrey: Ashgate, 2008.
God Kanbengdayhke Kadberre. Canberra: The Bible Society of Australia, 1992.
Gold, Lisa. *Music in Bali: Experiencing Music, Expressing Culture*. New York: Oxford University Press, 2005.
Grant, Catherine. *Music Endangerment: How Language Maintenance Can Help*. New York: Oxford University Press, 2014.
Gulliford, Andrew. "Bones of Contention: The Repatriation of Native American Human Remains." *The Public Historian* 18, no. 4 (1996): 119–43.
Harris, Amanda. "Hearing Aboriginal Music Making in Non-Indigenous Accounts of the Bush from the Mid-20th Century." In *Circulating Cultures: Indigenous Music, Dance and Media across Genres in Australia*, edited by Amanda Harris. Canberra: ANU E Press, 2014: 73–100.
———. Representing Australian Aboriginal Music and Dance 1930–1970. New York: Bloomsbury Academic, 2020.
Harris, Joshua. "Hidden for Sixty Years: The Motion Pictures of the American–Australian Scientific Expedition to Arnhem Land." In *Exploring the Legacy of the 1948 Arnhem Land Expedition*, edited by Martin Thomas and Margo Neale. Canberra: ANU E Press, 2011: 239–252.
Harvey, Mark. *A Grammar of Gaaudju*. Berlin; New York: Mouton de Gruyter, 2002.
Haskins, Victoria. "Beth Dean and the Transnational Circulation of Aboriginal Dance Culture: Gender, Authority and C. P. Mountford." In *Circulating Cultures: Exchanges of Australian Indigenous Music, Dance and Media*, edited by Amanda Harris. 19–44. Canberra: ANU Press, 2014.
Hiatt, L. R. *Kinship and Conflict: A Study of an Aboriginal Community in Northern Arnhem Land*. Canberra: A.N.U. Press, 1965.
Hussey, Genevieve. "Celebrated Homecoming," *7:30 Report Northern Territory*. Australian Broadcasting Corporation, 30 July 2011. http://www.youtube.com/watch?v=M8Y2jhMsJLQ.
Ivory, Bill. "Kunmanggur, Legend and Leadership: A Study of Indigenous Leadership and Succession Focussing on the Northwest Region of the Northern Territory of Australia." PhD thesis, Charles Darwin University, 2009.
James Dawson, Peter, and Noeletta McKenzie. "Inagurual Lurr'a Festival Comes to Maningrida." *The West Arnhem Wire*, 31 October 2013. http://westarnhem.nt.gov.au/the-wire-news/2013/10/31/inagurual-lurra-festival-comes-to-maningrida. Accessed January 2014.
Jones, Trevor A. "Arnhem Land Music. Part II: A Musical Survey." *Oceania* 28, no. 1 (1957): 1–30.
———. "The Didjeridu." *Studies in Music* 1 (1996 James Dawson 7): 22–55.
Kalarriya, Jimmy Namarnyilk [sound recording]. "Jimmy Namarnyilk Interviewed by Martin Thomas". The Oral History Collection, National Library of Australia, Canberra. http://nla.gov.au/nla.oh-vn5299380
Kapchan, D. A. "Performance." *Journal of American Folklore* 108, no. 430 (1995): 479–508.
Keen, Ian. *Aboriginal Economy & Society: Australia at the Threshold of Colonisation*. South Melbourne: Oxford University Press, 2004.

———. *Knowledge and Secrecy in an Aboriginal Religion*. Oxford; New York: Clarendon Press, 1994.

Kell, Jodie, Rachel Djíbbama Thomas, Rona Lawrence, and Marita Wilton. "Ngarrangúddjeya Ngúrra-mala: Expressions of Identity in the Songs of the Ripple Effect Band." *Musicology Australia* 42, no. 2 (2020): 161–78. https://doi.org/10.1080/08145857.2020.1948730.

Keogh, Raymond. "Nurlu Songs of the West Kimberleys." PhD thesis, University of Sydney, 1990.

———. "Process Models for the Analysis of Nurlu Songs from the Western Kimberleys." In *The Essence of Singing and the Substance of Song: Recent Responses to the Aboriginal Performing Arts and Other Essays in Honour of Catherine Ellis*, edited by Linda Barwick, Allan Marett and Guy Tunstill, 39–51. Sydney: University of Sydney (Oceania Monograph 46), 1995.

Knopoff, Steven. "Yuta Manikay: Juxtaposition of Ancestral and Contemporary Elements in the Performance of Yolngu Clan Songs." *Yearbook for Traditional Music* 24 (1992): 138–53.

Lamilami, Lazarus. *Lamilami Speaks, the Cry Went Up: A Story of the People of Goulburn Islands, North Australia*. Sydney: Ure Smith, 1974.

Linden-Jones, Anthony. "The Circle of Songs: Traditional Song and the Musical Score to C. P. Mountford's Documentary Films." In *Circulating Cultures: Exchanges of Australian Indigenous Music, Dance and Media*, edited by Amanda Harris. Canberra: ANU Press, 2014: 45–72.

MacGregor, Tony. "Birds on the Wire: Wild Sound, Informal Speech and the Emergence of the Radio Documentary." In *Exploring the Legacy of the 1948 Arnhem Land Expedition*, edited by Martin Thomas and Margo Neale. Canberra: ANU E Press, 2011: 87–112.

Macknight, C. C. "The View from Marege: Australian Knowledge of Makassar and the Impact of the Trepang Industry across Two Centuries." *Aboriginal History* 35 (2011): 121–43.

———. *The Voyage to Marege: Macassan Trepangers in Northern Australia*. Carlton: Melbourne University Press, 1976.

Magnat, Virginie. "Can Research become Ceremony?: Performance Ethnography and Indigenous Epistemologies." *Canadian Theatre Review* 151 (2012): 30–36.

Magowan, Fiona. *Melodies of Mourning: Music and Emotion in Northern Australia*. Crawley: UWA Press, 2007.

Malinowski, Bronislaw. *Argonauts of the Western Pacific: An Account of Native Enterprise and Adventure in the Archipelagos of Melanesian New Guinea*, Routledge, 1922/2014. Available at: ProQuest Ebook Central, https://ebookcentral.proquest.com/lib/unimelb/detail.action?docID=1675940, Accessed 7 January 2020.

Marrala, Khaki. *Kindi Ngamin Nuwung? What Do I Call you? A Guide to Kinship and Address*. Jabiru: Iwaidja Inyman and West Arnhem Shire Council, 2008.

Marett, Allan. "Ghostly Voices: Some Observations on Song-Creation, Ceremony and Being in North Western Australia." *Oceania* 71, no. 1 (2000): 18–29.

———. *Songs, Dreamings, and Ghosts: The Wangga of North Australia*. Middletown: Wesleyan University Press, 2005.

———. "Vanishing Songs: How Musical Extinctions Threaten the Planet." *Ethnomusicology Forum* 19, no. 2 (2010): 135–275.

Marett, Allan, Linda Barwick, and Lysbeth Ford. *For the Sake of a Song: Wangga Songmen and Their Repertories*. Sydney: Sydney University Press, 2013.

Marshall, Alan. *Ourselves Writ Strange*. Melbourne; London: Cheshire, 1948.

Mauss, Marcel. *The Gift: The Form and Reason for Exchange*. London; New York: Routledge, 1954/2002.

May, Sally K. *Collecting Cultures: Myth, Politics, and Collaboration in the 1948 Arnhem Land Expedition*. Lanham: AltaMira Press, 2010.

May, Sally K., D. Gumurdul, J. Manakgu, G. Maralngurra, and W. Nawirridj. "'You Write It Down and Bring It Back…That's What We Want' – Revisiting the 1948 Removal of Human Remains from Gunbalanya (Oenpelli), Australia." In *Indigenous Archaeologies: Decolonising Theory and Practice*, edited by Claire Smith and H. Martin Wobst. London: Routledge, 2005: 102–121.

May, Sally K., Paul S. C. Tacon, Alistair Paterson, and Meg Travers. "The World from Malarrak: Depictions of South-East Asian and European Subjects in Rock Art from the Wellington Range, Australia." *Australian Aboriginal Studies* 1 (2013): 45–56.

McConvell, Patrick, and Nicholas Thieberger. "State of Indigenous Languages in Australia." Australia: State of the Environment Second Technical Paper Series (No.1 Natural and Cultural Heritage), 2001.

McIntosh, Ian S. "Islam and Australia's Aborigines." *The Journal of Religious History* 20, no. 1 (1996): 53–77.

McKenzie, Kim. *Waiting for Harry* [videorecording]. Canberra: Australian Institute of Aboriginal Studies, 1980.

McKeown, C. Timothy. "Considering Repatriation as an Option: The National Museum of the American Indian Act (NMAIA) & the Native American Graves Protection and Repatriation Act (NAGPRA)." In *Utimut: Past Heritage – Future Partnerships: Discussions on Repatriation in the 21st Century*, edited by Mille Gabriel and Jens Dahl. Copenhagen: Danish Ministry of Foreign Affairs and Greenland National Museum & Archives, 2008: 134–147.

McLaren, Glen, and William Cooper. *Distance, Drought and Dispossession: A History of the Northern Territory Pastoral Industry*. Darwin: Northern Territory University Press, 2001.

Memmott, Paul and Robyn Horsman. *A Changing Culture: The Lardil Aborigines of Mornington Island*. Wentworth Falls: Social Science Press, 1991.

Merlan, Francesca. "Catfish and Alligator: Totemic Songs of the Western Roper River, Northern Territory'." In *Songs of Aboriginal Australia*, edited by Margaret Clunies Ross, Tamsin Donaldson and Stephen A. Wild, 143–67. Sydney: University of Sydney: Oceania Publications, 1987.

"Mewal Song Project" [webpage]. Batchelor Institute for Indigenous Tertiary Education, 2015. Available at https://call.batchelor.edu.au/projects/mewal-song-project. Accessed 1 September 2021.

"Mindil Beach LongGrassBand", YouTube video, uploaded by 'adminwhereisthelove' on 30 October 2007. Available at https://www.youtube.com/watch?v=7e_i57cXdzU. Accessed 1 September 2021.

Morphy, Howard. *Journey to the Crocodile's Nest: An Accompanying Monograph to the Film Madarrpa Funeral at Gurka'wuy*. Canberra: Australian Institute of Aboriginal Studies, 1984.

Morphy, Howard, and Frances Morphy. "Afterword: Demography and Destiny." In *Mortality, Mourning and Mortuary Practices in Indigenous Australia*, edited by Katie Glaskin, Myrna Tonkinson, Yasmine Musharbash and Victoria Burbank, 209–15. Surrey: Ashgate, 2008.

Mountford, C. P. *Aboriginal Music from the Northern Territory of Australia, 1948, with Annotations by Professor A. P. Elkin*, (twelve 12-inch discs, PRX2809–10, PRX2645–52), Australian Broadcasting Commission (processed by Columbia Gramophone), Sydney, 1949.

———. "Aborigines of the Sea Coast" [videorecording], Lindfield: Film Australia, 1951. Youtube video, uploaded by NFSA Films, 26 May 2013, https://www.youtube.com/watch?v=seh0-_JMBuQ

———. *American–Australian Scientific Expedition to Arnhem Land 1948*, (nine 78 rpm discs), Australian Broadcasting Commission, Sydney, 1949.

———. "Arnhem Land," [videorecording], Australian Commonwealth Film Unit: Film Australia, 1950.

———. "Birds and Billabongs," [videorecording], Australian National Film Board: 1951. Youtube video, uploaded by NFSA Films, 28 June 2010, https://www.youtube.com/watch?v=R09Cy0CMi-c

———. "Exploring Stone Age Arnhem Land." *National Geographic Magazine* 96, no. 6 (1949): 745–82.

———. *Records of the American-Australian Scientific Expedition to Arnhem Land: Vol. 1: Art, Myth and Symbolism* (1956).

Moyle, Alice M. "North Australian Music: A Taxonomic Approach to the Study of Aboriginal Song Performances." PhD dissertation, Monash University, 1974.

———. Songs from the Northern Territory Companion booklet for five 12 inch LP discs (Cat No. I.A.S M-001/5). Canberra: Australian Institute of Aboriginal Studies, 1967.

———. "Songs from the Northern Territory" Vol. 1. [LP disc recording re-released on audio compact disc]. Australian Institute of Aboriginal and Torres Strait Islander Studies, 1997.

———. "The Australian Didjeridu: A Late Musical Intrusion." *World Archaeology* 12, no. 3 (1981): 321–31.

Mulvaney, John. *Paddy Cahill of Oenpelli*. Canberra: Aboriginal Studies Press, 2004.

Murdoch, Lindsay. "Repatriated Aboriginal Remains Are Buried." *Sydney Morning Herald*, 20 July 2011, http://www.smh.com.au/photogallery/national/repatriated-aboriginal-remains-are-reburied-20110719-1hn0t.html?aggregate=&selectedImage=0.

———. "Stolen Spirits Brought Home to Be at Rest." *The Sydney Morning Herald*, 2011 http://www.smh.com.au/national/stolen-spirits-brought-home-to-be-at-rest-20110719-1hnbv.html.

Myers, Fred. "Ways of Place-Making." *La Ricerca Folklorica* 45 (2002): 101–19.

Nabageyo, Eileen, Eric Mardday, and Reuben Brown. *Kun-borrk Kore Kunbarlanja, Korroko Dja Bolkkime* (*Kun-borrk* at Gunbalanya, Then and Now), unpublished paper presented at the Stone Country Festival, Gunbalanya, 2012.

Nayinggul, Jacob [sound recording]. "Jacob Nayinggul interviewed by Martin Thomas." The Oral History Collection, National Library of Australia, http://nla.gov.au/nla.oh-vn5299383

Neale, Margo. "Epilogue: Sifting the Silence." In *Exploring the Legacy of the 1948 Arnhem Land Expedition*, edited by Martin Thomas and Margo Neale, 423–37. Canberra: ANU E Press, 2011.

O'Keeffe, Isabel. "Kaddikkaddik Ka-wokdjanganj 'Kaddikkaddik Spoke': Language and Music of the Kun-Barlang Kaddikkaddik Songs from Western Arnhem Land." *Australian Journal of Linguistics* 30, no. 1 (2010): 35–51.

———. "Manifestations of Multilingualism in the Classical Song Traditions of Western Arnhem Land." PhD thesis, University of Melbourne, 2016.

———. "Sung and Spoken: An Analysis of Two Different Versions of a Kun-Barlang Love Song." *Australian Aboriginal Studies* 2 (2007): 46–62.

Phipps, Peter. "Performances of Power: Indigenous Cultural Festivals as Globally Engaged Cultural Strategy." *Alternatives* 35, no. 3 (2010): 217.

Poignant, Roslyn, and Axel Poignant. *Encounter at Nagalarramba*. Canberra: National Library of Australia, 1996.

Raymond, Des Kootji, "Wrap Me up in Paperbark," [videorecording]. Macumba Media Enterprises, 1999.

Reid, Janice. "A Time to Live, a Time to Grieve: Patterns and Processes of Mourning among the Yolngu of Australia." *Culture, Medicine and Psychiatry* 3, no. 4 (1979): 319–46.

Roberts, Richard G., Rhys Jones, and M. A. Smith. "Thermoluminescence Dating of a 50,000-Year-Old Human Occupation Site in Northern Australia." *Nature Publishing Group* 345 (1990): 153–55.

Rose, Deborah B. *Dingo Makes Us Human: Life and Land in an Australian Aboriginal Culture*. Cambridge: Cambridge University Press, 2009.

Ross, Margaret Clunies, Tamsin Donaldson, and Stephen A. Wild, eds. *Songs of Aboriginal Australia*. Sydney: University of Sydney, 1987.

Ross, Margaret Clunies, and Stephen A. Wild. "Formal Performance: The Relations of Music, Text and Dance in Arnhem Land Clan Songs." *Ethnomusicology* 28, no. 2 (1984): 209–35.

Russell-Smith, Jeremy, Peter J. Whitehead, and Peter Cooke. *Culture, Ecology and Economy of Fire Management in North Australian Savannas: Rekindling the Wurrk Tradition*. Melbourne: CSIRO Publishing, 2009.

Simpson, Colin. *Adam in Ochre: Inside Aboriginal Australia*. Sydney: Angus & Robertson, 1952.

———. *Aboriginal Music from the Northern Territory of Australia, 1948, with Annotations by Professor A. P. Elkin*, (twelve 12-inch discs, PRX2809-10, PRX2645-52). Sydney: Australian Broadcasting Commission (processed by Columbia Gramophone).

Singer, Ruth. "Agreement in Mawng: Productive and Lexicalised Uses of Agreement in an Australian Language." PhD thesis, the University of Melbourne, 2006.

———. Mawng Dictionary, *Mawng Ngaralk* website, http://www.mawngngaralk.org.au/main/dictionary.php, Accessed 16 April 2015.

———. "The Wrong T-Shirt: Configurations of Language and Identity at Warruwi Community." *The Australian Journal of Anthropology* 29, no. 1 (2018): 70–88.

Singer, Ruth, and Salome Harris. "What Practices and Ideologies Support Small-scale Multilingualism? A Case Study of Warruwi Community, Northern Australia." *International Journal of the Sociology of Language* 241 (2016): 163–208.

Singer, Ruth, and Isabel O'Keeffe [depositors]. *A Collection of Musical Terms in Mawng and Their Translations Archived with Songs of Western Arnhem Land Australia*. http://elar.soas.ac.uk/deposit/arnhemland-135103, 2012.

Singer, Ruth, Nita Garidjalalug, Rosemary Urabadi, Heather Hewett, and Peggy Mirwuma. *Mawng Dictionary*. Canberra: Aboriginal Studies Press, 2021.

Sleath, Emma. "Island Festival Revives the Spirit of 'Jamalak'." Australian Broadcasting Corporation, 2013. http://www.abc.net.au/local/photos/2013/08/27/3835177.htm. Accessed 9 April 2014.

Spencer, Baldwin. *Kakadu People*, ed. David M. Welch. Australian Aboriginal Culture Series 3. Virginia: David M. Welch, 2008.

———. *Native Tribes of the Northern Territory of Australia*. London: Macmillan, 1914.

Stanner, W. E. H. "The Dreaming." In *The Dreaming and Other Essays*, 57–73. Collingwood: Black Inc. Agenda, 1953.

Stubington, Jill, and Peter Dunbar-Hall. "Yothu Yindi's 'Treaty': Ganma in Music." *Popular Music* 13, no. 3 (1994): 243–59.

Sutton, Peter. "Materialism, Sacred Myth, and Pluralism: Competing Theories of the Origin of Australian Languages." In *Scholar and Sceptic: Australian Aboriginal Studies in Honour of L. R. Hiatt*, edited by John Morton Francesca Merlan and Alan Rumsey, 211–42. Canberra: Aboriginal Studies Press, 1997.

Sykes, Jim. *The Musical Gift: Sonic Generosity in Post-War Sri Lanka*. Oxford: Oxford Scholarship Online, 2018.

Tamisari, Franca. "Dancing for Strangers: Zorba the Greek Yolngu Style: A Giullarata by the Chooky Dancers of Elcho Island." *La ricerca folklorica* 61 (2010): 61–72.

———. "Writing Close to Dance: Reflections on an Experiment." In *Aesthetics and Experience in Music Performance*, edited by Elizabeth MacKinlay, Denis Collins and Samantha Owens, 165–90. Newcastle: Cambridge Scholars, 2005.

Tedlock, Barbara. "From Participant Observation to the Observation of Participation: The Emergence of Narrative Ethnography." *Journal of Anthropological Research* 47, no. 1 (1991): 69–94.

Thomas, Martin. "'Because It's Your Country': The Repatriation of Human Remains from the Smithsonian Institution to an Aboriginal Community in West Arnhem Land." *Life Writing* (2013): 203–223.

———. "Expedition as Time Capsule: Introducing the American–Australian Scientific Expedition to Arnhem Land." In *Exploring the Legacy of the 1948 Arnhem Land Expedition*, edited by Martin Thomas and Margo Neale, 1–33. Canberra: ANU E Press, 2011.

———. "Return to Arnhem Land" [radio program] *Radio Eye*, presented by Brent Clough, 2 June 2007, http://www.abc.net.au/radionational/programs/radioeye/return-to-arnhem-land/3250548

———. "Taking Them Back: Archival Media in Arnhem Land Today." *Cultural Studies Review* 13, no. 2 (September 2007): 20–37.

———. "The Crackle of the Wire: Media, Digitization, and the Voicing of Aboriginal Languages." In *Voice: Vocal Aesthetics in Digital Arts and Media*, edited by Norie Neumark, Ross Gibson and Theo Van Leeuwen, 71–90. Cambridge, MA: MIT Press, 2010.

———. *The Many Worlds of R. H. Mathews: In Search of an Australian Anthropologist*. Crows Nest: Allen & Unwin, 2011.

———. "Turning Subjects into Objects and Objects into Subjects: Collecting Human Remains on the 1948 Arnhem Land Expedition." In *Circulating Cultures: Exchanges of Australian Indigenous Music, Dance and Media*, edited by Amanda Harris. Canberra: ANU Press, 2014: 129–169.

———. "Unpacking the Testimony of Gerald Blitner: Cross-Cultural Brokerage and the Arnhem Land Expedition." In *Exploring the Legacy of the 1948 Arnhem Land*

Expedition, edited by Martin Thomas and Margo Neale, 377–403. Canberra: ANU E Press, 2011.

Thomas, Martin, and Margo Neale, eds. *Exploring the Legacy of the 1948 Arnhem Land Expedition*. Canberra: ANU E Press, 2011.

Thomson, Donald. *Economic Structure and the Ceremonial Exchange Cycle in Arnhem Land*. Melbourne: Macmillan, 1949.

Toner, P. G. "Home among the Gum Trees: An Ethnography of Yolngu Musical Performance in Mainstream Contexts." In *Landscapes of Indigenous Performance: Music, Song and Dance of the Torres Strait and Arnhem Land*, edited by Fiona Magowan and Karl Neuenfeldt, 29–45. Canberra: Aboriginal Studies Press, 2005.

Toner, Peter. "Ideology, Influence and Innovation: The Impact of Macassan Contact on Yolngu Music." *Perfect Beat: The Pacific Journal of Research into Contemporary Music and Popular Culture* 5, no. 1 (2000): 22–41.

———. "Tropes of Longing and Belonging: Nostalgia and Musical Instruments in Northeast Arnhem Land." *Yearbook for Traditional Music* 37 (2005): 1–24.

———. "When the Echoes Have Gone: A Yolngu Musical Anthropology." PhD dissertation, Australian National University, 2001.

Tonkinson, Myrna. "Solidarity in Shared Loss: Death-Related Observances among the Martu of the Western Desert." In *Mortality, Mourning and Mortuary Practices in Indigenous Australia*, edited by Katie Glaskin, Myrna Tonkinson, Yasmine Musharbash and Victoria Burbank. Surrey: Ashgate, 2008: 37–54.

Treloyn, Sally. "Scotty Martin's *Jadmi Junba*: A Song Series from the Kimberly Region of Northwest Australia." *Oceania* 73 (2003): 208–20.

———. "Songs That Pull: *Jadmi Junba* from the Kimberley Region of Northwest Australia." PhD thesis, University of Sydney, 2006.

———. "'When Everybody There Together… Then I Call That One': Song Order in the Kimberley." *Context* 32 (2007): 105–21.

Treloyn, Sally, and Andrea Emberly. "Sustaining Traditions: Ethnomusicological Collections, Access and Sustainability in Australia." *Musicology Australia* 35, no. 2 (2013): 159–77.

Treloyn, Sally, Matthew Dembal Martin, and Rona Googninda Charles. "Cultural Precedents for the Repatriation of Legacy Song Records to Communities of Origin." *Australian Aboriginal Studies*, no. 2 (2016): 94–103.

Trudgen, Richard. *Why Warriors Lie Down and Die: Towards an Understanding of Why the Aboriginal People of Arnhem Land Face the Greatest Crisis in Health and Education since European Contact*. Darwin: Aboriginal Resource and Development Services Inc., 2000.

Turnbull, Paul, and Michael Pickering, eds. *The Long Way Home: The Meanings and Values of Repatriation*. New York: Berghahn Books, 2010.

Turner, Victor. "Dramatic Ritual/Ritual Drama: Performative and Reflexive Anthropology." *Kenyon Review* 1, no. 3 (1979): 80–93.

Turner, Victor, and Edith Turner. "Performing Ethnography." In *The Performance Studies Reader*, edited by Henry Bial, 265–79. New York: Routledge, 2004.

"Wakwak: a wurrkikandjarr performance" [videorecording]. Batchelor Institute for Indigenous Tertiary Education, 2015, available at: https://ictv.com.au/video/item/3125, accessed 1 September 2021.

Walker, Clinton. *Buried Country: The Story of Aboriginal Country Music*. Sydney: Pluto Press, 2000.

Walsh, Michael. "Australian Aboriginal Song Language: So Many Questions, So Little to Work with." *Australian Aboriginal Studies* 2 (2007): 128–44.

———. "Will Indigenous Languages Survive?". *Annual Review of Anthropology* 34 (2005): 293–315.

Warner, Lloyd W. *A Black Civilization: A Social Study of an Australian Tribe*. Rev. ed. Gloucester, MA: P. Smith, 1969.

Watkins, Joe. "Artefactual Awareness: Spiro Mounds, Grave Goods and Politics." In *The Dead and Their Possessions: Repatriation in Principle, Policy, and Practice*, edited by Cressida Fforde, Jane Hubert and Paul Turnbull. New York: Routledge, 2004: 149–159.

Webb, Steven. Survey of Remains in the Northern Territory Museum Repatriated from the Smithsonian Museum, Washington, [unpublished report]. Bond University, 2011.

Weiner, Annette. *Inalienable Possessions: The Paradox of Keeping-While-Giving*. Berkeley: University of California Press, 1992.

———. "Reproduction: A Replacement for Reciprocity." *American Ethnologist* 7, no. 1 (1980): 71–85.

Wild, Stephen, and L. R. Hiatt, eds. *Rom, an Aboriginal Ritual of Diplomacy*. Canberra: Australian Institute of Aboriginal Studies, 1986.

Wildflower. "Kabbari." From the album *Manginburru Bininj*. Skinnyfish Music. Compact disc. Recorded in 2009.

Wilson, Ronald. *Bringing Them Home: Report of the National Inquiry into the Separation of Aboriginal and Torres Strait Islander Children from Their Families*. Sydney: Human Rights and Equal Opportunity Commission, 1997.

Wilson, Shawn. *Research Is Ceremony: Indigenous Research Methods*. Halifax, Winnepeg: Fernwood, 2008.

Index

Note: **Bold** page numbers refer to tables; *italic* page numbers refer to figures and page numbers followed by "n" denote endnotes.

Aboriginal art: bark paintings 76–77, 98n14, 154, 194; 'contact art' 44; rock art 4, 9, 33n20, 44, 72, 74, 167, 187
Aboriginal languages *see* languages and language groups, Aboriginal
Agalara, Russell *25*, **28**, 39, *41*, 41–42, 49, *49*–50, 55, 63, 86, 92, 94, 110, 121, 123, 132, 141–142, **143**–146, 149, 179, 186, *190*, 201, 214, 221, 228n14; grandfather of *see* Nawudba, Michael
Altman, Jon 106
Amagula, Thomas 82
Amartjitpalk (place name) 40–*41*, 43, 46, 48, 51, 57, 61, 63–65, 223
American-Australian Scientific Expedition to Arnhem Land (AASEAL) 4–5, 15–16, 23, 30, 75–76, *76*–78, 153, 156, 159–162, *162*, 163–169, **170**, 180, 209
Amurdak (language) 20, **28**, 109
Anbarra people 108
ancestral country: ties to 6, 10, 12, 43, 64, 158, 223
ancestral spirits 6–7, 8–10, 14–15, 23, **28**, 40, 43, 50–51, 54, 61, 64, 68n40, 75, 77–82, 86–91, 94–96, 106, 109, 131–135, 139–140, 142, 145–146, 149, 180, 207, 214, **216**–218, 222–225, 227; agency of 79–80; creative exchange with 10, 41, 50–51, 64, 132, 145–146, 215; *mimih* (stone country spirits) 6–7, 9–10; *namarrkon* (lightning Dreaming ancestor) 9, 61; *namorrorddo/yumparrparr* (giant/shooting star) 118, 122, 139, 217, 232–233; performing for 23, 145, 149, 223; *warra ngurrijakurr* (mangrove-dwelling spirits) 10, 40; *yingarna* (creation mother) 9, 33n22
ancestral stories 6, 9, 43–44, 50, 65, 102, 136, 191
Anglicanism: ministers 82, 92; missions 21; *see also* Church Missionary Society
Annual Symposium for Indigenous Music and Dance 109, 111, 124, 127n13, 231
Apted, Meiki 135
arawirr see didjeridu
archival collections of song and dance: creation 15, 17; importance 177; repatriation 13–16, 153, 157–160, 180–181, 211n11, 215, 222–223, 229n20
Arnhem Land: central 18, 26, **28**, 58, 108, 111, 136, 150n22, 154, 172, 197, **202**; eastern 7, 21, 23, 26, **28**, 43, 45, 67n37, 99n40, 102, 111, 132, 136, 149n2, 155, 172, 183n39, 201, 209; northeastern 23, 26, 75, 134, 136, 204; *see also bunggurl*; *manikay*
Arnhem Land Expedition *see* American-Australian Scientific Expedition to Arnhem Land (AASEAL)
Arrkuluk: Camp 73, **83**, 86, 154, 157, 171; Hill 73, 78, 86–87, 89, 156, 191, 209
Asera, Dave *see* bands, Reggae Dave

Australian Broadcasting Commission 16, 86, 153, 155–156, 161; radio archives 155–156, 165
Australian Institute for Aboriginal and Torres Strait Islander Studies (AIATSIS) 108, 113

Balir Balir, Bob 37n94, 164–165, 169–**170**
bands: Bininj Band **202**, 204; Black Arm Band 203–**204**; Jess Ribeiro and the Bone Collectors **203**, 204; Mambali Band **202**; Matter of Soul 190, *190*, 201, **202**, 205; Nabarlek Band 201, **202**, 205, 225; Nawarddeken Band 201, **202**; New Generation **203**–204; Northern Gentlemen 193, 201–**202**, 205; performing in ceremonial body paint 190, *190*; reframing Indigenous song traditions 192, 201; Reggae Dave (Dave Asera) **203**; Ripple Effect Band 48; Rock Wallaby Band 201–**202**; singing in Kunwinjku/Mawng 187, 190–191, **202**; Soft Sands 201, 205; Sunset Liverpool River **202**; Sunrize Band 201–**202**; Tjupi Band **203**–204; West Arnhem Boss **202**, 204; Wildflower Band 48, 158, 190–191, **202**; women performing in 191; Yothu Yindi 194, 201, 204; Young Guns **203**–204; Yugul Voice **202**, 204
Barunga 24, 194
Barwick, Linda 4, 14, 17, 43, 51–*52*, 53–*56*, 57, 103, 111–*112*, 123–124, 127n13, 160, 168–169, 171, 173, 184n78, 201, 214, 216–217
Bascoe, Keith **28**
Bassett-Smith, Peter 16
Batjamalh (language) 124, 150n19, 169–**170**, 171, 173, 185n89
Bauman, Richard 27
Belyuen 134, 150n19, 171, 173
Bennett, Lou 4
Berger, Gus 109, 112
Berndt, Catherine 75
Berndt, Ronald 9–10, 12, 17, 51, 68n40, 75, 113, 126n1, 127n2
Beswick 24, 67n22, 155, 193
Bijon, Béatrice 112
Bilinyarra 50, 164–165, 169–**170**
bilma see clapsticks

bim see Aboriginal art, rock art
Bininj Kunwok dialect chain 20–21, 155, 182n5, 191, 201; Kuninjku 20, 28; Kunwinjku 17–18, 20–22, **28**–**29**, 31, 36n82, 61, 63, 65, 73, 81, 87–89, 92, 103, 106, 108, 126, 135, 137, **137**–138, 140, 153, 155–156, 158, 164–166, 168–169, **170**–172, 174, 176–177, 181, 182n5, 187, 190–191, **202**, **216**, 230–231; Kundedjnjenghmi 20, **28**, 172; Kundjeyhmi 20–21, 109, 159, 192, 195; Kune 20, **28**; Mayali 20–21, 176
Birch, Bruce 51–*52*, 53, 67n21, 77, *112*, 112, 127n19, 160, 217
Blitner, Gerald 38n108, 166
body paint *see* ochre
Bracknell, Clint 14
Bray, John 161, 183n39
Brown, Archie 109, *112*, 114, 127n19, 185n90
Brown, Jackie **170**
Brown, Jason *120*
Brown, Reuben *105*, *112*, *231*
Buffalo Dance (song-set) 29, 136–**137**, 140
buffalo shooting and skinning camps 21–22, 35n67, 45–46, 48, 154–155, 157, 161–165
Bugurnidja (language) 88
Bull, Nabulanj Paddy 163, 165, 169–**170**, 174, 177
Bulman 25, 155
bunggurl 26, **28**, 58, 129, 131, 136–**137**, 172, 194–195, 197–198, 201–**202**, 216
Bunungurr, Bobby **28**, 188, 195, 210–211n2, 212n13
Burarra people 107, 126n4, **202**
Burnyila, Roy **28**, 195, 211n1
Burrenjuck, Kenny 123, 198
Burrenjuck, Tommy (Barrtjap) 123, 198
Burrwanga, Johnny **28**, 136

Cahill, Paddy 45–46, 67n27, 164
Campbell, Genevieve 136
Campbell, Glenn 81
Canberra 108, 113, 214
Cassar-Daly, Troy: 'Gunbalanya' 138
ceremonies: building opening 40, 48; circumcision 48, 111, 181; as expression of identity 64, 106, 113, 125, 142, 148; graduation 48; reburial

17, 23, 71–75, 77–82, **83–85**, 86–90, 92–96, 105, 122, 192, **219**, 222, 225; secret-sacred 16, 30, 67n33; smoking **85**, 92, 94, 109, 134, **137**, 150n4, 232; *see also* diplomacy/exchange ceremonies; funeral ceremonies
ceremony leaders 1, 23–24, 75, 95, 107–108, 112, 114, 124, 142, 171, 192–194, 210–211, 216, 218, 221–222, 225, 231–232
Charles, Rona 231
Christianity 10, 46, 92, 130, 132–133, 135, 137, **137**–138, 140, 148; *see also* Church Missionary Society; hymns; missions
Christie, Michael 29
Church Missionary Society (CMS) 21
clan names *see* names, skin and clan
clan songs: Galpu **28**, 136–**137**; Gurrumba Gurrumba **28**, 195–**196**, *197*, 197, 212n16, **219**; Wurrkigandjarr **28**, 136–**137**, 139; Yirritja moiety **28**
clapstick beating: accompanying song 1–2, 8, 23, 42, 48–49, *52*–*55*, *56*, 58, 82, 89–90, 92, 103–105, 114–**116**, 117–119, *120*, 131, 136, 155, 158, 161, 168, 178, 198, 201, 205, 224; relationship to dance 7, 58, 60, 64, 87, 89, 114, 117–122, 130, 186, 188, 210; rhythmic modes 24, *52*–*55*, *56*, 58, 87, 92, 114–**116**, 117–119, 122, 141–142, 173, **175**–**176**, 178–**179**, 198, 200, 220; in rock music 205; tempo 55–*56*, 87, 90, 103, 114–115, **116**–119, 130, 198, 217; terminating pattern 53, 58, 90–91, 178–**179**, 179, 219, 223
clapsticks (*man-berlnginj/nganangk*) 2, 9, 40, 42, 92, *107*, *120*; boomerang 168
Cobourg Peninsula 26, 44–45, 109, 163–165
Compass, Nabulanj Paddy 185n90
composition *see* song creation
contact history, Aboriginal: between Aboriginal groups 224; European 43–46, 64, 106, 209, 225; Japanese 44–45, 106, 156, 186, 209, 225; Malay 44; Macassan 29, 36n81, 43–45, 47, 66n11, 91, 106, 156, 209, 224
Cook, Mr 157
Cooke, Peter 108
Cooper, Harrison 118, *120*, 123

Cooper, Joe 164
Cooper, Reuben 164–165
Cooper, Toby *200*, 200
Corn, Aaron 204
corroborees 23, 48, 58, 161, 165–168, 192
Croker Island (Minjilang) 18, 24–26, 46, 51, 108–109, 114, 135, 156, 160, 164–165, 169–**170**, 171, 181, 189, 200, **202**, 204
cultural traditions, Indigenous: loss of 225–226

Daly region 14, 26, 51, 79, 110, 123, 127n16, 134, 150n22, 158, 160, 165, 169–**170**, 177, 181, 198, 201, 204, 218, 224, 232; *see also lirrga*; *wangga*
dance: body paint *see* ochre; calls 58–*59*, 64, 87, 118–119, 121, 130, 198–**199**, 232; comical 63–64, 123, **216**; costume 30, 87–88, 104, 140; ground, preparation of 48, 103, 187; leader ('dance captain') 130, 141, 150n3, 186, 232; learning 65, 122, 125, 141–142, 200, 210, 222; *namorrorddo/ yumparrparr* (giant) 118, 122, 139, 217, 232–233
dancers: Gurrumba Gurrumba clan 195; Karrbarda 7, 50, 87, **137**, 188, 195; Milyarryarr/Mirrijpu (Goulburn Island) *200*, 200; Mimih 195; *see also* women, dancers
dance style: female 55, 64, 87, 119, 125, 139; 'freestyle' 60, 65; male 55, 125, 189; movements 7, 24, 53–54, 57–**59**, 60, 87–88, 91, 105, 114, 118–119, *120*–123, 125, 130, 136, 186, 189, 200, *200*; performed by Balanda (Euro-diasporic) 57, 61, 65, 123, 188–189, 192, 198, 214; performed by tourists 186, 188–189, 192, 200; spontaneity in 121, 124; synchronicity in 54, 57, 60–61, 65, 70n82, 103, 198
Darwin 46, 48, 109, 124, 134, 155–156, 164, 187, 193, **203**–205, 207, 210, 230–231
Dawu, Michael 188
De Heer, Rolf 188, 211n2
delek see ochre, white
didjeridu (*mako/arawirr*): accompanying song 2, 7, 11, 23–24, 41–42, 47–48, 51–*52*, 53–54, 58, 61, 63, 65, 86,

89–90, 92, 104, 115, 118, 121, 123–125, 130, 136, 141, 155, 158, 161, 166, 172, 177, 179, 188, 190, 198–**199**, 201; circular breathing 2; overblown notes/overtones 69n68, 136, 172, 188; paintings of 9; rhythm 41–42, 55–*56*, 69n68, 118, 124, 188, 219–220; in rock music 190, 205
didjeridu players 1, 22, 39–*41*, 49–50, 58, 61, 63, 86, 92, 103, 114–*115*, 118, 121, 123, 141, 163, 166, 169–**170**, 189, 198, 205, 215, 218, 223, 226–227, 233
Dingala, David 195
diplomacy/exchange ceremonies (Mamurrng; Rom) 11, 13, 23, 106–107, *107*–108, 113, 126n1, 181; *see also* Mamurrng
Divilli, Johnny 232
Djalama clan 103, 156, 169–**170**
Djalarra clan **137**
Djalawarrurru people 172
Djambunuwa *162*
Djinang (language) **28**
Djok clan 169–**170**
Djorlom, Esther *112*
Djorlom, Robert 111
Djulibing, Frances 188, 210, 211n2, 212n13
Dreaming/Dreamings 9–10, 13, 53, 61, 65, 79, 136, 223; and song composition 8, 10, 50–51, 65, 68n40, 68n44, 109, 132, 134–135, 140, 145, *174*–*148*, **170**–171, 174, 191, **202**, 210, 223–224, 233
Dumoo, Frank 123
Dunbar-Hall, Peter 201
Dunkley, Aub 163
Dusty, Slim: 'We've Done Us Proud' 138

Elkin, A. P. 176
Ellis, Catherine 8, 32n16, 57
Ellison, Alf 75
Erre (language) 21, 73, 88, 195
ethnography, performative 30–31
Evans, Nicholas 21, 24, 51–*52*, 53, 100n60, 217, 229n28
exchange: of gifts 11–13, 15–16, 106, 110–114, 125, 223; modes of 22, 215, 223–224; *see also* diplomacy/exchange ceremonies; Wurnan
exchange ceremonies *see* diplomacy/exchange ceremonies

festival: Barunga Festival (1988) 194; Garma Festival 193–194, 211n11; Gurruwiling Festival 193; Jamalak Festival 193; Lurr'a Festival 193; Mahbilil Festival 186, 192–193, 195–196, **196**, 201–**202**, **203**–204, 209, 212n15; Mowanjum Festival 193–194, 212n12, 231–232; Stone Country Festival 153, 158, 183n29, 187–190, *190*, 192–193, 195–196, **196**–*197*, 201, **202**–**203**, 204, 209–211, 212n15; Yugul Mangi Festival 193
festivals, Indigenous cultural 4, 11, 23, 49, 158, 181, 186–196, 201, **202**–**203**, 204–205, 209–211; audiences at 186–189, 192–194, 196, 200–201, 205, 209–210; ceremonial performances at 187–189, 195–200; as cultural maintenance 193–194, 210; as expressions of identity 190, 193–194, 210; funding of 192, 195; as intercultural exchange 188–189, 192, 209–210, 223; political functions of 194; sustainability of 211, 226
films: *Aborigines of the Sea Coast* 16; *Arnhem Land* 16; *Birds and Billabongs* 16; *Charlie's Country* 211n2; *Etched in Bone* 75; *Ten Canoes* 188; *Waiting for Harry* 96n3; *see also* National Geographic Society
footsteps, metaphor of 2, 6–8, 11, 22, 24, 27, 31, 54, 65, 157, 214–215
Ford, Payi Linda 14, 55–*56*, 216
funeral ceremonies 11, 18, 23, 27, 49, 63, 72–73, 78–82, 88, 90–92, 97n7, 113–114, 118, 129–137, **137**–142, **143**–**144**, 145–149, 181, 187, 217–218, 222–224; bough shelters 48, 90, 118, **137**, 139, *139*–141, 187, 217, 232; *kun-woning* (cleansing ceremony) **137**; *lorrkkon* 73, 96n3, 133, 150n12; mourning rituals 129–135, 139–140; processions 82–**83**, 86–87; rag-burning 132, 160; significance of 133; *see also* ceremonies, smoking
Furlan, Alberto 204

Gaagadju (language) 21, 37n84, 88, 96n2, 100n60, 150n13, 195
Galaminda, Isaac *120*
Galaminda, Jay *190*, 214
Galpu clan 43, 136–**137**, 138

Gameraidj, Joseph 163
Gameraidj, Stanley 103, 114, *120*–121, 124
Ganalbingu (language) **28**
Ganawa, Solomon 4, 49, *49*–50, 205, 220–221
Garde, Murray 16, 51, 70n77, 126n3, 160, 172–176, 191
Gawaraidji, Alfred 1–*3*, 4, 7, *25*, **28**, 31, 46, 86, 92, 94, 141, 189, 198, 210, 226
Gawayaku, Maurice 39–*41*, 47, 57, 60, 63, 65, *120*
gift economies 12, 106; *see also* exchange, of gifts
Giimbiyu language family 21; *see also* Erre (language); Mengerrdji (language); Urningangk (language)
Giles, Raymond 16, 153, 156, 160–*162*, 162–165, 180–181, 222
Goulburn Island: South (Martpalk) 18, 20–21, 24–26, 35n67, 39, 42–47, 61, 64–65, 66n11, 107–109, 111, 119, 123, 135, 140, 145, 156, 165, 169–**170**, 171, 178, 180, 186, 189, 195, 201, 207, 219, 221, 232; North (Weyirra) 21, 39, 41–42, 61, 65, 155–156, **170**
government: Australian 75, 77, 141; officials 71, 86, 108
Groote Eylandt 38n108, 75–76, 82, 98n31, 153, 166, 195
guitar, electric 187, 190–191, 201, 205
Gulamuwu, James 1–2, *3*–4, 23, 26, **28**, 31, **85**, 92–93, *93*–*94*, 94, 105, 109, 122, 135, **219**, 226–227, 230
Gulamuwu, Theo 230
Gulliford, Andrew 98n32
Gumardir people 46, 67n22, 161
Gumatj clan 136
Gumbula, Joe 82
Gumurdul family 169
Gumurdul, Gabby 169
Gumurdul, Victor 82, 88
Gumurdul, Yvonne 88
Gunambarr, Jason **28**
Gunbalanya 1, *3*–4, 8, 14, 16–21, 23–26, 30–31, 35n67, 39–40, 45–46, 48, 65, 67n36, 71–76, *76*–82, **83**, 86–88, 95–96, 102–103, 106, 109, 111–112, 119, 122–123, 126, 129–131, 134–137, **137**–140, 153–155, 157–*162*, 162–167, 169–**170**, 171–174, 177, 180–181, 186–187, 191–192, 195–196, **202**, 204, 209–211, 215, 217, 221–223, 225, 230

Gurruwiwi family **28**, 136
Guymala, Stuart 201
Guymala, Terrah **28**, 195, 201, 210, 225
Gwadbu, John *62*–*63*

Harney, Bill 162–163
Harris, Amanda 4, 30, *112*, 112, 157, 161, 180, 183n39, 214
Hawke, Prime Minister Robert 194
Hiatt, Les 96n3, 113
Hill, Mirrie 184n62
Hillier, Len 163
Hondo, Adis 75
Houghton, Suze 75
human remains: repatriation of 4, 14, 71–96, 98n28; theft of 4–5, 14–15, 23, 73–75, 77–79, 89, 95–96, 157, 217, 230; *see also* ceremonies, reburial
hymns, Christian **29**, 133, 135, 137, **137**–138; in Kunwinjku **29**, 92, 135, 137, **137**–138, 140

Ilakkilak, Marayika *49*–50
Ilarri (singer) 169–**170**
Ilgar (language) 20, **28**, 221
Injalak Arts and Crafts (IAC) 4, 17, 72, **85**, 92, 153–154, 156, 187, 230
Injalak Hill 1, *3*–5, 22–23, 31, 42, 72–73, 76, *76*–78, **85**–87, 109, 156–157, 180, 187, 191, 209, 226, 230
International Council for Traditional Music World Conference 232
Inyjalarrku 'mermaid' (song-set) 17, 21, *25*, 26, **28**, 53, 58, **84**–**85**, 90, 92, *93*–*94*, 103–106, 108–109, 114–115, **116**, 118, 120–123, 125, 135, **137**, 139–140, 169, 171, 178, 190, 198, **202**, 214, 217, **219**, 219–220, 230, 232
Itpyitpy 'grasshopper' (song-set) **170**, 174, **175**
Ivory, Bill 71–72, 74, 80–81
Iwaidja (language) 20–21, **29**, 51, 53, 77, 106, 109, 127n19, 136, 164, 169–**170**, 171, 179

Jabiru 19, 21, 24, 96, 128n40, 158–159, 186–187, 191–192, 195, **202**, 204, 210, 222, 225
Jawoyn (language) 109, 169
Johnson, David 77, 158
junba 15, 54, 68n44, 70n90, 100n66, 194, 212n12, 217, 227n2, 229n20, 231–232

Index

Kakadu National Park 19, 21, 25, 74, 138, 159, 193
Kalarriya, Jimmy 14–15, 17, 73, 95, 97n5, 101n73, 153–160, 163–165, 169, 171–174, 177, 180, 182n5, 182n22, 187, 201, 225, 230; brother, Mukudu 155–157
Kapchan, Deborah 30
Karrbarda 'long yam' (song-set) 7–8, 26, **28**, 49–50, 55, *56*, 58, **83–84**, 86–92, 130–131, 135, **137**, 139–141, **143**, 175–177, 186, 188, 195, **196**, **197**, 197–198, **219**, 219–220, 225, 230
Kerinaiua, Wesley **29**, 136
Kimberley region 15, 51, 54, 68n44, 194, 231–232; *see also junba*
kinship system 18, 22, 31, 35n66, 45, *49*–50, 126, 132–133, 149n1, 154, 161; *see also* names, skin and clan
Kolobarr 'big red kangaroo' (song-set) 165, 168, **170**
Kun-barlang (language) 21, **28**, 51, 106, **170**, 174, 176–177
Kunbarlang (song-set) 164–165, 169, 175–**176**, 176–177, 181
kun-borrk see song; songs; song-set; dance
Kurddal, Crusoe **28**, 37n95, 195, 201, 210
Kurri 'blue tongue lizard' (song-set) 163, **170**, 177–**179**, 220
kurrula (saltwater country) 7, 26, **28**, 86, 88, 109, 119, 126, 140, 156, 196; song-sets from **28**, 91–92, 96, 140, 158, 169–**170**, 171, 178–179, 181, **203**, **216**–217

Lambudju (song-set) **170**–171
Lambudju, Bobby Lane **170**–171, 173
Lamilami, Lazarus 6, 44, 46–48, 67n30, 107, *107*, 111, 113
Lane, Bobby *see Lambudju*, Bobby Lane
languages and language groups, Aboriginal 19; maintenance of 48; map of western Arnhem Land languages and communities *19*; multilingualism 20, 26, 72, 126, 174, 221; spirit languages 27–**28**, 61, 134–135, **170**–172; *see also* Amurdak (language); Batjamalh (language); Bininj Kunwok dialect chain; Bugurnidja (language); Djinang (language); Erre (language); Gaagadju (language); Ganalbingu (language); Giimbiyu language family; Ilgar (language); Iwaidja (language); Jawoyn (language); Kun-barlang (language) Marri Tjevin (language); Marrku (language); Marrku/Malwakardi (language); Mawng (language); Mengerrdji (language); Morrdjdjanjo (esoteric language); Ndjébbana (language); Ngumbar (language); Northern Aboriginal Kriol (language); Tiwi (language); Umbugarla (language) Urningangk (language); Yolngu Matha (language family)
Lee, Roderick 60, 103, *105*, 114, 123, *190*
Lee, Shannon 60, 103, 114
lirrga 53, 68n54, 216–217, 229n20

MacGregor, Tony 182n20
Madjalkaidj, Nangarridj Tommy 7, *25*–26, **28**, 46, 135, 140–141
Madjalkaidj, 'Tommy' *162*–163, 169–**170**, 225
Magowan, Fiona 217
Majakurdu clan 61, 204
Makanawarra, Eileen 50
mako see didjeridu
Malinowski, Bronislaw 11
Mamurrng 11–12, 27, 39, 49, 104–105, *105*, 106–112, *112*, 113–114, 117–126, 192–193, 209, 212n14, 214, **219**, 222–224, 230–*231*; *mamurrng* (pole) 12, 103–107, 110–111, 113, 117–120, *120*–122, 124–126, 128n41, 217
Manangkardi (language) 20–21, **28**, 41, 61–62, 65, 145, 156, **170**–172, 205, 207–209, 213n36, 221–222
Manbam (song-set) 61
man-berlnginj see clapsticks
Mandji, Billy **170**–171, 173–174
Mangirryang, Roy 119, *120*
Mangulda, Charlie **28**, 104, 106, 109–111, 114, 118, *120*, 120, 124, 127n19
manikay 7, 23, 26, **28**, 32n12, 82, 96, 136–**137**, 138, 140, 172, 201, 216–217
Manilakarr clan 78, 149n1, 162–163
Maningrida 21, 24, 26, 36n71, 71, 107–109, 126n3, 129, 135–136, 193, 195–196, 201–**202**, 204

Index 255

Maningrida Arts and Crafts 108
Manmoyi 195–196, 201, **202**, 210
Manmurulu, David 26, **28**, 103, 106, 109–112, 114–115, 117–118, 121–124, 135, 138–139, 214, **219**, 230–*231*, 232
Manmurulu family 127n19, 171, 214, 231
Manmurulu, Jenny 103–104, 113, 121, 123–124, 214, 230–*231*, 232
Manmurulu, Renfred 26, 103, 114, 135, 169, 230–*231*, 232
Manmurulu, Reuben 232
Manmurulu, Rupert 26, 40, 103, 114, 117, 119–120, *120*–123, 135, 138–139, 214, 230–*231*, 232
manyardi see song; songs; song-set; dance
Manyawko 'box tree' (song-set) 177
Marangurra, Jonathan ('John') 154, 163, **170**
Marawana, Larry 160, *162*, 163–169, **170**, 172–173, 180, 184n76, 209, 225; children of *190*
Mardbinda, Rodney 112
Mardday, Eric 7–8, 18, 26, **28**, 31, 49–50, 87, 89, 101n73, 131, 141, 150n3, 186, 188, 210, 230
Marett, Allan 4, 8, 27, 51, 54–*56*, 68n44, 79, 91, 103, 109–*112*, 123–126, 127n13, 131–132, 146, 150n19, 160, 168–169, 171, 173, 198, 216, 218, 224
Marrawiwi 'salmon' (song-set) 7, 21, *25*, 26, **28**, 140–141, **143**, 196, **196**, **219**, 219
Marrgam, Brendan 39–40, *41*–42, 57–58, 60, 103, 114, 121, 123–124
Marri Tjevin (language) 79, 123, 150n19
Marrku (language) 20, **28**, 169–**170**
Marrku/Malwakardi (language) 156
Marrwakara/Mularrik 'goanna/frog' (song-set) 17, 26, **28**, 39, 41, 43, 61, *63*–64, 70n84, **170**–172, 177, 181, 193, 201, **202**, 208, **219**, 219, 224
Marshall, Allan: *Ourselves Writ Strange* 166
Martin, Lorna 187
Martin, Matthew 15, 17, 231
Martin, Scotty 68n44, 227n2
Martpalk *see* Goulburn Island, South (Martpalk)
Mauss, Marcel 11
Mawng (language) 1, 5n6, 6, 20–21, **28**, 36n80, 40, 42, 44, 47, 51, 53, 55, 61–62, 65, 89, 107, 111, 122, 126, 135, 140–141, 156, 169–**170**, 171–172, 179, 181, 190, 201–**202**, 205, 207, 209, **216**, 218, 225, 231; Mayinjinaj 21, 67n22, 204, **216**; Ngurtikin 21, **216**; *see also* Manangkardi (language)
May, Sally 74, 77
McArthur, Margaret 159, 161
McCarthy, Frederick 76, 98n14, 98n31, 161
McCarthy, Malarndirri 86
McIntosh, Ian S. 91, 160
melodic forms 8, 54, 132, 146–149, 178, 208, 224
Melville Island 45, 136, 151n28, 163–164
Mengerrdji (language) 21, 73, 80–81, 88, 96, 99n46, 174, 177, 195
Methodism 10, 45–47, 67n26, 75, 107
'Mewal songs' *see* clan songs, Wurrkigandjarr
Mibarndal (place name) 156–157, 165
Mikkinj Valley outstation 19, 24, 110, 129, 131–132, 137, **137**–139, *139*, 141–142, **143**, 145, 149
Miller, Bob 161
Millie (singer) 163–165
Milpurr, Jamie *231*
Milyarryarr 'black heron' (song-set) 26, **28**, 50–51, *56*, 61, 192, 195–196, **196**–198, *200*, 200, **219**, 219–221
mimih see ancestral spirits, *mimih*
Mimih/Yawkyawk 'stone country spirits/mermaid' (song-set) **28**, 37n95, 195–**196**, *197*, 197, 201–**202**
Minjilang *see* Croker Island
Mirarr clan 21, 33n19, 78, 169, 230
Mirrijpu/Yalarrkuku 'seagull' (song-set) 4, 17, 21, 26–**28**, 39–43, 47, 49, *49*–50, 54–55, 58–*59*, 60–61, 63, 65, 70n84, **83**, **85**–86, 91, 94, 123, 132, **137**, 139, 141–142, **143**, 145–147, *147*–*148*, 149, 171, 178, 186, 193, 195–196, **196**, **197**, 201–**202**, 205, 208, 214, 218–**219**, 219–221, 224, 228n10, 232
missions 21–22, 35n67, 36n80, 40–41, 44–48, 75, 91, 107, 130, 133–134, 154–157, 159, 163, 165–166; *see also* Anglicanism; Methodism
Morphy, Howard and Frances 133, 217
Morrdjdjanjno 168, 172; esoteric language of **170**

Morton, Samuel 98n32
mother song (*ngalbadjan/nigi*) 61, **84–85**, 89–92, *93–94*, 94, 96, 105, 121–122, **137**, 139–140, 142, 145, 149, 178–**179**, 197, **216**, 218, 220, 222, 228n10
Mountford, Bessie 161–163, 165
Mountford, Charles 16, 30, 75–77, 97n14, 153–154, 161, 167
Mowanjum Art and Cultural Centre 194, 212n12
Moyle, Alice 9, 135, 169, 174
multilingualism *see* languages and language groups, Aboriginal, multilingualism
Mulvaney, John 164
Mun.gi, Nym **170**–171, 174
Murumburr clan 21
Museum and Art Gallery of the Northern Territory 72
Museums Victoria 74, 97n7
Myers, Fred 9–10, 13

Nabageyo, Ganbaladj 188
Nabageyo, Geoffrey 86, 188
Nabageyo, Shane 86
Nabarlek 'rock wallaby' (song-set) **28**, 195–196, **196**, **197**, 201–**202**
Naborlhborlh, Lewis 173
Naborlhborlh, Winston 201
Nadjamerrek, Allan 157
Nadjamerrek, Donna 18, 24, 35n66, 71–72, 81, 86, 101n73, 104, 111–*112*, 230; daughters of 123
Nadjamerrek, Lofty 72
Nadjamerrek, Reverend Lois **29**, 92, 137, **137**, 140
Nadjamerrek, Rhonda 102, 104, 111–*112*
Nagalarramba (place name) 107–108
Nagurrgurrba, Isaiah 18, 78, 81, 109, 133, 153–160, 180, 182n22, 187–188, 195–196, 201, 209, 230
Nakodjok Namanilakarr *see* Nayinggul, Jacob
Namagarainmag, Tom 49, *49*
Namarnyilk, Shaun 163, 230
namarrkon see ancestral spirits, *namarrkon*
Namayiwa, Johnny 1, *3*–4, 26, **28**, 31, 39, 50, *112*, 179, 189, 192, 198, 210, 217, 226
names, skin and clan 18, 31, 35n66, 103, 149n1, 154, 166, 183n28, 230

namorrorddo see ancestral spirits, *namorrorddo/yumparrparr*
Namornkodj, Nakangkila Frank Djendjorr 169–**170**, 177–**179**
Namundja, Don 153–155, 160, 180
Namunurr, Nabulanj Billy 155–156, **170**–171, 225
Nangamu, Cain 50
Nangamu, Solomon 1, *3*–4, 7–11, 17–18, 22, 24–*25*, 26, **28**, 31, 39–*41*, 41–42, 46, 49, *49*–50, 55, 61, *62*–*63*, 63, 65, **85**–87, 92–95, 101n73, 110–111, *120*–121, 123, 132, 136–137, 141–142, **143**, 145–146, 148, 156, 171–172, 179, 186, 189, 201, 205, 210, 214, 218, 220, 222–223, 225–227, 230–*231*, 232
Narndal, Julie 88
Narorrga, Dominic 191
Narul, Darren *190*
National Geographic Society 30, 75, 77; film footage 16, 154–155, 157, 159–160, 163, *190*
Nawaloinjba, Billy 171
Nawudba, Michael 49, *49*–50, 146, 149, 214, 221; daughter of (Mary) 49, *49*
Nayinggul, Alfred 82, 88, 110, 138, 215
Nayinggul, Connie 80, 99n46, 110, 130–131, 169, 174, 177
Nayinggul family 169
Nayinggul, Jacob 71–75, 78–82, 86–89, 92, 94–96, 109–110, 129–132, 134–136, **137**–142, **143–144**, 145, 148–149, 149n1, 163, 169, 187–188, 225; mother of (Priscilla) 140, 169; children of 94, 130
Nayinggul, Olamatta 163
Nayuku, Nangarridj Philip 163, 169–**170**, 178–**179**, 185n85
Ndjébbana (language) 21, 107, **202**
Neidji, 'Big Bill' 33n21, 100n60
ngalbadjan see mother song (*ngalbadjan/ nigi*)
nganangka see clapsticks
Nganaru (song-set) **170**–171, 232
Nganjmirra, Jill 191, **202**
Nganjmirra, Joey 130, 141, 186–189
Nganjmirra, Thompson 159; mother of 159
ngaya see song-set, daughter song
Ngili 'mosquito' (song-set) 190, **202**
Nginji 'giant' (song-set) 122, 190, **202**, 232

Ngumbur (language) 21
nigi see mother song (*ngalbadjan/nigi*)
Northern Aboriginal Kriol (language) 20–21, 182n5
Northern Land Council 74, 97n7, 138, 193
North Goulburn Island *see* Goulburn Island, North (Weyirra)
Nulgit, Pansy 231

ochre: red 72, 81, 94, 104–*105*, 150n4; white (*delek*) 6, 87, 102–104, 122, 129–130, 141, 190, *190*, 193
O'Connor, Pete 232
Oenpelli *see* Gunbalanya
O'Keeffe, Isabel 17, *62–63*, 112, 127n19, 174, 176
Orzech, Rachel 102, 104, 111–*112*, 230

Pacific and Regional *Archive* for Digital Sources in Endangered Cultures (*PARADISEC*) 27, 219
Pamurrulpa, Kevin 112
paperbark 43, 49, 65, 73, 81–82, 88–89, 230
Phipps, Peter 209
Poignant, Axel 106–110
Poignant, Axel and Roslyn: *Encounter at Nagalarramba* 108
Poignant, Roslyn 108
popular music 48, 138, 158, 192, 201, **202–203**; country and western songs 135, **137**–138; hip hop **202**; reggae 189, 194, 201–**202**, 225; rock 'n' roll 187, 189, 190–191, 193–194, 201, **202–203**, 205, 225; *see also* rock songs; rock albums
Pride, Charlie: 'Blue Ridge Mountains' 138

radio features: *Expedition to Arnhem Land* 16, 153, 156
Raiwalla 13
Ramingining **28**, 188, 193, 195–196
Rankin, Stanley Djalarra **28**, 129, 131, 136, 151n24
Red Lily Billabong 78, 138, 157–158, 161–*162*, 162–166
repatriation *see* archival collections of song and dance, repatriation
rhythmic mode 24, *52*–55, *56*–59, *59*–61, **83–85**, 86–87, 89, 92, 100n64, 106,
114–115, **116**, 117–119, 121–125, 132, 142, **143–144**, 146, 149, **175–176**, 177–178, **179**, 183n41, 192, 196–**199**, 200, 210, 212n16, 215–**216**, 216–224, 227, 232
Rioli, Dean 136
rock albums: *Manginburru Bininj* (Wildflower Band) 191; *Tribal Voice* (Yothu Yindi) 201
rock songs: audience participation in 194, 205, 209; 'Kabbari' (Wildflower Band) 191; 'Long Grass Man' (Northern Gentlemen) 193, 205–209; subject matter of 205, 209; 'Treaty' (Yothu Yindi) 194, 201
Rom *see* diplomacy/exchange ceremonies (Mamurrng; Rom)

sacred sites 23, 43, 54, 230
Saint-Clare, Joel 158, 195
saltwater country *see kurrula*
Saltwater Fish (song-set) **170**–171, 179
Sandy Creek (Wajpi) 19, 39, 44, 46–47, 102, 112
Schrire, Carmel 78
Scrymgour, Marion 86
Seeger, Anthony 13
Setzler, Frank 4, 16, 30, 75–76, *76*–78, 98n24, 98n31, 109, 155, 157, 180; photographs by 16, 155, 157, 180
Simpson, Colin *162*, 167; *Adam in Ochre* 155, 160, 166, 181n20; recordings made by 16, 34n56, 135, 153, 155–156, 158, 160–169, 174, 179, 180–181, 183n44, 184n78, 222
Singer, Ruth 151n39
Smithsonian Institution 16, 72, 75, 77–78, 96; National Museum of Natural History 78
song analysis 26–27, 29, **52**, 55–*56*, 57, **199**, 205–209; duration 51, 178, 197, 212n18; instrumental sections *52*–54, *59*–60, 114–**116**, 117–*120*, 124, 177–**179**, 190–191, 198–**199**, 216, 219–220; structure 51–*52*, 53, *59*, 115–**116**, 172, **175–176**, 179, 198–**199**; *see also* melodic forms; rhythmic mode; song texts; tempo; tessitura
song creation 10, 42, 149; 'spontaneously-composed' 165–166, **170**, 174; *see also* Dreaming/Dreamings, and song composition

song performance 8, 51, 103; by Balanda 65, 123–124; children 55, **170**–171; 'practising' 1, 8, 41–42, 103, 114; repetition in 42, 61, 142; 'tuning in' voice 2

songs: 'Bangany-nyung Ngaya' 124; *bobo* (goodbye) 27, **84–85**, 89–91, 96, 105, 113, 122, **143–144**, 145, **216**, 218; daughter song (*ngaya*) 143, 145; 'going down' **144**, 145; *kiwken* (boss) song **83**, **85**–86, 94, **143–144**, 145, 218; Kolobarr song 165, 168, **170**, 172–173; *manme* (tucker) 9, **143–144**, 145; 'morning star' song **85**, 94; Mularrik Mularrik song 7, 41; 'new' 8, 50–51, 132, 140, 145–149, 210, **216**, 218; 'old' 8, 50–51, **83**, 115, 132, 140, 145–149, **216**, 218; 'open domain' 172; 'Truwu' 123; *warramumpik* ('love') **143**, 145, 169–**170**, 174, 177; "Winbalung Song" ("Gunbalang Sweetheart" song) 164, 184n62; *see also* clan songs; mother song (*ngalbadjan/nigi*)

songs, choice of 51, 54, 106, 140, 145, 148, 180, 197, 215–**216**, 216–217; order of 8, 24, 53–55, 65, 70n90, 106, 142, 146, **216**–218

song-sets: 'aural identity' of 124, 181, 219–220; definition of 6, 32n4, 68n49; number of songs 51, 218–219, **219**; spirit language 27–**28**, 61–62, 134–135, **170**–172, 181, 208, 218, 222; transmission 49–50; *see also* Buffalo Dance (song-set); Inyjalarrku 'mermaid' (song-set); Itpyitpy 'grasshopper' (song-set); Karrbarda 'long yam' (song-set); Kolobarr 'big red kangaroo' (song-set); Kunbarlang (song-set); Kurri 'blue tongue lizard' (song-set); *kurrula* (saltwater country): song-sets; Manbam (song-set); Manyawko 'box tree' (song-set); Marrawiwi 'salmon' (song-set); Marrwakara/Mularrik 'goanna/frog' (song-set); Milyarryarr 'black heron' (song-set); Mimih/Yawkyawk 'stone country spirits/mermaid' (song-set); Mirrijpu/Yalarrkuku 'seagull' (song-set); Nabarlek 'rock wallaby' (song-set); Nganaru (song-set); Ngili 'mosquito' (song-set); Nginji 'giant' (song-set); Saltwater Fish (song-set); *wardde-ken* (stone country): song-sets; Wurramu (song-set); Yanajanak 'stone country spirits' (song-set)

songs, recording of 1, 41, 57, 70n77, 160–165, 167–168, 180

song texts 8, 51–*52*, 53, 57, *59*, 61–62, **116**, 142, **143–144**, 146–148, 171–174, **175–176**, 175–176, **199**, 205–209, 218

song transmission: gifting 4, 8, 11, 15, 22, 142, **144**; inheriting 7–8, *49*, 49–50; learning 8, 50–51, 55, 57, 63, 65, 125, 146; memorizing 2, 65; recordings 4, 14, 15, 17, 65, 153, 155, 157; *see also* archival collections

South Goulburn Island *see* Goulburn Island, South (Martpalk)

Spencer, Baldwin 48, 67n27, 67n33, 78, 96n2, 134, 151n28

spirit language *see* languages and language groups, Aboriginal

Stanner, W. E. H. 9–10

Stokes, John Lort 45

stolen generation 141

stone country *see wardde-ken*

Stone Country Festival *see* festival

storytellers 39, 167

Stubington, Jill 201

Sykes, Jim 12

Tamisari, Franca 7, 58, 213n38

tempo 24, 37n91, 41–42, *52*, 55, 61, 65, 70n90, **83**, 87–92, 100n64, 103, 114–**116**, 117–118, 120, 130–132, 137, 139, 141–142, **143–143**, 145, 148, 178–**179**, 179, 188–189, 192, 197–**199**, 212n16, 212n21, 215–**216**, 217–221, 224, 227, 228n10; tempo bands 55, 114, 178, 220–221; *see also* clapstick beating, tempo

tessitura 123, 137

Thomas, Martin 4, 16, 72, 75–78, 80–82, 86, 109, 112, 159–160, 182n20

Thompson, Dallas 204

Thomson, Donald 13

Tiwi (language) **29**

Tiwi Islanders 45, 132; songs of **29**, 136–137, 140–141, 183n37

Toner, Peter 140, 217

Torres Strait Islanders 39, 65, 193

Index 259

Treloyn, Sally 15, 100n66, 194, 212n12, 227n2, 232
Trudgen, Richard 67n28
Turner, Victor 31

Umbagai, Folau 232
Umbugarla (language) 21
Urabadi, Rosemary 104, 111–*112*, 169
Urningangk (language) 21, 73, 88, 195

vocables 7, 51–*52*, 53, 90–91, **116**, 147, 166, 172, 174, 178–179, 198–**199**
vocal timbre 165, 224

Wajpi *see* Sandy Creek
Walker, Howell 16, *76*–*77*, 155, 162–163, 184n78
Walsh, Michael 80
wangga 14, 51, 53–55, 79, 123–126, 128n28, 132, 169–**170**, 173, 177, 185n105, 198, 216, 218, 220, 224, 229n20, 232
Wardaga, Charlie 210
wardde-ken (stone country) 26, **28**, 87, 109, 119, 126, 136, 140, 192, 195, **203**; song-sets **28**, 87, 90–91, 96, 106, 136, 158, 169–**170**, 171, 176–178, 181, **216**–217
Warner, W. Lloyd 91
Warrabin, Harold 26, **28**, 39, *41*, 41–42, 47, *62*–*63*, 63–64, 102, 123, 172, 201, 205, 221
warra ngurrijakurr see ancestral spirits, *warra ngurrijakurr*
Warruwi 4, 14, 18–21, 25–26, 31, 35n67, 36n80, 39–40, 43, 46–48, 61, 66n11, 75, 103, 106, 108–110, *112*, 112–114, 117, 123–126, 135–136, 138, 169, 189–190, 193, **202**, 204–205, 217, 221, 223–225, 230–233

Washington DC 82, 96, 97n4, 222, 225
Watson, Birdibob 201
Watson, Reverend James 45–46, 67n22, 67n27, 66n28
Webb, Steven 72, 81, 97n4
Wees, Sam 39–*41*
Weiner, Annette 12
Western Arnhem Land Song Project (WALSP) 24, 27
Weyirra *see* Goulburn Island
Wickham, John Clements 45
Wild, Steven 108
Wilson, Shawn 29
Winunguj, George 107, *107*–109, 122, 225
Wirlirrgu clan 21
women: dancers 7, 47–50, 55, 58, 87, 89–90, *107*, 119–123, 125, 139, 188–189, 198, **216**–217, 232; singers 48, 50, 191; *see also* bands, women performing in; dance style, female
World War Two 155–156, 182n10, 188, 225
Wurnan 15, 17
Wurramu (song-set) 91
Wurrik clan 166, 169–**170**

Yalbarr, Micky 39–*41*, 41–42, 61, 63
Yanajanak 'stone country spirits' (song-set) **28**, *56*, 106, 109, 117–120, *120*, 121, 123–125, 185n105, **219**
Yirrkala 46, 75, 82, 194
Yolŋu Matha (language family) 21, **28**–29, 48, 67n37, 201
Yolŋu: *people* 7, 13, 23–24, 44, 75, 82, 106, 140, 193–194, 201, 204, 209, 212n38; law (*rom*) 7, 193, 204
yumparrparr see ancestral spirits, *namorrorddo/yumparrparr*; dances, *namorrorddo/yumparrparr* (giant)